ON "STRANGERS NO LONGER"

On
"Strangers No Longer"

PERSPECTIVES ON THE
HISTORIC U.S.-MEXICAN CATHOLIC BISHOPS'
PASTORAL LETTER ON MIGRATION

EDITED BY Todd Scribner AND J. Kevin Appleby

Paulist Press
New York / Mahwah, NJ

Cover images by: *top*, Suzanne Tucker / Shutterstock.com;
bottom, ruskpp/Shutterstock.com
Cover design by Sharyn Banks
Book design by Lynn Else

Library of Congress Cataloging-in-Publication Data

On Strangers no longer : perspectives on the historic U.S.-Mexican Catholic bishops' pastoral letter on migration / edited by Todd Scribner and J. Kevin Appleby.
     pages cm
     ISBN 978-0-8091-4828-8 (alk. paper) — ISBN 978-1-58768-289-6 (ebook)
     1. Catholic Church. Conferencia del Episcopado Mexicano. Strangers no longer. 2. Church work with immigrants—Catholic Church. 3. Church work with immigrants—United States. 4. Mexicans—Religious life—United States. 5. United States—Emigration and immigration—Religious aspects—Catholic Church. 6. Mexico—Emigration and immigration—Religious aspects—Catholic Church. I. Scribner, Todd. II. Appleby, J. Kevin.
     BX2347.8.I46O5 2013
     261.7—dc23

                                                                    2013011456

ISBN 978-0-8091-4828-8 (paperback) — ISBN 978-1-58768-289-6 (e-book)

Published by Paulist Press
997 Macarthur Boulevard
Mahwah, New Jersey 07430

www.paulistpress.com

Printed and bound in the
United States of America

Contents

Contents

Preface

The United States' and Mexican bishops involved in the respective migration committees of the U.S. and Mexican episcopal conferences began meeting informally in early 2000 to discuss mutual concerns regarding migration between the two neighboring countries. Deeply troubled by the deaths of migrants in the Mexican and American deserts as well as the family separation induced by flawed migration policies and practices in both countries, the U.S. and Mexican bishops decided to speak jointly against these injustices. As a result, *Strangers No Longer: Together on the Journey of Hope*—the first joint pastoral statement of the U.S. and Mexican bishops—was approved by the full bodies of each episcopal conference in 2002 and released in 2003.

Since that time, both episcopal conferences have worked to change immigration laws in their respective countries and, together with our brother bishops in Central America and the Caribbean, regionally. Despite slow progress toward reform of our immigration laws, we have continued, with the Lord's help, to raise the voice of the Church on this important humanitarian issue.

Each year, millions of human beings in our countries and throughout the world migrate in order to support their families or to escape persecution. They are subject to physical and emotional abuse by smugglers, human traffickers, organized crime, unscrupulous employers, and even enforcement personnel. Their basic human rights are not protected, yet their labor is used to benefit the common good of all. They are victims, not beneficiaries, of the new age of globalization, in which goods, capital, and communication are exchanged among nations regularly, yet human beings—who produce the labor that connects these elements—often are not provided legal and safe passage.

Such an immoral status quo must change. We will continue to raise our voices and defend our fellow human beings until change is achieved, both in our individual nations and across the hemisphere. His Holiness Pope Benedict XVI exhorted us: "Brother Bishops, I want to encourage you and your communities to continue to welcome

vii

the immigrants who join your ranks today, to share their joys and hopes, to support them in their sorrows and trials, and to help them flourish in their new home" (National Shrine of the Immaculate Conception, Washington, DC, April 16, 2008).

This volume commemorating the tenth anniversary of *Strangers No Longer* is another attempt to highlight the injustices of the status quo and to educate Catholics and others about the current realities of migration. Using the pastoral letter as a starting point, Catholic scholars and policy experts from the United States and Mexico examine issues of migration in the context of Catholic teaching, providing critical analysis and directions for the future. Of particular interest are their suggestions for how the Church can better assist migrants pastorally, socially, and as advocates. We extend our heartfelt thanks to these contributors and look forward to working with them in the future.

As a global institution devoted to the basic human dignity and human rights of the person, as imbued by the Lord our God and his Son, Jesus Christ, the universal Church can make a difference in the lives of those who are on the move, so that their God-given rights are protected. We invite our fellow Catholics and others to join us in this pursuit. Working together in solidarity, we look forward to the day in which the dignity and rights of the migrant are respected and defended throughout the world.

Most Reverend José H. Gomez
Archbishop of Los Angeles
Chairman of the U.S. Conference of
Catholic Bishops' Committee on
Migration

Most Reverend Rafael Romo
Archbishop of Tijuana, Mexico
Chairman, Committee on Mobility,
Episcopal Conference of Mexico
March 2013

Abbreviations and Sources

Most citations of official Catholic Church documents will be provided in the text. The common abbreviation of the document will be set in parentheses, followed by a number that designates the location in the document. For example, (SNL 26) signifies section 26 in the pastoral letter *Strangers No Longer: Together on the Journey of Hope*. Below are a list of documents and abbreviations used throughout the book. Unless otherwise noted below the English translations of documents issued by the Vatican and used herein can be found at their website: http://www.vatican.va/. Documents issued by the United States Conference of Catholic Bishops can be located at their website: www.usccb.org.

AA   *Apostolicam Actuositatem*, Decree on the Apostolate of the Laity, Second Vatican Council, November 18, 1965

CV   *Caritas in Veritate*, Charity in Truth, Encyclical Letter of Pope Benedict XVI, June 29, 2009

CCC   *Catechism of the Catholic Church*, promulgated on August 15, 1997 in the by John Paul II in the Apostolic Letter *Laetamur Magnopere*

CA   *Centesimus Annus*, On the Hundredth Anniversary of *Rerum Novarum*, Encyclical Letter of Pope John Paul II, May 1, 1991

CSDC   *Compendium of the Social Doctrine of the Church*, Pontifical Council for Justice and Peace, 2004

DCE   *Deus Caritas Est*, On Christian Love, Encyclical Letter of Pope Benedict XVI, December 25, 2005

EA   *Ecclesia in America*, On the Encounter with the Living Jesus Christ: The Way to Conversion, Communion and Solidarity in America, Apostolic Exhortation of Pope John Paul II, January 22, 1999

EJA   *Economic Justice for All*, Pastoral Letter on Catholic Social Teaching and the U.S. Economy, National Conference of Catholic Bishops, 1986

EM	*Encuentro and Mission: A Renewed Pastoral Framework for Hispanic Ministry*, United States Conference of Catholic Bishops, November 13, 2002
EMCC	*Erga migrantes caritas Christi*, The Love of Christ Towards Migrants, Pontifical Council for the Pastoral Care of Migrants and Itinerant People, Vatican City, 2004
EN	*Evangelii Nuntiandi*, Evangelization in the Modern World, Apostolic Exhortation of Pope Paul VI, December 8, 1975
EF	*Exsul Familia Nazarethana*, On the Spiritual Care to Migrants, Apostolic Constitution of Pius XII, August 1, 1952; available in *The Church's Magna Charta for Migrants*, ed. Rev. Giulivo Tessarolo, PSSC (Staten Island, N.Y.: St. Charles Seminary, 1962)
FNC	"From Newcomers to Citizens All Come Bearing Gifts," USSCB Committee on Migration, September, 1999
GS	*Gaudium et Spes*, Pastoral Constitution on the Church in the Modern World, Second Vatican Council, December 7, 1965
JIW	Justice in the World, Synod of Bishops, 1971.
LE	*Laborem Exercens*, On Human Work, Encyclical Letter of Pope John Paul II, September 14, 1981
LG	*Lumen Gentium*, Dogmatic Constitution on the Church, Second Vatican Council, November 21, 1964
NMI	*Novo Millennio Ineunte*, At the Close of the Great Jubilee of the Year 2000, Apostolic Letter of Pope John Paul II, January 6, 2001
OHT	"On Human Trafficking," USCCB Committee on Migration Statement, 2007
PM	*Pastoralis Migratorum*, New Norms for the Care of Migrants, Pope Paul VI, August 15, 1969
PP	*Populorum Progressio*, On the Development of Peoples, Encyclical Letter of Pope Paul VI, March 26, 1967
PT	*Pacem in Terris*, On Establishing Universal Peace in Truth, Justice, Charity, and Liberty, Encyclical Letter of Pope John XXIII, April 11, 1963
SNL	*Strangers No Longer: Together on the Journey of Hope*, A Pastoral Letter Concerning Migration from the Catholic Bishops of Mexico and the United States, January 22, 2003

SRS   *Sollicitudo Rei Socialis*, On Social Concern, Encyclical Letter of Pope John Paul II, December 30, 1987

WSAU   *Welcoming the Stranger Among Us: Unity in Diversity*, The National Conference of Catholic Bishops, November 15, 2000

Introduction

J. Kevin Appleby and Todd Scribner

In January 2003, the Mexican and U.S. bishops issued the joint pastoral letter *Strangers No Longer: Together on the Journey of Hope* that looked at migration in the Americas as a "sign of the times" (SNL 1). A recent study released by the Migration Policy Institute (MPI) reinforced the appropriateness of this observation by highlighting the significant amount of migration that has occurred in recent years between Central America, Mexico, and the United States. Since 1970, when about one million migrants from Mexico and Central America's Northern Triangle (El Salvador, Guatemala, and Honduras) lived in the United States, MPI now estimates that the total number increased to nearly fourteen million by 2009.[1] Nearly thirty-three million Hispanics living in the United States are either immigrants from Mexico or trace their family origin to Mexico.[2] Despite a drop in migration from Central America and Mexico to the United States following the onset of the economic recession that began in 2008, migration between these various regions has proven to be an important dynamic in modern life and will likely continue to be for decades to come.

For their part, the bishops of the United States and Mexico have affirmed that the movement of people between their two countries has been a generally beneficial process, not to mention an almost inevitable phenomenon given their geographical proximity, but were troubled by the fact that "many persons who seek to migrate are suffering, and, in some cases, tragically dying; human rights are abused; families are kept apart; and racist and xenophobic attitudes remain" (SNL 2). Their recognition of this problem points to the politically contentious nature of the immigration debate and the real world consequences that immigration policy can have on immigrants and their communities. How these decisions affect migrants, their families, and the neighborhoods in which they live has motivated the bishops to comment extensively homes in on one of the more contentious areas related to legislative debates over immigration policy: the question of the legalization of undocumented populations. Here she argues that the "deportation by attrition" strategy that has predominated over the past two decades has failed. She then challenges readers to support a legalization process for those who are currently in the United States in unauthorized status and does so by appealing to moral principles that are embedded in Catholic social teaching.

While debates rage on the American side of the border regarding the question of legalization, in chapter 5 Patricia Zamudio examines some of the factors that underlie a person's decision to migrate in the first place. In particular, she examines two types of migration: authorized forms of migration in the context of guest worker programs and unauthorized forms of migration, as seen in Central American migrants who pass through Mexico to the United States and Canada. In this chapter she brings to light some of the difficulties that migrants and their families face when deciding to migrate, not to mention the dangers that threaten when they do.

Building indirectly on Zamudio's essay, Don Kerwin looks more closely at some of the underlying causes that give rise to migration patterns in the first place. The reasons why people leave their homeland for another is a complex phenomenon that is informed by a wide range of push and pull factors. There are, in short, root causes that drive migration, one of which is globalization and economic underdevelopment. With globalization, the world has become increasingly interdependent and yet, at the same time, the disparities between the developing and the developed world have become all the more apparent. In chapter 6 Kerwin picks up on the centrality of this issue as it relates to migration and proceeds to explore how, as he puts it in his essay, "the bishops' vision deepens and complements the migration and development dialogue, and how migration-related development can animate the principles set forth in *Strangers No Longer*."

Kerwin's essay highlights the point that migration patterns are reinforced by global pressures that extend beyond any one country's borders. For this reason it is insufficient to focus only on American policies as they relate to immigration; it is as important to understand how policies beyond America's southern border address and affect migrants and their communities. Given the complex interdependence of these two countries, political decisions in one can have important consequences in the other. In light of this, Leticia Calderon Chelius examines how Mexican governmental policies on immigration have contributed to the movement of peoples both within Mexico and northward to the United States and Canada. This will be the focus of chapter 7.

Part III drills deeper down into the debates over policy by examining specific populations of concern to the bishops and examines their advocacy efforts on behalf of two populations in particular: victims of human trafficking and undocumented minors eligible for the DREAM Act. Chapter 8 will pick up on the issue of human trafficking, or modern day slavery. Here Terry Coonan examines the manner in which both policymakers and Church officials have taken on this issue. Chapter 10, authored by Colleen Cross, examines a specific segment of the undocumented migrant minor population that is eligible for what is popularly referred to as the DREAM Act.

Part IV will take an opportunity to look back at *Strangers No Longer* in its entirety and take stock of how the moral framework that the bishops have developed in their pastoral letter can inform their advocacy efforts in the years to come. Immigration is an obviously complex phenomenon that has in recent years become a politically contentious topic of discussion; the positions staked out by the bishops in their advocacy efforts have often elicited some controversy, both inside and outside the Church. In chapter 11 Mark Ensalaco focuses on some of the criticisms that have been aimed at the bishops' pastoral letter and in doing so highlights some of the issues related to immigration that may deserve further attention by the Church.

Finally, in the last chapter, J. Kevin Appleby reflects on the bishops' call for the passage of comprehensive immigration reform and traces the history between the publication of *Strangers*, the attempt to achieve passage of comprehensive reform legislation, and some of the reasons why Congress has so far failed to do so. He then highlights some of the challenges to which immigration reform proponents will have to respond to overcome resistance to such reform and the important role that the Catholic Church can play in this process.

NOTES

1. Marc Rosenblum and Kate Brick, *US Immigration Policy and Mexican/Central American Migration Flows: Then and Now* (Washington, DC: The Migration Policy Institute, 2011).

2. Seth Motel and Eileen Patten, "Statistical Profile: Hispanics of Mexican Origin in the United States, 2010" (Washington, DC: Pew Hispanic Center, 2010), http://www.pewhispanic.org/2012/06/27/hispanics-of-mexican-origin-in-the-united-states-2010/ (accessed August 28, 2012).

3. Pew Forum on Religion and Public Life, "U.S. Religious Landscape Survey" (Washington, DC: Pew Forum on Religion and Public Life, 2008), 36, 45.

4. Ibid., 53.

PART I

HISTORICAL, PASTORAL, AND THEOLOGICAL PERSPECTIVES

CHAPTER 1

Immigration as a "Sign of the Times": From the Nineteenth Century to the Present

Todd Scribner

In the often-quoted first sentence of his book *The Uprooted*, Oscar Handlin wrote, "Once I thought to write a history of the immigrants in America. Then I discovered the immigrants *were* American history."[1] If this can be accurately said of America, it is particularly apt in its application to the Catholic Church in America. In a little over a century the number of American Catholics increased nearly four hundred fold. With a population of less than forty thousand in 1790, and in the midst of a non-Catholic populace that was nearly a hundred times larger, Catholicism was very much a minority religion. By 1815 the Catholic population in America had increased to about two hundred thousand, and by 1865 had become the largest single denomination in the country with more than three and a half million members. Forty-five years later in 1910 it had again quadrupled to approximately sixteen million.[2]

The significant growth of the Church during the nineteenth century was primarily due to the waves of Irish, German, Italian, and Polish immigrants who entered the United States. First were the Irish, who began to arrive en masse following the potato famine of the 1840s and who were soon accompanied by an influx of Germans by the middle decades of that century. Beginning around 1890, this demographic began to shift as large numbers of Italian and Eastern European immigrants began to make their way to the United States over the next three decades. Although much of the literature on the subject focuses on the European immigration, Latino and Hispanic Catholics were also an indispensable part of the American-based Church from its earliest years. From the establishment of the St. Augustine settlement (1565), then under the Spanish crown, to the annexation of large swaths of Mexican land by the United States following the Treaty of Guadalupe Hidalgo in 1848, large numbers of Hispanic Catholics were brought into America and consequently played an essential role in the formation of American Catholic life.[3]

Given the important role that immigration has had in the life of the Catholic Church in America, it is not surprising that Church leadership has traditionally taken a pointed interest in the treatment of Catholic immigrant communities and the formation of immigration policy on both the state and national level. From the earliest days, the hierarchy has sought to protect the faith of newly arriving immigrants and to ensure that their pastoral needs were continually met. Their engagement on policy questions was at different times motivated by institutional self-interest, moral principle, and a pragmatism that recognized both the limits of their influence on Capitol Hill and the influence of external factors that helped shape the policymaking process. Given the expanse of this topic and the need to limit it for purposes of space, this essay will focus primarily on the institutional Church's engagement with immigration policy.

FROM THE IMMIGRANT CHURCH TO THE NATIONAL CATHOLIC WELFARE CONFERENCE

Historians of American Catholicism have often referred to the period from the mid-nineteenth century to the early decades of the twentieth as the age of the "immigrant Church." Throughout this era, Catholics often encountered an adversarial culture that was at times antagonistic toward their interests, not to mention their very presence in America. The immigrant Church that surfaced in reaction to the non-Catholic, nativist culture often turned inward and sought to establish a protective haven that would allow Catholics to practice their faith in a safe environment.[4] In his seminal work on American nativism, John Higham defined this disposition as an "intense opposition to an internal minority on the grounds of its foreign (i.e., "un-American") connections."[5] Beginning around the late 1830s, one factor that contributed to nativist sentiment was a deeply rooted anti-Catholicism that was born with the Reformation and brought to the United States during the colonial period. Throughout the nineteenth century many American Protestants accused the Church of espousing an authoritarianism that was irreconcilable with American democracy and its tradition of political and religious liberty. The significant influx of Catholic immigrants exacerbated these concerns and left the impression of a Catholic invasion sent by the pope to undermine the integrity of American political institutions.

The reaction to mass immigration among the native-born, predominately Anglo-Saxon population was often swift and harsh, as nativist movements sought to limit the influx of immigrants for both religious and cultural reasons. From the burning of the Ursuline convent in Charlestown, Massachusetts, following a fiery, anti-Catholic sermon by Lyman Beecher, to bloody riots in New Orleans, St. Louis, Louisville, and Philadelphia in later years, anti-Catholic nativism was in full swing by the mid-nineteenth century. During the 1850s, nativist sentiment was growing and found expression in the Know-Nothing Party, which took advantage of anti-Catholicism as a way to establish an influential political constituency.[6]

Bishops responded in diverse ways to Protestant hostility. Some, like Bishop Francis Patrick Kenrick of Philadelphia, took a more conciliatory tone in an attempt to defuse tensions between Catholic and Protestant communities. Others, including Bishop John Hughes of New York, were more confrontational. Following the Philadelphia riots in May 1944, during which several people were killed and two Catholic churches burned down, native-born Americans planned to hold a rally in New York City's Central Park. Anticipating violence similar to what had occurred in Philadelphia earlier that year, Bishop Hughes warned the mayor that if "a single Catholic church were burned in New York, the city would become a second Moscow," and proceeded to place a thousand armed Catholic men in a local church, commanding them to defend the building with their lives.[7]

While Protestant animosity aimed at Catholics was one problem confronting Church leadership, the heterogeneous character of the Catholic community and its changing population—from the predominately Irish and German immigration at mid-century to Polish and Italian influx just a few decades later—proved to be another difficulty. Not only did Church leadership have to respond to the nativist backlash against the Church, they also had to develop an infrastructure that could handle the arrival of millions of immigrants of various nationalities who spoke many different languages. Given the ethnic diversity that comprised the American Church, it was important to balance the ethnic interests of these various communities. One of the central ways Catholic leadership did so was through the national parish. For its part, the Holy See encouraged the formation of national parishes as a mechanism to protect the immigrants' faith, although noted that such a construct should only serve as a "temporary concession" so long as national differences remained strong. The purpose of the national parish was not to reinforce discrete, national identities, but was simply a useful mechanism to protect the faith.[8]

In contrast to the geographical location that ideally defines the size and scope of a given parish community, the distinguishing characteristic of the national parish was language. As the historian Jay Dolan noted, "The large influx of immigrants from various nations, speaking different languages, necessitated the adoption of the national parish to satisfy the religious needs of each group."[9] These parishes helped to provide a buffer between different ethnic communities and an opportunity for diverse groups to use their native tongue in liturgical and other Church-related celebrations. Paired with parochial schools that often accompanied the rise of individual parishes, each served a shared end: to reinforce and protect the religious identity of newly arriving immigrants.

While essential to this effort, both the parishes and their sister schools did not have the capacity on their own to ensure that the needs of an increasingly large Catholic community were consistently met. For this reason, extra-parochial institutions emerged, including hospitals, welfare agencies, settlement houses, port programs, and rural colonization programs, each of which responded to the unique needs of the various Catholic populations that were arriving.[10] Catholic societies of different stripes, including the Knights of Columbus and the St. Vincent de Paul Society helped to coordinate efforts aimed at the care of immigrants. One of the primary characteristics of these outreach efforts prior to World War I was that they were "carried on in individual dioceses under the local ordinary that was most effective in meeting the immigrants' day to day needs."[11]

While effective in the provision of pastoral care, by virtue of the local and diocesan character of the Church's immigrant work it was difficult to coordinate efforts on issues related to immigration policy on a national level. Throughout this period the Church "had no efficient organization at the national level to unify their work until 1917 when the National Catholic War Council was formed."[12] The absence of a centralized institution did not pose much of a problem throughout most of the nineteenth century given that federal immigration policy was still in its infancy; throughout most of this period such policies continued to be handled on the state level. As immigration policy became increasingly federalized in the late nineteenth and early twentieth centuries it became important for the Church to respond accordingly.

With the onset of World War I, Catholics responded to President Wilson's call to support the war effort in numbers that were disproportionately high compared to their total population. With large numbers of Catholic men joining the military, the hierarchy recognized the importance of initiating a nationally centralized organization that would coordinate the Catholic war effort. Following the war's end the bishops continued to affirm the value of a centralized institution in Washington, DC, that could keep the government apprised of the Church's interests, respond to any legislative efforts that were contrary to those interests, and coordinate its activities on a national level. It was also at this time that the National Catholic War Council was restructured and became the National Catholic Welfare Conference (NCWC). The formation of a national Catholic institution that was in charge of representing the bishops' policy positions could further function as a counterweight to nationally oriented Protestant organizations like the Federal Council of Churches that were pushing political agendas of their own.[13]

One issue that became of particular interest early on to Conference leadership was immigration. Within a year of the NCWC's founding, the bishops established the Bureau of Immigration as a way to respond to concerns that had been raised regarding the treatment of Catholic immigrants arriving at Ellis Island. In late 1920, Rev. John Burke, then General Secretary of the Conference, began to receive complaints regarding rumors that the YMCA had been given the responsibility by the federal government to greet immigrants as they arrived in the United States. Putting Catholics under the care of Protestant groups intensified the NCWC leadership's apprehension that these groups would engage in proselytization of Catholic immigrants as they arrived and in doing so convert many away from the fold.[14]

It was quickly decided that a director of immigration should be hired and stationed in Washington, DC. Further, it was agreed upon to appoint sub-directors to the ports of New York, Boston, Philadelphia, Baltimore, and Providence, who would greet and provide support to newly arriving Catholic immigrants. The primary responsibilities of the NCWC agents were "to act as an interpreter, legal adviser, and liaison between immigrant and government at the port of entry."[15] These decisions signified the first step in the creation of the Bureau of Immigration, which was the first iteration of what is today the Department of Migration and Refugee Services at the United States Conference of Catholic Bishops.[16]

In January 1923, the bureau expanded its activities to the Mexican border and established an office in El Paso. As was the case with other points of entry, NCWC leadership were concerned that Protestant organizations already active on the border were reaching out to Catholic migrants with the hope of winning them away from the Catholic faith. Additional efforts commenced soon thereafter across the border in Juarez, Mexico. These included the provision of medical and welfare referrals, pastoral care, and support related to the provision of visas and other legal services. NCWC staff worked closely with government officials in both the United States and Mexico to expedite entries, along with coordinating education efforts with the Mexican Catholic Church for immigrants who were hoping to gain entry into the United States.[17]

In each of these cases, whether the immigrants entered via the southwestern border or through one of the eastern port cities, the NCWC implemented a follow-up program in the destination diocese, "the main purpose of which was to assure for the new arrival the retention of his Catholic Faith. This can only be done by seeing that he mingles with Catholic people in his community, that he makes the acquaintanceship of his pastor, and that he attends Mass and receives the sacraments regularly."[18] Explicit efforts by the NCWC to form contacts in dioceses where immigrants were placed and who would report to the Conference on pastoral and material support resulted in only limited success. Some dioceses proved to be more responsive than others in their follow-up efforts, thus leading to inconsistent information nationally. Regardless of its effectiveness, the efforts made by the Conference in this regard demonstrated their interest in securing the faith of immigrant communities and, in doing so, ensuring the continued vitality of the Catholic Church in America.[19]

In addition to the more strictly institutional concerns of the Church, particularly as it applied to Protestant proselytization of Catholic faithful, following World War I, federal-level immigration policy became an important point of emphasis. Throughout most of the nineteenth century and into the early decades of the twentieth the federal government, while at times threatening to do so, did not become deeply enmeshed in the passage of restrictive immigration legislation. Individual states, however, did make some efforts to entice and, at times, inhibit immigration. Efforts were made to induce migration, partly in response to labor shortages in mines, industry, and agriculture, and partly because of the need to increase the population in territories seeking statehood.[20] On the opposite side of the spectrum, state legislatures also passed laws that sought to restrict the entry of immigrants who were criminals, paupers, or infected with contagious diseases.[21]

The 1875 Supreme Court ruling *Henderson v. The Mayor of New York* nullified state laws that required shipmasters to post a bond or head tax for passengers. The majority decision in the *Henderson* case held that "state regulations were an unconstitutional usurpation of exclusive congressional power to regulate foreign commerce."[22] This ruling severely limited the ability of states to pass immigration related legislation. Following the decision, many state level leaders, particularly along the eastern seaboard, pressured Congress to pass into law provisions that would help to regulate immigration. In 1882, Congress adopted a bill that built on earlier state level restrictions and prohibited certain categories of immigrants from entering the United States, including convicts, lunatics, and public charges. Further legislation, *The Chinese Exclusion Act*, was passed that same year that prohibited Chinese immigration and banned the naturalization of Chinese immigrants. The exclusion of the Chinese was eventually expanded to include a prohibition on Asian immigration altogether. In 1885 and 1891, Congress further consolidated federal authority over immigration policy with the passage of new legislation that respectively prohibited contract labor immigration and expanded the category of excludable populations to include polygamists and people suffering from contagious diseases.[23]

Attempts to further restrict immigration waxed and waned during the final decades of the nineteenth century, often in response to political tensions and economic insecurity. Economic depressions, paired with the conviction that immigrants were exacerbating the economic insecurity of the native born, contributing to the slum problem, and straining traditional morality enhanced restrictionist sentiment. Given the diversity of social ills that were attributed to high levels of immigration, reformers looked to immigration restriction as an important component of the solution. Restrictionist sentiment climaxed in the 1890s, although with the exception of the 1891 law that expanded the list of excludable migrants, nothing of substance passed. Nevertheless, by mid-decade a new proposal had gained prominence, calls for which would resurface repeatedly over the following two decades: the literacy test. Such a test would exclude the admission of all adult males who were unable to read and write in their own language.[24] Proponents of the legislation tapped into the "widespread belief that a literacy test would stem the increasing tide of immigration from southern and eastern Europe while not seriously affecting immigration from the 'Anglo-Saxon' nations of Northwestern Europe."[25] Although the literacy test initially passed in both houses of Congress in 1896 and appeared headed for law, President Grover Cleveland vetoed it. In his veto message, he contended that literacy does not afford a proper standard to determine the desirability of an arriving immigrant and that, furthermore, such a standard was often used as a smokescreen to hide more malicious grounds for exclusion.[26]

Between 1896, when it was first proposed in Congress, and 1917, when it eventually became law, the literacy test was debated on at least four separate occasions. In early 1913 and 1915, Congress again passed a version of the literacy test, but in both cases the legislation was vetoed by Presidents Taft and Wilson, respectively. In 1917, Congress finally enacted the legislation over the veto of President Wilson. For its part, the Catholic Church opposed the legislation almost universally, although there were some prominent individuals who favored its passage. Fr. John Ryan, for example, who became a leading expert on economic and labor issues at the National Catholic Welfare Conference during the 1920s and 1930s, endorsed the bill. He did so recognizing that it was a flawed piece of legislation that was often supported by bigots, but argued that unskilled immigrant labor tended to reduce the standard of living of domestic-born workers. His concern that immigration undermined the economic well-being of the domestic worker contributed to his support for the literacy test. It was, in short, "his long advocacy of a just living wage that led him to consider restriction as the *sine qua non* of improved living conditions for workers."[27]

Other higher-ranking Church officials took a contrary view to that of Ryan. In 1913, the *New York Times* ran a story that highlighted the Vatican's opposition to the literacy test as proposed and stated that the "Papal Authorities make no secret of their conviction that the bill was conceived from deliberately anti-Catholic motives, and it is sincerely hoped that the U.S. Senate will kill it."[28] On at least two separate occasions America's leading prelate, Cardinal James Gibbons of Baltimore, spoke out against the literacy test. In 1915 and 1917, he issued statements declaring his opposition following its passage in Congress. At the later date, Gibbons urged Wilson to veto the bill, stating that intellectual attainment is not the test of virtue and if the United States had "refused such illiterates from the beginning of our Government, our country would have lost the benefit of their virtue, thrift, industry, and an enterprising spirit."[29] Although Wilson heeded his call, Congress quickly overturned the veto and the literacy test became law.

THE ERA OF IMMIGRATION RESTRICTION

The high point of immigration restriction came with the passage of the 1921 and 1924 quota legislation. The quota legislation was influenced by the findings of the Dillingham Commission that had, more than a decade earlier, spent over three years, more than a million dollars, and employed a staff of more than three hundred people to produce forty-two volumes that supported restrictionist sentiment. The Commission's findings were largely based on a racial logic that deemed the "New Immigration" from southern and eastern Europe as inferior to the stock of immigrants from the "Old Immigration" that was of a more Anglo-Saxon and northern European variety. Paired with a newly minted nationalist sentiment following World War I, fallout from the Red Scare in the war's immediate aftermath, and high unemployment, conditions were ripe for restriction.[30]

The 1921 law limited European immigration to three percent of the total number of foreign-born population of a given country based on the 1910 census. In 1924, the restrictionist measures were further tightened by Congress, which moved to use the 1890 census and cut the quota from three to two percent of the foreign-born population. There was some concern among restrictionists that using an arbitrary cut-off date to achieve a desired form of discrimination was a crass and artificial way to protect the proportion of the old native stock.[31] In its place, a new mechanism—the national origins formula—was passed in 1924 but did not go into effect until later that decade. The national origins plan "calculated quotas not on the composition of the foreign-born population at a given census but on the 'national origins' of the American population as a whole."[32]

The NCWC remained relatively silent in the face of the 1921 immigration restriction legislation and did not make it a priority in their legislative agenda.[33] But by 1924 Conference leadership had become more vocal in their opposition to immigration restriction, so much so that the *Congressional Record* listed it as a "'distinguished organization' that opposed the restrictionist elements of the national origins plan."[34] In early 1924, the General Secretary of the NCWC, Rev. John Burke, submitted a letter to Representative Albert Johnson who was a cosponsor of the quota bill. Here Burke stated that the NCWC was not opposed to immigration restriction as such, but held that the legislation currently proposed was "distinctly un-American" because of its discriminatory basis.[35] That same year the Bureau of Immigration's Director, Bruce Mohler, testified before the House Committee on Immigration and Naturalization on the topic of the national origins legislation, during which time he lauded the desire of immigrants to Americanize and the work that the NCWC had engaged in to assist in this process. Unfortunately, given its discriminatory basis he argued that the proposed legislation undermined Americanization efforts and had sent the world a message not of "good will and equal justice to all, but of discrimination, of difference, and of dislike." While not opposed to restriction in principle, Mohler noted that any efforts in this direction should be based on "moral, humane, and economic grounds."[36]

Efforts by the NCWC to prevent passage of the legislation that year failed, but in the following decades, Conference leadership consistently opposed the national origins quota system. A February 1928 memo to Bruce Mohler, the General Secretary of the NCWC, for example, stated bluntly that the Administrative Committee, which had broad oversight over the work of the Conference, is "definitely against the National Origins Clause as it now stands."[37] Reviewing the work of the Bureau of Immigration over thirty years later during testimony before President Harry Truman's Commission on Immigration and Naturalization, Mohler declared that, in regard to the NCWC's opposition to the quota legislation, there "was hardly a year since the 1920s in which similar representations were not recorded."[38]

The quota legislation resulted in a significant decrease in the volume of immigration into the United States from Europe. With the onset of the Great Depression and World War II, traditional forms of immigration were further disrupted. In 1930, about two hundred forty-one thousand immigrants entered the country, while just three years later that number dropped to twenty-three thousand. The sociologist Douglas Massey put the effect of the Depression on immigration in perspective when he noted that "with mass unemployment in the United States, the demand for immigrant workers evaporated and during the 1930s total immigration fell below 1 million for the first time since the 1830s. Only 528,000 immigrants entered the United States from 1931 to 1940, yielding an annual average of only 53,000."[39] World War II provided yet another barrier to international migration from Europe, with only about forty thousand immigrants entering the United States on average during the war years of 1939–1945. Beginning to dwindle as early as the 1910s, within a few short decades later, mass immigration from Europe had come to an end.[40]

In contrast to the dwindling number of European immigrants, Catholic theologian Timothy Matovina has argued that Hispanic immigration witnessed a "counter-trajectory" in that "just as European immigration diminished to relatively miniscule numbers as a result of restrictive immigration legislation in the 1920s, Hispanic immigration began in earnest with the Mexican Revolution."[41] In the years immediately preceding World War I, southwestern agriculture began to rely more on Mexican migrants as a labor source. Responding to complaints expressed by the agricultural sector, Mexican migrant labor was temporarily exempted from the 1917 literacy test and other restrictive laws, thus making it easier to import labor from Mexico. Furthermore, western hemisphere migrants were exempt from the quota limitation implemented in the 1921 and 1924 quota legislation.[42] With demand for Mexican labor high, migrants from Mexico began to enter the United States in significant numbers.

From the first to the third decade of the twentieth century, immigration from Mexico jumped from fifty thousand to four hundred sixty thousand.[43] The influx of Mexican immigrants was further spurred following the Mexican Revolution and a period of aggressive anti-Catholicism that followed.[44] By 1927, the Mexican government began to deport members of the hierarchy, priests, and religious men and women. Soon thereafter, streams of religious refugees clamored for entry into the United States, many of whom were Catholic. In response, the NCWC helped to channel immigrants toward Mexican communities that were already established in the United States, an activity that was done for some years in coordination with the Church's continuing work on the border.[45]

With the onset of the Great Depression and the absence of employment opportunities, immigration from Mexico declined for a time, but again reemerged following an increase in the labor demands precipitated by the United States' entry into World War II. In 1942, the United States and Mexican governments negotiated an agreement that resulted in the establishment of the Bracero Program. The program was initially launched as a wartime measure to respond to labor shortages in the agricultural industry and provide cheap labor in abundance. In 1947, Congress allowed the statutory basis for the program to expire, although administrative efforts continued the program until 1951 when Congress formally sanctioned it.

Over the next decade critics argued that abuses were taking place in the system. For example, in 1951 President Truman's Commission on Migratory Labor reported that employer abuses and lax enforcement produced deplorable working and living conditions for braceros." Its recommendations to restrict contract labor went unheeded.[46] That same year the Mexican government threatened to abrogate the agreement reforms that would provide greater protections for migrant workers.[47]

The Catholic Church joined criticisms of the program during the 1950s. In March 1959, Msgr. George Higgins, director of the NCWC's Social Action Department, was asked to participate on the Eisenhower Administration's Committee on Migratory Labor and tasked to analyze continuing legitimacy of the Bracero Program. The Committee's final report focused on the damage that the program had done to the domestic labor force, its tendency to depress domestic wages, and its "deleterious effect on working conditions."[48] In testimony provided that same year, Higgins declared that Catholic farmers are required in good conscience to refuse participation in the program. During the same hearing, Fr. James Vizzard, a representative from the National Catholic Rural Life Conference, described the "bracero program as a 'not too subtle substitute for slavery.'"[49] The program was finally terminated in 1964.[50]

Parallel to the establishment of the Bracero Program in the early 1940s, World War II initiated another serious crisis that forced a reassessment of migration related policy. Beginning in the mid-1930s the proliferation of displaced persons or, in more modern parlance—refugees—posed a new challenge. The takeover and consolidation of power in the German government by Hitler and his Third Reich led to widespread political persecution that rapidly expanded over the course of the decade. The ravages of World War II further contributed to dislocation, as millions of people were driven from their homes, and eventually forced into refugee camps that dotted the European landscape. By the mid-1930s, the bishops had taken steps to respond to the refugee crisis but they did not become immersed in these efforts until after the war's end. Considerations of space prohibit us here from exploring in depth the Catholic Church's activities regarding these populations. For our purposes, the challenges raised in this regard are important insofar as they intersect with immigration policy during this period.

The quota system, already discussed above, provided a serious obstacle for anyone hoping to help move refugees out of camps in Europe and resettle them into the United States. Until 1980, there was no separate process that dealt with refugee resettlement on the one hand, and the admission of immigrants on the other. According to the quota legislation each migrant, whether a "traditional" immigrant or a refugee, was counted against the pre-existing quota limit of a country. Given the small annual quota of some countries, resettling refugees in large enough numbers to make any sort of impact on the problem was next to impossible. To respond adequately to the problem and resettle refugees in sufficient numbers, one had to either eliminate the quota system altogether or pass emergency legislation that would provide an exception for displaced populations. This became particularly pronounced in the post-war period when the numbers of displaced persons in Europe increased dramatically.

Given that at this time the elimination of the quota was not a realistic option, proponents of refugee resettlement pursued emergency legislation that could provide some degree of relief. The Catholic Church was active in advocating for legislation of this sort and for their simultaneous efforts to build an infrastructure on the diocesan level that could assist in the resettlement process. Their efforts eventually paid off with the passage of the Displaced Persons Act of 1948. During the four years in which the Act was in place, the NCWC assisted in the resettlement of nearly two hundred thousand refugees.[51]

Four years after the passage of the 1948 Displaced Persons Act, Congress enacted another important piece of migration related legislation: the Immigration and Nationality Act of 1952. More popularly known as the McCarran-Walter Act, the legislation was the culmination of a multiyear undertaking by Congress to codify and streamline existing immigration law. The final version of the bill eliminated some of the restrictive measures that had been a part of immigration policy, including racial barriers and the easing of restrictions on the admission of men and women religious. Nevertheless, the McCarran-Walter Act reinforced and strengthened the quota system that had been in place for nearly three decades. One might assume that the given the long-standing moral objection to the quota system, the Catholic Church would be hesitant to support legislation that reinforced its legitimacy. Yet, despite their objections, the NCWC eventually endorsed the legislation. Such support highlights the extent to which pragmatic considerations played a role in the conference's deliberations on immigration policy.

In early 1952, NCWC leadership called a meeting to discuss the legislative strategies related to migration policy. At this time, three overarching priorities were decided upon. First, work to amend the

McCarran bill so that it contained less restrictive provisions. Second, secure additional emergency legislation similar to the 1948 Displaced Persons Act, which was set to expire later that year. Third, develop a national education campaign that would inculcate a Christian attitude on immigration.[52] As already noted, the final version of the McCarran-Walter Act, while maintaining the quota system, eliminated some of the restrictive elements that had been established through earlier legislation. Consequently, while limited in its reach, some progress was made on the first priority.

At the same time that the McCarran-Walter bill was being considered, the Conference was continuing to advocate on behalf of further emergency legislation that would allow for the admission of more refugees from Europe. During this period NCWC leadership was purportedly informed that if the immigration legislation failed to pass, emergency legislation aimed at refugee resettlement would also be killed.[53] Their intelligence on Capitol Hill also made it clear that some of the more liberal alternatives being promoted in place of the McCarran-Walter Act had no chance of passage at that time. The Conference was thus confronted with a precarious either/or: Support the passage of the McCarran-Walter Act, weaknesses and all, or oppose the bill and, if successful, be stuck with the status quo. Further complicating matters, opposition to the bill's final passage and enactment could put into jeopardy any further emergency refugee legislation. Given this predicament, NCWC leadership finally concluded that "the practical choice, therefore, was one between the McCarran-Walter bill or the status quo, and, bad as the McCarran-Walter bill is, the status quo is worse."[54] In the summer of 1952, the NCWC came out in support of the legislation.

Following the McCarran-Walter Act's eventual passage, and given the absence of any major immigration legislation throughout the rest of the decade, the NCWC continued to focus on refugee crises that emerged. These included the crises in Hungary following its attempted revolution in 1956 and problems associated with Cuba in the years following Castro's rise to power. The Church also continued to engage in its long term educational program that aimed to bring about immigration policies that were consistent with the moral vision of the Church and which was listed as its third priority during the 1952 meeting on the McCarran-Walter Act. Its long-term goal remained the elimination of the quota system and its replacement with legislation that was more immigrant and family friendly. By the mid-1960s, an opportunity to realize this objective was at hand.

THE END OF IMMIGRATION RESTRICTION? ...NOT SO FAST

In the spring of 1965 an unnamed representative from the NCWC testified before the House and Senate Immigration Committees in regard to pending immigration legislation. Here the representative took the opportunity to denounce the racially discriminatory immigration policy currently in place, applaud attempts to emphasize family reunification, and commend Congress for setting aside a specific annual quota designated for refugee populations.[55] Shortly after the testimony, the newly installed Director of the Department of Immigration, John McCarthy, authored a memo to Msgr. Paul Tanner, the General Secretary of the NCWC, informing him of a national public relations campaign that would push for an overhaul of the immigration system. According to current intelligence, it appeared that the Administration was on the verge of supporting legislation that both mirrored the interests of the NCWC and which apparently had the support of both houses of Congress. Garnering grassroots support for such legislation within the Catholic community would be an important step to ensure its passage.[56]

While initially hesitant to pursue immigration reform, the Johnson Administration eventually came to support the elimination of the national origins quotas. This was partly due to the perceived damage the policy inflicted on American credibility internationally and partly because of its connection to the civil rights movement and the discriminatory basis that underlay the original quota legislation. Jack Valenti, a close advisor to the president, later admitted that the president "eventually recognized that existing immigration law and in particular national origins quotas created many decades before on racist grounds, as inconsistent with civil rights and racial justice."[57] In place of the national origins quotas, new legislation made family reunification the centerpiece of America's immigration policy. It ended the long-standing ban on Asian immigration. For the first time, an annual visa ceiling of one hundred twenty thousand was also imposed on immigrants originating in the Western Hemisphere. Given the new emphasis on family reunification, spouses, unmarried minor children, and parents of U.S. citizens were exempted from the overall ceiling limit.[58] Just days before President Johnson signed the 1965 Immigration Act into law, an internal memo was circulated within the NCWC noting that Church leadership was "fairly well satisfied" with the new legislation, particularly given its elimination of the national quota system.[59]

The 1965 Act helped to alter the landscape that had previously informed debates over immigration and its role in American life. One important shift had to do with a significant increase in Latino and Asian immigration. With the removal of the prohibition on Asian immigration, paired with the new emphasis on family reunification, immigration from Asia witnessed significant growth in the following decades. This increase was in part due to "chain migration" in which immigrants took advantage of the emphasis on family reunification and were able to bring family members into the United States to live.[60] Further contributing to the increase in Asian populations was the refugee crisis that occurred following the fall of Saigon and the admission of hundreds of Southeast Asians into the United States. The emphasis on family reunification also contributed to an increase in Latino immigration. In 1999, six hundred fifty thousand legal immigrants were accounted for by the Immigration and Naturalization Services (INS), of which 70 percent were of either Asian or Latino heritage.[61] Taken together, this signified a notable increase in the prevalence of these populations living in the United States. The next chapter in this volume, authored by Fr. Allan Deck, will examine some of the pastoral challenges confronting the Church that emerged in the face of this changing demographic, as many of these new immigrants were Catholic. We will thus not address this issue here, but instead focus on some of the policy challenges that arose following the 1965 Immigration Act.

In addition to the demographic changes brought on by the 1965 immigration bill, debates over immigration in the early 1970s also witnessed increasing concerns about illegal immigration. In 1960 the INS apprehended approximately twenty-three thousand unauthorized immigrants, a number that increased to more than a million by 1980.[62] The reasons behind this growing problem were manifold. One of the immediate causes had to do with the elimination of the Bracero Program in 1964. For more than twenty years, American agricultural enterprises had grown accustomed to cheap Mexican labor. With the program's discontinuation, this dependence did not end but rather was pushed underground, thus contributing to the presence of an unauthorized migrant labor population.

A second contributing factor to the rise in illegal immigration was the implementation of the annual quota ceiling of one hundred twenty thousand placed on immigrants from the Western Hemisphere. Prior to the 1965 Act there was no official cap placed on Western Hemisphere entrants. One consequence of the cap was that the demand for visas continually outstripped the supply, thus leading to more lengthy waiting periods. This in turn increased the likelihood that those who wanted to find work or reunite with family members already living in the United States, but who could not secure a visa, would enter illegally.[63] Echoing this concern, Archbishop Robert Sanchez of Santa Fe, New Mexico, declared during testimony to Congress that this Western Hemisphere ceiling had led to significant waiting times for migrants who were seeking entry into the United States "and has contributed substantially to unlawful immigration."[64]

Economic concerns played an important role in heightening the visibility of illegal immigration and help to explain its growing importance in the arena of policymaking during the 1970s. Within a few years after the implementation of the 1965 Act, critics worried that immigrants who either entered the country illegally to find work or who remained after the expiration of their visas "displace low-income American workers, hamper unionizing efforts, encourage employers to disregard wage, hour, and working conditions statutes, and generally depress the labor market."[65] As early as 1971, Congressional leaders began to propose legislation that would address some of these concerns, many of which included a focus on how to remove the economic incentives that attracted migrants to enter the United States illegally. Such proposals generally emphasized the efficacy of imposing sanctions on employers who knowingly hired unauthorized immigrants.[66]

Entering into the ninety-third Congress (January 3, 1973– January 3, 1975), Representative Joshua Eilberg (D-PA), the new chair of the House Subcommittee on Immigration and Nationality, announced that one of the priorities for his subcommittee was to assert control over the influx of illegal aliens. In line with this objective, Representative Peter Rodino (D-NJ) offered H.R. 982, the major thrust of which "was to remove the economic incentive which causes aliens to enter the United States to engage in illegal employment and to remove the incentive for employers to exploit this source of labor."[67] The bill was passed in the House but never made it out of the Senate Subcommittee on Immigration. In 1975, a similar bill was offered up in the House, at which point Msgr. George Higgins testified on behalf of the U.S. Catholic Conference (USCC). At the core of his testimony he called on Congress to increase economic assistance to Latin American countries and to provide an "across the board grant of amnesty with the necessary residency cut-off date for eligibility and adjustment of status, without chargeability against the numerical ceilings."[68] The increase in foreign aid would presumably aim at establishing economic stability in sending countries on which migrants could depend, thus avoiding the pressures to migrate elsewhere to provide for the needs of themselves or their families. In this view, the disparity between the economic conditions of the migrant's home country and America function as important push and pull factors that help to drive migration. Reducing this disparity would help to alleviate the pressures that promote movement across borders.

The rationale supporting Higgins' call for amnesty was twofold. First, the failure of the American government to enforce its immigration laws for years, taken alongside the willingness of American employers to hire unauthorized immigrants regardless of their status, placed a heavy share of the responsibility on both entities for the chaotic state that currently existed. A deportation-only strategy would not incorporate the more complex moral analysis that would apportion blame evenly among the various actors. Second, the failure to provide an amnesty would likely only drive unauthorized populations further underground and in doing so create a permanent subculture in the American economy. Higgins closed his testimony by recognizing that some sort of employer sanctions might be incorporated into a wider immigration reform bill, but if they were, he emphasized that such sanctions be applied only to prospective hires and not retroactively. Furthermore, regulations would have to be developed to ensure that employers did not discriminate when screening and hiring new employees.[69]

A few months later and in anticipation that immigration legislation focusing on employer sanctions would be passed out of the House, Bishop James Rausch issued a statement that developed some of the central themes of Higgins' earlier testimony. Like Higgins, Rausch referenced the importance of establishing more stable economic conditions in the developing world. He also expressed concern that the employer sanctions provision as currently expressed would put the onus on employers to enforce immigration laws that the government had for years failed to enforce, either as a matter of policy or incompetence. This dynamic would, he continued, likely result in widespread discrimination because "legal aliens and minority group citizens will be denied employment simply because employers will not want to run the risk of inadvertently violating the law."[70]

Suspicious of employer sanctions, during the 1970s the bishops provided an alternative approach to deal with the problem of illegal immigration. According to conference leadership the first step in dealing with this problem was to address those who were already here illegally, allow them to adjust their status, and then turn attention to hiring practices that attracted immigrants to come here illegally. This would in effect "wipe the slate clean" and provide the conditions on which an effective *verification* system could be used to avoid this problem in the future. Such a system was at least in principle already in effect. By virtue of legislation passed in 1972, the Social Security Administration was required to screen all applicants for employment by reviewing Social Security cards to determine eligibility. One conference spokesman noted that "if amnesty were granted, for example, to all who are in the United States today, or as of January 1, 1973, then the Social Security card would become the proof of the right by the holder to take up employment."[71] In contrast, enacting an employer sanctions strategy would lead to the dislocation of hard working immigrants who were members of long standing communities and who had families who were dependent on them for their basic economic sustenance. Such an approach would be "inhumane" and "immoral."[72] Despite the bishops' efforts and those of Congress, no meaningful legislation was passed that decade.

The failure to pass legislation contributed to Congress' decision to establish the Select Commission on Immigration and Refugee Policy (SCIRP) in 1978. Democratic leaders, who had initially supported the formation of such a commission, hoped that it "would broker an effective compromise package on illegal immigration while renewing support for robust legal immigration."[73] Its final report wrestled with these concerns and recommended that the U.S. government should "close the back door to undocumented/illegal migration, open the front door a little more to accommodate legal migration in the interests of this country," and clarify the objectives and the processes through which U.S. immigration policies could be adjudicated more fairly.[74] To do so, the Committee report suggested increased funding for the border patrol, the establishment of employer sanctions that would make it illegal for employers to hire undocumented workers, the provision of additional visas that would help to clear preexisting backlogs, and the implementation of a legalization process for migrants who were currently in the country illegally.[75]

The recommendations made by SCIRP laid the groundwork for the eventual passage of the Immigration Reform and Control Act (IRCA), which was signed into law on November 6, 1986 by President Reagan. Consistent with the SCIRP's suggested course of action the legislation provided a multipronged approach to deal with illegal immigration. First, to eliminate the jobs magnet an employee sanctions process was put into place that would penalize employers who hired unauthorized immigrants. Second, to inhibit immigrants from attempting to cross the border, increased security measures were instituted and resources were provided to strengthen the reach of the border patrol. Third, legal residency was given to undocumented immigrants who could prove they had lived in the United States for at least five consecutive years and had arrived in the United States prior to January 1, 1982.[76]

From the early years of the Carter administration and into the mid-1980s, in both official statements and in testimony before Congress, the Catholic bishops reiterated their desire to have a broad amnesty as the centerpiece of any sort of reform.[77] Only then would the USCC support the implementation of additional enforcement mechanisms. On the eve of IRCA's passage the National Conference of Catholic Bishops issued a resolution on immigration reform. Here they revisited the issue of employer sanctions and emphasized that any immigration reform "must be based on legalization as its foundation, rather than as an ancillary and conditional component," and that, furthermore, "only when legalization is treated as the centerpiece of immigration reform is it conceivable that the bishops will judge employer sanctions tolerable."[78] In addition, the statement posited that any sanctions that were implemented would have to be accompanied by clearly defined and enforceable anti-discrimination legislation, the development of a secure and uniform employment-identification system, and assurances that enforcement efforts would not focus disproportionately on employers who hire predominately minority populations.[79] Given that employer sanctions were included in the legislation under discussion and would almost certainly be included in any bill, the bishops were likely being realistic in their approach to the bill and trying to frame its eventual implementation.

In a statement released following the passage of IRCA, then Archbishop Roger Mahony noted that the U.S. Catholic Conference's "support of IRCA was mixed since we opposed and continue to oppose the negative components of the new law."[80] Mahony reiterated concerns that the employer sanctioning elements of the new legislation would lead to discriminatory practices but expressed support for the legalization process that would regularize the status of large numbers of the unauthorized population.[81] While the legalization process was a positive development "the final version of the Immigration Reform and Control Act of 1986 offered legalized status only to individuals who had resided continuously in the United States since before January 1, 1982. This 1982 cutoff date was too restrictive. It left an ineligible population of post-1982 arrivals that many estimated was as large as the eligible population."[82] In response, the bishops called for an expansion of the cut-off date that would cover post-1982 arrivals. Because of the overly restrictive cut-off date and the severe consequences that any sanctions would have on the remaining undocumented population the bishops again reasserted their opposition to employer sanctions. As reflected in earlier statements, they worried that legal immigrants would also suffer discrimination at the hands of employers concerned that they might mistakenly hire an undocumented alien and suffer economic consequences for doing so.[83]

On the opposite side of the spectrum, restrictionist critics of the legislation argued that President Reagan failed to impose a viable enforcement regime that would decrease illegal immigration over the long term; in short, the employer sanctions and border enforcement strategies imposed by IRCA were thought to be inadequate to address the problem.[84] While well intended, IRCA did not permanently resolve the issue of illegal immigration; within a matter of a few years the issue again resurfaced as a contentious point of debate.[85] By the early 1990s a new regime of enforcement had replaced the more nuanced approach that had prevailed in the 1986 legislation. For more than a decade, "enforcement-only" became the rallying cry of immigration restrictionists and was increasingly embodied in federal policy.

Beginning with the Immigration Act of 1990, emphasis was placed on enhanced border security and the provision of funding to hire new border patrol agents, increased sanctions on employers hiring undocumented workers, and increased penalties for immigration violations.[86] One of the most "promising" tactics developed to secure the border originated in El Paso under the direction of Border Patrol Chief Sylvester Reyes. At the time, the urban area surrounding El Paso was a popular crossing point for unauthorized immigrants. Under his watch, enforcement resources were poured into the surrounding area and, as a result, unauthorized immigration through the El Paso area was substantially reduced.

Following the implementation of "Operation Blockade," the designation of Reyes' enforcement efforts, the bishop of El Paso, Raymundo Peña, issued a statement that was critical of the strategy. Bishop Peña noted that while the Church does not condone law breaking, laws must be constructed in such a way that they reflect the reality on the ground. Most people who crossed the border on a daily basis were day laborers who were merely trying to provide a better life for their families and who "we allowed...into our homes, into our gardens, into our farms and into our businesses."[87] They were not criminals but in fact, hard workers who wanted to improve their families' living conditions and who, through their work, were contributing to the improvement of our own lives on the American side of the border. In short, the blockade strategy disrupted long standing migration and economic patterns and undermined the well-being of the surrounding community, both on the American and Mexican sides. Peña concluded by calling for a moratorium on the blockade and an opportunity to work with federal and local officials to develop a system that would adequately respond to the complexity of the economic conditions on the border.[88] His calls went unheeded.

The apparent success of Reyes' efforts was not lost on bureaucrats in Washington, DC. Similar tactics were put into place on a long stretch of land around San Diego, California the following year. As in El Paso, unauthorized border crossings in the San Diego area were reduced; the border appeared in these areas to be, once again, under control. In response, funding provided to the Border Patrol and to the INS increased dramatically from the mid-1980s through the first decade of the twentieth century. In 1986, the Border Patrol's annual budget was $151 million and the Immigration and Naturalization Service's budget was $451 million, but "by 2002 the Border Patrol's budget had reached $1.6 billion and that of the INS stood at $6.2 billion, 10 and 13 times their 1986 values, respectively."[89] By 2011, the Border Patrol budget was $3.6 billion, an increase of more than double that of the 2006 budget.[90] Further, between 1992 and 2009, the number of U.S. Border Patrol officers more than quadrupled from approximately three thousand five hundred to over twenty thousand officers.[91]

Given the substantial increase in border enforcement during this period, one might assume that there would be a parallel decrease in the number of unauthorized entries. The numbers say otherwise. Throughout the 1990s, annual illegal immigration rates increased substantially at the same time that funding for the Border Patrol increased multiple times. A study by the Pew Hispanic Forum found that in 1993 approximately four hundred thousand unauthorized migrants came into the United States. The figure peaked in 2000 at approximately six hundred sixty-seven thousand, at which point the numbers dropped following 9/11. In 2002, the number of unauthorized migrants dropped to levels that were roughly equivalent to the early 1990s. By 2004 unauthorized entries again began to creep upward, but remained lower than the numbers in the mid- and late 1990s.[92]

Throughout this period the bishops repeatedly criticized the increasingly restrictionist approach to immigration policy that was finding expression both in state and federal level legislation. In a statement issued by the USCC's Committee on Migration in 1993, the bishops expressed concern over the animosity "toward immigrants evident now in some parts of society and even, sad to say, supported by some public officials," and rejected policies that they argued fostered "greed," "racism," and "cultural bias."[93] Policies that unduly emphasize enforcement only and ignore the flesh and blood circumstances that give rise to illegal immigration, not to mention the communities within which unauthorized immigrants reside, undermine human dignity, unnecessarily divide families, and violate the fundamental notions of fairness and equal protection.[94]

In testimony before the House Judiciary Subcommittee on Immigration, Auxiliary Bishop DiMarzio of Newark, New Jersey, argued that these tendencies were exacerbated with the passage of the 1996 immigration legislation that expanded the grounds for deportation, eliminated administrative and judicial relief for immigrants, and established mandatory detention provisions.[95] The bishops continued to respond critically against welfare reform measures that they deemed unduly prejudicial to immigrants and their families,[96] and criticized state level legislation that denied health, education, and other services to undocumented immigrants.[97] By the mid-1990s, at the very latest, the bishops had begun to recognize that, in contrast to the enforcement only dynamic that had become the dominant paradigm a more comprehensive approach to immigration reform had to occur.

CONCLUSION

On the eve of the new millennium and in advance of the 2000 election cycle, the U.S. bishops published *Faithful Citizenship*. Here they laid out a framework related to immigration that had evolved over the previous three decades and that they argued should provide the basis for future immigration related legislation. In the document they called on Congress and the president to support "a more generous immigration and refugee policy based on providing temporary or permanent safe haven for those in need; protecting immigrant workers from exploitation; promoting family reunification; safeguarding the right of all peoples to return to their homelands; ensuring that public benefits and a fair and efficient process for obtaining citizenship are available to immigrants; extending to immigrants the full protection of U.S. law; and addressing the root causes of migration."[98]

This framework was developed more systematically three years later in the joint pastoral letter issued by the American and Mexican bishops titled *Strangers No Longer: Together on the Journey of Hope (SNL)*. During the official release of the pastoral letter on January 24, 2003, Auxiliary Bishop Thomas Wenski of Miami, Florida stated that, "we call attention to the simple fact that our current immigration system is broken and must be reformed. The consequences of this flawed system—the exploitation, abuse, and even the death of migrants—are morally unacceptable."[99] Since its publication, the pastoral letter has functioned as a blueprint for the bishops' advocacy efforts in relation to immigration, particularly during the debates that occurred over comprehensive immigration reform. In the final chapter of this volume, J. Kevin Appleby will explore the concrete way in which the bishops engaged in these debates and how the moral framework expressed in *SNL* informed this engagement. In anticipation of this, the intermediate chapters will pick up on some of the central themes of the pastoral letter and develop their significance in light of the bishops' policy and pastoral priorities and in their relationship to Catholic social teaching.

NOTES

1. Oscar Handlin, *The Uprooted* (Philadelphia: Little Brown and Company, 1951), 3.

2. José Casanova, "Roman and Catholic and American: The Transformation of Catholicism in the United States," *International Journal of Politics* 6, no. 1 (Autumn 1992): 76.

3. Timothy Matovina, "Remapping American Catholicism," *U.S. Catholic Historian* 28, no 4 (Fall 2010): 36–43.

4. David O'Brien, *Public Catholicism*, 2nd Edition (Maryknoll, NY: Orbis Books, 1996), 38–41.

5. John Higham, *Strangers in the Land: Patterns of American Nativism, 1860–1925* (New Brunswick, NJ: Rutgers University Press, 1955), 4. In addition to anti-Catholicism, Higham also isolated the fear of foreign radicalism and, by the turn of the twentieth century, a racial nationalism that was built on the notion of Anglo-Saxon superiority as feeding nativist sentiments.

6. O'Brien, 47–55.

7. Gerald Fogarty, "Public Patriotism and Private Politics: The Tradition of American Catholicism," in "American Catholics:

Patriotism and Dissent in War and Peace," special issue, *U.S. Catholic Historian* 4, no. 1 (1984): 8–10; Casanova, 83.

8. Stephen D'Giovanni, "The Apostolic Delegate in the United States and Immigration, 1892–1896," in "The Apostolic Delegation/Nunciature 1893–1993" special issue *U.S. Catholic Historian* 12, no. 2 (Spring 1994): 57.

9. Jay Dolan, *The Immigrant Church: New York's Irish and German Catholics, 1815–1860* (Notre Dame, IN: University of Notre Dame Press, 1975), 21.

10. Jay P. Dolan, "A Critical Period in American Catholicism," *The Review of Politics* 35, no. 4 (October, 1973): 526–28.

11. Richard Linkh, *American Catholicism and European Immigrants* (Staten Island, NY: Center for Migration Studies, 1975), 68.

12. Ibid.

13. Douglas J. Slawson, *The Foundation and First Decade of the National Welfare Conference* (Washington, DC: The Catholic University of America Press, 1992), 46–48.

14. Letter from Dudley Wooten to Msgr. John J. Burke, October 29, 1920, National Catholic Welfare Conference: International Affairs: Immigration, 1920–1922, Box 39, File 25, The American Catholic History Research Center and University Archives (Citations referring to the American Catholic History Research Center will hereafter be designated as ACHRCUA); Letter from Msgr. John J. Burke to Judge Dudley Wooten, November 5, 1920, National Catholic Welfare Conference: International Affairs: Immigration, 1920–1922, Box 39, File 25, ACHRCUA.

15. Slawson, 235.

16. In the spring of 1921, Bruce Mohler was hired as the director of the Bureau of Immigration, a position in which he served for more than four decades. In 1953 the Bureau of Immigration was restructured as a department and, twelve years later in 1965, renamed Migration and Refugee Services.

17. General statistical information related to the port programs, along with observations regarding trends in migratory patterns, can be found in the annual reports published by the NCWC during this period. They are available at ACHRCUA.

18. "NCWC Annual Report," 1924/1925, NCWC: Annual Report, ACHRCUA.

19. Ibid.

20. John Higham, "American Immigration Policy in Historical Perspective," *Law and Contemporary Problems* 21, no. 2 (Spring 1956): 214.

21. Gerald Neuman, "The Lost Century of American Immigration Law (1776–1885), *Columbia Law Review* 93, no. 8 (December 1993): 1840–1993.

22. Daniel Tichenor, *Dividing Lines: The Politics of Immigration Control in America* (Princeton, NJ: Princeton University Press, 2002), 68.

23. Ibid., 67–70; for an exceptional overview of the dynamics surrounding the Chinese Exclusion Act, see Andrew Gyory, *Closing the Gates: Race, Politics and the Chinese Exclusion Act* (Chapel Hill, NC: The University of North Carolina Press, 1998).

24. John Higham, "The Politics of Immigration Restriction," *Immigration and Nationality Law Review* 1 (1976/1977): 12–14.

25. James Pula, "American Immigration and the Dillingham Commission," *Polish American Studies* 37, no. 1 (Spring 1980): 7.

26. Grover Cleveland, "Veto Message," March 2, 1897. Online by Gerhard Peters and John T. Woolley, *The American Presidency Project*. http://www.presidency.ucsb.edu/ws/?pid=70845 (accessed August 19, 2012).

27. Linkh, 175.

28. "Indignation at the Vatican," *New York Times* (February 17, 1914), 3.

29. "Denounce Literacy Test," *New York Times* (January 25, 1915), 7; "Cardinal Urges Veto," *New York Times* (January 26, 1917), 9.

30. Pula, 8–11.

31. Higham, "The Politics of Immigration Restriction, 27–28.

32. Tichenor, 145.

33. Jeanne Danielle Petit, "Building Citizens: Women, Men and the Immigration Restriction Debates, 1890–1929" (PhD dissertation, University of Notre Dame, 2000), 153–54.

34. Ibid., 147.

35. Reverend John Burke, "Letter from Burke to Representative Albert Johnson," January 10, 1924, International Affairs: Legislation, Box 42, Folder 1, 1920–1926. ACHRCUA.

36. "Testimony before the House Committee on Immigration and Naturalization," January 7, 1924, International Affairs: Legislations, Box 42, Folder 1, ACHRCUA.

37. "Memo to Bruce Mohler," February 21, 1928, NCWC: Office of the General Secretary Box 42, file 1, ACHRCUA.

38. Testimony of Bruce Mohler to the President's Commission on Immigration and Naturalization in *Hearings before the President's Commission on Immigration and Naturalization* (Washington, DC: Government Printing Office, 1952), 1738–40.

39. Douglas S. Massey, "The New Immigration and Ethnicity in the United States," *Population and Development Review* 21, no. 3 (September 1995): 636–37.

40. Ibid.

41. Matovina, "Remapping American Catholicism," 35. For a more extensive treatment of Hispanic/Latino Catholicism in the United States, see Timothy Matovina, *Latino Catholicism: Transformation in America's Largest Church* (Princeton, NJ: Princeton University Press, 2011).

42. Kitty Calavita, "U.S. Immigration and Policy Responses: The Limits of Legislation," in *Controlling Immigration: A Global Perspective*, eds. Wayne Cornelius, Philip Martin and James Hollifield (Stanford, California: Stanford University Press, 1994), 58–59.

43. Massey, 636.

44. Douglas Slawson, "The National Catholic Welfare Conference and the Church-State Conflict in Mexico, 1925–1929," *The Americas* 47, no. 1 (July 1990): 57.

45. Julia Young, "Cristero Diaspora: Mexican Immigrants, The U.S. Catholic Church, and Mexico's Cristero War, 1926–1929," *The Catholic Historical Review* 98, no. 2 (April, 2012): 274–83.

46. Ibid., 2.

47. Marco Prouty, *César Chávez: The Catholic Bishops, and the Farmworkers Struggle for Social Justice* (Tucson, Arizona: The University of Arizona Press, 2006), 10.

48. Prouty, 20; George G. Higgins, "The Migratory Worker in American Agriculture," *Review of Social Economy* 19, no. 1 (March 1961): 43–56.

49. Joe Brown, "End of Bracero Program Would be Bad for Us," *Lodi News Sentinel* (August 22, 1959), 7.

50. Kitty Calavita, *Inside the State: The Bracero Program, Immigration and the I.N.S.* (New York: Routledge Publishing, 1992), 1–3.

51. James Norris, "The International Catholic Migration Commission," *Catholic Lawyer* 4 (1958): 122.

52. Meeting on Immigration Problems, Notes, February 27, 1952, Box 40, International Affairs: Immigration, 1952, Jan-March, ACHRCUA.

53. Msgr. Paul Tanner to Bishops Joseph Ritter, June 23, 1952, International Affairs: Immigration, NCWC, Box 42, folder 4, ACHRCUA. For a more in-depth analysis of the debates that ensued surrounding the passage of the McCarran-Walter Act and the internal deliberations of the NCWC's leadership and their eventual endorsement, see Todd Scribner, "Negotiating Priorities: The National Catholic Welfare Conference and United States Migration Policy in a Post–World War II World, 1948–1952," *American Catholic Studies* 121, no. 4 (2010): 61–86.

54. Ibid.

55. Testimony before the House and Senate Immigration Committees, March 26, 1965, NCWC: International Affairs: Immigration: Legislation, Box 41, Folder 16, ACHRCUA.

56. Memo from John McCarthy to Msgr. Paul Tanner, June 1, 1965, NCWC: International Affairs: Immigration, Box 41, Folder 16, ACHRCUA.

57. Jack Valenti quoted in Tichenor, 213. Johnson had enthusiastically supported the McCarran-Walter act in 1952 and thus there was some trepidation within pro-immigration reform circles about his intentions on this issue.

58. For a more in-depth analysis of the new framework guiding immigration policy, see Tichenor, 213–18.

59. Memo from John McCarthy to Msgr. Paul Tanner, October 1, 1965, International Affairs: Immigration: Legislation, Box 41, Folder 16, ACHRCUA.

60. Tichenor, 218.

61. Roger Daniels, *Guarding the Golden Door* (New York: Hill and Wang, 2004), 147.

62. Kitty Calavita, "The New Politics of Immigration: 'Balanced Budget Conservatism' and the Symbolism of Proposition 187," *Social*

Problems 43, no. 3 (August 1996): 289. One point of contention related to the contemporary immigration debate has to do with how to reference those who are here illegally; should one refer to them as "undocumented immigrants," "illegal aliens," "illegal immigrants," or something else? Throughout this essay, I try to hew closely to the language used in the specific text, testimony, statement, or other item being referenced. Where I am not referring to a specific text, I will default to the term "unauthorized immigrant."

63. William Hartley, "United States Immigration Policy: The Case of the Western Hemisphere," *World Affairs* 135, no. 1 (Summer 1972): 61–66.

64. Archbishop Robert Sanchez, "USCC Testimony on Proposed Legislation to Reform U.S. Immigration," reprinted in *Origins* 5, no. 43 (April 15, 1976).

65. Hartley, 66.

66. Donald Hohl, "Attempts at Immigration Reform: 94th Congress," *International Migration Review* 10, no. 4 (Winter 1976): 524.

67. Donald Hohl, "The Illegal Alien and the Western Hemisphere Immigration Dilemma," *International Migration Review* 7, no. 3 (Autumn 1973): 323.

68. Msgr. John Higgins, Testimony before the U.S. House Judiciary Committee's Subcommittee on Immigration, *Origins* 4, no. 41 (April 3, 1975).

69. Ibid.

70. Bishop James Rausch, "Illegal Alien Bill Criticized," *Origins* 5, no. 11 (September 4, 1975); see also Archbishop Robert Sanchez, "USCC Testimony on Proposed Legislation to Reform U.S. Immigration Laws," *Origins* 5, no. 43 (April 15, 1976).

71. Archbishop Robert Sanchez, Testimony before the Senate Judiciary Committee's Subcommittee on Immigration and Naturalization," *Origins* 5, no. 43 (April 15, 1976).

72. Rausch, "Illegal Alien Bill Criticized."

73. Tichenor, 239.

74. Select Commission on Immigration and Refugee Policy, *U.S. Immigration Policy and the National Interest* (Washington, DC: U.S. Government Printing Office, 1981).

75. Ibid.

76. Douglas S. Massey, "Backfire at the Border: Why Enforcement without Legalization Cannot Stop Illegal Immigration," *Trade Policy Analysis*, CATO Institute: Center for Trade Policy Studies (June 13, 2005), 4.

77. See, for example, Bishop Thomas Kelly, "U.S. Catholic Conference Reacts to Carter Immigration Plan, *Origins* 7, no. 10 (August 25, 1978); Msgr. Daniel Hoye, "The Status of Undocumented Aliens," *Origins* 12, no. 15 (September 23, 1982).

78. National Conference of Catholic Bishops, "Resolution on Immigration Reform," *Origins* 15, no. 25 (December 5, 1985).

79. Ibid.

80. Archbishop Roger Mahony, "The Church and Illegal Aliens: Serving Those Who Do Not Receive Amnesty," *Origins* 16, no. 47 (May 7, 1987).

81. Ibid.

82. U.S. Catholic Bishops, "Statement on Employer Sanctions," *Origins* 18, no. 25 (December 1, 1988).

83. Ibid.; the same concern was expressed in USCC's commentary on the Republican and Democratic Platform of 1988, Frank Monahan, "USCC Platform Testimony to Democratic and Republican National Convention Party Platforms," *Origins* 18, no. 5 (June 6, 1988).

84. Tichenor, 262–64; see in particular chapter four in Nicholas Laham, *Ronald Reagan and the Politics of Immigration Reform* (Westport, CT: Praeger Publishing, 2000).

85. Massey, "Backfire at the Border," 4.

86. Douglas S. Massey, Jorge Durand, and Nolan J. Malone, *Beyond Smoke and Mirrors: Mexican Immigration in an Era of Economic Integration* (New York: Russell Sage Foundation Publications, 2003), 91.

87. Bishop Raymundo Peña, "A Call to Reassess Operation Blockade," *Origins* 23, no. 21 (November 4, 1993).

88. Ibid.

89. Massey, "Backfire at the Border," 5.

90. Chad Haddall, "Border Security: The Role of the U.S. Border Patrol," Congressional Research Service, March 3, 2010, 4–5.

91. Ibid., 21.

92. Jeffrey Passel and Robert Suro, "Rise, Peak, and Decline: Trends in U.S. Immigration 1992–2004," *Pew Hispanic Center Report* (Washington, DC: Pew Hispanic Center, 2005), 4–5, 29.

93. U.S. Bishops' Committee on Immigration, "The Injustice of Anti-Foreign Sentiment," *Origins* 23, no. 24 (November 25, 1993).

94. Ibid.

95. Bishop Nicholas DiMarzio, "Testimony on the Detention of Immigrants," *Origins* 28, no. 41 (April 1, 1990).

96. USCC Administrative Board, "Moral Principles and Policy Priorities on Welfare Reform," *Origins* 24, no. 41 (March 30, 1995).

97. California Catholic Conference, "State Ballot Initiative Promotes Fear of the Stranger," *Origins* 24, no. 16 (September 29, 1994); National Conference of Catholic Bishops, "Statement on Proposition 187 and the Immigration Debate," *Origins* 24, no. 25 (December 1, 1994).

98. USCC Administrative Board, *Faithful Citizenship: Civic Responsibility for a New Millennium* (Washington, DC: United States Catholic Conference, 1999).

99. Archbishop Thomas G. Wenski, "Historic Mexican-U.S. Joint Statement On Migration Released: Calls for Reform of 'Broken' System," January 24, 2003, United States Conference of Catholic Bishops.

CHAPTER 2

Pastoral Perspectives on Migration

Immigrants as New Evangelizers

Allan Figueroa Deck

INTRODUCTION

This chapter focuses on the universe of relatively recent Catholic immigrants in a new way, not primarily as objects of concern but as agents, subjects of both their own lives and important players in the Church and society in the United States. For much too long there has been a tendency to speak about so-called minority groups and immigrants as persons of need, even victims of injustice and oppression. There is truth to this charge, of course. But this is not the whole truth. In failing to note that they are also human beings with agency and actually important contributors to Church and society despite many limitations, including sometimes the lack of proper authorization to be in the country, we disempower and dehumanize them and ignore the fact that they are already assuming roles of service and leadership in a host of ways.

Nevertheless, it is important to point out that the bishops of the United States and Mexico produced a historic joint pastoral letter on migration titled *Strangers No Longer*. This comprehensive review of the pastoral context of U.S.-Mexico migration issues focused on the religious and moral underpinnings of the Catholic Church's concern for the human dignity of migrants. It also stressed the urgent need for comprehensive revision of existing U.S. immigration laws. In the intervening years since its publication, the document has provided a sound basis for the many cooperative efforts of the bishops of both countries to engage their respective governments in dialogue and advocacy regarding this fundamental concern for human rights and dignity. The bishops' focus on pastoral care is primary. This chapter's focus, moreover, on the contributions of immigrants, what they accomplish despite their precarious situation in U.S. society and the Church, is not meant to distract from the primary concerns of pastors, Christian communities, and society in general regarding the challenges they face every day in responding justly and compassionately to the reality of undocumented immigrants.

Immigrants unquestionably need pastoral care, yet they also provide it for others, and not just to their own people, but to the wider community, in the Church and society day after day. They labor to make the economy work for the good of all. They are serving in parishes, dioceses, and apostolic movements all over the nation. Indeed, they are the agents of a new way of being Catholic and American. They play an essential role in the Church's contemporary call for a New Evangelization.

At least one-third of all Catholics in the United States are immigrants, and they can be grouped as follows: Latin Americans, Asian and Pacific Islanders, and persons from Africa, the Caribbean (Haiti and the English-speaking islands), and a smattering of Irish and Eastern Europeans. If one adds up all these groups, immigrants and succeeding generations, together with black Catholics, Native Americans, and U.S.-born Hispanics with whom they have some issues in common, for instance, socioeconomic and political marginality, they constitute well over half of all Catholics in the country.[1]

This chapter looks at the broad range of pastoral circumstances that affect the lives of these cultural/racial families including their U.S.-born children who are closely linked to their immigrant parents. Within this universe, I will stress the largest group, which is Hispanic/ Latino, both documented and undocumented, since this group constitutes by far the largest cohort of immigrants and is the one with which I am most familiar.[2]

THE CHURCH: A HOME FOR MIGRANTS AND REFUGEES

Thirty-four years ago, as administrator of a *barrio*, an immigrant parish in Santa Ana, California, I published an article on migration titled "A Christian Perspective on the Reality of Illegal Immigration."[3] At that time the nation was initiating yet another cycle of debate tainted by a great deal of nativism and negativity. I was concerned about a lack of familiarity among Catholics, including the clergy, regarding the Church's long-standing teachings on migration and its challenges to public policy and pastoral practice.[4] This cycle of public controversy ended satisfactorily with President Reagan's signing of the Immigration Reform Act of 1986, commonly known as the Simpson-Rodino Law. Perhaps three million immigrants and eventually many more family members were able to regularize their status and reunite. In the intervening years these migrants have become productive members of U.S. society.

The Church's diligence—bishops, various offices of the USCCB, diocesan offices of Hispanic and ethnic ministries, social ministries, Catholic Charities, and other community organizations—significantly contributed to a successful outcome. There is no question but that concern for immigrants has been and continues to be a *defining mark* of the leadership that Catholicism has contributed to the American experiment. The Church's track record of pastoral and social justice engagement around complex issues of human mobility demands respect. U.S. Catholics of whatever origin should be particularly proud of it.[5] Nevertheless, twenty-five years after the Simpson-Rodino immigration reform and amnesty, many subsequent immigrants, the majority of them Hispanic/Latino, have not achieved legal immigration status for one, two, or even three decades. Thousands of children and youth among them who know no country other than the United States and speak little or no Spanish have been caught in a frustrating limbo and tragically deprived of access to higher education.

There are many other immigrant groups besides Latinos, however. Let us consider some of the others as well. Close to a third of all refugees, many fleeing political persecution or war and authorized to immigrate by the U.S. government, are resettled under Catholic auspices every year whether they are Catholic or not.[6] We can think of the now familiar presence of Vietnamese Catholics and the contributions they make to the Church's life. For example, the fact that almost a third of the diocesan priests in the Diocese of Orange in California are of Vietnamese descent is not insignificant. Certainly there are more than a thousand Vietnamese priests in the United States today. The presence, moreover, of Vietnamese in the ranks of religious congregations of men and women is notable. The origins of this development are found in the wrenching experience of the people fleeing their war-ravaged homeland in the 1970s. Other immigrant groups—Koreans and Chinese, for example—as well as continuing migrations of Poles, Hungarians, and other Eastern and Central Europeans, are bringing new life to the Catholic Church in the form of vocations to the priesthood, the religious life, and lay leadership.

The Haitian immigration is due undoubtedly to the chronic instability of that island nation. It is stimulated by several causes: political persecution, violence, dire economic need, or, as in the case of the 2010 earthquake, the largest in Haitian history, plain physical survival. No one can deny the profound faith and spirit of Haitian Catholics over the centuries despite the ordeals they have experienced![7] These communities and other immigrant groups not mentioned are among the brightest stars on the horizon of U.S. Catholicism. The coming of Catholics from Africa is a phenomenon somewhat under the radar. Yet we know that they are among the most educated immigrants to come to the United States.[8] All one has to do is witness the annual meeting of the African Conference of Catholic Clergy and Religious in the United States (ACCCRUS) attended by scores of African priests and women religious working throughout the United States, or participate in magnificent African parish liturgies to realize how much vigor and vitality these communities are laying at the U.S. Church's doorstep. The Church's response to all these immigrants at the highest levels and locally in the parish—the frontline of her presence—must be one of hospitality and true inclusion in every ecclesial aspect including pastoral leadership. To conceive of the challenge as opportunity is to think strategically in terms of the Church's evangelizing mission.

Perhaps the largest group of Asian and Pacific Islander Catholic immigrants are Filipinos, strong Catholics and significant bridge-builders for the Church and for the civic communities in which they

39

live. Having experienced U.S. political and cultural influences for many decades, the Filipinos tend to be relatively comfortable with the U.S. cultural scene and experienced in cultivating intercultural relationships. Filipino Catholics usually speak English and are found dispersed throughout the country with the single largest number living in California. Interestingly enough, their vibrant Catholicism has roots similar to those of Mexican Catholics, a circumstance which contributes to their familiarity and ease with the Hispanic immigrant's popular religiosity which shares many of the same Spanish roots: a strong focus on the Virgin Mary and on the suffering Christ. Filipinos are consequently key players in many of the multicultural contexts in which the U.S. Church finds itself today. The relatively high level of education and professionalization among these immigrants, moreover, allows Filipinos to hold their own in many contexts of ministerial leadership open to laity today. The presence of more than a thousand Filipino priests throughout the country and their leadership in serving both the English and Spanish-speaking communities is a major boon for U.S. Catholicism.

The coming of tens of thousands of Arab Catholic refugees to the United States creates a new presence among the various Eastern Catholic ecclesiastical jurisdictions like the Chaldean, Maronite, Ruthenian, and Byzantine Churches that serve a growing number of immigrants from Eastern Europe and the Middle East. Nor should we forget the growing Indian Catholic population, some of whom practice the Roman Rite and others the ancient rites of the Syro-Malabar and Syro-Malankara Churches that are in union with Rome.

One of the underreported success stories about U.S. Catholicism has to do with the gradual rise in the number of immigrant women religious of non-European origin in the country. Under the leadership of Cardinal Francis George and the Office for the Vicar of Religious of the Archdiocese of Chicago, native Latin American sisters and some of Latin American origin born in the U.S. have formed the Association of Hispanic Religious Congregations of Women in the United States. More than one hundred of these women religious representing thirty-five congregations met in August 2011 in Alhambra, California. If one adds the growing ranks of Filipina, Vietnamese, Korean, Chinese, and African sisters ministering in the United States today, there is good reason to think that new life is in the making for women religious in this country. These women are often much younger than their U.S. counterparts, wear a modified religious habit, and do not identify a great deal with the aging mainstream of sisters or with the groups that prefer to wear a full religious habit. These women from the developing world are not antagonistic to either of those groups, but merely have distinctive backgrounds, approaches, and priorities. Anecdotally, one hears of Catholic grade schools once again being staffed by women religious. While there are very few of them—one in Chicago and another in Los Angeles of which I am aware—this may be signaling something positive. These women are serving both immigrant and non-immigrant communities and doing it well.[9]

Another encouraging story pertains to the rise of Hispanics and other non-European Catholics, often immigrants, in the ranks of the permanent diaconate. Of the almost eighteen thousand permanent deacons in the United States, more than three thousand are Hispanic, while a growing number are of Asian ancestry. There is no question that the permanent diaconate is on the rise and that this trend is being significantly fed by immigrant groups.[10] There are, moreover, an increasing number of dioceses in which deacons outnumber priests. In this connection it should not be forgotten that in a real sense the Church often gets "two for the price of one" when it ordains married deacons. The high regard in which deacons' wives are held is palpable in parishes and dioceses since they too accompany their husbands and sometimes even exceed them in ministerial productivity.

A VIEW OF PASTORAL CONTEXTS

How can one characterize the pastoral reality of these diverse groups, each of which is at a very different moment of its presence in the United States? In some cases the local bishops are invoking the tried and true pastoral approach called the personal parish—what U.S. Catholics call the national parish. This approach is often but not always used to organize pastoral care for the Vietnamese, Korean, or Chinese Catholic communities that speak languages that are particularly challenging for Westerners, are often relatively recent immigrants, and have a special need to be ministered to in a way that stresses homogeneity rather than heterogeneity. As time goes by, of course, it may not be as necessary to provide this much separation from the parish or diocesan mainstream. One circumstance to acknowledge is that the children of many Asian groups, Vietnamese, Korean, Chinese, and Filipinos, for example, are often among the most academically success-ful students. They rise in levels of educational attainment more quickly than any other group including the European American. A byproduct of this educational success is a relatively high level of assimilation to U.S. culture on the part of many Asian and Pacific Islander youth. This circumstance, as one might imagine, leads to considerable stress between the immigrant parents and their assimilating children. The Church is sometimes caught in the middle. Pastors and other pastoral leaders need to be prepared for handling this tension since they are often called upon to mediate among generations.

Local bishops and pastors have discretion to choose between the options of a national or personal parish as the 1983 Code of Canon Law refers to it, or a multicultural approach, as circumstances allow. Flexibility is of the essence due to the many variables, financial, prac-tical and cultural, which are at play. The old pastoral strategy—so suc-cessful in the United States—of the national parish began to fall out of favor after World War II, and so we have seen the close of many of them or the combining of them into shared or multicultural parishes. This is particularly so in the Eastern and Midwestern United States where there is a decline in population, a displacement due to death rates and internal migration to the South and the Southwest. This trend has been exacerbated by financial constraints leading to the clos-ing or clustering of parishes. In turn, this contributes to the combining of cultural and linguistic groups that were previously served separately. This trend, it must be noted, is not as relevant to the Asian groups as it is to the European communities, the Germans, Italians, Poles, and Hungarians, or perhaps even to Hispanics/Latinos, who preceded the Asian communities. The pastoral care of Vietnamese and Korean Catholics is often done in the form of national parishes. There are exceptions however, as in the Diocese of Orange, which has the largest population of Vietnamese Catholics of any diocese in the United States. From the beginning of the Vietnamese migration, the diocesan bishops there have opted to organize the ministry within existing parishes while establishing a Vietnamese Center that does not function as a parish. Thus in the Orange diocese there are several multi-tracked parishes that attend to Vietnamese, and/or Koreans, Hispanics, and European Americans in the same venue.

In many parts of the United States, there has arisen a new and distinctive pastoral reality that is challenging bishops, pastors, and lay leaders in general, namely, parishes shared among several language and cultural groups. While perhaps the majority of the immigrant communities are still being served in their separate communities, as time goes by this approach evolves into something different. What has emerged, therefore, is the *intercultural* parish. This means that all the groups often find themselves in a situation where they are not isolated in tracks or silos, but more or less continuously rub shoulders. Parishioners of whatever background, immigrant or native-born, are not finding a straightforward, culturally homogenous situation as they may have experienced or expected in the "good ol' days" of the national parish on the one hand or the assimilating suburban parish, where everything was done in English and conformed to the rising middle-class norm, on the other. In a growing number of pastoral situations it is no longer a matter of working with just one or perhaps two languages and/or cultures. Less and less do we find pastors, parochial vicars, lay ecclesial leaders, and Church volunteers coming mainly from a dominant group, as minorities of various kinds taken together become a majority. For example, several Vietnamese priests are pastoring Hispanic parishes, not to mention all the mainstream European American parishes served by African, Indian, Hispanic, or Vietnamese priests and lay pastoral agents. In these shared parishes, one needs to have a sense of how three, four, or more groups might interact.

As pastoral leadership evolves, and Hispanic/Latino, Vietnamese, or African Americans, for that matter, assume roles of leadership not only on behalf of their particular communities but more broadly for the entire Catholic community, they are being forced out of their silos willy-nilly. For example, there are many dioceses where the majority of catechists are Hispanic/Latino. They are the catechetical leaders of the *entire* community including European Americans. While no one proposes forcing this intercultural dynamic upon anyone, it is simply happening on the ground because of several factors, among them demographics, finances, generational changes, and a declining interest among European American Catholics in priesthood, religious life, and other forms of ecclesial service.

Perhaps the U.S. bishops' decision to create the Secretariat of Cultural Diversity with a mandate to serve all the racial/ethnic and cultural families, including the European American, was providential. This development brought about a context within the Bishops' Conference itself whereby the ecclesiological imperative of unity, an ecclesiology of communion, is clearly signaled. The bewildering diversity of racial, cultural, and language groups that make up U.S. Catholicism must willingly and gradually enter into sustained relationship, get a bit closer, as it were, and find ways to collaborate in the creation of participation in the Church's life and mission. Communion in difference or diversity is an *ecclesiological imperative* for Catholicism, not an option, and it is painfully, but gradually, being forged on the frontlines of multi- and intercultural ministries throughout the country.

MOVING BEYOND THE SILOS

Moving beyond the comfortable silos in which racial/cultural ministries have tended to function historically, for many necessary and good reasons, seems an unavoidable next step. At the same time, there must be concern and sensitivity to how some non-immigrant Catholic communities feel about the shifts taking place in the U.S. Church and society. African American, Native American, and other Catholic communities that have struggled for attention and resources within society and the Church for generations have legitimate concerns about these shifts and what they mean within their own groups The history of U.S. blacks, to make this point clear, is one of intense, ongoing struggle to attain recognition and space, resources, and opportunities, and form their own leaders in circumstances of persistent racism and attitudes of white privilege in both Church and society. Today in inner-city as well as suburban contexts black Catholics find themselves regularly outnumbered by clergy and faithful of diverse backgrounds who often have good will but no cultural and little historical sense about African American Catholics. There is often a lack of understanding about particular issues that affect the lives of black people in the United States and a tendency to sometimes push blacks off one's radar screen.

Similarly, the status of Native American Catholics is a matter of grave concern. The bishops whose dioceses serve Native Americans have expressed deep regret about the decline in ministers, lack of native people in positions of ecclesial leadership, and the many social problems affecting the lives of the community.[11] The USCCB raised the Ad Hoc Committee on Native American Affairs to the status of a permanent Subcommittee of the Committee on Cultural Diversity. Native American Catholics understandably have reservations (no pun intended) regarding the flow of immigrant groups that may contribute to Native American pastoral care disappearing from the Church's and larger society's vision. These concerns of both Native American and African American Catholics must not be swept under the rug.

Nevertheless, Native American and African American Catholics must realize that it works both ways: they as well often have little familiarity with the new people on the American block, and must in turn learn about others and experience Christian solidarity with brothers and sisters who also have needs. This is a delicate situation that demands considerable pastoral wisdom on all sides. It demands more effort, knowledge, hospitality, and more positive attitudes, on the part of everyone. A survey of the pastoral care of immigrants must raise this observation since the concern for serving immigrants must not unwittingly result in pastoral insensitivity or injustice to others.

These concerns lead us to insist that a healthy pastoral response to today's interculturality in the context of ministry to immigrants should not be taken as an invitation to pursue a certain misguided multiculturalism that relegates diverse groups into a huge, generic, multicultural box. Such an approach is inconsistent with the important missiological principle that a local church is not strong unless it develops its own proper leadership. A certain kind of multiculturalism can unintentionally limit the ability of each culture, race, and ethnicity to develop its own proper styles and ecclesial leadership (clerical and lay) and necessary ministerial resources. The *particularity* of each family must be honored. To fail in this is to misunderstand the challenge and opportunity of the present moment in U.S. Catholic Church history. Bishops and pastors must prudently decide on the model they wish to use in their particular pastoral contexts and discern how models of parish organization and ministry and the necessary *intercultural competencies* may better assure the respectful participation of all. While the organizational model of the USCCB's Cultural Diversity Secretariat was judged to be appropriate for carrying on the business of the Bishops Conference, it was not meant necessarily to provide a paradigm for parishes or dioceses that experience many different circumstances and levels of ecclesial integration among particular Catholic communities.

In an age of growing diversity in several different variables—social class, culture, language, and generation—"one-size-fits-all" pastoral and organizational approaches are often ill-advised. Indeed, it stands to reason that an age of growing diversity in the Church will also be an age of diversity in pastoral methods, expressions, and approaches. Moreover, the Church's current focus on the New Evangelization requires precisely that—not a retreat to only one formulation, style, and practice of the faith, much less a business-as-usual mentality, but rather a full-scale retrieval of the Catholic tradition in all its richness and pluralism along with a thoughtful adaptation to truly new circumstances.[12] The Hispanic bishops clearly cautioned against a simplistic multicultural approach in their 2000 document titled *Encuentro and Mission* when they wrote: "This model often dilutes the identity and vision of Hispanic ministry and those of other ethnic ministries. It can reduce effectiveness in dioceses, parishes, and Catholic organizations and institutions" (EM 4).

THE GOAL: ECCLESIAL INTEGRATION

The option taken by the U.S. bishops for ethnic ministries of every kind is expressed best by the phrase "ecclesial integration."[13] They do not speak of assimilation, much less of Americanization. This is not the Church's function. The Church exists to evangelize which means proclaiming the good news and engaging all cultures, including the paradigmatic modern and U.S. cultures, with the transcultural core of values and convictions of Christian faith. Secular society and even some pastors have mistakenly assumed or proposed assimilation as the Church's task. Experience shows that this is an error because the core of Catholic values and identity in each of the various racial, ethnic, and language groups that constitute the universal, Catholic family must be preserved and respected. In his magisterial *Evangelii Nuntiandi,* Pope Paul VI reminded us that Christian anthropology requires that preaching and teaching always engage the people's core values and penetrate their cultural identity not externally as a thin layer of varnish but rather down to the very soul of it (EN 20). If this core identity is undermined, the faith is undermined, because the faith has to become life for the believer precisely in his or her own culture. This does not mean that adaptation is out of the question for newcomers, or that critiques of the immigrants' cultures are inadmissible. Such critiques are inevitable and even good. What is required, however, is a cultural discernment that preserves the core identity, especially if it is Catholic, while adapting to whatever is good or even better in the new U.S. culture. Pope Benedict XVI often referred to the process of evangelization as a "give and take." The Church gives from the font of revelation and in turn receives from the distinctive humanity of each and every culture.

Experience has shown that the proposition of the Americanists of the late nineteenth and early twentieth centuries to the effect that the Catholic Church in the United States must become "American" was more problematic than originally envisioned by its defenders. [14] A century or more down the pike we realize that unfortunately the existence of a bottom line, a consensus among mainstream Catholics, regarding Catholic identity and what it means to be a Catholic in the United States is exceedingly questionable. There are many reasons to say that we are in the midst of a search for a new bottom line for U.S. Catholic identity. The battle is being fought for the minds and hearts of younger, so-called mainstream Catholics as well as for the burgeoning and youthful Latino, Asian and Pacific Islander, and other immigrant Catholic populations. That is why the question of pastoral care that empowers these new American Catholics must give priority to intercultural competencies and awareness that enables rising new generations to negotiate their participation in the U.S. experiment with knowledge, attitudes, and skills that promote a robust Catholic identity.

A myriad of factors influence the Church's prospects today. The broken immigration system not only makes life miserable for many millions of Catholic immigrants who give to the nation as much as they receive from it, but also threatens to deprive the Church of new life blood and the U.S. economy of an exceptionally productive, reliable, and necessary work force. It must be recalled that much is happening in the world, for example, ongoing migrations, economic downturns, unemployment, displacement of people, and an all-pervasive globalization. In the meantime, people's lives go on as best they can in concrete

47

pastoral contexts like the parish community, the diocese, and apostolic movements.

In the remaining sections of this chapter, I reflect on some of these circumstances, especially in the Hispanic/Latino context, for the purpose of gaining more clarity regarding today's challenges and opportunities as this complex and thorny subject evolves. As Cardinal Avery Dulles points out, what is at stake may be the Church's influence on American culture. He stated the challenge in these words: "...the immigration flows from culturally Catholic areas such as Latin America...have the potential for increasing the church's influence on American life." He adds, however, the ominous observation that "...the prognosis is uncertain since there is a serious danger that this Hispanic American population, intent upon success in American terms, will forget or repudiate its own roots and adopt the prevailing American values of individualism, professionalism, and worldly success."[15] The good cardinal makes it abundantly clear that the critical factor regarding the pastoral care of immigrants, Hispanic/Latino or any others, hinges on the nature of their *ecclesial integration* and not on their acculturation to the American experience.

IMMIGRANTS: GIVING AND RECEIVING

Hispanics/Latinos have gone on to become "the leading indicator of the Catholic Church's future in the United States," to use the words of Harvard University's Robert Putnam.[16] More than four thousand of the 17,500 parishes in the country have services in Spanish and the majority of dioceses have organized Hispanic/Latino or multicultural offices. Hispanic/Latino priests for the first time in U.S. Catholic Church history have become a critical mass numbering well over three thousand. About 40 percent of U.S. seminarians are not of European ancestry and of these the majority is foreign born—from Latin America, Asia, or Africa. A significant and growing number of priests are themselves immigrants, and the demographic transformation of some presbyterates is remarkable as they turn from being predominantly European American to being a fascinating combination of Asians, Pacific Islanders, Africans, and Hispanics in the majority. Similarly the ranks of immigrant and non-European American lay pastoral agents have swollen over the years. Despite the fact that immigrant lay leadership tends to function with an ecclesiology that conceives of the laity's role as fundamentally volunteer and only occasionally professional, there is a rising tide of lay ministers from among the immigrant ranks, many of them pursuing certification and higher degrees. The Federation of Pastoral Institutes (FIP) convenes various organizations—some diocesan or regional and others based in a university or religious congregation—for the purpose of professionally advancing Hispanic ministers, the majority of whom are immigrants. In addition to serving in parish-based ministries like the roles of catechist, lector, Eucharistic minister, and youth, young adult and social minister, immigrants account for much of the vitality and success of apostolic movements such as the Cursillo, Charismatic Renewal, Marriage Encounter, and Christian Family Movement, to name only a few. These movements are veritable schools of ministry and leadership.[17] The development of effective leaders from among immigrant communities, nevertheless, faces some difficult challenges.

HOSPITALITY AND MUTUALITY

One of the first challenges can be expressed this way: *both* the faithful themselves and their clergy often need orientation to the U.S. context. In 1999, the U.S. bishops issued *Guidelines for Receiving Pastoral Ministers* which recommended the provision of appropriate orientation programs for such ministers. In 2003 they revised and reissued the *Guidelines*, but everyone would agree today that (1) not a great deal of attention was paid to them and (2) they are now somewhat dated given, for example, the changes in U.S. immigration law affecting religious workers after the 9/11 tragedy. While there are effective orientation programs like Loyola Marymount University's *Cultural Orientation Program for International Ministers* (COPIM), and an even larger program at Oblate School of Theology in San Antonio, by and large international priests serving immigrant communities are in need themselves of some of the same mentoring that the immigrant faithful need. It must be insisted that orientation programs, if they are to be well received and effective, must reflect a real sense of hospitality and mutuality. The challenge is not merely a question of the outsiders adapting to a new in-group. The Church conceives of intercultural encounters as always involving openness to the other as well as a sense of giving and a receiving. While international priests, religious and lay ministers will have to adapt to a new culture, the receiving U.S. culture must itself be open to adaptation to others, receiving something new and perhaps better from the rising tide of international ministers—priests, deacons, religious, and lay pastoral agents.

WHAT'S THE PLAN?

Over the past several decades a process of learning has taken place in the United States. Organized pastoral ministries came into existence in Texas and California as well as in large urban centers like New York, Chicago, and Miami. Sometimes parishes took the lead; other times the diocese did so. In 1945 the first national office for Hispanic ministry was established in San Antonio and later moved to Washington, DC, where it exists today in the form of the Sub-Committee on Hispanic Affairs of the Committee on Cultural Diversity. As the decades passed and the Hispanic community became even more rooted in the United States, the care of migrants had to be distinguished from the care of Hispanics who are settled whether they be U.S.-born or immigrants who have resided in the United States for many years. This distinction is reflected in the structure of the USCCB offices where one finds the Committee on Cultural Diversity's Subcommittee on Hispanic Affairs just mentioned, and another called the Committee on Migration. This latter committee is concerned with immigration policy and the immediate challenges facing migrants and refugees, not the long-term issue of pastoral care.

Hispanic ministry received much of its original encouragement from the need to serve recently arrived immigrants, many of whom were *braceros* or migrant farm workers. Now it has gone well beyond that and become Hispanic ministry, a standard feature of diocesan organization throughout the country. Of course, there continue to be migrant farm workers whose pastoral concerns are often addressed by the Subcommittee on the Pastoral Care of Migrants, Refugees and Travelers of the Cultural Diversity Committee. There is also a professional organization called the Catholic Farm Worker Ministry Network which accompanies the needs and issues in this demanding area of ministry.

More than any other, current scholar Timothy Matovina has chronicled the evolution of Hispanic ministry and its crucial role in the Catholic Church in *Latino Catholicism*. He demonstrates the high stakes involved in the current transformation taking place in the Church as a result of dramatic demographic shifts now underway.[18]

Large numbers of Hispanic Catholic immigrants are found virtually everywhere in the United States as are significant numbers of Asian, Pacific Islander, Caribbean, and African Catholic immigrants. Of course, there are many dioceses in several states in which the majority of faithful are Hispanics, notably Los Angeles, the largest archdiocese in the nation, and there will be more where Hispanic ministry addresses the needs of the majority not the minority.

The need to envision and plan for the rapidly growing ministry with and to Hispanics/Latinos led to one of the most distinctive historical chapters in U.S. Catholicism called the *Encuentro* process. It consisted of three national pastoral gatherings (*encuentros*) and three groundbreaking documents: The 1983 pastoral letter of the U.S. bishops titled *The Hispanic Presence: Challenge and Commitment*, the 1987 *National Pastoral Plan for Hispanic Ministry*, and in 2002, *Encuentro and Mission: A Renewed Pastoral Framework for Hispanic Ministry*. These three documents were the fruit of national pastoral *encuentros*, which gathered significant numbers of representatives of the Hispanic/Latino communities, perhaps the majority of them immigrants. What stands out among several other factors is the broad vision, perceptive ecclesiology, and influence these documents have exercised over subsequent pastoral policies and practices since their original formulation. To this day, they capture the fundamental pastoral vision of the U.S. bishops regarding the present and future of the Hispanic Catholic communities in the nation.

Unfortunately, as is true in the case of many Church teachings, older and younger generations of Catholics, including the clergy, often know little about this outstanding legacy of twentieth-century U.S. Catholicism. Certainly the cogency of these resources owes much to the spirit of the Second Vatican Council which inspired them, as well as to the significant and unprecedented influence of events in Latin American Catholicism, for example, the Episcopal Conferences of Medellín, Puebla, and Santo Domingo, together with the explosion of contextualized theological reflection on that continent called Libera-

51

tion Theology.[19] The spirit of the *Encuentro* process and its Latin American sources have faded as new generations of Latino laity and clergy arise who have no recollection of the process. Yet its vision continues to inspire the latest iteration of the pastoral vision in *Encuentro and Mission*.

MINISTRY AMONG HISPANIC IMMIGRANTS: KEY CONCEPTS

The reality of Hispanic ministry in the United States is vast and complex. The largest group of Hispanics being served are the relatively recently arrived immigrants. They tend to find in the Church a friendly, recognizable face in an otherwise often inhospitable environment. While enjoying too few priestly vocations from among their own ranks, U.S. Hispanics have benefitted from the presence of hundreds of priests as well as women religious from Latin America. Some Hispanic/Latino parishes are national parishes that have been established by local bishops to care for Hispanics in an entire diocese or region of a diocese. Many Latino parishes are what could be called *de facto* national parishes.[20] They serve communities that are overwhelmingly Latino. A large number of these are in inner cities, but there is a trend toward suburbs as well. Indeed the majority of U.S. Hispanics/Latinos live in suburbs despite considerable talk about *barrios*. In these areas, the Latino presence often has to mingle with other cultures, not just the European American but also the Asian, African, African American, or English-speaking Caribbean. There are also increased possibilities of mingling among the urban Hispanic working class and the more affluent professional middle- to upper-class European American Catholics.

The Diocese of Orange in California, for example, is quite fascinating because of the long history of serving two, three, or even four tracks in the same parish. While this has not necessarily resulted in a truly integrated parish, the highest level of communion in difference, it has, over decades, created familiarity and mutual acceptance among diverse cultural groups and social classes—no small achievement. The rising number of individuals marrying outside their own cultural/racial group, contributes to what has already been noted, namely, the increased interculturality of U.S. society in general including the churches.[21]

These circumstances suggest that Hispanic ministry is anything but static. It always has been a dynamic, changing reality that requires pastoral vigilance and adaptability—today more than ever. Hispanic ministry can only be part of a larger picture, a dialogical process, which is the evangelization of U.S. culture across the board. The point is that ultimately Hispanics/Latinos will enter the mainstream, so the critical question for the Church is what kind of mainstream that will be in terms of core values. Having said that, however, there are certain fundamentals that need to be kept in mind and which still serve to orient pastors and other pastoral agents to effective pastoral care of Hispanic immigrants as they negotiate their relationship to the larger American experience. Here is a list of some major concepts that need to be kept in mind as the challenges unfold:

- Hispanic popular Catholicism is the usual form in which Catholicism exists in Hispanic/Latino cultures, not the middle-class U.S. form one might take as the paradigm from seminary or university study.
- The standard and relatively modern Catholicism of the United States contrasts with a more ancient Hispanic/Latino Catholicism in several significant ways: for example, emphasis on Mary and the saints; additional rites beyond the seven sacraments; distinctive ways of celebrating Advent, Lent, and Holy Week.
- Focus is on celebration or fiesta with emphasis not on intellectualizing or a propositional/apologetic approach to the faith, but a performative approach, that is, one that demonstrates faith in practice, for example, forming small faith-sharing communities, celebrating feasts, stressing *convivencia* (community socializing), highlighting the beauty and drama of liturgical seasons, and valuing the parish's expressivity of faith as much as or more than its organization.
- Conceive of the Church as community of families more than a gathering of individuals.
- Realize that Hispanic/Latino communities are extraordi-

narily youthful. Hispanic ministry truly is youth and young adult ministry.

- Hispanic immigrants experience a great deal of *anomie*, that is, disorientation regarding how to adapt, how to raise their children, what to value, etc. They need mentoring in the area of *cultural discernment*. To serve as mentor, however, ministers must have a deeper appreciation of their own culture and grasp the transcultural thrust of the Gospel. Many ecclesial leaders are unfortunately not yet equipped for this.
- Hispanic/Latino immigrants do not relate to either progressive or conservative U.S. Catholicism, but prefer an affective, sacramental, and ritual practice rather than the seemingly cerebral and ideological Catholicism of middle-class European Americans.

As Hispanic and other immigrants integrate into the U.S. Church mainstream, they find themselves challenged to serve the whole Church, not just their particular group. This is happening as relatively youthful Hispanic/Latino, Asian and Pacific Islander, Haitian, English-speaking people of the Caribbean, and also African American Church leaders—bishops, priests, deacons, and lay ecclesial ministers—learn to effectively communicate and relate to their increasingly diverse ecclesial communities. The process is difficult and does not succeed without suitable knowledge, attitudes, and skills. In 2000, in celebration of the Jubilee Year, the U.S. bishops convened *Encuentro 2000: Many Faces in God's House* in Los Angeles. They expressly acknowledged the defining role that cultural diversity would play in the Church of the Third Millennium. Eight years later, the U.S. bishops established the clear pastoral priority of the recognition of cultural diversity. Among the activities they authorized for pursuing this priority was the development of *Guidelines for Intercultural Competence*, which was approved by the Committee on Cultural Diversity in 2011.[22] In 2010, the USCCB sponsored the Catholic Cultural Diversity Network Convocation at the University of Notre Dame which modeled some of the practices that lead to greater unity in Church settings. For the purpose of disseminating the *Guidelines* and making them palpable for Church leadership, a five-module workshop was designed. It unpacks the topic of interculturality in terms of attitudes, knowledge, and skills.

What exactly is meant by attitudes, knowledge, and skills appropriate for ministering among immigrants today? The simple five-module workshop developed by the USCCB Committee on Cultural Diversity proposes first of all that all ministers be able to frame the topic of intercultural relations in the language of the magisterium. It has been noted in talking about immigrants and matters of cultural diversity in the United States that there is a tendency to rely on rationales, terms, and language coming from the field of multiculturalism as it has developed over several decades. This rhetoric arose in the world of public education and business. Certainly it has much to offer, but the foundations of openness to diversity are also found in Catholic Tradition itself, in the Scriptures, first of all, and then in fundamental doctrines of the Church regarding the nature of the Trinity, of ecclesial communion, and of the evangelizing and missionary character of the Church. It makes sense for ecclesial leaders to ground the need and desire to learn about intercultural relations and communications in the Church's very identity and mission and not merely in some secular ideology like multiculturalism. This is the first point upon which the bishops insist in the *Guidelines*.

While the limits of this chapter do not allow us to go into detail regarding the *Guidelines*, even a brief glimpse of the first one reveals how vital they are to advancing our practice of Hispanic ministry in fidelity to what is unique about our Catholic faith. For the Church to pursue its ministry with and to Hispanics/Latinos without firmly grounding this enterprise in Catholic identity and mission is merely to get on secular society's bandwagon of diversity and multiculturalism, rather than drawing deeply from the springs of Sacred Scripture, Tradition, and the still-unrealized vision of the Second Vatican Council.

Today and increasingly, it will be necessary and appropriate for Catholic immigrant groups, other diverse cultural and racial communities, and the European-American leadership of the Church to raise the bar on cultural proficiencies of every kind. The field of intercultural studies, which is quite developed, provides many insights into this subject and a theology of intercultural relations will ground this effort in the central doctrines of Catholic faith. Implicit in this observation is the realization that immigrant groups must view themselves as subjects of ecclesial life, not mainly as objects or receivers of the goodwill and activities of others. While immigrants are often limited by a lack of familiarity with their new circumstances, *anomie*, and a lack of leadership and resources, a healthy sense of subsidiarity demands that they be empowered to respond to their own needs as quickly as possible.

In the case of Hispanics, the development of adequate ecclesial leadership has been particularly daunting. The primary deficit facing Hispanic immigrants is educational in nature, namely, the enormous gap between the Hispanic community's level of educational attainment and what is necessary to adequately function as leaders in U.S. society and the Church. While Hispanic immigrants are exceedingly generous as volunteers in parishes and apostolic movements, they often lack the credentials that allow them to assume roles of leadership. The educated Hispanic middle class, sometimes immigrants but often second or third generation, do not come forward for ecclesial ministries as much as the working, especially immigrant, class who have a keener interest in the faith. Access to better K–12 education is crucial for Hispanic immigrant children and youth as a recent Notre Dame study demonstrates.[23] Catholic schools can play a decisive role in educational advancement of Latinos and other immigrants. For the most part, however, it is the public schools that will perpetuate or bridge the enormous chasm in educational attainment between Latinos and so many other groups in the nation. Catholic universities, dioceses, and pastoral institutes have responded to this educational gap in various ways and formation opportunities in pastoral leadership have grown over the years.

The considerable success, it should be noted here, that evangelical and Pentecostal denominations have had in attracting Hispanic/Latino and other immigrants to their ranks has something to do with the investment these groups make in the formation of ministers and in empowering them to assume leadership roles. While vocations to the priesthood, diaconate, religious life, and lay ministries among Hispanic/Latinos continue to grow, recruitment levels are still far below what they should be given that Hispanics constitute more than 50 percent of the entire U.S. Catholic population under the age of thirty-five.[24]

Nevertheless, the growing number of Hispanic/Latino permanent deacons and the growth of international priests from Spanish-speaking countries have created a critical mass of Hispanic of clergy for the first time in U.S. history. The fact that many of the international, immigrant priests are not incardinated, however, means that they do not necessarily have the stability and influence to exercise full leadership potential within their dioceses. There are several thousands of international priests in the United States, which constitute about 15 to 25 percent of the total number. The largest groups of international priests are from Latin America, India, the Philippines, and various African nations, especially Nigeria. In thirty-five dioceses, more than 50 percent of the presbyterate is constituted by international priests.[25] The situation will improve as the international priests gain permanence in their assignments. Efforts are underway to assist these priests and other ministers in their proper orientation to society and the Church in the United States. In this process, several departments of the USCCB, led by the Secretariat of Clergy, Consecrated Life and Vocations, are serving as a clearinghouse for addressing the highly complex issues around international ministers.

Recent surveys indicate that immigration from Mexico has abated.[26] This suggests that at least in the case of persons of Mexican origin, attention must continue to shift from recently arrived immigrants to their native-born children. There will certainly continue to be a great need for ministry in Spanish, but the emphasis on serving the first-generation youth who often prefer English must grow. This does not mean that these children can merely be turned over to the dominant English-speaking community, since Hispanic/Latino youth who speak English still share many of the same values, approaches, and customs of their parents.[27] What is needed is bilingual as well as intercultural knowledge, attitudes, and skills to work with such a hybrid reality.

CONCLUSION

The United States, among the various nations of the earth, is at the vanguard of the pastoral care of immigrants. Planning to respond to the ongoing challenges and developments in this field demands a great deal of attention to the diversity among immigrants themselves. As we have seen, even Hispanic/Latino immigrants are extremely diverse in terms of national origin, generation and social class. The coming of fairly resourceful Latin American middle-class immigrants—Venezuelan Catholics found in Miami or Houston, for instance—leads to new and untested pastoral practices. For example, some Venezuelan Catholics in Houston have organized a virtual ministry whereby they form intentional small faith communities that are regularly linked by the Internet to the Church in Venezuela. Such a thing would have been impossible only twenty-five years ago. Mexican Catholics have succeeded to some extent in creating links over many decades, not on the Internet, but by yearly visits back home to the *rancho* or by the yearly visits to the United States of the parish priest, local bishop, or religious image of devotion from one's hometown or region. U.S. pastors have often been astonished to see, when they visit their parishioners back home, how local Mexican churches are supported by U.S. immigrants: new building projects, remodeling, or new church furnishings abound as a result of immigrants' remittances of their hard-earned dollars.

These developments suggest that pastoral care of migrants has many dimensions in a world characterized by globalization, travel, social media, and cyberspace. They enrich and complicate the exercise of pastoral care. The variety of pastoral options will increase in relation to the number of different contexts pastors must confront in ministry with immigrants in the pluralistic environment of the United States. Moreover, change is constantly going on. This ministry more than ever responds to an ever-moving target. A business as usual, one-size-fits-all, or univocal mentality just will not do. In such a situation what is most important is a clear and compelling vision for evangelization and a pastoral plan, along with keeping one's eyes open and one's feet on the ground. Ultimately, ministry with immigrants must be linked to the over-arching challenge of evangelizing mainstream U.S. culture, since all immigrant groups, and especially their children, adjust one way or the other to the prevailing or dominant culture. The result of straightforward assimilation, it would appear, is too often a distancing from the life of the Church and the faith, not its intensification.

For success in ministry from an ecclesial perspective, all Catholic immigrants need formation and resources to truly *discern* what kind of people—American of this or that origin *and* Catholic—they wish to be. Is our preaching, catechesis, and Catholic education up to speed and ready to meet the challenge? If this question is not *explicitly* raised and seriously tackled, pastoral care of immigrants will in many cases not accomplish its true evangelizing mission. For evangelization means changing one's way of thinking, living, and behaving to conform to the values of the Gospel. It is not about imparting a superficial outer coating of faith on some generic U.S. Catholic prototype. That is why the pastoral care of immigrants must be inspired by the New Evangelization which demands a more intentional and discerning focus on the part of all the faithful and their pastors on the cultivation of a distinctive Catholic way of life. A robust sense of Catholic identity and what it requires—a *new bottom line* is essential if Catholics, immigrant or native-born, are going to really make a difference and not be merely well-adjusted Americans, but rather the true missionary disciples of the Lord they are called to be by virtue of baptism.[28]

NOTES

1. For more information on the wide range of activities related to immigrants see the Secretariat of Cultural Diversity, Migrant Refugee Services and other pertinent USCCB departments at http://www.usccb.org (accessed July 1, 2012).

2. The Pew Research Center announced that Asian immigration to the United States is growing the fastest. Asian immigrants have surpassed the Latino immigrant population not in numbers but in terms of growth rate. See Kirk Semple, "In a Shift, Biggest Wave of Migrants is Now Asian," *New York Times*, June 18, 2012.

3. Allan F. Deck, "A Catholic Perspective on the Reality of Illegal Immigration," *Social Thought*, Fall 1978, 39–52.

4. Church teaching on the rights and dignity of migrants is hardly something new. This topic is a fundamental theme of biblical Christianity as well as of the reflection of bishops and theologians from the patristic age to the present. The Holy See dedicates an entire department of the Vatican to this ministry: the Pontifical Council for the Pastoral Care of Migrants, Refugees and Itinerant People. The latest major document of the Roman magisterium on this topic is found in *Erga Migantes Caritas Christi (On the Love of Christ Toward Migrants)* issued by Blessed Pope John Paul II in 2004.

5. See Allan F. Deck, "Conferenza Episcopali—Stati Uniti d'America" in *Migrazioni: Dizionario Socio-Pastorale*, Graziano Battistella, ed. (Milan: The International Migration Institute of the Scalabrinian Missionaries, 2010), 272–76.

6. See USCCB Migrant Refugee Services at http://usccb.org (accessed July 1, 2012).

7. See Terry F. Buss with Adam Gardner, *Haiti in the Balance* (Washington, DC: Brookings Institution Press, 2008), 1–10.

8. See Aniedi Okure and Dean Hoge, *African and Caribbean Catholics in the United States*, A Study Conducted for the Subcommittee for the Pastoral Care of Migrants, Refugees and Travelers (PCMRT) by the Life Cycle Institute of the Catholic University of America (Washington, DC: USCCB Publications, 2008).

9. See report of Sister Hilda Mateos, MGSpS, at http://www.ushispanicministry.com/archives/1044 (accessed July 1, 2012).

10. See Statistics at Center for Applied Research in the Apostolate (CARA) at http://cara.georgetown.edu (accessed July 1, 2012).

11. See *Native American Catholics at the Millennium*, USCCB Ad Hoc Committee on Native American Affairs (Washington, DC: USCCB Publications, 2002).

12. In this connection one might recall Pope John Paul II's definition of the New Evangelization as "proclaiming the Gospel with new expressions, methods and ardor." See *Redemptoris Missio*, no. 3.

13. Alejandro Aguilera-Titus provides useful parish models for pursuing the process of ecclesial integration. See Hispanic ministry and *Building Intercultural Competence for Ministers (BICM)* at http://usccb.org (accessed July 1, 2012).

14. The term *Americanist* refers to U.S. Catholic Church thinkers and leaders of the late nineteenth and early twentieth centuries who sought to promote constructive engagement between U.S. culture and Catholic identity. They supported the concept of Americanization for the droves of Catholic immigrants in order to assure influence and acceptance of Catholics by the dominant WASP society. They got their wish. U.S. Catholics did attain recognition and status, especially after World War II, having proven their loyalty to the nation, and definitively in 1960 when the first Catholic president, John F. Kennedy, was elected. The subsequent defection from the Catholic faith by many Catholics of European American heritage suggests that Americanization as put forth by "Americanists" is an ambivalent proposal and should not be uncritically championed as a strategy for Catholicism's engagement with U.S. culture. For a cogent reflection on what it means to forge a U.S. Catholic identity today, see Cardinal Francis George, "Evangeliz-

ing American Culture," in *The Difference God Makes* (New York: Crossroads Publishing Company, 2009), 25–41.

15. Avery Dulles, "The Impact of the Catholic Church on American Culture," address at the John Paul II Cultural Center, Washington, DC, November 13, 2001, as reported in *America* 185 (December 3, 2001), 5.

16. Memorandum of Robert D. Putnam and David E. Campbell to Fr. Allan F. Deck, SJ, dated May 22, 2008, reported in *Catholic Review*, Archdiocese of Baltimore, at http://catholicreview.org, last accesses July 1, 2012.

17. See Marina Herrera, "The Context and Development of Hispanic Ecclesial Leadership," 166–205, and Edmundo Rodríguez, "The Hispanic Community and Church Movements: Schools of Leadership," 206–39, in *Hispanic Catholic Culture in the U.S.*, ed. Jay P. Dolan and Allan Figueroa Deck (Notre Dame: University of Notre Dame Press, 1994), also Hosffman Ospino, *Hispanic Ministry in the 21st Century* (Miami: Convivium Press, 2010).

18. See Timothy Matovina, *Latino Catholicism: Transformation in America's Largest Church* (Princeton, NJ: Princeton University Press, 2011); Moisés Sandoval, *On the Move: A History of the Hispanic Church in the U.S.* (Maryknoll, NY: Orbis Books, 2006); and "The Organization of an Hispanic Church," in Jay P. Dolan and Allan F. Deck, *Hispanic Catholic Culture in the U.S.*, 131–65.

19. While Liberation Theology was pointedly criticized by the Congregation for the Doctrine of the Faith under Cardinal Joseph Ratzinger before he became Pope Benedict XVI, it was never condemned in its entirety. On the contrary, Pope John Paul II himself speaking to the Brazilian bishops said of it: "…we are convinced…that the theology of liberation is not only timely but useful and necessary. It should constitute a new state—in close connection with former ones—of the theological reflection initiated with the apostolic tradition, and continued with the great fathers and doctors, by the ordinary and extraordinary magisterium and, in more recent years, by the rich patrimony of the church's social doctrine, expressed in documents from *Rerum Novarum* to *Laborem Exercens*." See "Pope John Paul II Letter to the Brazilian Episcopal Conference, April 9, 1986" in *Liberation Theology: A Documentary History* (Maryknoll, NY: Orbis Books, 1990), 503.

20. For more comprehensive views of Hispanic ministry see Charles W. Dahm, *Parish Ministry in a Hispanic Community* (Mahwah, NJ: Paulist Press, 2004); or Allan Figueroa Deck *The Second Wave: Hispanic Ministry and the Evangelization of Cultures* (Mahwah, NJ: Paulist Press, 1989).

21. Pew research finding, "The Rise of Intermarriage," reported at http://pewresearch.org (accessed Feb. 16, 2012).

22. The five guidelines are (1) frame issues of diversity theologically in terms of the Church's identity and mission to evangelize, (2) seek an understanding of culture and how it works, (3) develop intercultural communication skills in pastoral settings, (4) expand one's knowledge of the obstacles which impede effective intercultural relations, and (5) foster ecclesial integration rather than assimilation in Church settings with a spirituality of hospitality, reconciliation, and mission. See "Catholic Cultural Network Convocation" and "Resources" at http://usccb.org (accessed July 1, 2012).

23. See *To Nurture the Soul of a Nation: Latino Families, Catholic Schools, and Educational Opportunity, A Report of the Notre Dame Task Force on the Participation of Latino Children and Families in Catholic Schools* (Notre Dame, IN: University of Notre Dame, 2009), and Latino Educational Equity, Institute for Latino Studies, University of Notre Dame, 2008, at http://latinostudies.nd.edu/equityindex (accessed July 1, 2012).

24. See Mark M. Gray, Study of Catholic Parishes, Center for Applied Research in the Apostolate (CARA), Georgetown University, 2011.

25. Ibid.

26. See Pew Hispanic Center Report, Washington, DC, "Net Migration from Mexico Falls to Zero—and Perhaps Less," April 23, 2012.

27. See Ken Johnson-Mondragon, *Hispanic Youth and Young Adult Ministry in the United States: Bridging Hispanic and Mainstream Ministry to Forge the Church Anew in the 21st Century* (Stockton, CA: Instituto Fe y Vida, 2010).

28. See Synod of Bishops XIII Ordinary General Assembly, *The New Evangelization for the Transmission of Christian Faith*, no. 10, Lineamenta, 2011.

CHAPTER 3

A Mission of Reconciliation

Theological Perspectives of Pilgrim People[1]

Daniel G. Groody

Shortly after the dawn of the new millennium, President Clinton held a historic press conference in the East Room of the White House. Attending were Craig Venter and Francis S. Collins, leaders of the Human Genome Project, who were about to announce the newly deciphered sequence of human DNA. The human genes contain the elemental building blocks that are intrinsic to every person, and if the code in this sequence were read at one letter per second, it would take thirty-one years to read. If printed out in a regular font it would yield a stack of paper the size of the Washington Monument. Remarking on the scope of this discovery, Clinton observed, "Without a doubt, this is the most important, most wondrous map ever produced by humankind.... Today we are learning the language in which God created life. We are gaining ever more awe for the complexity, the beauty, and the wonder of God's most divine and sacred gift."[2]

We are just beginning to understand the ramifications and implications of such a discovery. It has changed the way we grasp who we are and from where we have come. Since then various research projects have launched, including the Genographic Project, which is a joint study conducted by National Geographic and IBM.[3] Coined as a "landmark study of the human journey," it seeks to generate new knowledge about the migratory history of human kind. By analyzing

63

DNA samples from indigenous tribes throughout the world, and comparing specific genetic markers on the DNA sequence with samples from other people, we can trace back one's migration history more than sixty thousand years. With almost half a million samples, this study is giving us new insight into the origins of humankind and how migration is literally *in our genes*.

Around the same time of this historic gathering, the United States Conference of Catholic Bishops also held a press conference. On January 24, 2003, Bishop Thomas Wenski of Miami, on behalf of the Bishop's Migration Committee, announced the publication of *Strangers No Longer: Together on a Journey of Hope*. It not only identified migration as a "sign of the times" that makes a claim on the human conscience, but also highlights how it is a perennial issue that is woven into our spiritual genes as well.

From the call of Abraham to the Exodus, from exile to return, from the incarnation to Jesus' ascension, from Jesus' call to his disciples to "follow him" to his sending them out into all nations, the theme of movement and migration are interwoven into the fabric of our relationship with God. So much so that the Second Vatican Council refers to the Church's own self-identity with the phrase "pilgrims in a strange land" (LG 7). We come from God and are called to return to God, and from beginning to end, the Scriptures reveal to us a God who migrates to his people, eliciting a response of faith that does justice in its homeward journey.

In response to the gospel message, the physical, emotional, and spiritual needs of migrants have been at the heart of the Church's mission everywhere. As noted in *Strangers No Longer*, "Our continent has consistently received immigrants, refugees, exiles, and the persecuted from other lands. Fleeing injustice and oppression and seeking liberty and the opportunity to achieve a full life, many have found work, homes, security, liberty, and growth for themselves and their families. Our countries share this immigrant experience, though with different expressions and to different degrees" (SNL 15).

The National Shrine of the Immaculate Conception, located adjacently to the current offices of the U.S. Conference of Catholic Bishops, holds a unique window into the Church's mission to migrants over many generations. This basilica, in its varied iconic, pictographic, and mosaic expressions, honors the manifold contribution of immigrants to the Church and society and the various religious communities that have assisted them in difficult times. When visiting the basilica on October 7, 1979, Pope John Paul II remarked,

> This Shrine speaks to us with the voice of all America, with the voice of all the sons and daughters of America, who have come here from the various countries of the Old World. When they came, they brought with them in their hearts the same love for the Mother of God that was characteristic of their ancestors and of themselves in their native lands. These people, speaking different languages, coming from different backgrounds of history and traditions in their own countries, came together around the heart of a Mother they all had in common. While their faith in Christ made all of them aware of being one People of God, this awareness became all the more vivid through the presence of the Mother in the work of Christ and the Church.[4]

Among the nationalities represented in the basilica's chapels are African, Austrian, Byzantine-Ruthenian, Chinese, Cuban, Czech, Filipino, French, German, Guamanian, Indian, Irish, Italian, Korean, Latin American, Lithuanian, Maltese, Polish, Slovak, Slovenian, and Vietnamese. Among the religious communities represented in the basilica are the Augustinians, Carmelites, Claretians, Dominicans, Franciscans, Jesuits, Montfort Missionaries, Oblates of Mary Immaculate, Redemptorists, Salesians, Sisters of Charity, Sisters of Providence, the Vincentians, and many others. Through its diverse array of culturally expressive chapels and oratories, this Basilica embodies the catholicity or universality of the Church in both its unity and diversity. But it also highlights its prophetic role in facing the unique social, political, and economic challenges of each generation, particularly those presented by the enduring and perennial issue of migration.

Although the theme of migration is intrinsic to our biological and spiritual origins, it is one of the most complex and controversial issues of our day. Its scope and scale today is unprecedented, touching virtually every aspect of human life. The International Organization of Migration estimates that more than two hundred fourteen million people are migrating around the world today;[5] this means that one out of every thirty-three people around the world is living away from their homelands. Approximately forty-two million migrants are forcibly uprooted, including sixteen million refugees outside their countries and twenty-six million who are internally displaced.[6] According to the International Organization of Migration, these total numbers could reach as high as four hundred five million by 2050.[7]

These flows of people affect not only migrants but receiving communities as well, making migration an increasingly volatile and contentious political issue. Questions about borders, security, identity, culture, resources, and legality prompt reactions from every sector, leaving us too often stagnating in the futile binary logic of citizen/alien, legal/illegal, and native/foreigner. In the process, we not only conflate and confuse issues related to national security and human insecurity, sovereign rights and human rights, civil law and natural law, but we leave waves of injustice in their wake.

In the face of these challenges and widespread resistance, the bishops have offered a faith-based vision on the issue of immigration reform that prioritizes people over profits, human costs over financial costs, and development and dignity over destructive and divisive rhetoric that degrades and dehumanizes. Drawing on the significant contribution of *Strangers No Longer*, my focus here is not to offer more information about migration but to offer a new imagination about it, which I hope can help us advance the conversation about migration in more creative ways and attend to those whose lives are most adversely affected.

Expanding on some of the core intuitions of the pastoral letter, I want to begin to do this by offering some theological insights on migration. In particular, I want to frame migration in light of the Church's mission of reconciliation. In doing so I want to focus on the search for justice, which, from a theological perspective, is not about courtrooms and scales as much as it is about building right relationships.[8] At its core, theology gives us a way to understand and create right relationships by overcoming (1) the human-inhuman divide; (2) the human-Divine divide; (3) the human-human divide; and (4) the country-kingdom divide. Each offers a way of thinking about theology and migration in light of the Church's ministry of reconciliation and the quest to become more human before God.

OVERCOMING THE HUMAN-INHUMAN DIVIDE

Throughout the world when migrants share with me the story of their experiences, I often ask them what is the most difficult part of their journey. Despite swimming across canals and oceans, hiding away in cargo ships and train cars, and enduring extreme temperatures in deserts and mountains, they often point to difficulties that go beyond the physical challenges. One migrant from Mexico said,

> I have stowed away on baggage compartments of buses and almost suffocated in a box car; I almost froze to death in the mountains and baked to death in the deserts; I have gone without food and water for days, and nearly died on various occasions. As difficult as these are, these are not the hardest parts of being a migrant. The worst is when people treat you like you are a dog, like you are the lowest form of life on earth.[9]

Such stories reveal that no wound cuts more deeply than the feeling that you are not even a human being, that you are no one to anyone. One of the most central issues facing migrants today is the struggle simply to reclaim their status as human beings, especially in the context of a world that demeans, diminishes, and dehumanizes them.

In the Book of Genesis we are introduced to *imago Dei* (image of God), a central truth, which emerges throughout the Scriptures, that human beings are created in the image and likeness of God (Gen 1:26–27; 5:1–3; 9:6; 1 Cor 11:7; Jas 3:9). This is not just another label for human beings but a way of speaking profoundly about human nature. Defining all human beings in terms of *imago Dei* provides a very different starting point for the discourse on migration and creates a very different trajectory for the discussion than commonly used labels from a sociopolitical sphere (alien, migrant, refugee, internally displaced person), or worse, the degrading stereotypes used by nativist groups. *Imago Dei* names the personal and relational nature of human existence and the mystery that human life cannot be understood apart from of the mystery of God.

On the surface it may seem basic to ground a theology of migration on *imago Dei*, but the term is often ignored in public discourse.

Defining the migrant and refugee first and foremost in terms of *imago Dei* roots such persons in the world very differently than if they are principally defined as social and political problems or as illegal aliens; the theological terms include a set of moral demands as well. Without adequate consideration of the humanity of the migrant, it is impossible to construct just policies ordered to the common good and which benefit society's weakest members. In *Strangers No Longer,* the bishops root their analysis not in models of political pragmatism, economic efficiency, nor cultural imperialism, but most fundamentally in the gospel message and Christ's proclamation of the kingdom of God.

In its efforts to safeguard the dignity of all people, Catholic social teaching has consistently argued that the moral health of an economy is measured not in terms of financial metrics like the gross national product or stock prices, but in terms of how the economy affects the quality of life in the community as a whole (EJA 14). Catholic social teaching states that an ordered economy must be shaped by three questions: (1) What does the economy do *for* people? (2) What does it do *to* people? and (3) How do people participate in it? (EJA 1). It puts strongest emphasis on what impact the economy has on the poor. It stresses that the economy is made for human beings, not human beings for the economy. In the immigration debate this means that the primary focus has to do first with human and relational costs; Catholic social teaching asks to what extent the economy of a country enhances the dignity of every human being, especially those who are vulnerable and deemed insignificant.

Imago Dei also means that people, by implication, ought to have available: "…everything necessary for leading a life truly human, such as food, clothing, and shelter; the right to choose a state of life freely and to found a family, the right to education, to employment, to a good reputation, to respect, to appropriate information, to activity in accord with the upright norm of one's own conscience, to protection of privacy and rightful freedom, even in matters religious" (GS 26). It is preferable for people to meet such needs in their homeland, but when these conditions cannot be met there, as John XXIII noted, people have a right to emigrate in order to "more fittingly provide a future" for themselves and their family (PT 106).

For many forced migrants, moving across borders is connected to finding a job. Writing against the backdrop of the exploitation of migrant workers and much global unemployment, John Paul II addressed the connection between human dignity, social justice, and work.[10] He noted that "the person working away from his native land, whether as a permanent emigrant or a seasonal worker, should not be placed at a disadvantage in comparison with the other workers in that society in the matter of working rights. Emigration in search of work should in no way become an opportunity for financial or social exploitation" (LE 1).

Catholic social teaching recognizes the right, and even the responsibility, of a state to control its borders, but it also argues that, when a state cannot provide the conditions necessary for human dignity, people have a right to migrate to foreign lands, even without proper legal documentation.[11] As noted in *Strangers No Longer*,

> Catholic teaching has a long and rich tradition in defending the right to migrate. Based on the life and teachings of Jesus, the Church's teaching has provided the basis for the development of basic principles regarding the right to migrate for those attempting to exercise their God-given human rights. Catholic teaching also states that the root causes of migration—poverty, injustice, religious intolerance, armed conflicts —must be addressed so that migrants can remain in their homeland and support their families. (SNL 28)

In their "Instruction on the Pastoral Care of People Who Migrate," the bishops of the United States have added that "any limitation on international migration must be undertaken only after careful consideration of the demands of international solidarity. These considerations include development, trade and investment programs, education and training, and even distribution policies designed to narrow the wide gaps between the rich and the poor."[12] In other words, controlling borders must be addressed only after the issues of distributive justice have been tackled; otherwise we end up looking at immigration as a problem in itself rather than a symptom of deeper social imbalances which precipitate the movement of people.

Most migrants leave their homes not only to realize a greater dignity for themselves but also for their families. Statistics on global remittances offer one indicator of the connection between migration and relationships. A recent study found that migrants sent home to their families, often in small amounts of $100 to $300 at a time, more than $325 billion in 2010.[13] Meanwhile, the total Overseas Development Aid from donor nations to poorer countries was $128 billion.[14] This means that migrants living on meager wages spent two and a half times as much money helping alleviate global poverty as the wealthiest countries of the world. Contrary to dehumanizing stereotypes, *imago Dei* is a two-edged sword that positively functions as an affirmation of the value and worth of every person and evaluates and challenges any tendencies to dominate or oppress the poor and needy, or degrade them through various manifestations of racism, nativism, and xenophobia. Sin disfigures the *imago Dei*, resulting in a fallen world that creates discord in relationships.

RECONCILING THE HUMAN-DIVINE DIVIDE

Christ is the perfect embodiment of *imago Dei* and the one who helps people migrate back to God by restoring in them what was lost because of sin. Karl Barth writes about the incarnation in terms of "the way of the Son of God into the far country."[15] He does not explicitly use the term "migration," but his reflections are a way of speaking about God crossing over into the dark territory of a sinful, broken humanity. What distinguishes the Christian God from other, false gods, Barth notes, is that they are not ready for this downward mobility, "this act of extravagance, this far journey."[16]

A theology of migration fundamentally is about God's migration into our sinful, broken existence, and our return migration to our ancestral, spiritual homeland, where at last we find our lives and our relationships made whole again. No aspect of a theology of migration is more fundamental, nor more challenging in its implications, than the incarnation. Through Jesus, God enters into the broken and sinful territory of the human condition in order to help men and women, lost in their earthly sojourn, find their way back home to God. As noted in the Gospel of John, migration shapes Jesus' own self-understanding: "Having loved his own who were in the world, he loved them to the end…Jesus, knowing that the Father had given all things into his hands, and that he had come from God, and was going to God" (John

13:1, 3). From this perspective, the incarnation is the great migration of human history: God's movement in love to humanity makes possible humanity's movement to God.

The sojourn of the *Verbum Dei* (Word of God) into this world is riddled with political and religious controversies, many of which are connected to narratives about migration. In Luke's Gospel, Jesus enters the world amidst a drama involving documentation (a census of the entire Roman world, Luke 2:1–5). In Matthew's account, Jesus and his family must flee a threat that endangers their lives, making them political refugees (Herod's plot, Matt 2:13–17, a parallel to a foundational migration in biblical history, Exod 1—14). In John's Gospel, many have trouble believing in Jesus precisely because of the place from which he emigrates (John 7:41–43, 52). In a fallen world, human beings find many compelling political, legal, social, and religious reasons to exclude—and reject—the migrant Son of God.[17] Nonetheless, the *Verbum Dei* manifests that, even as human beings erect barriers of every sort, God walls off no one from divine fellowship. Christ reaches out to all those considered, in Barth's terms, "alien life."[18] In the journey into otherness and vulnerability, Jesus enters into total identification with those who are abandoned and alienated.

Although the incarnation saves, Barth notes that it also "offends." It offends precisely because it brings into question the disordered values of a society that has lost its sense of *imago Dei*. It challenges especially those who exclude on the basis of superficial notions of private property, legal status, and personal or even national rights without any social, moral, or divine reference point, or any regard for the exigencies of distributive, contributive, and restorative justice that flow as a natural consequence from divine gratuity. The incarnation moves people beyond a narrow, self-serving identity into a greater identification with those considered "other" in society, particularly those like migrants and refugees who are poor and regarded as insignificant. In becoming neighbor to all in the incarnation, that is, all who live in the sinful territory of a fallen humanity, God redefines the borders between neighbors and opens up the possibility for new relationships. Migration becomes a descriptive metaphor for the movement of God toward others in the human response of discipleship.

HEALING THE HUMAN-HUMAN DIVIDE

A central dimension of the *missio Dei* (mission of God) is Jesus' ministry of reconciliation which deals largely with overcoming human constructions that divide the insider from the outsider, particularly those generated by law in its various forms. The *missio Dei* challenges a tendency that very often human beings have to idolize the state, religion, or a particular ideology and use it as a force that excludes and alienates, even when it does so under the guise of obedience to a greater cause. Jesus' openness to Gentiles, his reaching out to the Syrophoenician or Canaanite woman (Matt 15:21–28; Mark 7:24–30), his response to the Roman centurion (Matt 8:5–13; Luke 7:1–10), and many other encounters illustrate Jesus' willingness to go beyond borders and narrow interpretations of the Law in obedience to a greater law of love (Mark 12:28–34).

From a theological perspective, the incarnation itself presents challenges to conventional understandings of the Law. Throughout the Scriptures we see how the Law is central to living out a covenantal relationship with God (see, for example, Deut 30:11–20a), but we also see ways in which our interpretation of that Law gets misdirected. It is worth a moment of contemplation to see the dimensions of law at work in God's migration to the human race. When God enters our world at the time Jesus is conceived, Mary is already betrothed to Joseph. When she becomes pregnant, she runs in haste to visit her relative Elizabeth. While Mary surely desires to see a dear relative, she may also be running in fear, knowing she could be stoned if found to be pregnant by someone other than her betrothed spouse (John 8:3–5). In addition to making Mary vulnerable to the punishment of death by stoning, impregnating another man's wife makes God, from the perspective of conventional analysis, the adulterer, which would make God—strange as it may sound—subject to the same punishment (Lev 20:10). But why would God choose to enter Mary's womb at this particular time? Perhaps, in some measure, to challenge the absolutist interpretation that is often given to the Law. In the incarnation, God breaks the Law in order to reveal the greater laws of mercy, love, and grace that will come to humankind through Jesus (John 15:9–13; Titus 3:4–7). This does not mean that the Law in its religious expression is unnecessary, but it does point us to the fact that often our understanding of that Law can be inadequate.

Jesus' fellowship with sinners (Matt 9:9–13), his concern for those outside the Law (Matt 8:1–4), and his praise of the righteous Good Samaritan (Luke 10:25–37) raise important questions about law, its purposes, misuses, and abuses. Jesus recognized the value of the Law (Matt 5:17–18), but he also challenged people to see the larger picture of the Law and understand its deeper meaning (Luke 13:10–17). In the Gospels, there are three parallel accounts of Jesus' disciples picking heads of grain on the Sabbath to assuage their hunger and of Jesus healing a man with a shriveled hand on the Sabbath. When challenged by the religious leaders and crowds about breaking Sabbath laws, Jesus responds that the Sabbath is made for man, not man for the Sabbath, and that the "higher law" is that it is lawful—even required—to do good on the Sabbath and, by extension, on every other day as well (Matt 12:1–14; Mark 2:23–3:6; Luke 6:1–22). By his words and actions, Jesus demonstrates that compassion requires a reading of the Law that gives primary consideration to meeting human needs.

No area is more divisive in the immigration debate than the issue of immigration law and public policy.[19] In public discourse, people commonly say they have no problem with immigration, but they do have a problem with people breaking the law. The problem with this perspective is that it makes no distinction between various kinds of law and assumes an equal binding force for all law. In Thomistic terms, there is divine law, eternal law, natural law, and civil law.[20] This confusion, resulting in a failure to differentiate, becomes particularly problematic when some, invoking supposedly Pauline theology (Rom 13:1–7), unquestioningly and mistakenly equate the current civil law and public policy with a divinely ordained mandate. The ordinances and regulations related to sovereign rights and civil law must be seen alongside the needs, duties, and responsibilities proper to human rights and natural law.[21] At the very least, law here must first be understood in light of the protection of human dignity. Catholic social teaching uses this line of reasoning in arguing that people have a right to migrate when their country of origin lacks the necessary means to provide them with the capacity and opportunity to provide for themselves.[22]

When thousands of immigrants and refugees die each year trying to cross areas like the deserts of the American Southwest or the waters dividing North Africa from Europe, the structures of a society must be seriously examined under the entirety of legal reasoning. Here many different kinds of law are at work: laws of nations that control borders; laws of human nature that lead people to seek opportunities for more dignified lives; natural law that deals with ethical dimensions of responding to those in need; and divine law that expresses the Creator's will for all people. The fact that so many migrants are dying in their efforts to meet basic human needs raises serious questions about current civil laws and policies and their dissonance with other forms of law. Quoting Aquinas, from a Birmingham jail Martin Luther King, Jr. put it this way: "An unjust law is a human law that is not rooted in eternal law and natural law";[23] it is violence against the *imago Dei*.

When people cross borders without proper documentation, most are not simply breaking civil laws but obeying the laws of human nature, such as the need to find work in order to feed their families and attain more dignified lives. Moreover, crossing international borders without papers in most countries is an administrative infraction, not a felony; it is not a violation of divine law or natural law, and in such cases undocumented immigration should in no way be confused with serious criminal activity or threats to national security.[24] Much misunderstanding and injustice occur when immigrants and immigration are perceived primarily as problems in themselves rather than as symptoms of more systemic social ills and inequities, as matters of national security rather than as responses to human insecurity, as social threats rather than as foreign neighbors.

Conventional wisdom that guided much of policymaking throughout history implied that dealing with the problem of undocumented immigrants will keep a country safer. Recent history shows, however, that such a rationale is untenable: the terrorist bombing of the Murrah Federal Building in Oklahoma City was perpetrated by American citizens, not by outsiders, and although the 9/11 attacks were carried out by people born outside the United States, all nineteen terrorists came into the country on legal visas. Rhetorically mixing criminals and terrorists with undocumented immigrants seeking work only inflames and distorts the debate and makes the vulnerable easy targets for a country's unrest and anxiety.

Jesus was particularly concerned with the Law as it took shape in religious form. His practice of table fellowship gives us a very important window into his understanding of the Law in light of the kingdom of God. Through table fellowship Jesus fulfills the message of the prophets, invites all people to salvation, and promises his disciples a place "at table" in God's kingdom (Luke 22:30). In sharing a meal with those on the fringes of society in order to create new communities, Jesus frequently crossed borders created by narrow interpretations of the Law. He reached out in particular to those who were marginalized racially (Luke 7:1–10), economically (Luke 7:11–17), religiously (Luke 7:24–35), and morally (Luke 7:36–50). His invitation to the table was good news for the poor and those deemed insignificant or rejected by society; others it confused or even scandalized.

Jesus' table fellowship with sinners and his rejection of social and religious categories of inclusion/exclusion is probably what prompted his critics to want to dispense with him because it affronted their religious vision. As Robert Karris put it, "Jesus got himself crucified by the way he ate."[25] In bringing scribe, tax collector, fisherman, and zealot into one community, Jesus challenged his followers to a new kind of relationship beyond humanly constructed borders, one based not on social status, the rules of a nation, or religious self-righteousness, but on a common hope for the coming of God's reign (Matt 8:11; 11:16–19). For Jesus, God's mercy could not be contained within the walls of limited mindsets (Matt 7:1–5; Matt 13:10–17), and he challenged people to realize a higher law based on God's uncalculating mercy rather than on their restricted notions of worthiness and unworthiness (Luke 6:27–38).

CROSSING OVER THE COUNTRY-KINGDOM DIVIDE

The way we perceive those considered as "other" in the phenomenon of migration is rooted not only in how we see those who are different from ourselves but also in the way we see God. Meister Eckhart says that the goal of Christian life is not so much to seek the *visio Dei* (vision of God) in heaven as to see things in this life as God sees them.[26] While our journey through this life is situated within the context of our citizenship in this world, ultimately it is grounded in our movement toward and citizenship in the world to come. In addition to pledging allegiance to a particular country, the *visio Dei* brings out that one's ultimate obedience is to God alone, which leads one beyond any national and political boundaries to ultimate fidelity to the kingdom of God. Our focus here is how this vision takes root in human history, how it influences social transformation, and how it transfigures the way we understand migrants and refugees.

A theology of migration seeks to articulate a renewed vision of God and human life as it is lived out between the eschatological horizon of faith and unbelief and a historical horizon of justice and injustice. Because Christian orthodoxy and orthopraxis emerge out of an understanding of God and God alone, the *visio Dei* shapes people's ethical dispositions and offers a new way of perceiving the *imago Dei* in those whose dignity is often disfigured by dehumanizing stereotypes and demeaning public rhetoric. In its care for all, especially those most in need, the Church not only goes beyond borders but unites itself with those on the other side of them, giving expression to its interconnectedness as the Body of Christ. In imitation of its founder, the Church serves all people regardless of their religious beliefs, their political status, or their national origins.

Because of the human tendency to make God into our own disordered image and likeness, however, *visio Dei* demands conversion, individually and collectively. Exodus 20:2 states, "I am the Lord your God, who brought you out of the land of Egypt, out of the house of slavery." The word *Egypt* (*mitsrayim*) literally means "double straits" (a reference to upper and lower straits that form the territory of Egypt through which the Nile flows), "narrow places," or "narrow confinement."[27] Beyond the literal reading of the word *mitsrayim*, the subsequent figurative interpretations are striking.

In its story of migration, Israel was delivered not only from a specific national territory but also from a narrow way of thinking. Liberation at Sinai means more than simply taking off the shackles. It involves a cognitive migration, taking on a new mindset, adopting a new way of looking at the world, living out a different vision, and ultimately learning to love as God loves. The migration of Israel after the Exodus was meant to help Israel re-envision how to live in the world, a task that proved more challenging than the geographical migration: it was easier to take Israel out of the *mitsrayim* than to take the *mit-*

srayim out of Israel. After coming to power and becoming more prosperous, Israel frequently forgot its history and subsequently those who came to them as strangers and immigrants.

The *visio Dei* comes into focus in the person of Jesus Christ and the kingdom he proclaimed. The kingdom of truth and life, holiness and grace, justice, love, and peace brings people into a different kind of social and ethical territory.[28] It is based not on geography or politics but on divine initiative and openness of heart, leading to a different kind of vision of the current world order, where many of the first are last and the last first (Matt 19:30; 20:16; Mark 10:31; Luke 13:29–30). Jesus clearly taught that many of the values and metrics people employ to measure others will be inverted and that the excluded will be given priority in the kingdom. The kingdom calls people into movement, making the Church exiles on earth, strangers in this world, and sojourners en route to another place.[29]

In Philippians 3:20 Paul describes Christians as living in this world but carrying the passport of another world: "But our citizenship is in heaven, and it is from there that we are expecting a Savior, the Lord Jesus Christ." The author of Hebrews speaks of the journey in hope toward a different place: "…here we have no lasting city, but we are looking for the city that is to come" (Heb 13:14). In the midst of recounting the stories of the major figures of biblical history, the author writes of their faith and hope:

> All of these died in faith without having received the promises, but from a distance they saw and greeted them. They confessed that they were strangers and foreigners on the earth, for people who speak in this way make it clear that they are seeking a homeland. If they had been thinking of the land that they had left behind, they would have had opportunity to return. But as it is, they desire a better country, that is, a heavenly one. Therefore God is not ashamed to be called their God; indeed, he has prepared a city for them. (Heb 11:13–16)

From the perspective of a theology of migration, no text in the New Testament is more central than Matthew 25:31–46.[30] While scholars continue to debate who are the "least" (*elachistōn*) in this passage, what is significant for my discussion here is that this text describes the social location of many migrants and refugees: hungry in their homelands, thirsty in deserts they attempt to cross, naked after being robbed of their possessions, imprisoned in detention centers, sick in hospitals, and, if they make it to their destinations, they are often estranged and marginalized. This text implies that crossing borders makes possible new relationships, and it puts the verdict of judgment, to a great extent, in people's own hands: the extent to which people cross borders in this life determines to what extent they will cross them in the next (Luke 16:19–31). Robert McAfee Brown adds that this text speaks of the judgment of not only individuals but also nations.[31] The *visio Dei* also challenges people to move beyond an identity based on a narrow sense of national, racial, or psychological territoriality. It holds out instead the possibility of defining life on much more expansive spiritual terrain consistent with the kingdom of God.

CONCLUSION: CROSSING OVER THE DEATH-LIFE DIVIDE

If the Exodus story is foundational to the Scriptures, the notion of "passing over" is also central to understanding the Church's ministry of reconciliation. A theology of migration is a way of speaking about the mission of the Church to build right relationships by crossing over from death to life, manifested in part through expressions of solidarity. The bishops through *Strangers No Longer* have asked people from all walks of life to evaluate how they can work at this mission of reconciliation no matter where they are:

> We ask our presidents to continue negotiations on migration issues to achieve a system of migration between the two countries that is more generous, just, and humane. We call for legislatures of our two countries to effect a conscientious revision of the immigration laws and to establish a binational system that accepts migration flows, guaranteeing the dignity and human rights of the migrant. We ask public officials who are in charge of formulating, implementing,

and executing immigration laws to reexamine national and local policies toward the migrant and to use their leadership positions to erase misconceptions about migration. We ask adjudicators who process immigrants' legal claims to create a welcoming atmosphere that does not threaten their confidence or security. We encourage the media to support and promote a genuine attitude of welcoming toward migrants and immigrants. (SNL 104)

This spirit of solidarity is given ritual expression each year in various ways through various services in which binational communities participate in liturgies such as the Way of the Cross and the Eucharist. Along the border between El Paso, Texas and Juarez, Chihuahua, for example, the Catholic community from both sides comes together to celebrate the Eucharist, led by the border bishops from both countries. They join the altar at the wall that divides the two countries from each other, not primarily to make a political statement but a spiritual one, which manifests that now and in the future, we gather as one in the Body of Christ.

On the cross, Jesus accomplishes this mission of reconciliation by crossing the border that divides human beings from God and each other, initiating a new creation characterized by right relationships. Paul puts it this way: "For he is our peace; in his flesh he has made both groups into one and has broken down the dividing wall, that is, the hostility between us." (Eph 2:14). Although Paul is referring to the hostility between Jews and Gentiles, the implications of his words are more universal in scope. Christ breaks down the wall that separates people and reconciles the world to himself through his death on the cross.

This mission is not just about what happens when we die but about how we deal with the forces of death in this life. In part this involves denouncing the structures and systems of society that divide and dehumanize people in order to foster human dignity in the poor and vulnerable. Reducing people to their legal or political status not only denies the incarnational dignity of those in need but also dehumanizes those who have the opportunity to help. The question, then, is not whether to allow or restrict migration, but whether our moral choices make us less human or more human. Ignoring those in pain and building walls of separation alienates people not only from each other but also from ourselves, from who we are truly meant to be.

Strangers No Longer reminds us that to limit compassion to the borders of one's nationality, one's family, or even one's self is a migration toward disintegration. For those on a trajectory toward disintegration, a theology of migration cannot make sense, since it will always be news from a foreign land. If the term "alien" is to be used at all, it would be descriptive not of those who lack political documentation but of those who have so disconnected themselves from God and others that they are incapable of seeing in the vulnerable stranger a mirror of themselves, a reflection of Christ, and a challenge to human solidarity.

NOTES

1. This chapter is drawn in part from two articles by Daniel G. Groody, "Crossing the Divide: Foundations of a Theology of Migration and Refugees," *Theological Studies* (September 2009): 638–67, and "Homeward Bound: A Theology of Migration," *Journal for Catholic Social Thought* 9, no. 2 (Summer 2012): 409–24.

2. Francis S. Collins, *The Language of God: A Scientist Presents Evidence for Belief* (New York: Free Press, 2006), 1–2.

3. For more on the Genographic Project, see https://geno graphic.nationalgeographic.com/genographic/index.html

4. See: http://www.nationalshrine.com/atf/cf/%7BB0534716-4524-407D-A065-B68C4BFCB4BE%7D/BASILICA%20BACK GROUNDER%20-%20as%20of%206-09.pdf, 2 (accessed August 19, 2012).

5. See: http://www.iom.int/jahia/Jahia/about-migration/facts-and-figures/lang/en (accessed August 19, 2012).

6. See: http://www.unhcr.org/4a3b98706.html (accessed August 19, 2012).

7. See: http://www.iom.int/jahia/Jahia/about-migration/facts-and-figures/lang/en.

8. For more on this topic, see Daniel G. Groody, *Globalization, Spirituality, and Justice: Navigating the Path to Peace* (Maryknoll, NY: Orbis Books), 2007.

9. Immigrant quotation from the author's personal interviews in the deserts, mountains, and canals along the U.S./Mexican border, par-

ticularly in the towns of Altar and Sasabe, Sonora, Mexico, and various parts of Arizona and California. Transcripts of interviews are in the author's personal files.

10. John Paul II, *Laborem Exercens*, 1.

11. Sacred Congregation for Bishops, "Instruction on the Pastoral Care of People Who Migrate" (Washington, DC: United States Catholic Conference, August 22, 1969), 7.

12. USCCB, *One Family Under God: A Statement of the U.S. Bishops' Committee on Migration*, rev. ed. (Washington, DC: USCCB, 1998), 6.

13. Migration and Remittances Fact Book 2011, 2nd Edition (Washington, DC: The World Bank, 2011), vii; http://siteresources. worldbank.org/INTLAC/Resources/Factbook2011-Ebook.pdf (accessed August 19, 2012).

14. See Organisation for Economic Co-operation and Development, "More Aid for Poorer Counties, But is it Better Aid?"; http://www.oecd.org/newsroom/moreaidforpoorcountriesbutisitbet teraid.htm (accessed August 19, 2012).

15. Karl Barth, *The Doctrine of Reconciliation: Church Dogmatics*, trans. G. W. Bromiley, ed. G. W. Bromiley and T. F. Torrance (New York: Continuum, 2004), 157–210.

16. Ibid., 159.

17. Jesus was rejected by many in his day including Herod who feared losing his power (Matt 2:1–13); Jesus' family, who thought he was out of his mind (Mark 3:20–21); his neighbors who failed to understand his origins (Matt 13:54–57; Mark 6:1–4; Luke 4:13–30); the rich young man, who had great wealth and did not want to share it (Matt 19:16–22; Mark 10:17–22; Luke 18:18–23); the religious leaders who envied Jesus' popularity with the people (Matt 26:3–4; John 11:47–53); Judas, who exploited Jesus for money and favor with those in power (Matt 26:14–16, 47–50; Luke 22:4–6; John 18:2–5); Peter, who feared the ramifications of association with him (Matt 26:69–75; Mark 14:66–72; Luke 22:54–62; John 18:15–18, 25–27); and the crowds who shouted "crucify him" and did nothing to redress injustice (Matt 27:15–18, 20–23; Mark 15:6–14; Luke 23:13–23; John 19:5–7, 14–15).

18. Barth, 171.

19. An important work on public policy and Christian values is Dana W. Wilbanks, *Re-Creating America: The Ethics of U.S. Immigration Refugee Policy in a Christian Perspective* (Nashville: Abingdon, 1996).

20. Aquinas understood "law" as "an ordinance of reason for the common good, promulgated by him who has the care of the community" (*ST* 1–2, q. 90). The eternal law governs everything in the universe: the divine law corresponds to the Old Law and new Law of the Hebrew Scriptures and New Testament; the natural law deals with ethical norms and human behavior; and the civil law deals with human codes used for social order. For an overview of natural law and its development within Catholic Tradition, see Stephen J. Pope, "Natural Law in Catholic Social Teachings," in *Modern Catholic Social Teaching: Commentaries and Interpretations*, ed. Kenneth R. Himes (Washington, DC: Georgetown University, 2005), 41–71. For a more extended treatment, see John Finnis, *Natural Law and Natural Rights* (New York: Oxford University Press, 2001).

21. For interdisciplinary perspectives on rights in Africa, see David Hollenbach, ed. *Refugee Rights: Ethics, Advocacy, and Africa* (Washington, DC: Georgetown University, 2008).

22. For more on Catholic social teaching regarding migration, see Michael A. Blume, "Migration and the Social Doctrine of the Church," in *Migration, Religious Experience, and Globalization*, ed. Gioacchino Campese and Pietro Ciallella (New York: Center for Migration Studies, 2003), 62–75.

23. S. Jonathan Bass, *Blessed Are the Peacemakers: Martin Luther King, Jr., Eight White Religious Leaders, and "The Letter from the Birmingham Jail"* (Baton Rouge: Louisiana State University, 2001), 244.

24. While "entry without inspection" has long been a criminal offense, it has traditionally been treated as an administrative violation, leading to civil deportation proceedings. In recent years, however, the Department of Homeland Security has referred for criminal prosecution increasing numbers of immigrants who have entered illegally and committed other immigration violations. For more on his topic, see Doris Meissner and Donald Kerwin, *DHS and Immigration: Taking Stock and Correcting Course* (Washington, DC: Migration Policy

Institute, February 2009), 40–41; http://www.migrationpolicy. org/pubs/DHS_Feb09.pdf (accessed August 19, 2012).

25. Robert J. Karris, *Luke: Artist and Theologian* (New York: Paulist, 1985), 47.

26. Bernard McGinn, "*Visio Dei*: Seeing God in Medieval Theology and Mysticism" in *Envisaging Heaven in the Middle Ages*, ed. Carolyn Muessig and Ad Putter with Garth Griffith and Judith Jefferson (New York: Routledge, 2007), 24–27.

27. See Laurel A. Dykstra, *Set Them Free: The Other Side of Exodus* (Maryknoll, NY: Orbis, 2002), 58. I am grateful to Lisa Marie Belz for this insight.

28. *Lumen Gentium*, 36.

29. Christine D. Pohl, "Biblical Issues in Mission and Migration," *Missiology* 31 (2003): 3–15.

30. For more on different ways in which Matthew 25:31–46 has been interpreted throughout history, see John R. Donahue, "The 'Parable' of the Sheep and the Goats: A Challenge to Christian Ethics," *Theological Studies* 41 (1986): 3–31.

31. Robert McAfee Brown, *Unexpected News: Reading the Bible with Third World Eyes* (Philadelphia, PA: Westminster, 1984), 127–41.

PART II

THE CHURCH AND IMMIGRATION POLICY

CHAPTER 4

Legalization and the Undocumented According to Catholic Social Teaching

Kristin E. Heyer

Over the past decade, the failure to pursue responses in line with those put forth in *Strangers No Longer: Together on the Journey of Hope* has issued dehumanizing consequences for undocumented migrants and deepened divisions within communities.[1] In contrast to the joint bishops' conferences call for the United States and Mexico to address root causes of and legal avenues for migration and to safeguard family unity, border enforcement has remained the primary focus. The consequent deportation-by-attrition practices and removal quotas along with the growth of the "immigration industrial complex"[2] have nevertheless failed to resolve the problem of a significant undocumented presence within the United States or the need for Mexican and other migrants to enter its borders. The global phenomenon of human mobility has only intensified: today, one person in nine lives in a country where international migrants comprise one-tenth or more of the total population.[3]

Archbishop Silvano Tomasi has argued that the plight of irregular migrants signals the moral failure of the international community to prevent the circumstances propelling dangerous, unbidden journeys.[4] Over the past ten years, the death toll of migrants crossing Mexico and the deserts of Arizona has steadily mounted, alongside unprecedented U.S.-Mexico border fortification.[5] As Gioacchino Campese puts it, despite Border Patrol search-and-rescue operations, "deaths continue to rise because it is the strategy itself—the rerouting of the immigrants toward the most dangerous terrains—that is causing the deaths."[6] The Inter-American Court of Human Rights ruled that the deaths of thousands of migrants from Mexico and Central America offer the strongest evidence that the United States continues to violate human rights by employing Operation Gatekeeper.[7]

As unaccompanied women undertake the journey in increasing numbers—about half of migrants worldwide and across the Americas are female—they face particular threats, from sexual assault by smugglers and officials, to abuse on the job, to manipulation in detention facilities. The majority of annual victims of human trafficking begin as economic migrants or refugees, and trafficked women become vulnerable to sexual violence and sexually transmitted infections, yet have little access to medical or legal services.[8] According to the U.S. Attorney General, an estimated fourteen thousand five hundred to seventeen thousand five hundred people are trafficked into the United States each year, and more than twenty thousand Mexican children are victims of sex trafficking annually, particularly in tourist and border areas.[9]

Dehumanizing conditions await those who do survive treacherous journeys: exploitation on the job or in detention facilities, threats of deportation and consequent family separation, and a climate characterized by a rise in anti-immigrant sentiment.[10] As the economic downturn beginning in 2007 hit, rising unemployment rates in the United States heightened anxieties about immigrant competition with native-born residents for jobs, and concerns about the deficit cast doubt on the country's ability to absorb additional low-wage workers.[11] The United States has typically alternated between peaks of anti-immigrant sentiment (during the 1840s, 1920s, 1970s, and, arguably, the 2000s) and more hospitable stances, typically during periods of economic growth.[12] The combination of these forces has produced paralysis for comprehensive immigration policy, and state and local governments have enacted legislation to attempt to redress matters at local levels. Ostensibly to take federal enforcement shortcomings into their own hands, states like Arizona, South Carolina, Georgia, and Alabama have recently enacted punitive measures that damage immigrant families as well as community safety, local economies, and constitutional protections.[13]

Amid this shifting milieu, marked by new fears along with more timeless reservations regarding power and security, the immigration debate in the U.S. context has been framed in hyperbolic and often misleading terms that distract from actual motives and consequences for migrants and communities. Talking points that highlight scarce resources, scheming lawbreakers, or demographic threats often fail to register the pervasive realities of ruptured family lives and gender-based violence. As the 2011 letter of the U.S. Hispanic/Latino Bishops to migrants laments, many Catholics resist their Church's advocacy on behalf of protections for immigrant workers and families. The credo in the United States that we pull ourselves up by our bootstraps and make our own fate in many quarters remains as entrenched as it is incompatible with a solidaristic idea that we share each other's fate. Hence the Catholic defense of the immigrant often strikes a countercultural chord.

Amid legitimate concerns about the cultural and economic impact of the estimated eleven million undocumented immigrants residing in the United States, the centrality of human life and dignity in the Catholic Tradition challenges death-dealing policies and practices driven not only by an individualistic ethos or emphasis on the rule of law, but oftentimes too by a market logic, xenophobia, and indifference to vulnerable populations. Despite changes in the global economy which have only intensified over the past decade, the United States has not significantly changed its legal immigration system for over twenty years and has not overhauled it since 1965.[14] The impact of the provisions of the nation's 1986 and 1996 immigration laws, the mismatch between its labor needs and available visas, and significant backlogs in current family reunification categories have produced a broken situation that cries out for just and humane reform.

Thus mounting border deaths and policies that compel and then punish irregular migration are profoundly at odds with Catholic commitments. In particular, the Tradition's understanding of human rights, the political community, and the universal destination of created goods squarely challenge the persistent reality that the vast majority of contributing and vulnerable migrants remain excluded from a viable, timely path to citizenship and its protections (PT 25, 106; GS 69, 71; PP 23; CCC 2402). Here we bring this need for legalization channels into relief in light of the Tradition's scriptural foundations as well as core Catholic understandings of the person and the state, and then outline consequent policy reforms that would serve justice and security alike.

CHRISTIAN DISCIPLESHIP AND JUSTICE FOR IMMIGRANTS

To what do the demands of discipleship call Catholics amid these human realities at our borders, in our fields, and within our parishes and civic communities? The Christian faith brings rich resources to bear on the complicated questions of immigration, perhaps unsurprisingly so since its central figure himself was a refugee fleeing Herod's terror and then an itinerant preacher. The formative liberation of Israel by God from enslavement by the Egyptians led to commandments regarding hospitality to strangers (Exod 23:9; Lev 19:33). Indeed, after the commandment to worship one God, no moral imperative is repeated more frequently in the Old Testament than the command to care for the stranger. When Joseph, Mary, and Jesus fled to Egypt, the émigré Holy Family became the archetype for every refugee family (EF). In Jesus' parables such as the Good Samaritan (Luke 10:25–37) and the Last Judgment (Matt 25:31–46), he identified neighbor love and just living with care for the vulnerable stranger among us. Hence, the Christian disciple "must become a neighbor to the despised stranger if she or he is to follow Jesus on 'the way.' In Jesus' reading of the law, 'the world with its sure arrangement of insiders and outsiders' is subverted by God's reign."[15] In *Deus Caritas Est*, Pope Benedict XVI noted that neighbor love enjoined by the Good Samaritan parable can no longer be limited to "the closely knit community of a single country or people." Rather, "Anyone who needs me, and whom I can help, is my neighbor...Love of God and love of neighbor have become one: In the least of the brethren we find Jesus himself, and in Jesus we find God" (DCE 15). Thus as Bishop Nicholas DiMarzio has noted, who constitutes our neighbors does not depend on birthplace or possession of documents.[16]

This centrality of neighbor love does not reduce the immigration paradigm to charity or largesse or move it out of the inclusive civic conversation. Rather, it enjoins justice. This summons does not circumvent basic fairness, which is already in short supply; the United States accepts their labor, taxes, and purchasing power, yet does not offer undocumented migrants the protection of its laws.[17] As the signs of the times over this past decade attest, undocumented immigrants

90

encounter legion examples of distributive, commutative, structural, and even legal injustice, which the Catholic tradition bids citizens to resist and redress. For example, the widespread exploitation of undocumented day laborers violates fundamental fairness in exchange (commutative justice). The regional juxtaposition of relative luxury and misery while basic needs go unmet challenges basic notions of distributive justice. The asymmetry and impact of free trade agreements and utterly outmoded visa policies impede rather than empower persons' active participation in societal life (social justice).

Neither does the Christian summons limit our moral understanding to adequately identifying our neighbor—strictly parsing out what we owe to whom, when, under what circumstances, and with what papers. Rather, Christians are invited to focus on "being the neighbor, 'selving as neighbor,'" in William O'Neill's words.[18] With a recollection of biblical narratives that recount humans' experience of God's hospitality, of our own being as gift (and ancestry as immigrant), we are called to restore the covenant in turn. "Taking the victim's side as our own,"[19] enjoins not only compassion but also liberation. For just as the Good Samaritan promises additional recompense to the innkeeper, Christians are called to enter the world of the neighbor and "leave it in such a way that the neighbor is given freedom along with the very help that is offered."[20] The "unfreedom" of present and would-be migrants detailed in this volume pointedly illustrates the urgency of this responsibility. In the contemporary U.S. context, this lack of freedom immigrants experience fundamentally stems from their exclusion from membership in civic society. Undocumented immigrants remain deprived of the primary good of membership, or the "right to have rights."[21]

CATHOLIC SOCIAL THOUGHT: A CASE FOR IMMIGRANT LEGALIZATION

> Through the process of naturalization, the immigrant is transformed from an immigrant into a U.S. citizen: no longer the stranger to political society, but now a full member free to assert all the rights and bear all the responsibilities of citizenship. (FNC)

91

THE CATHOLIC VISION OF THE PERSON: DIGNITY BEYOND BORDERS

A Catholic immigration ethic is grounded not only in a scriptural heritage but also, significantly, in its vision of the person as inherently sacred and made for community. In the Catholic tradition, a person imaged in a relational, trinitarian God is endowed with human rights understood not as absolute claims made by radically autonomous individuals, but rather, claims to goods necessary for each person to participate with dignity in society's communal life.[22] Thus, whereas a Christian anthropology does not compromise autonomy, it understands humans as profoundly relational and interdependent. Flowing from this vision, Catholic principles of economic and migration ethics protect not only civil and political rights, but also more robust social and economic rights and responsibilities. This understanding of human rights and the nature of the political community ground a defense of twin rights to emigration and immigration that generally privileges reception over exclusion. As *Strangers No Longer* details, the Catholic Tradition's affirmation of social and economic rights establishes persons' rights *not to migrate* (fulfill those rights in their homeland) and *to migrate* (if they cannot support themselves or their families in their country of origin) (PT 106; SNL 34–35). The state's purpose is to protect the common good of its citizens, and when the common good remains so distant from attainment that a population is deprived basic human rights, people may seek a new home elsewhere.

Once migrants do seek life in new lands under such circumstances, a Catholic anthropology profoundly critiques patterns wherein stable receiving countries accept the labor of millions of immigrants without offering legal protections or viable paths to citizenship. The bishops' conferences and others have repeatedly critiqued such "shadow" societies as risking the creation of a permanent underclass, harming both human dignity and the common good. From Pope Leo XIII's 1891 warnings that neither human nor divine laws permit employers to exploit for profit another's need, to Pope Benedict XVI's condemnations of global economic practices that hinder authentic development, the protection of human dignity remains the central criterion of economic justice. The encyclical tradition makes clear that "every economic decision and institution must be judged in light of whether it protects or undermines the dignity of the human person...realized in community with others" (EJA 1, 14). In *Laborem Exercens*, for example, Pope John Paul II roots his condemnation of the social and financial exploitation of migrant workers in the principle that "...the hierarchy of values and the profound meaning of work itself require that capital should be at the service of labor and not labor at the service of capital" (LE 23).

Hence the Catholic social tradition explicitly protects the basic human rights of undocumented migrants in host countries in light of longstanding teachings on human and workers' rights, which do not depend on citizenship status.[23] The tradition promotes rights to just wages, benefits, safe working conditions, and health care assistance, especially in the case of on-the-job injuries, and rights to association (LE 19–20). Within the U.S. labor market, the pervasive exploitation of undocumented immigrants in terms of substandard wages and protections, disproportionately unsafe conditions, wage theft, and a lack of mechanisms to enforce humane protections thus constitute basic violations.[24] Offering unauthorized immigrant laborers and their family members a viable path to legalization remains the best hope for countering this pervasive exploitation in an effective and enduring way. At the same time, such avenues would provide stability and augment productivity in the workforce.[25]

POLITICAL COMMUNITIES IN SERVICE TO THE GLOBAL COMMON GOOD

From Pope John Paul II's *Ecclesia in America*, to the Mexican and U.S. bishops' *Strangers No Longer*, to the ongoing advocacy of the Catholic Church on local, national, and international levels, the tradition insists that the Church must remain a vigilant advocate on behalf of the rights of migrants and their families without documentation. Beyond its foundation in the social and economic rights flowing from a relational anthropology, the Catholic right to migrate is also rooted in the universal destination of created goods. As the tradition holds, state sovereignty "cannot be exaggerated" to the point that access to land is denied to needy people from other nations, provided that the national common good "rightly understood" does not forbid it (EF Introduction; PT 106). Flowing from the understanding of rights

93

articulated above and this notion of the goods of creation, a key component of the Catholic right to migrate remains its inclusion of economic rights violations alongside political oppression as legitimate causal factors.[26] While the social tradition recognizes the right of sovereign nations to control their borders, the right is not understood to be absolute in nature. In *Strangers No Longer*, the U.S. and Mexican bishops' conferences emphasize the presumption of migration and reception over sovereignty in light of the contemporary situation of global poverty and persecution. The bishops' conferences assert that the right of a sovereign state to control its borders in order to promote the common good and the human right to migrate in order to realize God-given rights are complementary, for while reasonable limits may be set, the common good is served when basic human rights are not violated.

Contemporary push factors continuing to drive much of the immigration to the United States and the treatment of the undocumented within its borders threaten the common good. In chapter 6 of this volume, Donald Kerwin highlights some of the push and pull factors that drive immigration, particularly as it applies to issues affecting economic development. The Catholic recognition of both the right of sovereign nations to control their borders and its temperance by conditions of social justice and the universal destination of created goods continue to warrant citizenship rights for many who remain within the United States without viable avenues to pursue this basic right and responsibility. Given the role the United States has played in shaping conditions that directly contribute to irregular migration, and its relative ability to absorb newcomers into its communities and economy, it has a particular obligation to the reception and accommodation the Catholic social tradition urges (SNL 36).

The economic and political realities judged by the joint bishops' conferences to warrant a presumption of migration and reception over sovereignty in 2003 have not appreciably improved.[27] In 2010, when bishops from Mexico, Central America, the Caribbean, the United States, and Canada met, they underscored the increased violence and drug smuggling along with connections between rising violence and economic insecurity in the region: "The lack of economic opportunity as well as the lack of a sense of social meaning, especially among younger adults, fuels the resort to underground and illicit activities in many of the countries of the hemisphere."[28] They renewed their call to the U.S. Congress for reform of immigration law in a manner that does not criminalize unlawful entry or separate families and that affords legal protection for those already working in the U.S. labor force. With more than 60 percent of undocumented immigrants in the United States having lived here for over ten years, over sixteen and a half million U.S. households home to mixed-status families, and two million undocumented students in primary and secondary schools across the country, a "double society" increasingly threatens the common good as the U.S. bishops warned in their pastoral statement *Together a People:* "...one visible with rights and one invisible without rights—a voiceless underground of undocumented persons."[29]

Given the unity of the human family, a person's citizenship in a particular state does not deprive her of "citizenship in that universal society" (PT 25). This sense of cosmopolitan citizenship and global solidarity challenges absolute understandings of sovereignty. For in contrast to the dominant political discourse absolutizing sovereignty claims, sovereignty and hospitality are mutually implicating in Catholic social thought, with legitimate exercises of sovereignty dependent upon prior demands of human rights protections and basic conditions of social justice (EF 51; CV 62).[30] Elevating narrow visions of sovereignty or rule of law divorced from the protection of human rights of the vulnerable continues to harm migrants under the guise of fundamental American values. Just as the Catholic Tradition rejects sovereignty as an expression of absolute power, so it cautions against idolizing security.[31]

Moreover, the legalization of eligible immigrants serves the ends of proportionate security in addition to human rights protections. Bringing unauthorized immigrants out of the shadows by means of opportunities to meet certain conditions and regularize their status would allow the U.S. government to account for its society's members and focus enforcement efforts on genuine security threats. Recent enforcement initiatives aiming, in part, to differentiate threat levels among undocumented immigrants residing in the United States (such as Immigration and Customs Enforcement's Secure Communities program) have raised significant concerns about civil rights abuses and the erosion of community trust.[32] Continuing to disallow viable paths to legalization for the majority of immigrants welcomed in the marketplace but not the voting booth, college campus, department of motor vehicles, or stable workplace, risks making permanent this underclass of disenfranchised persons, undermining not only Christian commitments but also significant civic values and interests.

Finally, a Catholic theory of nationality calls for new immigrants (as all community members) to concretely contribute to dignified life in the community of all—demonstrating solidarity with their fellow residents and contributing to society. Rather than fearfully navigating in the shadows or hitting the "ceiling" of high school or rare college scholarships, a path to legalization would allow immigrants to work, advance in their studies, and to secure basic health services and police protection, thereby furthering the good of all. In the Catholic Tradition, rights fundamentally secure participation in the life of the community, and imply correlative responsibilities. As Donald Kerwin puts it, "Rights do not just allow, but *require*, immigrants to contribute to their new communities."[33] Hence the Catholic vision of the person and their consequent rights and responsibilities—civil, political, economic, social, cultural, and religious in nature—confer not only rights of protection in one's homeland, migration where these remain unrealized, reception and dignified conditions in countries of destination, but also meaningful participation in the life of one's new community. Whereas membership in a political community remains "the primary good we distribute to one another,"[34] critical to the fundamental "right to have rights," the array of rights affirmed by the Catholic social tradition depend upon a path to citizenship particularly for immigrants who contribute in many positive ways to the shared life of their communities of destination. The bishops' clear support for an earned legalization program for immigrants in *Strangers No Longer* remains urgently needed, serves justice and security alike, and appropriately considers immigrants as bearers of dignity "broken by the law."[35]

POLICY IMPLICATIONS: REFORM THAT SERVES JUSTICE AND SECURITY

Whereas a Christian immigration ethic requires more than a policy response, it necessarily entails attention to the politically possible in light of the stakes of ongoing suffering. At a concrete level, then, what are receiving nations' responsibilities in justice? Justice requires, negatively, that countries refrain from creating or substantially contributing to situations that compel people to emigrate and that host countries refrain from exploiting or extorting undocumented laborers. Positively, receiving immigrants fleeing situations of dire economic need, offering citizenship protections to those they do employ, and developing policies that reflect actual labor needs and hiring practices and protect family unity are obligations in justice.[36]

Given these demands of justice, the United States has obligations to redress its role in abetting irregular migration and to offer those who live and work within its borders a viable path to earned legalization. Often dismissed as an amnesty that rewards lawbreakers, earned legalization proposals typically yoke lawful permanent residence to conditions such as continuous employment, payment of a fine, rigorous criminal background and security screenings, and English proficiency.[37] Earned legalization programs should safeguard against imposing disproportionately burdensome requirements; for example, undocumented women and children may be adversely impacted by employment, language competency, or continuous residency based requirements. Just as through community involvement (long-term residence and "good conduct"), undocumented residents can work toward citizenship in other countries,[38] migrant workers in the United States, likewise embedded in and contributing to their host society, should be afforded permanent residency with the possibility of U.S. citizenship. Given nearly two-thirds of undocumented immigrants living in the United States have resided in the country at least ten years, mass deportation is impractical and unjust. At a minimum, a path to legal residency for those minors brought to the United States like the one offered by the DREAM Act is long overdue. For more on this topic, see Colleen Cross' chapter in this volume (chapter 10), which traces out some of the political and theological implications of the DREAM Act.

In 2009 the Council on Foreign Relations' Task Force on U.S. Immigration Policy noted that the trend over the first decade of the twenty-first century of approximately eight hundred thousand total undocumented immigrants arriving per year with the large majority finding employment indicates the legal migration system "has not remotely reflected market demand."[39] In view of such outdated allocations a new worker visa program responsive to actual employment needs (for both agricultural and non-agricultural low-wage workers) is also urgently needed. Whereas temporary or guest-worker programs have historically proven vulnerable to abuses, many migrants continue to express the desire for legal avenues for seasonal (agricultural or construction) work in the United States. Approaches in this vein would improve upon the present de facto guest-worker program of undocumented labor, but should include labor protections with adequate enforcement, job portability, and personal mobility.

Reform of family visa backlogs and inadequate country quotas to allot more Western Hemisphere visas will help expedite family reunification; at present the United States allocates the same number of visas to neighboring Mexico as to Botswana and Nepal.[40] Unjust costs to migrants and to communities necessitate reforming border security and enforcement regimes that respect core principles of due process and reflect the nature of civil violations as well as mitigating the local costs of accommodation (for example, federal revenue sharing should disperse funds to states with large immigrant populations, by having populations used in the revenue formula reflect foreign-born residents). Establishing a standing commission on immigration to advise Congress regularly on warranted adjustments on an ongoing basis would provide flexibility and help ensure the United States not reinvent the immigration reform wheel every few decades.[41] Mechanisms that offer enforcement authorities more ability to exercise discretion in immigration cases are also warranted, in light of the complex factors and relationships that pressures to fill detention beds or fast-track deportations now override.

Most immigrants to the United States hail from middle-income countries whereas most development aid is targeted toward low-income countries (each of which faces a distinct set of issues). Given the inability of those in greatest need to migrate, pursuing trade equity and longer-term development and investments that do not replicate the destructive patterns of the recent past would align reform efforts toward more future-oriented solutions with a wider reach. In the service of protecting human rights, wealthy states' substantial duties to admit outsiders in need coexist with their duty to collaborate toward a more just global order.[42]

Domestically, care must be taken that reform efforts not accomplish greater justice for new immigrants at the expense of low-wage native-born workers. Legislative efforts should carefully consider the interplay between U.S. obligations to those in need beyond its borders and to its own citizens. Earnings inequalities within the U.S. labor market have increased dramatically in recent decades. The economic downturn beginning in 2007 has further exacerbated such effects, "as the rates of job destruction outpaced those of job creation for more than two years, leading to the net loss of several million jobs."[43] Additionally, globalization trends have reduced the availability of well-paid jobs in the goods-producing sectors, such as durable manufacturing, which have traditionally paid good wages to workers with a high school level education or less.[44] Whereas economists differ on whether undocumented immigration suppresses wages, fills needed gaps, or stimulates economies (and complex variables alter the dynamics in various locales), it is essential that duties to lower-wage citizens be considered alongside the impact of proposed reforms. Regularizing workers presently laboring in the informal sector, with such care taken, can potentially prevent native-born, low-wage workers from being undersold by unscrupulous employers looking to exploit the vulnerability of those without documents. To this end, reforms should incorporate an extension of core federal labor protections to unauthorized workers and strengthen penalties for violations to promote compliance.[45] Solutions that thus "raise the floor" for all workers must be sought.

Immigration policies including legalization provisions will invariably need to achieve compromise in piecemeal fashion at first, given the challenge of achieving legislative consensus. Pitting constituents against one another—whether native-born vs. immigrant workers, or "innocent children" vs. "guilty parents" in the case of DREAM Act proposals—does violence to the common good and neglects to consider pieces of the immigration puzzle in light of its whole. In some cases, recognizing the moral priority of relative need (gravity and imminence of harm) will be necessary in elaborating policy guidelines, given particular vulnerabilities and complicities.[46]

Ultimately, an approach rooted in Catholic commitments must both reduce the need to migrate and protect those who find themselves compelled to do so as a last resort. Taken together, such comprehensive measures not only serve justice and approximate hospitality, they better reflect the nation's own founding principles. The past decade's failed reform efforts in the United States prompt reflection on questions of national identity: for example, what does it honor by awarding personhood to corporations and excluding its tax-paying workers from labor protections? Policy inaction, local initiatives, and political rhetoric on the immigration issue too often betray a retributivist posture with divisive and damaging effects, an outlook directly at odds with a Catholic emphasis on restoring right relationships. The protection of human rights in service to the common good and reconciled communities squarely challenges migrants' relegation to a shadow existence as well as unequal interdependence among nations that abets extralegal flows. A reform agenda with a viable path to citizenship as its centerpiece is well poised to serve justice and security alike.

NOTES

1. Portions of this chapter appeared in Kristin E. Heyer, *Kinship Across Borders: A Christian Ethic of Immigration* (Washington, DC: Georgetown University Press, 2012) and are reprinted with permission. Other sections are adapted from "Reframing Displacement and Membership: Ethics of Migration," *Theological Studies* 73 (March 2012).

2. Whereas in the United States private companies control nearly half of total detention beds and seven of eleven British detention centers are run by for-profit contractors, Australia has entirely outsourced its enforcement to a succession of three publicly traded companies since 1998. For a genealogy of "immigration industrial complex," which alludes to the conflation of national security with immigration law enforcement and "the confluence of public and private sector interests in the criminalization of undocumented migration, immigration law enforcement, and the promotion of 'anti-illegal' rhetoric," see Tanya Golash-Boza, "The Immigration Industrial Complex: Why We Enforce Immigration Policies Destined to Fail" *Sociology Compass* 3 (February 2009): 295ff.

3. Forty years ago, the ratio was 1:29; see Aaron Terrazas, *Migration and Development: Policy Perspectives from the United States* (Washington, DC: Migration Policy Institute, 2011), 1; http://www.migrationpolicy.org/pubs/migdevpolicy-2011.pdf (accessed July 17, 2012).

4. Silvano Tomasi, "Migration and Catholicism in a Global Context," in *Migration in a Global World* (Concilium 2008/5), ed. Solange Lefebvre and Luiz Carlos Susin (London: SCM Press, 2008), 22.

5. The Arizona press reported that by the end of 2009, there were "3,300 agents, more than 200 miles of fences and vehicle barriers, and 40 agents assigned to the agency's search, rescue and trauma team, Borstar, yet illegal immigrants [were] still dying while trying to cross the Border Patrol's 262-mile-long Tucson Sector. Border-county law enforcement, Mexican Consulate officials, Tohono O'odham tribal officials and humanitarian groups [said] the increase in fencing, technology and agents has caused illegal border crossers to walk longer distances in more treacherous terrain, increasing the likelihood that people [would] get hurt or fatigued and left behind to die." Brady McCombs, "No signs of letup in entrant deaths." This article appeared in the December 27, 2009, *Arizona Daily Star*, unfortunately web access to the text no longer exists.

6. Gioacchino Campese, "*¿Cuantos Más?* The Crucified Peoples at the U.S.-Mexico Border," in *A Promised Land, A Perilous Journey: Theological Perspectives on Migration*, ed. Daniel G. Groody and Gioacchino Campese (Notre Dame, IN: University of Notre Dame, 2008), 278.

7. John Fife, "Civil Initiative," in *Trails of Hope and Terror: Testimonies on Immigration*, ed. Miguel A. De La Torre (Maryknoll, NY: Orbis, 2009), 174.

8. UNFPA: United Nations Population Fund, "Linking Population, Poverty and Development: Migration, A World on the Move," http://www.unfpa.org/pds/migration.html (accessed July 17, 2012).

9. U.S. Department of State, *2004 Trafficking in Persons Report* (June 14, 2004) www.state.gov/documents/organization/34158.pdf (accessed August 1, 2012).

10. From 2004–2008 the number of anti-Hispanic hate crimes rose 25 percent, according to the FBI, as reported in Jessica Ramirez, "When Hate Becomes Hurt," *Newsweek* (March 10, 2008), 14. Hate groups exploiting the issue of illegal immigration have also been on the rise in recent years. See Christians for Comprehensive Immigration Reform, "A House Divided: Why Americans of Faith are Concerned about Undocumented Immigrants" (November 2007) for their discussion of the proliferation of hate crimes/groups as documented by the Southern Poverty Law Center and Anti-Defamation League, 4–8,

http://www.immigrationpolicy.org/sites/default/files/docs/Christiansf orCIR.pdf (accessed July 17, 2012).

11. Kate Brick, A. E. Challinor, and Marc R. Rosenblum, *Mexican and Central American Immigrants in the United States* (Washington, DC: Migration Policy Institute, 2011), 16.

12. Aaron Terrazas, *Migration and Development: Policy Perspectives from the United States* (Washington, DC: Migration Policy Institute, 2011), 10. Noah Pickus cautions that whereas "economic interests have played a significant role in regulating the admission and incorporation of immigrants," they do not fully account for the treatment of newcomers in the United States: "Waves of restriction have not followed the turns of the economy. Neither the Naturalization Act of 1790 nor the National Origins Act of 1924 was passed in a period of extensive economic turmoil." Noah Pickus, *True Faith and Allegiance: Immigration and American Civic Nationalism* (Princeton: Princeton University Press, 2005), 11.

13. On April 23, 2010, Governor Jan Brewer of Arizona signed into law an especially broad and stringent immigration bill (S.B. 1070), criminalizing the failure to carry immigration papers and granting police wide latitude to detain anyone suspected of being in the country outside of legal channels. See Randal C. Archibold, "Arizona Enacts Stringent Law on Immigration," *New York Times* (April 24, 2010), A1. The 287(g) programs and the state measures like S.B. 1070 and imitative measures raise concerns about the potential for racial profiling, dismantling community members' trust in local law enforcement officials, and diversion of resources.

14. Donald Kerwin and James Ziglar, "Fixing Immigration: Start by making legal immigration benefit everyone," *America* (December 12, 2011).

15. William R. O'Neill, and William C. Spohn, "Rights of Passage: The Ethics of Immigration and Refugee Policy," *Theological Studies* 59 (1998): 103, citing Bernard Brandon Scott, *Hear Then the Parable: A Commentary on the Parables of Jesus* (Minneapolis: Fortress, 1989), 202.

16. Bishop Nicholas DiMarzio, Chair, U.S. Bishops' Committee on Domestic Policy, "Labor Day Statement 2006," *Origins* 36, no. 13 (September 7, 2006): 204.

17. Cardinal Roger Mahony, "For Goodness Sake: Why America Needs Immigration Reform," *The Tidings* (February 11, 2011).

18. William R. O'Neill, "Anamnestic Solidarity: Immigration from the Perspective of Restorative Justice" paper delivered at the annual convention of the Catholic Theological Society of America, Halifax, Nova Scotia (June 5, 2009).

19. Ibid.

20. John R. Donahue, *The Gospel in Parable* (Philadelphia: Fortress Press, 1988), 133.

21. See Hannah Arendt, *The Origins of Totalitarianism* (New York: Harcourt, Brace & World, 1966), chapter 9.

22. Michael J. Himes and Kenneth R. Himes, *Fullness of Faith: The Public Significance of Theology* (New York: Paulist Press, 1993), 46.

23. Pope John Paul II's *Ecclesia in America* "reiterates the rights of migrants and their families and the respect for human dignity 'even in cases of non-legal immigration." *Ecclesia in America* (Washington, DC: USCCB, 1999), 65. Over recent decades social encyclicals have enumerated migrant rights to life and a means of livelihood; decent housing; education of their children; humane working conditions; public profession of religion; and to have such rights recognized and respected by host of government policies. See 1969 Vatican *Instruction on Pastoral Care* (7); 1978 *Letter to Episcopal Conferences* from the Pontifical Commission for the Pastoral Care of Migrant and Itinerant peoples (3); Pope Paul VI, *Octogesima adveniens* (17); Pope John XIII, *Pacem en Terris* (106); National Council of Catholic Bishops, *Resolution on the Pastoral Concern of the Church for People on the Move* (Washington, DC: USCCB, 1976) and endorsed by Pope Paul VI; and *Strangers No Longer*, 38.

24. For an analysis of day labor abuses in terms of Catholic social thought and social sin, see Kristin Heyer, "Strangers in Our Midst: Day Laborers and Just Immigration Reform," *Political Theology* 9, no. 4 (2008): 425–53.

25. Donald Kerwin and Charles Wheeler, "The Case for Legalization, Lessons from 1986, Recommendations for the Future." This article originally appeared in *Issues in Immigration*, Vol. 1 (Center for Migration Studies, 2004). It was reprinted by *Bender's Immigration Bulletin*, vol. 12, no. 3 (February 1, 2007).

26. The 1969 *Instruction on Pastoral Care* asserts that "where a state which suffers from poverty combined with great population cannot supply such use of goods to its inhabitants…people possess a right to emigrate, to select a new home in foreign lands and to seek conditions of life worthy of man." Sacred Congregation for Bishops, *Instruction on Pastoral Care*, 14. For a helpful discussion of Catholic teaching on economic refugees, see Drew Christiansen, "Sacrament of Unity: Ethical Issues in the Pastoral Care of Migrants and Refugees," in Office of Pastoral Care of Migrants and Refugees, Bishops' Committee on Migration, National Conference of Catholic Bishops, *Today's Immigrants and Refugees: A Christian Understanding* (Washington, DC: United States Catholic Conference, 1988), 90–91.

27. Ibid., no. 39.

28. Catholic Bishops' Regional Consultation on Migration, "Cooperation among Governments in Region, Economic Development Key Factors: U.S. Should Afford Protection to Foreign Workers," June 4, 2010; http://old.usccb.org/comm/archives/2010/10-118.shtml (accessed July 17, 2012).

29. National Conference of Catholic Bishops, *Together a New People, Pastoral Statement on Migration and Refugees*, November 8, 1986, 10.

30. Anna Rowlands, "On the Temptations of Sovereignty: The Task of Catholic Social Teaching and the Challenge of UK Asylum Seeking," *Political Theology* 12 (2011): 860. Since the time of Pius XII, official Catholic social teaching has "so thoroughly contested the right of sovereign powers of states to unqualified control of their borders that any assertion of sovereign rights in this area must be judged, from the point of view of Catholic social ethics, a secondary or residual right, not one of primary importance." The presumption in favor of state control of borders and regulation of the movement of peoples across its borders holds only "in exceptionally grave circumstances." Christiansen, "Sacrament of Unity: Ethical Issues in the Pastoral Care of Migrants and Refugees," 88–89.

31. Donald Kerwin, "The Natural Rights of Migrants and Newcomers: A Challenge to U.S. Law and Policy," in Groody and Campese, *A Promised Land, A Perilous Journey*, 204.

32. See, for example, the USCCB's Migration and Refugee Services/Office of Migration Policy and Public Affairs, "287(g) and

Secure Communities: The Facts about Local Immigration Law Enforcement" (May 2011); http://www.usccb.org/issues-and-action/human-life-and-dignity/immigration/stateandlocalimmigrationenforcement.cfm (accessed July 17, 2012).

33. Donald Kerwin, "Toward a Catholic Vision of Nationality," *Notre Dame Journal of Law, Ethics & Public Policy* 23 (2009): 205.

34. Michael Walzer, *Spheres of Justice: A Defense of Pluralism and Equality* (New York: Basic Books, 1983), 31.

35. Bishop Thomas Wenski has noted, "The so-called 'illegals' are so not because they wish to defy the law, but because the law does not provide them with any channels to regularize their status in our country—which needs their labor; they are not breaking the law, the law is breaking them." Most Reverend Thomas Wenski, "U.S. immigration policy outdated and unjust toward working Immigrants," Diocese of Orlando, FL website (May 13, 2005), http://www.orlandodiocese.org/en/btw-columns/item/228-us-immigration-policy-outdated-and-unjust-toward-working-immigrants-%E2%80%93-may-13-2005 (accessed July 17, 2012).

36. David Hollenbach forwarded similar priorities at the Woodstock Center's meeting on migration in Fairfield, CT (July 19, 2007).

37. Five major proposals for earned legalization were introduced in the U.S. Congress from 2006–2011.

38. Saskia Sassen, *Territory, Authority, Rights: From Medieval to Global Assemblages* (Princeton, NJ: Princeton University Press, 2008), 295.

39. National Council on Foreign Relations (Jeb Bush and Thomas McLarty III, chairs, Edward Aldin, Project Director), *U.S. Immigration Policy*, Independent Task Force Report No. 53 (Washington, DC: National Council on Foreign Relations, 2009), 50.

40. Congress' imposition in 1976 (on the logic of "formal equality") of country quotas of twenty thousand on the Western Hemisphere and closure of a loophole in the law that had permitted undocumented Mexican immigrants with U.S.-born children to legalize their status, effectively recast Mexican immigration as illegal. Mae M. Ngai notes that the transfer of Mexican migration from legal to illegal form should have been expected, given that in the early 1960s annual "legal" Mexican migration "comprised some 200,000 *braceros*

and 35,000 regular admissions for permanent residency...."
Deportations of undocumented Mexicans rose by 40 percent in 1968,
to one hundred fifty-one thousand; then in 1976, when the twenty
thousand per country quota was imposed, it rose to seven hundred
eighty-one thousand, whereas the combined total number of appre-
hensions for all others in the world remained below a hundred thousand annually. Mae M. Ngai *Impossible Subjects: Illegal Aliens and the
Making of Modern America* (Princeton, NJ: Princeton University Press,
2004), 261. See also Douglass S. Massey, "Forum" (response to Carens)
in Joseph Carens, *Immigrants and the Right to Stay* (Cambridge, MA:
MIT Press, 2010), 78.

41. This recommendation is made in the Brookings-Duke
Immigration Policy Roundtable; its use here does not signify concur-
rence with all recommendations from that report. See William
Galston, Noah Pickus and Peter Skerry, *Breaking the Immigration
Stalemate: From Deep Disagreements to Constructive Proposals* (Washington,
DC: The Brookings Institution and Durham, NC: The Kenan
Institute for Ethics, 2009); http://kenan.ethics.duke.edu/breaking-
the-immigration-stalemate/ (accessed July 17, 2012).

42. Jonathan Seglow, "The Ethics of Immigration," *Political
Studies Review* 3 (2005): 329. The comprehensive claim rights recognized by Catholic social thought and some cosmopolitan approaches
far exceed the principles of human rights law regarding migrants.

43. Harry J. Holzer, Julia I. Lane, David B. Rosenblum, and
Fredrik Andersson, *Where Are All the Good Jobs Going? What National
and Local Job Quality and Dynamics Mean for U.S. Workers* (New York:
The Russell Sage Foundation, 2011), 3.

44. In fact, the share of U.S. workers employed in durable manufacturing has fallen from about 12 percent in 1970 to 6 percent in 2008
as both technology and globalization reduced the demand for domestic labor in these jobs." Holzer, et al., 7.

45. See Donald Kerwin, *Labor Standards Enforcement and Low-
Wage Immigrants: Creating an Effective Enforcement System* (Washington,
DC: Migration Policy Institute, 2011); www.migrationpolicy.org/
pubs/laborstandards-2011.pdf (accessed July 17, 2012).

46. O'Neill, "Anamnestic Solidarity."

CHAPTER 5

Migrant Abuses and Migrant Worker Programs in the Context of Catholic Teaching

Patricia Zamudio

INTRODUCTION

When people migrate, they find themselves involved in very difficult situations. Because they are seen as different, as lacking recognizable social bonds, they are deprived of the social solidarity we encourage for those who are members of our communities. As the Mexican and American bishops note in their pastoral letter *Strangers No Longer*, "in both our countries we see much injustice and violence against them and much suffering and despair among them because civil and church structures are still inadequate to accommodate their basic needs" (SNL 5). Migrants are often seen as intruders, and as such, are denied the benefits of belonging. And that denial puts them in a position to be taken advantage of by many, even by those who should protect them, such as the state institutions of the host or transit countries. In contrast, the bishops invite us "Catholics and persons of good will in both nations to exercise [our] faith and to use [our] resources and gifts to truly welcome the stranger among us" (SNL 7).

In the last decade (2002–2012), migration has increased globally to unprecedented highs, from one hundred fifteen to two hundred fourteen million international migrants per year.[1] A good proportion of migrants have enjoyed the benefits of a regular status. Such is the case for participants in temporary worker programs. In 2009, for example,

Canada received twenty-six thousand workers under the Canadian Seasonal Agricultural Worker Program (SAWP),[2] and the U.S. Office of Foreign Labor Certification (OFLC) approved 86,014 H-2A positions.[3]

In addition to these documented workers, however, a low but significant proportion of migrants reside in their host countries in undocumented status. According to the International Organization for Migration, it is estimated that the percentage of irregular (undocumented) migrants is between 10 and 15 percent—that is, between twenty-one and thirty million people.[4]

Such a massive movement of people across international borders and the suffering that often follows challenges us as Catholics to find ways to diminish it. In the face of such difficult times, we maintain faith by reading "the signs of the times" (Matt 16:3) and understanding the message God is sending, so we can identify the response he expects us to give as a sign of his love (GS 4). Catholic pastors have reminded us that we should "contemplate [in migrants] the image of Christ who said, 'I was a stranger and you made me welcome' (Mt 25:35)" (EMCC 12).

This is what the Church is doing: welcoming migrants in any way possible, through the work of pastoral groups all over the world. In addition to the priests and nuns that guide such service, thousands of laypeople participate in different ways, many times generously volunteering their time. Most of them have a sense of mission, seeing their work as a way to respond to God's call to demonstrate their Christian values and help construct a humane and just world, as a sign of the presence of the kingdom of God among us. The Gospel is the main inspiration for their work; however, a number of doctrinal documents like the pastoral letter *Strangers No Longer: Together in the Journey of Hope* (SNL), guide their actions and also help them to give meaning to an often dangerous mission.

The main objective of this chapter is to analyze two kinds of migration experiences: guest-worker programs and transit migration. I will explore the various kinds of abuses committed against people who participate in these forms of migration, and the ways the Catholic Church responds to the challenges these situations present. Through analysis of migrants' experiences and the response of the *pastores* (pastors) of the Pastoral Dimension of Human Mobility[5] (DPMH) in

Mexico, I will show how migration has given us opportunities to construct a better world, and how Catholic teaching provides a practical and very human expression of Jesus' message in the Gospel of Matthew: "Truly I tell you, just as you did it to one of the least of these who are members of my family, you did it to me" (Matt 25:40; see also SNL 26).

READING "THE SIGNS OF THE TIMES" IN THE EXPERIENCE OF OUR MIGRANT BROTHERS AND SISTERS

> We judge ourselves as a community of faith by the way we treat the most vulnerable among us.
>
> —*Strangers No Longer*

The motivations that trigger migration are diverse, but at the heart of most migratory movements is the desire to improve living conditions for the migrant and his or her family. Elsewhere, I have called migration "a strategy for the construction of futures."[6] In all my years as a migration researcher, I have found that migrant people acknowledge that, in general, they can survive the present day in their communities of origin with more or less (economic) trouble; they can still make ends meet. However, in their eyes, merely "making ends meet" without the possibility of enjoying a comfortable life is not the way a human being should live—most of all, it is not the way their children should live. These hard-working people want a dignified future for their families and acknowledge that the local conditions of their communities do not provide opportunities for significant change in their social and economic conditions.

In the light of Catholic teaching, these people should be able to migrate and construct the lives they want, exercising all their rights—civil, political, social, economic, and cultural—but most of all, they should have the option of remaining in their communities, enjoying the company of their family and friends, and *still* being able to exercise their rights (SNL 28; PT 25). In other words, they should be able to exercise their God-given human rights no matter what, whether they choose to leave or to stay in their communities. The problem is, precisely, that they cannot stay in their communities if they want to improve their lives, but if they decide to migrate to another country to work, they confront innumerable obstacles.

The purpose of this section is to characterize two kinds of migration: guest-worker programs and transit migration. I will identify relevant aspects of people's migration experience and will describe the abuses migrants experience during their journey. I will also describe the strategies, protocols, and projects the DPMH has developed in order to lovingly welcome migrants as brothers and sisters, demonstrating to them that they can find "a homeland everywhere in the Church" (SNL 41).[7]

I will start by exploring the factors underlying international migration, emphasizing the difficulties people face in making the decision to migrate. I will then examine each type of migration already noted above: documented migration within the context of guest-worker programs and undocumented migration during the transit from one country to another. With regard to the first type of migration (guest-worker programs), I will focus on Mexican migrants participating in programs in the United States and in Canada. For the second type of migration (undocumented transit migration), I will focus on Central American migrants during their transit through Mexico.

THE DECISION TO MIGRATE

With the hope of providing a better life for their families in mind, people consider migration as an option, but it is an option unlike any other. Migration provides an opportunity for them to make significant changes in their lives, but at the same time it risks suffering for themselves and separation from their families. This is not an easy decision to make: Separation hurts everybody. As the bishops note in their pastoral letter *Strangers No Longer*, "We witness the vulnerability of our people involved in all sides of the migration phenomenon, including families devastated by the loss of loved ones who have undertaken the migration journey…" (SNL 4). For those who leave—usually the father—saying goodbye to their loved ones is always painful:

> You feel an emptiness that cannot be filled with anything. I said to myself: The day and the hour we have to leave has

come...."Don't you dare cry!" I told [my mother]. "Don't make it harder," I told her. "I don't cry," I said, "I don't want you to cry." When we finally left it was hard, but you have to get strength from wherever you can so [your family] doesn't see you cry, so they don't cry. Once we were leaving and I said farewell to my wife...You see her sad-looking little face and you just stay there, just choking back, with the cry in the stomach; but you do not let it go, you hold it in (Beto).[8]

For those who remain in the communities of origin, the suffering is also profound. For women, the absence of their husbands means uncertainty and an increase in their responsibilities: "When her partner decides to migrate, the woman who remains in the community of origin needs to assume, besides her own duties, those that he will no longer be able to do, among others [diverse kinds of contributions, mainly]."[9] Rosa[10] resides in San Juan Huiluco, Puebla (in Mexico); she speaks of her feelings about her husband's absence and, at the same time, her understanding of the necessity of his migration:

Well, sometimes, when there are problems, I would like him to be here with me. I almost always want him to be here...But he's not. Because of the necessity, he almost does not want to be here because he earns a little bit more there, because it is not possible to make it here. Besides that, he has not come back [for a while] because of the crossing [of the border]....[11]

These examples point to the fact that "[m]igration under certain conditions can have a devastating effect on families" and so "support of the family that is left behind is also needed" (SNL 46). With this in mind, the DPMH has implemented various strategies to help families within their communities and, at the same time, to help them maintain contact with their family members abroad. Among the pastoral works the DPMH performs in migrants' communities of origin is helping people search for family members who have disappeared, either while migrating or after establishing themselves at their destination. In doing so, the DPMH shows migrants' families that the loneliness they might feel because of their loved one's absence does not mean they are alone. The nuns' and priests' solidarity with them is a sign of hope and a confirmation that the Christian values they have been taught can be practiced in their everyday lives, particularly in difficult times (EMCC 83).

Children also suffer the absence of their parents, but with some ambiguity. At the beginning they feel abandoned, but when the remittances start coming and they see the economic benefits they may accept the situation more easily. The following dialogue between Evelin and Doris, participants in a photography project developed in El Tamarindo, a rural community in El Salvador, highlights this ambiguity:

> Doris: How is it that migration is bad [if you get so many gifts]?
> Evelin: Because one loses their family.
> Doris: How is it that you lose them? You don't lose them because they come back.
> Evelin: The majority of the time, they don't come back.
> Doris: But, if you could leave El Tamarindo to be with them, would you?
> Evelin: Yes, of course.[12]

A person's desire to reunite with her parents and other family members can make her own decision to migrate (now or in the future) much more likely. Despite the acknowledgement of the negative effects of migration on the family, many people see the decision to leave their communities and countries as the only way to improve their precarious lives.

In addition to the negative effects of family separation, migrants have to face the consequences of laws and politics aimed at limiting their movement. Despite economic globalization that has tended to open borders to commodities and capital, labor has not enjoyed this benefit (EMCC 4).[13] Even within the framework of multi-country communities like the European Union, the experience of migrant workers is usually one of precariousness. Furthermore, in the face of economic crises, one of the first strategies countries employ as a protection is to close their borders to migrants.[14] Some analysts suggest that among the objectives driving laws and policies against opening borders to labor is the possibility of having available a mass of flexible

112

and legally unprotected laborers that can be disposed of when the demand for commodities decreases and taken back when it increases.[15]

This is happening in a world context of increasing inequality between rich and poor, population increase, and a mass of people who find themselves in socioeconomically perilous conditions. In terms of basic human needs like food, for example, the number of malnourished people in the world has increased from eight hundred thirty million in the period 2000–2002 to nine hundred twenty-five million in 2010.[16] It is in this context of inequality and political and legal restrictions that people make the decision to migrate. It is also in this context that they enjoy some of the benefits of their decisions and suffer the negative consequences of those decisions. In light of the economic disparities afflicting rich and poor nations and the political and cultural resistance to migrate in parts of the developing world, the Church is called to be "a sign of hope for a world that ardently desires justice, freedom, truth, and solidarity, that is peace and harmony" and to "become aware of [our] call to be always and repeatedly a sign of fraternity and communion in the world" (EMCC 102).

VULNERABLE BY LAW: MIGRANTS IN GUEST-WORKER PROGRAMS

One avenue available to people who want to migrate with the proper documentation is a "guest-worker program." Mexican migrants use guest-worker programs to get jobs mainly in Canada and the United States. This is considered by many the proper way to manage migration of low-skilled workers, because it is supposed to offer a reliable legal structure to all the parties involved. First, the worker gets a contract to temporarily work with a specific employer—the time and labor conditions are defined, and the worker has a proper migratory document to reside in the country. Second, the employer obtains a worker with the necessary skills, so it is possible to organize the work to meet production needs. Finally, the host government ensures that its migratory laws are respected, and both governments get either jobs for their poor citizens (home country) or a work force for production (host country). The programs I reference here are geared to hiring unskilled laborers, mainly but not exclusively, in agriculture.

The main antecedent for Mexican workers participating in a guest-worker program was the Bracero Program, which began in 1942 through an agreement between Mexico and the United States. It offered workers seasonal jobs and had a series of provisions meant to protect them. For example, the workers signed individual contracts to earn at least minimum wage and were provided with housing. The Mexican and U.S. governments supervised the rules of the program. It was abolished in 1964, partly in response to concerns over racism and human rights violations, after having given work to an almost half a million *braceros*.

Despite the abuses migrant workers experienced within the framework of the Bracero Program, the involvement of the Mexican government in facilitating the application process for the program made it their preferred option for migrating to the United States. When the Bracero Program ended, migrants turned to the H-2 program for unskilled workers. It started in 1943, bringing migrants from the Caribbean to work on the sugar cane plantations in Florida. In this program, workers are employed for up to ten months a year, after which they have to go back to their home countries and hope to be employed the following season. In 1986, as part of the Immigration Reform and Control Act (IRCA), the program changed to incorporate nonagricultural work and was divided into two categories: H-2A for agricultural work, and H-2B for nonagricultural work.[17] The H-2A program included a guaranteed minimum wage, a guarantee of at least three quarters of the employment time agreed upon in the work contract, provision of living facilities, and reimbursement of the recruiting fee and transportation expenses (bus or plane from the workers' place of origin, plus food consumed during the trip). The H-2B program only guarantees full-time employment with a wage of at least the prevailing wage rate.[18]

Canada has also developed guest-worker programs. The Canadian Seasonal Agricultural Worker Program (SAWP) started in 1966 in response to labor shortages in the agriculture industry. It is a multilateral treaty program "to allow foreign agricultural [workers] from signature countries to work up to eight months a year at Canadian agricultural operations." This program has grown from eighteen thousand migrant workers in 2001 to twenty-six thousand in 2009. Ontario is one of the main importers of this kind of foreign labor. The program is operated at a federal level by the ministry of Human Resources and Social Development (HRSDC). Being a multilateral agreement, only the Canadian and sending governments, along with lobbying groups for employers, can determine the workers' wages, labor, and living conditions. Mexico signed the memorandum of understanding with Canada in 1974. The main sending countries are Mexico, Jamaica, Barbados, Trinidad and Tobago, and the Organization of Eastern Caribbean States (Grenada, Antigua, Dominica, Saint Kitts and Nevis, Saint Lucia, Saint Vincent and the Grenadines, and Montserrat).[19]

Much like the United States, the Canadian government incorporated a second program that provided less protection for the workers: the Temporary Foreign Workers Program for Occupations Requiring Lower Levels of Formal Training (TFW). In this program, employers can hire migrant workers year-round. This program has dropped many benefits that workers enjoyed under SAWP; for example, workers must pay for their own housing, half of their return fare, and often exorbitant fees to employment brokers. Because this program has fewer protective provisions for workers, it is becoming the preferred one for employers.

Advocates of migration control who support guest-worker programs seem to be looking only at the formal benefits of those programs and then comparing them to the various problems that undocumented migration brings to migrants, host governments, employers, and the host society in general. However, these advocates seem to be overlooking the fact that these programs have significant problems of their own, especially from the perspective of the worker. First, the programs provide only temporary jobs that lack the certainty of continuity, since these jobs depend mainly on the employer's production needs and their satisfaction with the worker's performance. Second, the worker is bound to her/his employer, which means the worker is not free to change to a different employer if she/he is not satisfied with the labor conditions or if she/he is suffering abuses from the employer. Finally, the programs do not provide any possibility for changing one's migratory status (no opportunity for permanent residency or citizenship), thus condemning the worker to a period (or a life) of circular (back and forth) migration.

These features are a constant reminder to the worker that she/he is not welcome in the country as a human being, but only a means of production, as part of the labor force, and as such does not have enough worth to ever be considered a potential fellow citizen. Even if the host government and employers do not consciously articulate such a conception of the worker, and even if they say they are only protecting the "common good" of Canadians or Americans, this exclusionary conception of the foreign worker is implicitly their rationale. Even if we don't question the political legitimacy of borders, we need to acknowledge that in this world they mean inequality and exclusion.

The Catholic Church understands the challenge of this conception of the foreign worker, and responds to it from its core teachings contained in the Gospel—the good news of the inclusion of all: "Then people will come from east and west, from north and south, and will eat in the kingdom of God" (Luke 13:29; see also EMCC 17): But not just yet.

THE GUEST-WORKER PROGRAMS AS LIVED EXPERIENCE

To take advantage of the guest-worker program employers must apply to the proper governmental institution to obtain permission to use foreign workers in advance of the work season. Once the application is approved, the employers use the services of a broker or recruiter (*enganchador*) to hire the workers. The recruiter can function in two main ways.[20] In the first instance the recruiter may visit various small communities to advertise the company, make the agreement with the workers, and help them get their visas. In the other, the recruiter may live in a single community and recruit in that community year after year. In both cases, the workers are subjected to various kinds of abuses. The main form of abuse is not getting what they were promised in terms of wages, guaranteed work, and/or labor conditions. In most cases, those abuses include the payment of a large fee to the recruiter, as in the case of Margarita, a woman from Zacatecas who went to the United States to work within the H-2A program:

> I was able to go [to the United States] thanks to a loan of five thousand pesos from the recruiter. With an interest of 15 percent [a month]…It took me some time before I could send

money to my children, because I had to pay the recruiter that amount of money. For me [the experience] was costly in sadness and tears. I did not have [enough] work. I came back almost immediately.[21]

Another case of being overwhelmed by one's debt to the recruiter is that of Alvaro Hernandez-Lopez, a guest worker recruited from Guatemala:

In 2001, at age 45, he came to the United States to work for Express Forestry Inc. in the Southeast. He continued coming for two more planting seasons. "What I earned planting trees in the States was hardly enough to pay my debt," he said. "It was really hard for us to fight to get to the States legally and then not earn any money. We were told we had to leave our deeds to get the job. On a blank paper we had to sign our names and hand over our deeds. They said that if we didn't sign this paper they wouldn't bring us to the States to work."[22]

Even workers who have worked for several seasons with the same employer have to use the recruiter's services, something they do not understand. The experience of Modesta, as related by a friend from the same town in Zacatecas, is telling:

She has been working for that company for twenty years and she still needs to pay almost ten thousand pesos to the [woman] recruiter. It is about a thousand dollars and *el patrón* (the boss) just takes the money away and does not reimburse it or anything. And [Modesta] feels that she has a right to something [after all those years]. But he does not.

I think *el patrón* could hire these women directly, since they are almost family. But she just gives her money away to the recruiter. They (the workers) know the way to get there and everything, and yet they still have to use an intermediary.[23]

Unfortunately for Modesta, who works under the H-2B program in the United States, her employer is not required to reimburse these fees. But even when the employers are required (as in H-2A or SAWP programs), many do not. The worker usually has no means for forcing the employer to pay what is required and often does not even have a legitimate mechanism through which they can file a complaint.[24]

Under the H-2A program, when the worker completes the contract the employer has to pay for the trip back home. But this, too, is often not done. For example, Manuel, a man who has worked in the citrus orchards of Veracruz since he was a child, decided to migrate to the United States to be able to make ends meet. He got an H-2A job to pick oranges in Florida. Eventually, he realized that the written rules were not going to be honored by his employer:

> When it came to the halfway point in the season, the employer decided to change the terms of the transportation reimbursement…"The boss said, 'I'll reimburse you, but then you have to pay me for where you live.' But how is that possible? We, the farmworkers, know we have the right to a house, transportation, stove, and a refrigerator. We didn't know why he was charging for that!" exclaimed Manuel.
>
> The loss of money for transportation and kickbacks left Manuel struggling to feed even himself, much less send money back home to support his family. "I didn't have anything to eat…I was starving," said Manuel. He left to return to Mexico two months before the contract was over, forced out by the employer for daring to voice his concerns.[25]

In this and many other cases, workers do not have the ability to complain and demand that the employer honor the contract. Unfortunately, for Manuel and many others, the few institutional resources available to them for this purpose are not easily accessible. Mexican consulates and governmental agencies in charge of supervising the functioning of the programs usually lack the human resources and/or the disposition to help the migrants.[26] In this situation, it is important that worker advocacy organizations help to monitor the programs, preventing abuses and/or helping victims to report them.

The Pastoral Dimension of Human Mobility has started to assist Mexican workers who participate in the H-2A program through its project "Jornaleros [Laborers] Safe with Visas H-2A," which was initiated in 2010. This project has the purpose of "knowing their situation better and accompanying them pastorally."[27] It is already functioning in five dioceses and is implementing strategies at various levels, including the provision of legal advocacy for migrants who have suffered abuses or whose contracts were not honored, and educating communities about the potential dangers of the program, especially the frauds that brokers can commit. The DPMH's strategies are rooted in the conviction that the best way to promote the dignity of the person is to help the worker to become her/his own human rights advocate: This is a way to evangelize through reminding workers that their dignity does not depend on how the laws see them or how employers treat them— dignity is theirs because they are children of God (SNL 9).

At the same time, the DPMH participates in promoting a better social understanding of the problem and in lobbying for the legal and political changes needed to decrease the vulnerability of workers who participate in the H-2A and other migrant worker programs. In doing this, they join the call issued by the bishops in *Strangers*, which asks public officials, legislators, and the media to do their job to support and assist migrants (SNL 104).

A major change needed in the programs is that workers should no longer be bound to one particular employer. The current system of binding a worker to one employer creates conditions similar to indentured servitude, in which the worker is subjected to the will of a person who holds the power to force him back home if he does not silently accept abuses. One of the most common abuses is related to wages. All the programs guarantee a minimum wage, usually higher than the officially determined minimum wage. In the H-2A program, the U.S. government even has the responsibility to provide an "Adverse Effect Wage Rate" (for example, if the prevailing wage is lower than the federal minimum wage). In the case of Manuel, he was told he was going to get $8.82 per hour.[28] He worked shifts of twelve hours or more in the fields. When his first paycheck arrived, he "learned that to keep his job he would have to kick back some of his promised pay to his employer":

> "When we came out of the bank, the boss was already on the bus waiting for us," remembered Manuel. The boss had a "blacklist" in his hand indicating how many tubs of oranges each worker had filled. Workers were forced to pay

back the difference between their piece rate earnings and the legally required Adverse Effect Wage Rate (AEWR)— also known as build-up pay—to the crew leader. "He was robbing us...he stole a lot of money," said Manuel, who had to kick back as much as $130 some weeks..."Many people wanted to complain but they were afraid...to have to come back to Mexico."[29]

In guest-worker programs, the threat of not being accepted for another season if the boss is dissatisfied plays an important role in the worker accepting violations of the contract. A study conducted with workers under the SAWP program in Ontario, Canada, found that "many...said that they had suffered some kind of abuse by their employers or supervisors, [but] preferred not to report the incident for fear that their employer would not request them for the following work season."[30]

A consequence of this "control mechanism" is that workers do not even have the "right" to get sick. Of course, getting sick means not being able to work and therefore not earning the money that was hoped for, which was the justification for all the troubles workers went through to migrate. But like complaining, getting sick can contribute to a bad record in their labor performance:

> Workers under contract know that power rests on the farmer and that the confrontations, complaints, and frequent sicknesses, denial to work overtime or weekends or calling the liaison functionaries can translate into negative reports at the end of the season and their expulsion from the program.[31]

In a study conducted in Canada, it was clear that at least half of the migrants had worked while sick or injured: they feared their employer's reprisal or threats to send them back.[32]

This problem is exacerbated given that the conditions in which migrants work often contribute to their likelihood of becoming sick; agricultural workers, for example, often find themselves in contact with pesticides and other chemicals, without any protective measures. Under the programs they are entitled to receive training about protective measures, but many report not having received any.[33] In a study of migrant workers from the state of Tamaulipas (a border state in

Mexico), workers expressed their regret that U.S. employers have no regard for foreign workers' health and do not provide them with the tools to reduce their exposure to toxic substances:

> ...They did not give us any protection, [no mouth covers or gloves], we were out there with our bare hands; and the chemicals they put on the plants to prevent infestations are strong. We were working behind the ones fumigating. That was difficult, because the poison is strong due to the chemicals they use. [34]

Though employers often fail to contribute to the health protection of workers, their continual evaluation of workers' performance ensures them a very stable, productive, and loyal labor force. That is what the workers are: each one is just a pair of hands that need to produce, not a human being with as much self-worth as anybody else, with a family to take care of and friends he grew up with. The home and host states have failed to do their job. They are not ensuring that migration is undertaken in a way that respects people's dignity.

Employers, their supervisors, and many in the host societies behave as though their workers are simply commodities to be used. Gonzalo, a farmworker in Johnston County, North Carolina, relayed this experience directly:

> You can see that the water is dirty. One day we were working with a guy who gave us water with ants in it. It didn't have any ice and it was over 95 degrees outside. He just said get to work. So what you get is poor treatment and no water. [35]

And to make sure they are working in the fields and doing nothing else, governmental officials and employers insist that workers do not have much interaction with the local community. Many are isolated and only go to town when the employer takes them, usually to buy groceries. When they are close to a town and go to stores or to other places, they often experience the suspicion of people in the community. This is the same for both countries and for all the programs. In Canada, for example, migrants working in Leamington complained of the local community's unwillingness to welcome them:

There are many people who look down on us, don't think we are worth anything. Some of them don't want us to work here.[36]

A Mexican man who has gone to work there for fifteen years says regretfully:

Even though they were nicer before, people in Leamington never really liked the Mexicans. They think we are all thieves....Here we go to Zeller's...and they stare at us to make sure we won't steal...There are some pubs where we are not allowed. Because I like dancing I used to go to pubs when I first came over, but women don't even want to dance with you. And they are rude. I understand it when a guy is drunk and he does not take "no" for an answer. But when you approach a girl and ask her to dance with you politely there is no reason for her to be rude.[37]

The reflection of this migrant worker is moving. After fifteen years of spending over six months in a place, workers become familiar with the environment and the community and they begin to develop a sense of belonging. But the sentiment is not mutual. Because of their impermanence—not to mention the fact they are foreigners—the community does not look at them as neighbors or as friends. The woman from Zacatecas said that Modesta was almost family to her employer, having worked for him for over twenty years. But from the employer's perspective, she was only another pair of hands with enough skills to clean crabs every season, not a woman with a name and a home of her own.

As we have seen, guest-worker programs have built-in legal provisions meant to protect workers, but they are regularly unenforced and thus not effective, and so workers suffer abuses within a context that was supposed to ensure their rights—at least their right to work for a just salary and with decent labor conditions. Instead, they find people ready to take advantage of any vulnerability they might have, of any legal ambiguity that can provide an opportunity to give less in exchange for more. Employers are ready to take advantage of the virtual absence of governmental institutions responsible for protecting the rights of workers.

This is why the role the Catholic Church can play is so important: The Church advocates for the welcome of migrants by their host communities, regardless of the duration of their stay, their migratory status, their socioeconomic conditions, or their ethnic background. The Church can function as an intermediary between the migrant and the broader community. Suspicions between cultures can be worked out, and ways of communication can be found. Public policies must help this process through encouraging a respectful dialogue between migrants and host communities. For the Catholic Church, it is important to help the host society accept its guests as brothers and sisters and welcome them: "With the help of social and pastoral workers, the local population should be made aware of the complex problems of migration and the need to oppose baseless suspicions and offensive prejudices against foreigners" (EMCC 41). In this way, members of host communities will be able to open their hearts and understand that "The love of God, while it gives humankind the truth and shows everyone his highest vocation, also promotes his dignity and gives birth to a community, based on the Gospel proclamation being welcomed, interiorized, celebrated and lived" (EMCC 36).

VULNERABLE BY DESIGN: UNDOCUMENTED MIGRANTS IN TRANSIT THROUGH MEXICO

Regardless of their status, migrating internationally is in itself an experience that places people in vulnerable situations: Being away from their community of origin and the country they belong to, their social and state protection diminishes. Even for those who are in a country with the proper documents, life is very difficult as they are subjected to the policies, laws, and rules of a country that only allow them to be there provisionally and under very restricted conditions that usually exclude the right to work.

Since the 9/11 attacks in 2001, border control policies in both the United States and Mexico have become more and more restricted in the interests of national security. For example, in 2002 Mexico and the

United States signed the "Smart Border Agreement" that included several provisions to "protect the citizens of both nations from terrorism, illegal drugs, and other dangers; facilitate and expedite legitimate cross border travel and commerce; and allow our governments to determine who crosses the borders."[38] In the same year, Mexico, Guatemala, and Belize signed an agreement to constitute the High Level Group for Border Security, with similar purposes. And in 2007, Mexico and the United States announced the Plan Mérida (Merida Initiative), a program designed "to fight organized crime and associated violence while furthering respect for human rights and the rule of law."[39]

The alleged benefits of these measures for promoting border security are highly questionable; their actual results have in fact been counterproductive. In the words of EMCC (7): "Even more ineffective [than unilateral migratory measures] would be purely restrictive policies, which, in turn, would generate still more negative effects, with the risk of increasing illegal entries and even favoring the activities of criminal organizations," and thus enormously increasing the vulnerability of migrants.

In a context of increasing fear of and suspicion toward foreigners, when migrants do not fulfill the legal requirements for entering a country they are liable to be portrayed as criminals and deprived of their basic rights as human beings (EMCC 6). Already in 2003, the Mexican and American bishops boldly presented the situation of migrants in transit through Mexico:

> Mexican enforcement of immigration laws, targeted specifically through racial profiling of migrants attempting to reach the United States, has been marked by corruption, police brutality, and systemic abuses of basic human rights. Migrants often are forced to bribe Mexican police to continue transit and, if unable to produce payments, are beaten and returned to the border. Because of the lack of rights and policies that drive undocumented migrants away from small urban areas, the migrants often are assaulted by bandits in the border area between Ciudad Hidalgo, Mexico, and Tecun Uman, Guatemala. We know of migrants from Central America who pay thousands of dollars to smugglers to shepherd them through Mexico but who, in some cases,

are kidnapped. Their families never hear from them again. (SNL 83)

Almost ten years later the situation has only worsened, both in terms of the level of rejection migrants experience and of the level of violence public officials, criminals, and even common citizens exert against migrants crossing the border irregularly.

It is difficult to calculate with certainty the number of undocumented migrants that go through Mexico every year, but there have been some estimates. According to the National Institute of Migration (INM), in 2005 there were about four hundred fifty thousand undocumented migrants in the country, while there were only one hundred seventy-one thousand in 2008, probably due to the economic crisis and the tightening control of undocumented migration in the southern border of the United States. The National Commission of Human Rights (CNDH), however, considered that the latter number from 2008 a low figure, estimating that the real number must be around four hundred thousand a year.[40] According to Amnesty International, more than 90 percent of undocumented migrants in Mexico come from Central America, mainly from El Salvador, Guatemala, Honduras, and Nicaragua, and most of them want to get to the Mexico-U.S. border.[41] To reach their destination, these people have to clandestinely cross national borders and go through territories that do not welcome them.

During the migrants' transit—the word *transit* referring to their journey from their community of origin to their desired destination— the briefness of their stay in any place largely deprives them of the sense of belonging that human beings develop when they maintain regular social relations and also deprives them of the solidarity we grant to our neighbors and fellow citizens. Central American migrants who cross Mexican territory on their way to the United States have an additional source of vulnerability: the precariousness of their economic situation forces them to use the cheapest means of transportation and, in many cases, they are forced to depend on charity to fulfill their basic human needs—water, food, rest, etc. The train is the cheapest way to cross Mexico and the most dangerous too.

Groups from the Pastoral Dimension of Human Mobility receive migrants at many points along the railroad routes. Starting in Tapachula, Chiapas, Tenosique, Tabasco, and other cities or towns close to the southern border, and continuing through the country up to the northern border states of Tamaulipas, Coahuila, and Chihuahua among others, the pastoral workers of the Catholic Church welcome migrants in various ways, from providing humanitarian aid (food, water, shelter, emergency medical attention, and so forth) to reporting crimes or violations of human rights committed against them.

The *Casas del Migrante* (Migrant's Homes) or other types of pastoral works—mainly *comedores* (soup kitchens)—offer migrants a place to enjoy (temporary) peace and a lively encounter with God through people who offer them total acceptance and total respect for their dignity as human beings. In this way, the pastoral works promote the human person, announce the good news of the Gospel, and create a place for the integration of everyone—that is, a place for a true communion (EMCC 100). Though migrants only stay in each of the *Casas* for a short time— usually no more than three days—they will surely find other pastoral works along their route in which they will experience again the Christian welcome announced in the Gospel: "for I was hungry and you gave me food, I was thirsty and you gave me something to drink, I was a stranger and you welcomed me, I was naked and you gave me clothing, I was sick and you took care of me, I was in prison and you visited me" (Matt 25:35–36). The pastoral works are tending a population that could be conceived of as being imprisoned by the continuous dangers of their journey, and who find freedom from those dangers only when they are welcomed by the pastoral agents. In between *Casas*, migrants return to the danger as they go back to boarding the train.

La Bestia ("the Beast")—as the train is called, as if it were a menacing animal—has become the primary way for undocumented migrants to cross Mexico, and it presents them with many hazards. The natural elements are always a problem: the migrants travel mostly on the roof, without any protection from sunlight, rain, cold, or heat. The website of *Hermanos en el Camino* (Brothers on the Road), a shelter in Ixtepec, Oaxaca, has a series of recommendations for migrants when they take the train. One recommendation: "While going through the tunnels or on very cold days, protect your hands with gloves or a piece of cloth, because in the cold the iron surface of the train freezes."[42]

The train's speed is also a source of danger: When it is running, just to be able to board it is a challenge. *Hermanos en el Camino* recommends, "Do not try to get on the train if it is going at high speed, because the speed creates a magnetic field that attracts bodies toward the train." This is what happened to Alma, a thirty-year-old woman from Honduras who, in 2002, after losing her job at a chain chicken restaurant in Tegucigalpa, decided to migrate to the United States. She lost her left leg and half of her right leg while trying to board the train in Huixtla, Chiapas. This is how Arturo Cano, a journalist from *La Jornada*, narrates the accident based on her testimony:

> The group started to run to climb onto the locomotive. The most agile jumped and quickly found themselves on top of the running train. Alma stretched her arms but never reached the hard metal. It was then when, as she says, the train *la jaló* (pulled her in). Alma supports her narration with a gesture: she draws in the air a power that wanted to suck her in toward death. Alma says that she pulled herself back, and maybe this was why she "only" lost ten centimeters of her right leg. The left one disappeared almost completely.[43]

If the migrants are lucky enough to get on board, they have to make sure not to fall asleep and they must hold tight to whatever they find if they want to avoid an accident. Similar to Alma's experience, many migrants have been mutilated when they fell from the train. This health crisis has been acknowledged by the International Committee of the Red Cross, which has decided to increase its humanitarian work to help Central American migrants with mobile hospitals along the routes and with aid for mutilated migrants who need artificial prostheses.[44]

The dangers of the transit are not only due to the characteristics of the train. Even worse are the constant assaults migrants suffer during their journey. Raids by agents of the INM are a source of danger because they often force migrants to jump off a moving train, with the consequences explained above. Such raids are a violation of the law and an opportunity for corruption.

This disregard for migrants' security is not at all justified by their irregular, undocumented migratory status. On the contrary—it is restrictive migration policies that create the irregularity and give the journey such a degree of danger. From a legal and political perspective, as a signatory to the International Convention on the Protection of the

Rights of All Migrant Workers and Members of Their Families—which entered into force in 2003—Mexico is obligated to protect the human rights of migrants. The Mexican Federal Constitution also enshrines the right to state protection of human rights for all people while they are in Mexican territory.[45] The actual situation on the ground, however, is one of constant violations to migrants' human rights and extreme violence against them. In 2011, the Reporter for Migrants' Human Rights of the Inter-American Commission of Human Rights (ICHR), Felipe González, expressed his concern for the situation, recommending that the Mexican government should take immediate measures to prevent more acts of violence and to ensure access to justice for migrants who have been victims of crimes and violations of their human rights.[46]

Due to the clandestine nature of their movement, migrants are the focus of constant harassment from migration related and other governmental authorities. Here is an example of the magnitude of state agencies' participation in acts of violence against migrants in transit:

> On 23 January 2010, three Federal Police vehicles stopped a freight train carrying more than one hundred irregular migrants. The train was travelling from Arriaga, in the state of Chiapas, to Ciudad Ixtepec, in the state of Oaxaca. According to several migrants, uniformed and armed police forced the migrants to get off the train and lie face down, and then stole their belongings. After going through the migrants' possessions, the police let the migrants go and told them that if they did not continue their journey on foot along the railway tracks, they would be killed.[47]

Furthermore, the context of violence that prevails in Mexico has increased the vulnerability of transit for undocumented migrants. There are real "networks of abuse"[48] that make migrants their preferred targets. They charge a "protection" fee, steal the migrants' money, attack them physically, rape women, and kidnap migrants *en masse* to force their relatives—in their home countries or in the United States—to pay a ransom.

Migrants enter the country in border areas of the states of Chiapas or Tabasco. Once they board the train, they continue their journey though routes that take them to the south of Veracruz, where most of the violence against them takes place, particularly around Coatzacoalcos. The state of Tabasco and the south of Veracruz have been identified as the most dangerous zones of the entire route. According to the Mexican National Commission of Human Rights, out of the 9,758 kidnapping incidents that were registered between September 2008 and February 2009, 2,944 took place in Veracruz and 2,378 in Tabasco, compared to fifty-two in Oaxaca and forty-two in Chiapas.[49]

According to the reports of "Posada Belén" (Shelter Belem) in Saltillo, Coahuila:

> [In Coatzacoalcos], [after making its first appearance in the border towns], organized crime returns to the scene to trick those who, out of necessity, are forced to trust in purported *coyotes* who promise them cheap trips which actually result in frauds and kidnappings....The degree of the mafia's impunity is such that kidnappings take place even in front of the police. In 2008 it was common for big and luxurious trucks or freight trucks to approach the tracks and take, through threats and shootings with machine guns, all the people who were there.[50]

The ordeals migrants experience during their transit are often unspeakable: from constant fear during their entire journey to extreme acts of violence against them. Besides the humanitarian help they give to migrants, pastoral workers have been crucial in registering and reporting the situation of violence and demanding that the government do something about it. For example, *Posada del Migrante* (The Migrant's Shelter) in Saltillo, Coahuila interviewed 828 migrants who stayed in the shelter between 2007 and 2008. It reports 3,924 different abuses, among them 1,266 acts of intimidation (threats, insults, shooting bullets in the air), 475 incidents of physical aggression, and forty-two incidents of sexual aggression or violence.[51] Through this reporting work, pastoral workers contribute to dignifying the migratory experience, an important aspect of their mission of promoting human dignity.

One of the worst manifestations of this web of violence, corruption, and impunity is the kidnapping of migrants. A chilling report about kidnappings (created by CNDH in 2009, with the collaboration of the DPMH) identifies 9,758 kidnapped migrants in a period of six months between 2008 and 2009, among them fifty-seven minors. The majority of these incidents took place on the cargo train route, mainly in the states of Chiapas, Oaxaca, Tabasco, Veracruz, and Tamaulipas. The report says that in Chiapas there were forty-three reported kidnapping incidents between 2009 and 2010, with fifteen of them against migrants.[52]

The experiences of migrants are very telling. The CNDH 2011 report presents many testimonies of those experiences, showing different aspects of the problem. First, the modus operandi of organized crime, in which migrants by the train tracks are taken and then brought to *casas de seguridad* (safe houses—meaning, safe for the criminals):

> I saw everything. It was when we arrived in Medias Aguas [state of Veracruz].
>
> They kidnap them [by the train tracks] and do not let them go, and they take money from their families. I was there when that happened; I was kidnapped for three days. They demanded with beatings that I give them my [phone] numbers in Honduras and in the north (the United States). They spoke with my brother—they wanted three thousand dollars to release me, or I would suffer the consequences.[53]

Migrants are treated like mere commodities, their bodies (and dignity) exchanged for money. And their impotence before all these abuses is made greater by the complicity of the police:

> I will never forget what I saw.
>
> …The municipal policemen were on the criminals' side. They used to pass by every day and, mmm, I guess [the criminals] gave them a fee. Because, I say that, if it were not so, then the policemen would have helped us to get out. *Y nada* (And nothing). They did not do anything…[54]

The migrants' disappointment is coupled with their feeling of impotence when they consider their alternatives, knowing that even the authorities participate in criminal acts. When they are detained by the migration authorities, they prefer not to report crimes against them, so they can avoid staying in the country during the judicial process. Besides, the law does not force the INM to make sure migrants have access to justice.[55]

The problem becomes even worse when the society itself denies migrants in transit even the least bit of solidarity. Recent events in the Estado de México (State of Mexico, a state just outside of Mexico City) help to illustrate this situation. On July 2012, the *Albergue* (shelter) San Juan Diego had to close down due to the attacks of the neighbors, forcing migrants to look for alternative places to take a break from their journey. Before continuing the story, a bit of history: On January 19, 2009, Catholic Church groups opened the shelter (the *Albergue* San Juan Diego) twenty meters from the train tracks. It accommodates one hundred migrants at a time, and the migrants who cannot stay inside have to look for a place to spend the night. In its first year, the shelter gave food and other care to more than seventeen thousand undocumented migrants. However, the increase in the number of undocumented migrants made the neighbors wary of the *albergue*. Worse, the shelter has attracted members of organized crime and corrupt public officials. The neighbors are afraid, and while they used to express solidarity with the migrants, they are now trying to get rid of them.

The effects of this fear have been devastating for everybody. In December 2011, eighty neighbors tried to assault the shelter team and the migrants.[56] Problems continue, and on July 9, 2012, the shelter had to be temporarily closed after a fight between migrants, shelter workers, and neighbors. Father Alexander Rojas, the coordinator of the shelter, then installed a temporary helping station (Sánchez, Casa del Migrante) under a bridge (Puente Independencia), but this had to be closed down after neighbors complained.

This case illustrates in an extreme way the antipathy a host society can develop toward migrants. It is important to consider, however, that an inherently conflictive situation—large numbers of undocumented migrants walking around and sleeping in the streets close to the shelter—is deepened by the harassment of migrants by the police and organized criminals. It is clear that the government must provide the resources needed to relocate the shelter to a place that is safe for the migrants and accommodates the needs of the neighbors as well. Adequate facilities with the necessary security measures must be built.

The bishop of Tultitlán, Monsignor Guillermo Ortiz Mondragón, and leaders of the Pastoral Dimension of Human Mobility are dialoguing with the government to find the best solution for all concerned. However, it will not be easy to reestablish peace between the host community and the migrants and their advocates.[57]

This situation presents a major challenge to Church pastors and to Catholics in general. It is precisely in situations like this that we can be reminded of our Christian values and, as EMCC (101) tells us, accept that "The 'foreigner' is God's messenger who surprises us and interrupts the regularity and logic of daily life, bringing near those who are far away. In 'foreigners' the Church sees Christ who 'pitches His tent among us' (cf. Jn 1:14) and who 'knocks at our door' (cf. Rv 3:20)...."

MIGRANTS' EXPERIENCES AS A SIGN OF HOPE

Exploring the experiences of migrants as participants in guest-worker programs or during their transit through Mexico makes us aware of the consequences of stigmatizing a group of people as foreigners who are unworthy of social solidarity. Like the Catholic Church, many individuals and groups, human rights advocates, and labor and migrant organizers have repeatedly warned the United States, Mexican, and Canadian governments of the dangers of ignoring the abuses various actors have committed against migrants during the last decade (and even before). However, no one was able to foresee the extreme levels that abuses and violence against migrants in transit would reach, nor did anyone anticipate the growing capacity that criminal groups would develop to incorporate different actors into their ranks, including the migrants themselves. Regarding migrants in guest-worker programs, the trend toward decreasing protective regulations and facilitating legal exploitation by employers has shown its adverse effects. If migrants are being abused so often under the current regulations, we can only expect that those abuses will increase if there are even fewer regulations. After all, these trends are not surprising in a world that places economic profit over human well-being.

This is why Catholic teachings about migration are so crucial at this moment in history. Because they help us maintain hope in the face of extremely difficult situations, they guide us to read "the signs of the times" and understand them not as a tragedy but as a gift: as an opportunity to respond to God with the best of our abilities, an opportunity to proclaim to our migrant brothers and sisters His message of love and reconciliation.

Now more than ever the promise of the Mexican and U.S. bishops is desperately needed:

> We commit ourselves to animate communities of Christ's disciples on both sides of the border to accompany you on your journey so that yours will truly be a journey of hope, not of despair, and so that, at the point of arrival, you will experience that you are strangers no longer and instead members of God's household. (SNL 106)

NOTES

1. International Organization for Migration (IOM), *Facts and Figures, Global Estimates and Trends: Estimated number of international migrants worldwide* (2010); http://www.iom.int/jahia/Jahia/about-migration/facts-and-figures/lang/en (accessed August 22, 2012).

2. United Food and Commercial Workers Canada (UFCW), *The Status of the Migrant Farm Workers in Canada 2010-2011* (UFCW: 2012), 9.

3. Farmworker Justice, *No Way to Treat a Guest. Why the H-2A Agricultural Visa Program Fails U.S. and Foreign Workers* (United States: Farmworker Justice, 2011), 19.

4. IOM, *Facts and Figures, Global Estimates and Trends*, 29.

5. I will use the name, "Pastoral Dimension of Human Mobility" and/or "DPMH" (acronym in Spanish) or only "Pastoral" to refer to the Pastoral of Human Mobility in Mexico. The DPMH is one of seven dimensions of the Social Pastoral of the Mexican Episcopate.

6. Patricia Zamudio, "International Migration and the Construction of Futures," *Ichan Tecolotl* Year 13, no. 147 (November, 2002): 1.

7. Taken from Pope John Paul II's annual message on World Migration Day, 1993; http://www.vatican.va/holy_father/john_paul _ii/messages/migration/documents/hf_jp-ii_mes_19930806_world-migration-day-93-94_it.html (accessed August 28, 2012).

8. Carolina Rosas, *Males at the Rhythm of Migration. International Migration and Masculinities: From Veracruz to Chicago* (Mexico: El Colegio de México, 2008), 215.

9. Patricia Zamudio, "Prologue" in Jaqueline García, Mónica Flores and Gabriela Martínez, *Manual of Emotional Health. The Creation of Self Help for Women Relatives of Migrants* (México and Puebla: Servicio Jesuita a Migrantes and Universidad Ibero Americana, 2012), 10.

10. Not her real name.

11. Josefina Manjarrez, "Migration and Change in Gender Relations in the Transnational Migratory Circuit San Juan Huiluco-New York," in *Between Local Contexts and Global Cities. The Configuration of Migratory Circuits Puebla-Nueva York*, eds., Marcela Ibarra and Liliana Rivera (Puebla: Universidad Iberoamericana-Puebla, 2011), 213.

12. Heather Bradley, *Through Their Own Lens. Children of Salvadoran Diaspora Reveal and Interpret Migration in their Lives* (El Salvador: UNPD-El Salvador, UNICEF, 2006), 13.

13. Institute of Studies and Dissemination about Migration, A.C. (INEDIM), *Security for Migrants. Building a Policy and Advocacy Agenda* (Mexico: INEDIM, 2011).

14. Isabel Yépez and Gioconda Herrera, *New Latinamerican Migrations to Europe: Balance and Challenges* (Quito, Ecuador: FLACSO-Ecuador, 2007).

15. Stephen Castles and Raúl Delgado, "Migration and Development: Perspectives from the South" in *Colección Desarrollo y Migración* (México: Miguel Ángel Porrúa, Universidad Autonoma of Zacatecas, and University of Oxford, 2007); Luin Goldring, "Temporary Worker Programs as Precarious Status: Implications for Citizenship, Inclusion and Nation Building in Canada," *Canadian Issues/Thèmes Canadiens* (Spring 2010): 50–54.

16. Food and Agriculture Organization, *The State of Food Insecurity in the World 2010* (FAO, 2010); http://www.fao.org/docrep/013/i1683e/i1683e.pdf (accessed August 27, 2012).

17. Southern Poverty Law Center (SPLC), *A Brief History of Guestworkers in America* (SPLC, 2007a); http://www.splcenter.org/publications/close-to-slavery-guestworker-programs-in-the-united-states/a-brief-history-of-guestwork (accessed July 28, 2012).

18. Southern Poverty Law Center (SPLC), *Close to Slavery. Guestworker Programs in the United States* (SPLC, 2007b), 8; http://cdna.splcenter.org/sites/default/files/downloads/Close_to_Slavery.pdf (accessed August 28, 2012).

19. UFCW, *The Status of the Migrant Farm Workers in Canada 2010–2011*.

20. Author's own fieldwork research in various periods from 2000 to 2012.

21. Center for Migrants' Human Rights, Inc. (CDM), *H2A Guest Worker Testimony—Zacatecas*, Mexico, September 2009; http://www.youtube.com/watch?v=tsTolNcJagk (accessed July 7, 2012).

22. Southern Poverty Law Center (SPLC), *Close to Slavery. Guestworker Programs in the United States*, 11.

23. Center for Migrants' Human Rights, Inc. (CDM), *H2A Guest Worker Testimony—Zacatecas*, Mexico, September 2009.

24. Farmworker Justice, 25–26.

25. Ibid., 24.

26. Ibid., 25–26; Manolo Abella, "Policies and Best Practices for Management of Temporary Migration," paper presented at the International Symposium on International Migration and Development, Population Division Department of Economic and Social Affairs, United Nations Secretariat, Turin, Italy, June 28–30, 2006; Gustavo Verduzco, "The Temporary Mexican Migrant Labor Program in Canadian Agriculture," *The Center for Comparative Immigration Studies*, University of California, San Diego, Working Paper 90, January 2004.

27. Pastoral Dimension of Human Mobility (DPMH), Report 2006–2012, *Being and Doing of the Pastoral Dimension of Human Mobility. Towards an Exercise of Systematization of Six Years of Work. Communion in the Mission: Inclusion of the Excluded* (Mexico: DPMH, 2012).

28. The minimum wage in Florida in 2008 was $6.79 and in 2009 was $7.25.

29. Farmworker Justice, 24.

30. Verduzco, "The Temporary Mexican Migrant Labor Program in Canadian Agriculture," 9.

31. Sherrie N. Larkin, *West Indian Workers and Ontario Farmers: The Reciprocal Construction of a Divided World*, Master Thesis, University of Western Ontario, London (Ontario), 1989, cited in Leigh Binford, "Agricultural Fields, Power Fields: Mexican State, Canadian Farmers and the Mexican Temporary Workers," *Migraciones Internacionales* 3, no. 3 (January–June 2006): 64.

32. Leigh Binford, "Agricultural Fields, Power Fields: Mexican State, Canadian Farmers and the Mexican Temporary Workers."

33. UFCW, *The Status of the Migrant Farm Workers in Canada 2010-2011*, 14.

34. Izcara Palacios, Simón Pedro, Andrade Rubio, and Karla Lorena. "Health problems of laborers from Tamaulipas employed with visas H-2A in the United States," *Mundo Agrario* XI, no. 22 (2011): 15; http://www.redalyc.org/src/inicio/ArtPdfRed.jsp?iCve=84521185007 (accessed July 7, 2012).

35. Oxfam America, *A State of Fear: Human Rights Abuses in North Carolina's Tobacco Industry* (Boston: Oxfam, 2011), 25.

36. Tanya Basok, "Human Rights and Citizenship: The Case of Mexican Migrants in Canada," The Center for Comparative Immigration Studies, University of California, San Diego, Working Paper 72, January 2003, 13.

37. Ibid.

38. White House, President George W. Bush, *Border Security U.S.-Mexico Border Partnership Agreement* (2002); http://georgewbush-whitehouse.archives.gov/infocus/usmxborder/ (accessed July 7, 2012).

39. Hillary Clinton, U.S. Secretary of State, *U.S. Department of State on Merida Initiative (2007)*; http://www.state.gov/j/inl/merida/ (accessed July 7, 2012).

40. I(dh)eas, Strategic Litigation in Human Rights, A.C., *In Nobody's Land: The Labyrinth of Impunity, Human Rights Violations of Migrant Persons in the Soconusco Region* (Mexico: I(dh)eas, 2011), 5.

41. Amnesty International (AI), *Invisible Victims: Migrants on the Move in Mexico* (UK: AI, 2010).

42. Brothers on the Road, Migrant Voice: "Tips for the Road"; http://www.hermanosenelcamino.org/voz-migrante.html (accessed August 28, 2012).

43. Arturo Cano, *Those Mutilated by the Trains* (Solidaridad. net, December 19, 2003); http://www.solidaridad.net/noticias.php?not= 968 (accessed August 28, 2012).

44. Rodrigo Soberanes, International Committee of the Red Cross (CICR). *The International Red Cross Announces More Support for Migrants in Mexico* (Thursday, March 1, 2012); http://mexico. cnn.com/nacional/2012/03/01/la-cruz-roja-internacional-anuncia-mas-apoyo-a-migrantes-en-mexico (accessed August 28, 2012).

45. Working Group on Migratory Legislation and Policy. (GTLPM). *Migratory Law Violates Migrants and Mexicans' Constitutional Guarantees* (Press Release, May 3, 2011).

46. Interamerican Commission of Human Rights (CIDH), *Preliminary Observations of the Relateur on Migrants' Human Rights from CIDH to Mexico* (Annex to the Press Release 82/11): 9; http://www.oas.org/es/cidh/prensa/comunicados/2011/ANEXO.82-11.pdf (accessed July 7, 2012).

47. Amnesty International, 29.

48. Ana Chávez and Antonio Landa, *Migrants in their Journey through Mexico: New Problematics, Routes, Strategies, and Networks* (circa 2012); http://www.somede.org/xireunion/ponencias/Migracion%20 internacional/147Pon%20Ana%20Ma%20Chavez-Antonio%20 Landa.pdf (accessed July 7, 2012).

49. National Commission of Human Rights (CNDH), *Special Report on Cases of Kidnappings Against Migrants* (Mexico: CNDH, 2009), 13.

50. Posada del Migrante Belén, *Fourth Report on the Situation of Human Rights of Migrants in Transit through Mexico* (Belén, Posada del Migrante, Humanidad Sin Fronteras and Frontera con Justicia, Saltillo, Coahuila, May 23, 2008), 5.

51. Ibid., 24.

52. CNDH, 64.

53. National Commission of Human Rights (CNDH). *Special Report about the Kidnapping of Migrants* (Mexico: CNDH, 2011), 84.

54. Ibid., 75.

55. National Institute of Migration (INM). *Rights and Rules of Foreigns' Convivency in the Migratory Station* (Mexico: INM, 2001).

56. Center for Human Rights Miguel Agustín Pro, "Más agresiones contra la Casa del Migrante de Lechería," *Analysis Pro,*

December 14, 2011; http://centroprodh.org.mx/sididh_2_0_alfa/?p=11931 (accessed August 28, 2012).

57. A new shelter in Huehuetoca, State of Mexico, was opened on August 29, 2012..

CHAPTER 6

Migration, Development, and the Right Not to Have to Migrate in the New Era of Globalization

Donald M. Kerwin, Jr.

The Catholic bishops of Mexico and the United States released *Strangers No Longer: Together on the Journey of Hope (SNL)* in the aftermath of September 11, 2001. The terrorist attacks radically shifted U.S. policy priorities and effectively ended the prospects for a "grand bargain" between the United States and Mexico on immigration and economic development. However, in the intervening decade, "migration and development" has emerged as the *lingua franca* of international migration discussions. In 2005, the Global Commission on International Migration (GCIM) made reinforcing migration-related development gains one of its signal recommendations to the United Nations (UN) Secretary-General and member states.[1] In 2006, the UN Secretary-General sponsored a High-Level Dialogue on International Migration and Development which underscored the need to maximize migration's development potential and to mitigate its negative consequences. Since 2007, hundreds of state representatives, civil society groups, and observers have convened annually to discuss migration-related development policies, practices, and opportunities at the intergovernmental Global Forum on Migration and Development (GFMD). In May 2011, the President of the UN General Assembly convened an informal debate on this theme. The General Assembly will hold a second High-Level Dialogue on International Migration and Development in 2013. Migration-related development has also been "mainstreamed" into other UN processes and conversations and into the anti-poverty and development plans of many nations. Beyond structuring international discussions, this framework has begun to generate investment, innovation, and significant partnerships.

In *Strangers No Longer*, the U.S. and Mexican bishops set forth a vision of migration defined by human flourishing, respect for rights, and promotion of the common good. This chapter describes how the bishops' vision deepens and complements the migration and development dialogue, and how migration-related development can animate the principles set forth in *Strangers No Longer*. The chapter will not review the literature or debates on the many contributions of immigrants (past and present) to the United States, or on the challenges, tensions, and unevenly shared burdens created by large-scale migration.[2] Rather, it will discuss how migration can contribute to the well-being of immigrants from developing countries, their families, and their ancestral homelands.

MEANING AND POTENTIAL OF MIGRATION-RELATED DEVELOPMENT

Migration-related development speaks to the many ways that the movement of people—and the processes put in motion by migration—can affect the well-being of immigrants, and their families, circles of association, and communities of origin and destination. The academic literature sets forth several theories—some overlapping, some complementary—on why people migrate: wage differences; cost/benefit analysis by potential migrants; decisions by families to maximize income and minimize risk; the labor demands of industrial countries; disruptions caused by capitalism and world markets; bi-national linkages established by trade, war, and colonial relationships; and the ways that migration flows perpetuate themselves.[3] In lay terms, most people migrate due to a combination of need, wish to improve the prospects of their families, and desire to realize their potential. Given these reasons, it is not surprising that migration-related development gains overwhelmingly accrue to migrants, their families, and their sending and receiving communities.

How does migration contribute to development? First, it allows immigrants from developing countries to earn more, to support their families, and to invest in their communities of origin. A 2006 report by the UN Secretary-General concluded that "[l]ow skilled migration has the largest potential to reduce the depth and severity of poverty in communities of origin."[4] According to one analysis, migration-related wage increases have the potential to exceed all known anti-poverty interventions in developing countries.[5] The development potential of migration can be illustrated by the size of annual remittance flows. In 2011, remittance levels rebounded from the global economic crisis to reach $501 billion worldwide, with $372 billion sent to developing countries.[6] These figures dwarf Overseas Development Assistance and, in many countries, remittances also exceed foreign direct investment. In 2009, remittances constituted between 35.1 percent and 15.7 percent of Gross Domestic Product (GDP) in the top ten remittance-receiving countries measured in this way.[7]

Remittances contribute to reductions in poverty and inequality: recipients primarily use them for immediate needs like food, housing, health care, and education. The resulting increases in consumption and investment, however, have multiplier effects and contribute modestly to overall development. In 2011, Mexico received $24 billion in remittances, the third highest total worldwide,[8] and the source of more than one-half of total income for the poorest one-tenth of Mexican households.[9]

Migration can also positively influence the labor market in countries of origin. A recent analysis suggests that a 1 percent decrease in labor supply in Mexico due to migration, increases wages on average by 0.4 percent, translating into migration-related wage increases between 1990 and 2000 of 8 percent.[10] In addition, migrants return home with skills and experience that allow them to earn more than they would otherwise have been able to earn had they not migrated.[11] Like exports, a robust remittance flow can also be an important source of foreign earnings, which can increase the capacity of states to import goods and services, to obtain more favorable interest rates on sovereign debt issues, to borrow on international markets, and to support development projects. Remittances can provide a more stable source of income than private debt and equity and foreign direct investment following economic downturns.[12] On a negative note, remittances have the potential to undermine the willingness of recipients to work, to reduce productivity, and to serve as a disincentive to continued schooling. They can also lead to inflation and reduce export competitiveness.

The potential of migration-related development can also be seen in diaspora humanitarian, business, cultural, civic, professional, trade, and other initiatives. Not surprisingly, both states of origin and destination have made diaspora engagement a high priority. A Migration Policy Institute (MPI) survey of states participating in the GFMD identified more than four hundred institutions in fifty-six nations that formally engage diasporas, and twenty-six countries with ministries exclusively devoted to this work.[13] In May 2011, the U.S. Department of State and MPI formally initiated the International diaspora Engagement Alliance (IdEA) in order to "promote diaspora-centered initiatives in entrepreneurship, volunteerism, philanthropy, diplomacy, and social innovation in countries and regions of diaspora origin."[14] The U.S. Agency for International Development maintains a Global Development Alliance Database, which lists diaspora and other agencies that offer disaster relief and development assistance. Diaspora groups often pool remittances for infrastructure and other development needs in communities of origin. These groups can address structural barriers to development more effectively than can individuals.[15] However, collective remittances represent only a small percentage of total remittances, and they support a range of non-development activities as well.

Disaster relief is a common form of diaspora activism and investment.[16] From disaster relief, it is not a great leap to investment in more formal, state-centered development initiatives, including diaspora-targeted bond issues to support development.[17] Diasporas may be more willing than those without knowledge or personal ties to invest in their communities of origin. They may also have higher expectations for development projects and be in a position to demand greater accountability for their successful implementation.

Saving levels also suggest the potential for diaspora development investments. In 2010, the World Bank estimated the savings of diasporas from developing countries to be in the $400 billion range, led by the Mexican diaspora with $47 billion in savings.[18] Diasporas have also extensively supported development, diplomacy, and reconstruction initiatives in areas depleted by war, civil unrest, and forced migration. Returning migrants have also assumed leadership roles in many fledgling democracies.[19]

Migration policies can create win-win scenarios by accommodating the potentially complementary interests of states and other stakeholders. For example, they can align the interests of developed countries that have aging and shrinking labor forces, with developing countries that enjoy higher birth rates and growing labor forces.[20] The World Bank projects, for example, that the labor force in sub-Saharan Africa will grow by three hundred twenty-eight million between 2005 and 2050, while it is projected to decrease over the same period in China, Europe, and North America by eighty-five million, sixty-seven million, and nine million respectively.[21] In contrast, Mexico may no longer prove to be a ready source of workers for the U.S. economy due to its plummeting fertility rate, from 7.3 children per woman in 1970 to 2.4 children in 2009, and the resulting increase in the median age of its citizens.[22]

CATHOLIC TEACHING AND THE MIGRATION AND DEVELOPMENT DIALOGUE

Strangers No Longer can be seen, in part, as a response to the deepened interdependence of people created by globalization. It speaks to the need to reduce poverty and inequality, expand living-wage jobs, target development assistance to communities that have been depleted by emigration, and shore up Mexico's agricultural sector and small businesses (SNL 61). It places development in the context of a larger vision of human flourishing, and contemplates an ideal in which nations create the conditions that allow their members to prosper at home (SNL 34). In these circumstances, migration would be "driven by choice, not necessity" (SNL 59). However, the U.S. and Mexican bishops also acknowledge that the conditions that compel migration— "poverty, injustice, religious intolerance, armed conflicts"—show few signs of abating (SNL 28). For this reason, *Strangers No Longer* establishes a presumption "that persons must migrate in order to support and protect themselves and that nations who are able to receive them should do so whenever possible" (SNL 39).

The migration and development dialogue likewise assumes that migration by necessity will continue and may well increase due to:

- Rapid shifts in capital, services, and goods that characterize globalization
- Global warming, natural disaster, and volatile weather conditions; poverty and wage disparities
- Political violence and upheaval
- The failure of states to develop immigration policies that reflect their labor and development needs
- Disruption in the agricultural sector which employs 1.3 billion persons in developing countries
- Widening differentials between states in development, demographics, and democracy[23]

In short, both frameworks couple vision with realism.

However, several themes from Catholic teaching can deepen the migration and development conversation. These include its teaching on the potential of migration to unify culturally diverse peoples; "integral" development; subsidiarity; the responsibilities that accompany rights; the universal or "border-less" common good; and the purpose of sovereign states.

THE POTENTIAL FOR UNITY THROUGH CULTURAL DIVERSITY

In its emphasis on "win-win" scenarios among the diverse stakeholders in the migration process, the migration and development dialogue may prove to be a fruitful way to discuss migration with a skeptical public. At the same time, Catholic teaching directly addresses widespread public concerns related to the loss of national culture and identity in a way that migration and development does not.

A 2007 survey of more than forty-five thousand persons in forty-seven nations found that majorities in all but one country feared loss of culture and traditional way of life, and supported taking steps to protect their way of life from foreign influence.[24] In the United States, 72 per-

144

cent worried about loss of their way of life, and 62 percent believed that their way of life needed to be protected. In Mexico, the numbers were 81 and 75 percent. The survey found a strong correlation between those who favored greater immigration restrictions and those who believed that their way of life needed to be protected.[25] A 2011 survey of U.S. and European public opinion found that only 55 percent of Americans (down from 65 percent in 2009) thought that immigration enriched U.S. culture, compared to 58 percent in five European countries.[26]

A telephonic survey in August 2011 similarly found that a significant minority of Americans believed that immigrants threatened American values and were changing American society for the worse. Fifty-three percent believed that immigrants strengthened American society, but 42 percent said that immigrants threatened "traditional American customs and values."[27] Of those who believed immigrants were "changing American society and way of life a lot" or "a little," 42 percent believed the change to be a bad thing.[28] Yet at the same time, Americans overwhelmingly believed that immigrants were "hard-working" (87 percent) and had "strong family values" (80 percent).[29]

How would *Strangers No Longer* respond to these concerns? The letter speaks to the need to accept newcomers based on "faith in the presence of Christ in the migrant" and "a conversion of mind and heart, which leads to a renewed spirit of communion and the building of structures of solidarity" (SNL 40). The process of conversion requires "confronting attitudes of cultural superiority, indifference, and racism: accepting migrants not as foreboding aliens, terrorists, or economic threats, but rather as persons with dignity and rights, revealing the presence of Christ and recognizing migrants as bearers of deep cultural values and faith traditions."[30]

The call to conversion should be viewed in the context of Catholic teaching on cultural diversity. The Catholic Church does not embrace all of the cultural beliefs and practices of immigrant groups or natives: it views its role as uplifting and evangelizing cultures in states of origin and destination (WSAU 28). At the same time, it teaches that people invariably express their deepest beliefs and values through their cultures and, therefore, that migration can lay the groundwork for unity based on an experience of the shared values of culturally diverse people.[31] In a world rife with division, it teaches that migration can play an essential role in promoting understanding and unity among people. In a world of migration exclusively by choice, migration (and cultural dialogue) would still be necessary to guard against the re-emergence of the pride and misunderstanding that can separate diverse peoples.[32]

THE MEANING OF DEVELOPMENT IN AN ERA OF GLOBALIZATION

Globalization is not a new phenomenon. People, goods, and knowledge have always moved. However, the speed of movement and advances in technology allow some people—for the first time in history—to straddle two or more places and to maintain strong ties to multiple communities simultaneously, a phenomenon that is expected to accelerate. As Benedict XVI recognized, globalization has extraordinary potential to contribute to human welfare and dignity, while at the same it could "cause unprecedented damage and create new divisions within the human family" (CV 33). As a human construct rather than a force of nature, globalization can be structured so that it better serves the human person. It can distribute wealth more equitably, create fewer "losers," and minimize disruption and hardship. At present, it has a certain logic, but it needs an ethic.[33] Moreover, its logic depends on free trade and movement of displaced workers. Yet, in practice, developed countries heavily subsidize certain industries and erect barriers to migration for those compelled to move by economic necessity.[34]

In the dawn of this new era of globalization, how should we think about development? The Brundtland Commission popularized the idea of "sustainable" development which speaks to the need to satisfy present human needs—particularly the needs of the poor—but in a way that does not compromise the ability of future generations to meet their needs. The familiar language of sustainability conveys a complex idea: it recognizes the interdependence of human beings over space (in its emphasis on equity among all people) and time (between current and future generations). The migration and development framework likewise embraces the idea of "human development," which speaks to expanding people's freedoms, choices, and capabilities.[35]

In 2009, Benedict XVI cautioned that laborers should never be viewed as a "commodity" or treated as a "factor of production" (CV 62). Robert Zoellick, President of the World Bank, subsequently urged the international community to consider jobs not as a "derivative of growth," but as vehicle to contribute to higher living standards, increased productivity, social cohesion, and positive social change. He argued that development should be democratized by:

- Emulating the practices and ideas not just of the North, but of the South
- Respecting the agency and contributions of the full range of players in the development process
- Giving voice to women who have been sidelined and silenced in these conversations
- Opening all forms of development, including private investment, to developing countries
- Extending credit and saving systems, and sharing data and information with all

To Zoellick, development is not about applying cookie-cutter strategies to every challenge, but about creating and adapting different models for different conditions. An essential ingredient is local ownership: the potential beneficiaries of development programs must be allowed to identity their own needs and approaches to meeting them.[36] Success in meeting one need invariably leads to prioritization of different needs that require different solutions. This is how development works. In short, the migration and development dialogue speaks to sustainable development over space and time; human development on a personal level; and democratized development strategies.

Catholic teaching deepens this conversation by insisting on development that honors human beings in all of their dimensions, and by calling for a moral response to the good of others that transcends borders. The Catholic analogue to "human development" is "authentic" or "integral" development, which speaks to "the development of each man and of the whole man" (PP 14). It is a tenet of Catholic anthropology that human beings become themselves in relation to God. Thus, "authentic" development must promote and safeguard the spiritual and religious dimensions of the human person.

A recently published study by Jesuit social centers on the effects of globalization on the world's poor concludes that to be sustainable development programs must account for the "cultural, moral, and religious values" that give meaning to people's lives and inform their choices.[37] Such programs must also respect the agency and dignity of the persons they purport to help: top-down approaches sow the seeds of their own failure. The study pointed out that the disintegration of cultural and moral values can undermine socioeconomic development. Conversely, values can spur socioeconomic development in even the grimmest situations. The study set forth case studies of individuals whose values influenced decisions to leave or remain with family members, to commit to workplace activism, and to engage in community-building activities.[38] Globalization set the context for their decisions, but economic considerations alone did not drive them.

Catholic teaching assigns to individuals the central responsibility for their own development. However, it also stresses the importance of solidarity in promoting the good of others. In response to the world's increasing interdependence, Catholic teaching has developed the concept of the "universal" or borderless common good. In 1965, Pope Paul VI said that "the common good ... takes on an increasingly universal complexion and consequently involves rights and duties with respect to the whole human race" (GS 26).[39] In 1987, Pope John Paul II spoke of a "moral" barrier to development that can only be overcome through "solidarity," which he famously defined not as "a feeling of vague compassion or shallow distress at the misfortunes of so many people, both near and far," but as "a firm and persevering determination to commit oneself to the common good; that is to say to the good of all and of each individual, because we are all really responsible for all" (SRS 38). In 1999, John Paul II highlighted the role of the universal common good in personal development, urging the Church in the Americas to work toward establishing "an economic order dominated by the pursuit of the common good of nations and of the international community, the equitable distribution of goods and the integral development of peoples" (EA 52).

RECALIBRATING RELATIONSHIPS IN THE MIGRATION PROCESS

Benedict XVI characterized international migration as "a social phenomenon of epoch-making proportions" that requires "close collaboration" between countries of origin and destination" and legal norms that safeguard "the needs and rights of individual migrants and their families, and at the same time, those of the host countries" (CV 62). Similarly, the migration and development frame looks for win-win scenarios based on cooperation between the diverse participants in the migration process, including receiving communities.[40]

Yet interests invariably become—or even start off—imbalanced, requiring that relationships between stakeholders be recalibrated. Immigrant laborers, for example, may receive pay and remit monies home, but they may be denied other benefits from the host society and be tied, indebted, and beholden to individual employers to the point that they can even be loaned to others.[41] The treatment of Asian workers, who effectively translated oil revenue into material well-being for the citizens of Gulf States, illustrates this point.[42]

In the United States, federal, state, and local governments unevenly share the benefits and costs associated with immigration. Over the long term, the tax revenue from immigrants (lawful and irregular) exceeds the cost of government services and benefits that they receive, but in the short term, the education, health care, and law enforcement costs incurred by states and localities for *irregular* immigrants exceeds the tax revenue from this population.[43] On the other hand, low-skilled immigrant workers increase profits for their employers and reduce the costs of goods and services to consumers.[44]

Subsidiarity, a Catholic organizing principle akin to the secular notion of devolution, can help to assign responsibility for making migration-related decisions and righting inequities. It provides that decisions should be pushed down to the individual, group, or competent authority that is closest to the issue. Migrants and their families, for example, would be in the best position to decide how to use individual remittances. Communities of origin and diaspora groups would be better suited to address barriers to the effective and intended use of remitted monies. Wealthy nations would be well-positioned and bear greater responsibility than other nations to admit persons displaced by their economic or foreign policies.[45] Finally, states must work collectively to reduce poverty and to achieve sustainable development.[46]

SOVEREIGNTY, RIGHTS, AND RESPONSIBILITIES

There is an enduring public sense—borne in part of the promiscuous use of "rights" language—that rights benefit some to the detriment of others. As the global immigration debate illustrates, there is also a widespread belief that rights turn on state membership and, thus, that irregular migrants have no rights. *Strangers No Longer* recognizes the authority of sovereign states to control their borders, to determine who can enter, and to regulate admission in furtherance of the common good (SNL 30). However, it qualifies this authority by providing that the common good cannot be served by denying entry to persons who have migrated to realize their God-given rights.

This teaching implicates the nature of sovereign states, which do not create rights, but exist to safeguard them and to promote the common good. Catholic teaching does not recognize sovereignty as an absolute value.[47] It understands the power of states to be limited by their very purpose, by the requirements of natural law, and by their treaty and other international obligations.[48] Sovereignty does not require the absolute control of borders and the populations inside them. To the Catholic Church, this concept locates responsibility for protecting rights and serving the common good, especially the rights and the good of persons in need.[49] It cannot be used to justify the exclusion of persons who sovereign states have failed to protect or to sustain.

Catholic teaching does not view the exercise of rights as a power grab by one group at the expense of another, but as a moral claim to a shared "good" that invariably carries responsibilities. Immigrants do not simply have a right to participate in the life of their new communities and nation: they have a responsibility to contribute. Social ("contributory") justice is as much their responsibility, as the responsibility of the states and communities that receive them.

Like Catholic teaching, the migration and development rubric recognizes the authority of states to determine membership, and to act in the best interests of their nationals. It also recognizes that states cannot maximize migration-related benefits and mitigate hardships in isolation.[50] By its nature, international migration involves multiple states and therefore requires supra-national solutions. Immigration is also a cross-cutting domestic issue that strongly influences educational, public health, labor, and other systems and policies. As a result, many nations now incorporate or "mainstream" migration into larger development and anti-poverty planning processes.[51] Mainstreaming "migration" does not subvert the legitimate authority of states, but allows them to achieve their objectives.

PROVIDING SHAPE AND CONTENT TO CATHOLIC TEACHING AND ADVOCACY ON MIGRATION

The migration and development rubric has the potential to illuminate Catholic teaching principles, strengthen the Church's advocacy, and enrich its diverse programs and ministries.[52] The teaching and policy principles set forth in *Strangers No Longer* have not been widely embraced or acted upon in public life. The "right not to have to migrate," for example, has not been an effective theme in the U.S. immigration debate. The migration and development dialogue provides substance to this aspiration and vision. It can advance Catholic teaching, advocacy, and ministries in at least nine ways.

First, it highlights the need to put in place the institutions, systems, and conditions that will maximize the development gains and potential of migration. It recognizes that migration does not constitute a panacea to broader development challenges. It will not solve, for example, the global unemployment crisis or obviate the need for national job-creation policies.[53] Progress in meeting the Millennium Development goals related to education, gender equality, environmental sustainability, and access to treatment for HIV/AIDs and other diseases can increase the development impact of migration. The necessary physical infrastructure, public institutions, and information systems also enhance migration's development potential. Migration can, in turn, modestly contribute to Millennium Development goals like reducing extreme poverty and hunger, and improving educational and health systems.

The "rule of law" may be an underappreciated development fundamental.[54] In the U.S. immigration debate, a narrow view of this concept is often evoked to justify the denial of core rights and benefits to irregular migrants.[55] An exhaustive index created by the American Bar Association's World Justice Project embodies a broader view. It requires:

151

- Government officials to be accountable to the law
- Clear, publicized, stable, and fair laws that protect fundamental rights, including the security of persons and property
- Protection of commercial activity and property rights
- Fair and efficient administration and enforcement of the law
- Non-discrimination in granting franchises, licenses, and public contracts
- Competent, independent, and ethical law enforcement officials, attorneys, and judges[56]

These conditions help to ensure that lawlessness does not force persons to migrate and can protect migrants in transit and in destination countries. They strengthen the integrity of public institutions, the business environment, public works projects, and health systems. They can also pave the way for diaspora investment, increase the odds that investments will be used as intended, and (thus) increase the likelihood of more extensive diaspora engagement in the future. As graphically illustrated by the horrific violence in Mexico in recent years, strong legal systems are particularly necessary in the transition from autocratic regimes that exercise comprehensive legal, social, and political control over societies, to nascent democracies.

The Catholic Church could take a leadership role in encouraging states to institute the systems and processes that underlie authentic development and that allow them to maximize migration-related development gains. Universal birth registration represents a case in point. In Mexico, an estimated seven million persons lack birth certificates and the resulting rights, protections, and benefits of citizenship. As a result, many are compelled to migrate and they become "doubly undocumented" in the United States and elsewhere.[57] The Church should make universal birth registration one its global priorities.

It should also advocate for reforms that would increase the impact of migration-related development, including lower remittance transfer fees (by opposing monopolistic practices); reduced recruitment costs of labor migrants; simplified immigration laws; and immigration policies that channel more migrants into legal migration streams and away from violent and predatory smuggling rings. It could also counter the potentially negative effects of remittances by, for example, pushing young people to pursue their educations and assisting the elderly guardians of children whose parents have migrated. Church entities could also partner with diaspora agencies on particular relief and development projects.

Second, migration and development moves the immigration debate beyond an instrumental view of development. Rather than treating development as a tool to stem migration, it views migration as a potential benefit for migrants and others. The idea of creating the conditions (through development assistance and other means) to allow people to stay at home has merit, as far as it goes.[58] However, the migration and development discussion starts from a different point. It asks how to extend the development gains *from* migration to all the participants in this process. It typically thinks of these gains in terms of individual and collective remittances, and diaspora engagement in its many forms.

It also provides a useful way to think about forced migration scenarios. From this perspective, even climate change can be seen as a potential development opportunity.[59] Global warming may exhaust the already modest resources of vulnerable persons and further marginalize them, making it more difficult to migrate. On the other hand, with long-range planning and sufficient international commitment, migration could improve the prospects of desperately poor persons from increasingly inhospitable environments.[60] The need to prevent forced migration and mitigate its effects has been a mainstay of Catholic advocacy. The migration and development dialogue suggests responses that go well beyond disaster relief. Even in the most difficult of circumstances, it views migration as a potential opportunity.

Third, this frame encourages states to see migration as a bellwether for the need to establish conditions that will allow their nationals to flourish at home, and that will attract and enhance migration-related investments.[61] The departure of skilled workers from developing countries, particularly health care workers, has garnered significant attention. Migration is often necessary for the personal and professional development of these workers. However, investing in basic infrastructure (roads, water systems, electrical grids), and in the health care systems in sending states can encourage skilled workers to stay at home and expatriates to return, either permanently or temporarily, as teachers, mentors, and direct care providers. The Church can advocate for the necessary infrastructure investments and for elimination of disincentives to diaspora engagement, including non-recognition of work credentials.[62] It can also help to erode the often arbitrary and damaging distinction between skilled and unskilled workers, and educate policymakers and others on the ways that "less skilled" immigrant workers bring, transform, and create knowledge.[63]

Fourth, migration and development emphasizes the need for sound, evidence-based migration policies. Migration is not a Millennium Development goal, perhaps in part due to the difficulties in developing indices to measure the success of migration policies. However, the UN Millennium Declaration provides for the protection of the rights of migrants and their families, humanitarian assistance to refugees, and the voluntary return and safe reintegration of refugees and other displaced persons.[64]

The challenges to creating and implementing sound immigration policies should not be understated. Many states do not consistently collect or track reliable data that would allow them to develop responsive immigration policies and to measure progress in meeting migration-related goals. Most do not "mainstream" migration considerations into development conversations on trade, foreign policy, and education.[65] Many do not sufficiently coordinate with other states on migration-related priorities that cannot be effectively addressed unilaterally.[66] Finally, many states lack the resources and infrastructure to realize their immigration policy goals. The Catholic Church's broad experience of diverse immigration systems ideally situates it to champion rights-respecting, effectively managed, and well-resourced immigration systems.

Fifth, circular migration emerges from the migration and development conversation as one of the immigration policies with the most development potential. Circular migration programs can increase and spread development gains, provided that they avoid the well-documented problems of past temporary worker programs. They must prioritize transparency (through pre-departure orientation of workers), job training, and recognition of credentials with the goal of increasing the benefits of migration and the well-being of migrants wherever they settle. They should also permit workers to move between employers, provide permanent workers a path to permanent status, allow for portable pensions and health benefits, pay sufficient wages so as not to undercut the wages of native workers, and avoid discrimination in pay, benefits, and worker safety and health. Temporary protection programs can likewise contribute to development through remittances and fostering stability in nations that cannot accommodate the return of large numbers of their nationals. El Salvador and other nations have long advocated on these grounds for the extension of temporary protected status (TPS) to their nationals in the United States.

In *Strangers No Longer*, the U.S. and Mexican bishops urged reform of the U.S. employment-based (permanent) immigration system. The bishops also set forth conditions for a temporary worker program that largely mirror the best practices identified in the migration and development dialogue (SNL 75). In addition, the bishops decried U.S. immigration policies that separate families,[67] as well as Mexico's under-registration of children at birth. They argued that a broad U.S. legalization programs would benefit both nations.

Sixth, the migration and development rubric gives pride of place to immigrant integration. Rights-respecting integration policies can create a virtuous circle: they help to maximize the impact of migration on development in communities of origin and destination.[68] Integration builds human capital, improves financial prospects, and allows immigrants to contribute more fully to their communities. The question becomes how to facilitate and expedite integration. The U.S. refugee resettlement program has been successful in promoting early self-sufficiency through employment. Family friendly immigration policies also contribute to integration. Legal status is a necessary but not a sufficient condition to integration.[69]

The Catholic Church's public policy positions on immigration reform are well known. In contrast, its work in promoting the successful integration of the seventy-three-million foreign-born U.S. residents and their children, and in strengthening receiving communities, is poorly understood by the general public, policymakers, and even Catholic agencies. Policymakers and others who oppose generous immigration policies argue that today's immigrants are not integrating like past populations precisely because they can no longer rely on traditional "mediating" institutions, like the Catholic Church, other faith communities, labor unions, civic organizations, the military, and public school systems. The Church can share its experience of successfully integrating refugees and its knowledge of the importance of family unity in contributing to successful integration. However, it would potentially benefit millions of persons—and greatly promote development in sending and receiving communities—if Church institutions could collectively increase and improve their response to the multifaceted integration needs of newcomers.

The migration and development dialogue also emphasizes the crucial role played by community-based organizations (CBOs) and hometown associations (HTAs) in helping to integrate immigrants. These entities offer linguistic, citizenship, and other services, serve as mediating institutions for immigrants to the larger society, and offer them skill-building and institutional leadership roles. They can also enhance the contributions of immigrants to their homelands through collective remittances and by addressing barriers to development. Beyond their contacts and knowledge of communities of origin, CBOs and HTAs bring high expectations to the development initiatives that they support. In Catholic terms, these initiatives can represent an expression of solidarity and an exercise of the preferential option for the poor.

Seventh, the migration and development rubric recognizes the diverse responsibilities of the multiple stakeholders and participants in the migration process. The World Health Organization's voluntary code of practice on the recruitment of health professionals represents a case in point. The code urges developed countries to assist developing countries to strengthen their health systems, recognizes the right of health personnel to migrate consistent with the law, and seeks "to mitigate the negative effects and maximize the positive effects of migration" on health systems in countries of origin.[70] It also calls on member states to create sustainable health care workforces through "planning, education and training, and retention strategies that will reduce their need to recruit migrant health personnel," and to facilitate training, professional education, and circular migration programs that benefit immigrant source and destination countries.[71] It discourages "active recruitment of health personnel" in countries facing "critical shortages."[72]

The Catholic Church should support and implement these principles through its own extensive networks of hospitals and clinics in developing and developed countries. It should also expand its work in serving those who are hardest hit by migration. If U.S. immigration policies cannot be meaningfully reformed, for example, it becomes even more important to meet the needs of detainees and children whose parents have been deported.

Eighth, the migration and development frame can build on and potentially align with substantial development progress spurred by the private sector. In 2011, the World Bank reported that $77 billion had been invested in telecom networks in sub-Saharan Africa over the preceding decade.[73] Over that time, the number of mobile subscribers increased from ten to four hundred million. Public/private partnerships can build on these successes. International organizations increasingly seek policies that facilitate legal migration as a way to build wealth, while states may be more concerned with social cohesion and wages and working conditions for native workers.[74] The Church can play an important role in establishing partnerships between different stakeholders that address their respective goals and concerns.

Ninth, the migration and development conversation highlights the need for research and the continual evaluation of relevant programs and policies in order to manage migration to the greatest advantage. To engage their diasporas effectively, states of origin must know where their expatriates live, who they are (including their socioeconomic characteristics), how they view their nation of birth, how they group themselves, and what projects they support.[75] Diasporas, in turn, need to understand the legal system and business opportunities in their communities of origin. States also need significant data to craft successful immigration and integration policies.[76]

CONCLUSION

Strangers No Longer can guide, deepen, and complement the migration and development dialogue. Its teaching on rights and responsibilities, the common good, solidarity, sovereignty, and culture respond to public concerns that this framework does not directly address. The migration and development process can, in turn, give rise to innovative policies and programs that lend content to the Catholic Church's policy principles and that strengthen its ministries and operational commitments. Migration and development dovetails with Catholic teaching in its emphasis on human development, its appreciation for the benefits of migration, its promise that these benefits might be expanded, and its commitment to mitigate the hardships created by migration. However, as *Strangers No Longer* teaches, these goals will only be achieved through authentic development, which begins by honoring the dignity of the persons at the heart of this timeless phenomenon.

NOTES

1. The Global Commission on International Migration (GCIM) was established by a Core Group of States with the encouragement of the UN Secretary-General. Its nineteen delegates were tasked with promoting debate among states and other actors on migration; analyzing gaps in policy approaches; examining linkages between migration and other global issues; and presenting recommendations to the UN Secretary-General.

2. Suffice it to acknowledge, as *Strangers No Longer* does, that the "labor, values, and beliefs of immigrants" have helped to shape and continually renew the United States (SNL 17).

3. Douglas S. Massey, Joaquin Arrango, Graeme Hugo, Ali Kouaouci, Adela Pellegrino, and J. Edward Taylor, "Theories of International Migration: A Review and Appraisal," *Population and Development Review* 19, no. 3 (1993): 431–66.

4. UN General Assembly, *International Migration and Development. Report of the Secretary-General.* A/60/871 (2006); http://daccess-dds-ny.un.org/doc/UNDOC/GEN/N06/353/54/PDF/N0635354.pdf?OpenElement (accessed July 15, 2012).

5. Michael Clemens, Claudio E. Montenegro, and Lant Pritchett, "The Place Premium: Wage Differences for Identical Workers across the U.S. Border" (Washington, DC: Center for Global Development, 2008); http://www.cgdev.org/files/16352_file_CMP_place_premium_148.pdf (accessed July 15, 2012).

6. Dilip Ratha and Ani Silwal, "Remittance Flows in 2011—an Update," *Migration and Development Brief 18* (Washington, DC: World Bank, April 23, 2012); http://siteresources.worldbank.org/INTPROSPECTS/Resources/334934-1110315015165/MigrationandDevelopmentBrief18.pdf (accessed July 15, 2012).

7. World Bank, *Migration and Remittances Factbook 2011, Second Edition* (Washington, DC: World Bank, 2011); http://siteresources.worldbank.org/INTLAC/Resources/Factbook2011-Ebook.pdf (accessed July 15, 2012).

8. Ratha and Silwal, "Remittance Flows in 2011—an Update."

9. Raymundo Campos-Vazquez and Horacio Sobarzo, *The Development and Fiscal Effects of Emigration on Mexico* (Washington, DC: Migration Policy Institute, 2012); http://www. migrationpolicy. org/pubs/RMSG-fiscaleffects-emigration.pdf (accessed July 18, 2012).

10. Ibid., 11.

11. Ibid., 4.

12. World Bank, *Migration and Remittances Factbook 2011*.

13. Kathleen Newland and Dovelyn Agunias, *Developing a Road Map for Engaging Diasporas in Development: A Handbook for Policymakers and Practitioners in Home and Host Countries* (Washington, DC: Migration Policy Institute; Geneva: International Organization for Migration, 2012); http://www.migrationpolicy.org/ pubs/thediaspora handbook.pdf (accessed July 15, 2012).

14. International diaspora Engagement Alliance (IdEA), "About Us" (U.S. Department of State, 2011); http://www.state.gov/s/partner ships/diaspora/index.htm (accessed July 15, 2012).

15. UN General Assembly, *International migration and development. Report of the Secretary-General.* A/65/203 (2010); http://daccess-dds-ny.un.org/doc/UNDOC/GEN/N10/470/04/PDF/N1047004. pdf?OpenElement (accessed July 15, 2012).

16. Man-made and natural disasters often lead to the creation and revitalization of diaspora agencies.

17. El Salvador, Ethiopia, India, Israel, Nepal, Nigeria, the Philippines, Rwanda, and Sri Lanka have issued or plan to issue diaspora bonds. The success of bond issues depends largely on the level of diaspora confidence in and support for the government in the country of origin.

18. Dilip Ratha and Sanket Mohapatra, "Preliminary Estimates of Diaspora Savings," *Migration and Development Brief 14* (Washington, DC: World Bank, February 1, 2011); http://siteresources.world bank.org/INTPROSPECTS/Resources/334934-1288990760745/

MigrationAndDevelopmentBrief14_DiasporaSavings.pdf (accessed July 15, 2012).

19. Global Commission on International Migration (GCIM), *Migration in an Interconnected World: New Directions for Action. Report of the Global Commission on International Migration* (Switzerland: Global Commission on International Migration, 2005), 9.

20. World Bank, *Shaping the Future: A Long-Term Perspective of People and Job Mobility for the Middle East and North Africa* (Washington, DC: The World Bank, 2009); http://siteresources.worldbank.org/INTMENA/Resources/Shaping_Future.pdf (accessed July 15, 2012).

21. Ibid., 54.

22. Jeffrey Passel, D'Vera Cohn, and Ana Gonzalez-Barrerra, "Net Migration from Mexico Falls to Zero—and Perhaps Less" (Washington, DC: Pew Hispanic Center, 2012), 30–31; http://www.pewhispanic.org/files/2012/04/Mexican-migrants-report_final.pdf (accessed July 15, 2012).

23. GCIM, 4, 12–13, 21.

24. Pew Research Center, *World Publics Welcome Global Trade—But Not Immigration* (Washington, DC: Pew Research Center, 2007), 21; http://pewglobal.org/files/pdf/258.pdf (accessed July 15, 2012).

25. Ibid., 26-28.

26. The German Marshall Fund of the United States, Compagnia di San Paolo, Barrow Cadbury Trust, and Fundación BBVA, *Transatlantic Trends Immigration: Topline Data 2011* (Washington, DC: The German Marshall Fund of the United States, 2011), 30; http://trends.gmfus.org.php5-23.dfw1-2.websitetestlink.com/wp-content/uploads/2011/12/TTI2011_Topline_final.pdf (accessed July 18, 2012). Only 30 percent of Americans and 18 percent of Europeans thought it was a "very good" or "somewhat good" idea to admit persons who did not speak the native language fluently and did not have "a good chance to fit in smoothly" with the national culture. Ibid., 21.

27. Robert P. Jones, Daniel Cox, William A. Galston, and E. J. Dionne, Jr., *What It Means To Be American: Attitudes in an Increasingly Diverse America Ten Years after 9/11* (Washington, DC: Public Religion Research Institute and Brookings Institute Governance Studies Program, 2011), 21; http://publicreligion.org/site/wp-content/

uploads/2011/09/PRRI-Brookings-What-it-Means-to-be-American-Report.pdf (accessed July 15, 2012).

28. Ibid., 21–22.

29. Ibid., 20.

30. Ibid.

31. John Paul II, Message for World Migration Day, *Migration and the Unity of the Human Family* (August 21, 1991), 3; http://www.smc.org.ph/religion/day1991.htm (accessed July 16, 2012).

32. Michele R. Pistone and John J. Hoeffner, "But the Laborers are...Many? Catholic Social Teaching on Business, Labor, and Economic Migration," in *And You Welcomed Me: Migration and Catholic Social Teaching*, ed. Donald Kerwin and Jill Marie Gerschutz (Lanham, MD: Lexington Books, 2009), 81–82.

33. J. Bryan Hehir, "With No Vision, People Perish," in *All Come Bearing Gifts: Proceedings of the National Migration Conference 2003* (Washington, DC: United States Conference of Catholic Bishops, 2003), 19.

34. GCIM, 21.

35. UN Development Programme, *Human Development Report 2011, Sustainability and Equity: A Better Future for All* (New York: United Nations Development Programme, 2011); http://www.undp.org/content/dam/undp/library/corporate/HDR/2011%20Global%20HDR/English/HDR_2011_EN_Complete.pdf (accessed July 15, 2012).

36. Remittances can be seen as the form of development that most respects the agency of those closest to the need, assuming that governments do not appropriate these funds. Robert B. Zoellick, "Beyond Aid," speech by World Bank Group President Robert B. Zoellick at George Washington University (September 14, 2011); http://web.worldbank.org/WBSITE/EXTERNAL/NEWS/0,,contentMDK:23000133~pagePK:34370~piPK:42770~theSitePK:4607,00.html (accessed July 15, 2012).

37. Gasper F. Lo Biondo and Rita M. Rodriguez, *Development, Values and the Meaning of Globalization: A Grassroots Approach* (Washington, DC: Woodstock Theological Center, 2012), 33.

38. The phenomenon of migration has also led to a growing body of theological reflection in recent years, as well as to literature that documents how migrants and newcomers draw on religious conviction to

sustain them and to frame their own experiences. Gioacchino Campese, "The irruption of migrants: theology of migration in the 21st century," *Theological Studies* 73, no. 1 (2012); http://www.read periodicals.com/201203/2594689701.html#b (accessed July 18, 2012).

39. While the "common good is chiefly guaranteed when personal rights and duties are maintained" (PT 60), rights do not exhaust the conditions that constitute the common good. These conditions include "everything necessary for leading a life truly human, such as food, clothing, and shelter; the right to choose a state of life freely and to found a family, the right to education, to employment, to a good reputation, to respect, to appropriate information, to activity in accord with the upright norm of one's own conscience, to protection of privacy and rightful freedom even in matters religious" (GS 26).

40. UN General Assembly, *International migration and development. Report of the Secretary-General.*

41. Azfar Kahn and Hélène Harroff-Tavel, "Reforming the Kafala: Challenges and Opportunities in Moving Forward," *Asian and Pacific Migration Journal* 20, no. 3–4 (2011): 293–313.

42. Philippe Fargues, "Immigration without Inclusion," *Asian and Pacific Migration Journal* 20, no. 3–4 (2011): 273–92.

43. Congressional Budget Office, "The Impact of Unauthorized Immigrants on the Budgets of State and Local Governments" (Washington, DC: Congressional Budget Office, 2007); http://www.cbo.gov/sites/default/files/cbofiles/ftpdocs/87xx/doc8711/12-6-immigration.pdf (accessed July 15, 2012).

44. Harry J. Holzer, "Immigration Policy and Less-Skilled Workers in the United States: Reflections on Future Directions for Reform" (Washington, DC: Migration Policy Institute, 2011); http://www.migrationpolicy.org/pubs/Holzer-January2011.pdf (accessed July 15, 2012).

45. David Hollenbach, "Migration as a Challenge for Theological Ethics," *Political Theology* 12, no. 6 (2011): 807–12; http://www.politicaltheology.com/PT/article/view/11223/10655 (accessed July 15, 2012).

46. UN General Assembly, *Summary of the informal thematic debate on international migration and development: Notes by the President of the General Assembly.* A/65/944 (2011); http://www.un.org/esa/population/migration/GA65944e.pdf (accessed July 15, 2012).

47. The purpose of sovereign states is not to confine people with national boundaries, but "rather to protect, above all else, the common good of the entire human family" (PT 98). States also provide a community in which their members can contribute, express their own aspirations, and become themselves.

48. "Sovereignty," in *New Catholic Encyclopedia*, 2nd ed. (Detroit, MI: Thomson Gale, 2003); Donald M. Kerwin, "Rights, the Common Good, and Sovereignty in Service of the Human Person," in *And You Welcomed Me: Migration and Catholic Social Teaching*, ed. Donald Kerwin and Jill Marie Gerschutz (Lanham, MD: Lexington Books, 2009), 93–121.

49. Similarly, the International Commission on Intervention and State Sovereignty (ICISS) has concluded that sovereignty, understood to encompass the responsibility "to respect the dignity and basic rights of all the people within the state," "has become the minimum content of good international citizenship." ICISS, *The Responsibility to Protect* (Ottawa, ON, Canada: International Development Research Centre, December 2001), 1.35; http://idl-bnc.idrc.ca/dspace/bitstream/10625/18432/6/116998.pdf (accessed July 18, 2012).

50. UN General Assembly, *Summary of the informal thematic debate on international migration and development: Notes by the President of the General Assembly.*

51. Global Migration Group (GMG), *Mainstreaming Migration into Development Planning* (Washington, DC: International Organization for Migration, 2010).

52. Agencies like Catholic Relief Services and the International Catholic Migration Commission (ICMC) have been leading participants in this dialogue. ICMC, for example, has organized civil society's participation at the GFMD.

53. GCIM, 20.

54. By contrast, the literature extensively covers migration governance issues. See, ibid., 65–78; *Global Migration Governance*, ed., Alexander Betts (Oxford: Oxford University Press, 2011).

55. Kerwin, "Rights, the Common Good, and Sovereignty in Service of the Human Person," in *And You Welcomed Me: Migration and Catholic Social Teaching*.

56. Mark David Agrast, Juan Carlos Botero, and Alejandro Ponce, *WJP Rule of Law Index 2011* (Washington, DC: The World

Justice Project, 2011), 9–10; http://www.worldjusticeproject.org/sites/default/files/wjproli2011_0.pdf (accessed July 15, 2012).

57. Karen Mercado Asencio, "The Under-Registration of Births in Mexico: Consequences for Children, Adults, and Migrants," *Migration Information Source* (Washington, DC: Migration Policy Institute, April 2012); http://www.migrationinformation.org/Feature/display.cfm?ID=888 (accessed July 15, 2012).

58. As a factual matter, development is often oversold as a tool to curb migration. In fact, increases in income in communities of origin typically lead to increases in migration. UN General Assembly, *International migration and development. Report of the Secretary-General.*

59. Foresight, *Migration and Global Environmental Change: Future Challenges and Opportunities. Final Project Report* (London: The Government Office for Science, 2011).

60. This framework has also led states to address difficult migration-related challenges like the absence of parents in migrant sending communities and the reintegration of deported nationals.

61. UN General Assembly, *International migration and development. Report of the Secretary-General.*

62. UN General Assembly, *Summary of the informal thematic debate on international migration and development: Notes by the President of the General Assembly.* Non-recognition of credentials also inhibits human development in countries of destination.

63. Natasha Iskander and Nichola Lowe, "The Transformers: Immigration and Tacit Knowledge Development" (January 1, 2011). *NYU Wagner Research Paper No. 2011-01*; http://papers.ssrn.com/sol3/papers.cfm?abstract_id=1745082 (accessed July 19, 2012).

64. UN General Assembly, Resolution adopted by the General Assembly, 55/2, United Nations Millennium Declaration, 25–26 (8 September 2000); http://www.un.org/millennium/declaration/ares 552e.htm (accessed July 16, 2012).

65. However, states as diverse as Bangladesh, Ghana, Jamaica, and Moldova incorporate migration into their broader development plans.

66. The issues that require bilateral and multilateral cooperation include regulating recruitment of workers, protecting migrants in transit, ensuring portability of health coverage and pensions, addressing

legal grievances of deported nationals, pursuing human traffickers, and enforcing border controls.

67. From a development standpoint, family separation can undermine immigrant integration in host communities and diminish the potential multiplier effects of remittances in communities of origin.

68. UN General Assembly, *International migration and development. Report of the Secretary-General.*

69. Irregular migration, in turn, prevents integration, exacts substantial financial and human costs, and contributes to the development of smuggling rings and other criminal enterprises.

70. World Health Organization, "The WHO Global CODE of Practice on the International Recruitment of Health Personnel: WHA63.16" (WHO, 2011), 3.4; http://www.who.int/hrh/migration/code/code_en.pdf (accessed July 16, 2012).

71. Ibid., 3.6, 3.8, 4.6, 5.1, 5.5.

72. Ibid., 5.1.

73. Zoellick, "Beyond Aid."

74. GCIM, 28–29.

75. Nor can receiving states develop effective integration policies—with all the attendant benefits—without knowing immigrants.

76. Integration emerges from the migration and development dialogue as a form of domestic development.

CHAPTER 7

The Changing Social and Political Context of Migration in Mexico

Is There Room for Hope?

Leticia Calderon Chelius

Although Mexico is a country with a long tradition of migration, historically the exodus was concentrated in certain areas of the country and, until relatively recently (less than three decades), among people of certain socioeconomic sectors.[1] In this way, with the migratory flow focused on some states—Jalisco, Guanajuato, Michoacan, Zacatecas, San Luis Potosi—Mexico, the nation with the largest migrating population in the world had, for decades, little awareness of migration.[2] This explains, in part, the inability of Mexican society to incorporate migration as a cross-sectional process, and also some of the social, economic, and cultural problems of the country. That ignorance has also provoked historically incomprehensible social and political reactions, both in regards to Mexican migrants (of which most go to the United States, which accounts for 94 percent of Mexican migration), and to foreigners coming into Mexico.[3] The attitude of Mexican society toward migration in its many facets and forms, although more evident because it is part of the national reality, continues to arouse ambiguous, aloof and, even at times, hostile positions.

Just as the pastoral letter *Strangers No Longer* examined the conditions related to migration in the United States, it is crucial to look

166

also at the conditions surrounding migration in Mexico. Mexican attitudes to migration fluctuate from mistrust to rejection and this can be found even in Mexico's own legislation. It is the juridical framework that best encapsulates many of the attitudes, reactions, and ambivalence that Mexicans feel toward migration, especially at a time like never before in their history—a time when migration is no longer the exclusive issue of *those who left*, and has become an everyday affair with an unprecedented increase in internal migration throughout the country. Additionally, new flows of foreigners have been settling in the country in relatively low numbers in the last two decades and, although they constitute less than 1 percent of the total Mexican population their very presence has been gradually modifying the collective imagination regarding foreigners in Mexico.[4] One needs to keep in mind that for decades references to foreigners were a glorious page in Mexican nationalism, repeated in the official gesture of solidarity that different presidential administrations gave the politically persecuted. Thus, the arrival of exiles from Spain (in the 1940s) and South America (in the 1970s) became historical landmarks in national pride, without diminishing the value of political courage and international solidarity shown by both the government and Mexican society.[5] Unfortunately, both diasporas over time became the only point of reference for the identities of foreigners living in Mexico. This prevented Mexican society from opening itself to an understanding of the new and gradual flows of immigrants that have been coming into the country in discreet but sustained ways from elsewhere.[6]

THE JURIDICAL LANDSCAPE OF MIGRATION IN MEXICO: ARE WINDS OF CHANGE BLOWING?

When Mexicans speak of migration, they almost automatically think of Mexicans living abroad. As mentioned earlier, by number and their impact on the country, the experience of those who have left is much more visible than of those who have arrived. This explains, in large part, why Mexican migration was not regarded as a comprehensive process that includes several stages (emigration, immigration, transit, and return), but one of departure and integration into the new host society. Hence, the Mexican government, beginning in the 1980s, began developing programs, projects, and legal reforms in certain areas—financial, consular protection, political rights—to better regulate the relationship of the state with its diaspora.[7] However, historically Mexico responded to foreigners, both residents and persons in transit, through administrative arrangements that sought to regulate these flows—always in a very selective and restrictive way—depending on national origin.[8] Thus, the situation of foreigners in the twentieth century was not regulated by specific laws. Except in the nineteenth century, in Mexico there was no migration law as such, so regulations regarding foreigners were inserted into the different versions of the General Population Law.[9] The 1974 version of the Population Law regulated the policy toward foreigners in Mexico for three decades, and was endorsed by the new General Population Law in 1990. This law had few changes from the previous one, except for the inclusion of refugee status not previously covered, reconfiguring what was up to then an uncertain and highly discretionary category in Mexican migration policy. In this way, Mexico's government for decades maintained the status quo regarding the topic of migration (programs, regulations, controls), although in different forums and discussions by experts and politicians, various administrations were urged to update the juridical framework for immigration.[10] "There must be an immigration law as such," was repeated insistently.

Finally, in early 2011, under the administration of Felipe Calderon Hinojosa (2006–2012), an immigration bill was announced that, at least in its filing statement, sought to leave behind the obsolescence of nearly half a century when the prevailing vision supported by the legislative statutes was a suspicious, controlling, and paternalistic vision about foreigners on the part of the Mexican state. Discussion forums recognized that laws, regulations, and administrative procedures regarding foreigners, now repealed, controlled their residential mobility, and even the motives for their sentimental relationships. Whether a foreigner was to move to another house or marry, he or she had to ask permission of the state for a review of their case. The Mexican state attributed to itself the right to address even the reasons why a foreigner would marry a Mexican: it was thought that a foreigner might be hiding some motive for personal gain at the expense of a

Mexican national. The overriding assumption was thus that the Mexican state should prioritize the protection of its nationals who were susceptible to being deceived, even in terms of love relationships.

THE NEW MIGRATION LAW

Although the debate on the Migration Law (2011) lasted more than a decade, it was only seriously considered during Felipe Calderon's administration. It was carried out parallel to the emergence of new circumstances related to migration and immediately went beyond the juridical proposal just approved. To understand the new Migration Law, it is thus necessary to consider the reality that emerged shortly before its development. The first, and perhaps most important factor, was the decriminalization of migration in Mexico in 2008. Until that year undocumented migration into Mexico was not considered an administrative offense but something punishable with all the weight of the law, including prison and economic penalties.[11] Unauthorized migration into Mexico was considered a crime. This explains why the debate to repeal these penal provisions stated that it was necessary to not consider migration as a criminal act because they were "provisions that severely criminalize the acts more frequently made in the context of undocumented migration; and this was inadmissible, since it distanced itself from the social requirements and respect for human rights of migrants; they also criminalize poverty and the pursuit of opportunities.... "[12] However, even in Mexico, a country of high migration that has faced the severity of restrictive immigration laws, especially in the United States where this trend has been increasing, the debate about repealing the articles that severely penalized undocumented entrance into the country lasted several years. Even after adoption, the mandate that repealed the articles regarding the penalties for undocumented entrance remained frozen for more than a year. After certain modifications, the Senate approved the repeal of the relevant laws on April 28, 2008. The next day the bill was referred to the House, where it was put to a new vote in the full assembly and passed unanimously on April 29, 2008.[13] It was not until then, in twenty-first-century Mexico, that undocumented migration ceased to be considered a criminal act by the state.[14]

Parallel to the change in Mexican legislation concerning undocumented immigration another legal reform deserves attention: the Law on Refugees and Complementary Protection (January 27, 2011), which is a substantive advance over the previous law on international refugees. This new version harmonizes Mexican law with international legal instruments in force and it ratifies agreements that Mexico has signed over the years, many of which were not implemented due to a lack of adequate legislation in related areas. This legislation "includes a comprehensive and complete definition of 'refugee' that will allow no sanctions against whoever enters the country in an irregular manner because of persecution; and those seeking family reunification in this manner will not be discriminated against." On the contrary, "Refugees will have the right to work, access to health care and education," and, for example, may join the Seguro Popular (Public Health Insurance). Despite the ambitious nature of the principles that it espouses, there have been fewer than five thousand applicants for refugee status despite deep crisis conditions affecting neighboring countries, and the legal framework that was extended to allow "family reunification" as the guiding principle for seeking refuge.[15]

In the same context of the debate on new immigration regulations, a third legislative element is the law against the slave trade. This law should be seen as a consequence of the increase in this cruel crime—privation of a person's liberty by enslavement—because of the context of extreme violence that Mexico has suffered in recent years and the change in the circular migration flow due to the closure of the U.S. border. Both organized crime and the Mexican state are incapable of controlling, through inaction, complicity, or incompetence, the networks benefiting from increased traffic of migrants, vulnerable due to their poverty, through Mexican territory. The framework of this law against the slave trade should be seen, in turn, as part of the context of the general approval of the Constitutional Reform on Human Rights on June 9, 2011, which for many is the most important approval of the last decades on matters of human rights in Mexico.[16]

WHAT IS NEW IN THE NEW MIGRATION LAW?

As noted, the Migration Law is actually the first concerted effort to create a legal framework for migration to and from Mexico (a subject that before was regulated by the General Law of Population). However, it is important to recognize that the law ended up being a framework for the regulation of immigration of aliens into the country, and practically left out of the debate the topic of emigration, which as noted, was the related issue most commonly mentioned. The migration process is so broad that the idea of confining it to a single juridical framework proved to be impossible. Thus, unless the issue of emigration (Mexicans living abroad), is taken up in a new specific juridical framework of its own, as it stands now, and given the limited framework in which it is mentioned in the Migration Law, the issue of emigration remains pending.

It should be noted that programs, regulations, and administrative functions developed for years by the Mexican state for this community representing 10 percent of the total Mexican population, are still in force.[17] We can therefore say that the Migration Law is actually a new immigration law, evidence of that newness is its statement of principles, and that throughout the text human rights are the basis of the whole law (an element that was lacking in previous versions). Also as part of the lexicon of the statement of principle, notions about shelter, family, and social integration have been incorporated. Furthermore, it is mentioned explicitly that there will be sanctions for those failing to follow the law. That is a breakthrough in terms of accountability.

In the preamble, where the objectives of the law are stated, these elements stand out:

- Aims to create a framework of safeguards to protect the rights of migrants in the country, facilitate and order migration flow to and from Mexico, giving priority to protecting and respecting human rights.
- Presents unconditional respect for the rights of Mexicans and foreigners, whatever their origin, nationality, gender, ethnicity, age, and immigration status.

- Empowers the National Immigration Institute to implement and execute migration policy and, in order to combat corruption within the institute, supports the professional training and certification of its personnel through a Center for Evaluation and Trust Control.
- The new law states that an irregular immigration status would never constitute a criminal act, nor would having committed a crime be reason for prejudgment (which, already mentioned above, was the case in 2008).[18] Another novelty, and its most relevant legal proposal, is that this legislation consolidates more than thirty categories of migration included in the General Population Law to only three:

  —*Visitor* immigration status to be granted to foreigners who remain in Mexico for short stays: tourism or business; visitors with permission to receive remuneration for stays of less than 180 days, or as visitors or workers in the border regions.
  —*Temporary Resident* status to be given to foreigners who wish to remain in the country for stays of less than four years. This category includes students who may stay in the country for the duration of their studies.
  —*Permanent Resident* status awarded to foreigners wishing to reside indefinitely in Mexico, for reasons of political asylum, recognition of refugee status, complementary protection, or family reunification.[19]

WHAT CRITICISM HAS THE NEW MIGRATION LAW RECEIVED?

The main criticism is that as a law it is a list of good principles that do not involve concrete actions until there are adequate, approved, and functioning regulations that match those principles. The law also raised negative reactions from civil society groups that have worked for years with migrants in Mexico because of these shortcomings:

1. Contrary to the spirit of the preamble it proposes to create a border police force under the Interior Ministry thus maintaining a level of police control of migration flows.
2. Although there is talk of creating a system for professionalizing and certifying migration personnel through an Assessment Center and Reliability Control, no rules are set to create a reliable space to effectively develop those improvements.
3. For many human rights groups, to offer new types of visas, excluding a transit visa, ignores the real problem of migration. Articles 34 and 47 of the law invalidated completely the discussion and analysis of the possible transit permit, eliminating the possibility of any type of migration status for trans-migrants. This preserves the invisibility of this group, the most vulnerable to organized crime and the authorities.
4. Home checks or operations without a warrant remain in place, leaving room for the authorities to abuse and intimidate migrants. It also allows the development of migration control operations at locations other than those for international traffic to check the immigration status of aliens.
5. Discretionary control is maintained to allow entry to the lawyers of migrants in detention centers in order to follow legal channels for their arrest and eventual freedom. Besides that, the new laws do not mention precise limits so that the detention would not constitute a disproportionate measure of time—periods in excess of what is legally permitted by the Magna Carta (Constitution)—and therefore there is no mention of programs alternative to detention that would shape a more balanced option to comply with the legitimate interest of the state.[20]
6. Despite the mention of human rights as part of the lexicon of the new law, some insist that there is no effective vision that cuts across all areas or includes basic rules regarding children. This is an issue of special interest to the various groups working in Mexico on this matter

who are concerned about increased flow of unaccompanied children in the contemporary migration process.

7. One point that stands out among the criticisms is the state's inability to create real mechanisms for dialogue and exchange, and to receive proposals from civil society groups that were organized for the enactment of the law and subsequent regulations. Especially when many of these organizations do much of the work that the same authorities end up delegating.

In summary, the points that aroused controversy as soon as the immigration laws were enacted and started a broad debate were:

- That an inclusive language should be maintained and terms should be standardized;
- The document should preserve throughout an emphasis on gender in addition to speaking of migrant girls, boys, and adolescents;
- There should be a review concerning the detention of migrants and due process throughout the entire follow up of detained migrants;
- The need to include transparency as a basic element of a culture of accountability, an issue that is not mentioned in the new law;
- To allow, clearly and unconditionally, unrestricted access to the detention centers by lawyers, a main demand of the lawyers themselves;
- To provide a framework for effective and transparent clarity in the Assessment and Control Centers trusted by the Instituto Nacional de Migración (INM—National Institute of Migration) (training of personnel and career professionals under truly objective supervision and outside the bureaucratic framework of the government).

In reaction to this first wave of criticism of the new immigration law, proposed changes in wording came from government offices, although these were mainly in the regulations, where many lawyers and activists within the migration debate have focused their efforts. They believe that the law will remain as a document of good principles, but that the regulations, which will determine the practical, daily juridical framework, can make a difference in the lives and dignity of migrants in Mexico. Small changes that were detected in early versions, now in the regulations and not so much in the law, included:

- The word "minors" replaced "boys, girls, and adolescents" in Article 71;
- Everything related to bail for freedom was eliminated in Article 98;
- A paraphrase was included stating that migratory reviews must be informed and motivated not by free will of a migration agent or mere assumption;
- References to "legal" were changed to "regular";[21]
- References to "expulsion" were changed to "deportation."[22]

THE NEW IMMIGRATION ACTIVISM

The debate about immigration law has led us to an interesting process, the encounter and partnership of many isolated groups, some of long standing and others of recent inception, that are working on the immigration issue in Mexico. Spontaneously, organizations from Mexican civil society came together to form a common front and made a public commitment to address the issue of migration in 2011. Unfortunately, the alliance was more a desperate cry in the face of a terrible, painful, and seemingly impossible situation than a simple organized answer to review the legislative framework of migration.

Mexico has a long history of violence against foreigners passing through its territory. The situation took on extreme emergency in the face of what some call the "migration holocaust."[23] Neither the Report of the Comisión Nacional de Derechos Humanos (National Human Rights Commission—CNDH) in 2009[24] nor the findings of mass murder in clandestine graves[25] were sufficient for a thorough review of the Mexican immigration enforcement model. The recurring criticism of the conduct of the authorities of the INM, by omission or action, was shrouded in scandal due to the increased number of officers dismissed, discharged, or temporarily put on leave, and accused of cover-ups, corruption, or direct involvement in crimes against foreigners who cross Mexican soil bound for the United States. The dismissal or confinement of offending authorities can be interpreted as positive, but it is a tragedy that even after their being made aware of the criminal behavior, it has been allowed to continue for years, under the very cover of the INM.

To give an example, in October 2011 there was an announcement dismissing and confining 121 INM service agents who were employed for years and were suspected of abuse. In extreme cases, it was known that they stopped trucks of clandestine migrants, chose those whom they considered most suitable, and sold them to organized crime. This tragic level of collusion and complicity can only be understood within an extensive network of corruption that permeates the country far beyond the actual migration flow. It is not exclusive to migration or limited to this area. What is exclusive to migration is that by the very condition of their vulnerability, undocumented aliens become invisible, hidden, and therefore disposable, which exacerbates the dangers of their situation. It has been shown that gangs, protected by the very state in the persons of these migration service agents and other public servants who guard the criminal gangs, are waiting for migrants. This is the clear image of the definition of organized crime: power as co-participant and guardian of criminals of all kinds.

The evidence for this situation has been reported by the CNDH and documented in 2009, 2010, and 2011. The authorities were unwilling to discuss the reports and discredit their testimony alleging "methodological issues."[27] Subsequent reports have done nothing but strengthen the hypothesis that has been known all along, and that has been shouted most loudly by the voices of survivors, families, advocates, migrant protectors, and some journalists.

But even within the festering darkness of migration in Mexico, there are signs of light. While the issue of foreigners, those who have taken up residence in the country or those just passing through, had not raised many voices internally, the status quo was repeatedly denounced by Dr. Jorge Bustamante, United Nations Special Rapporteur on the Human Rights of Migrants, appointed in 2005 and serving through July 2011.[28] What has been surprising is the avalanche of activism that has occurred in Mexico concerning the rights and protection of migrants, especially those who are in transit through the country. This does not include a broad sector of society but only small groups of activists. However, given their small number, the various groups and advocates that have taken up the cause of immigration in Mexico have managed to turn the national migration debate around. The cause of immigration in Mexico enables groups that operate in different ways to work together. Through the initiatives of journalists, media, and the website 72migrantes.com, the stories of those killed since the first murders uncovered by the discovery of mass graves in 2010, crimes perpetrated directly against foreigners, have been disseminated.[29] The killings were known to have been taking place for some time, to the great shame that overwhelms us, as Mexicans. Other groups have managed to mobilize in multiple locations and in forms and styles typical of the variety that makes up Mexican civil society,[30] especially those interested in the migration issue.[31]

There are several groups that despite their historical existence were overshadowed in the Mexican political scene on the issue of migration, but who suddenly came to light as some of the most traditional, experienced, and consistent proponents for the defense of the most vulnerable populations such as migrants. They are different members of the Mexican Episcopal Conference (CEM), who coordinate those representing the Progressive Church of Mexico in a clear, organized action with the rest of the continent's dioceses to raise their voices as one. Names such as Alejandro Solalinde, Director of Brothers on the Way shelter in Oaxaca; Miguel Concha, Director of Human Rights Center Fray Francisco de Vitoria; Pedro Pantoja, Director of Belen, Casa del Migrante; and Raul Vera,[32] Bishop of Saltillo, have become the reference points and the more courageous voices, faces, and attitudes who speak in defense of migrants.[33]

The unusual nature of this activism has been based[34] on their ability to become allies and unite without putting their religious affiliations first. As individuals and as a group they have become the leaders calling and uniting sectors of civil society who have led the debate on the law and the situation of migration in and through Mexico. They work at a high technical level, as the work group on immigration legislation, and as allied voices but without being pushy nor giving religious overtones to such an important cause as the protection of migrants. At the same time, they have become high profile personalities in their unrestricted activism, as is the case with Alejandro

Solalinde, both to insure that the Migration Law will not be trapped in the bureaucracy of the Mexican Congress, as well as to openly denounce the continued abuse and threats against his life because of his advocacy for migrants. As Emilio Ruiz Parra points out in a memorable report in the journal GATOPARDO, "after only four years coordinating the shelter *Hermanos en el Camino* (Brothers on the Way), Solalinde became one of the most notable figures not only of the Catholic Church but of human rights defenders. Thin, soft-spoken, and of courtly manners, he is a magnet for controversy."[35]

HOW IS THIS KIND OF ACTIVISM A CHALLENGE?

Given the national emergency in Mexico, since 2009 there has been widespread social activism shown in demonstrations against violence and for peace,[36] against enforced disappearance, and for the defense of human rights advocates—a group particularly attacked and victimized with impunity in the country.[37] In the case of migration the vulnerability of migrants in transit through the country has become more apparent than ever. The "migration holocaust" became the raw and powerful image of the plight of migrants. Given the evidence, and especially because the brutality that was discovered after 2009 far exceeded this description, it became impossible for the authorities to continue to gloss over or dismiss such imagery.[38]

To establish the emergence of an alliance and foothold for advocacy and activism, it is necessary to understand that in Mexico different groups are becoming valuable components in the work on immigration, specifically the debate about the law and the resurgence of violence. On the one hand, within the organized groups of civil society there are sectors of young activists, mostly Mexicans, but also foreigners, who are professionals who have a cosmopolitan vision of the world and a belief in the unrestricted defense of human rights. Despite their small numbers in a country overwhelmed by poverty and poor access to education, their presence, capacity, and ability for intelligent dialogue has contributed an important counterbalance to power. As professionals in their field, these young activists are capable of a technical

178

level of discourse that allows them to challenge and put into question the strong opinions that are issued from the law firms that write migration law and its regulations.[39] This type of challenge to power is very influential because there is no way to neutralize it without arguments, and to argue one has to think. On the other hand, there are also established activists whose prestige makes them impossible to ignore as legitimizers of any agreement that would advance a bill. And immigration law requires the daily work of these activists, as advocates, in the detention centers, and in the socialization and integration processes.[40] These activists, unlike the officials, know the field and the officials, therefore, cannot simply dismiss them.[41]

Another form of activism that adds its strengths to this effort and has had a definite impact on the new Mexican migration scenario is the one formed by the humblest activists, the everyday ones, as is the case with many groups such as *Las Patronas*[42] representing the poorest and helping others, poorer than themselves. In this case, it is a community that has become recognized and respected for its selfless work with migrants. These are groups that do not receive or seek anything from the state, and instead offer their solidarity, sometimes even challenging their own society. Their goal is not to influence political processes or laws, but their work has such an impact that they sit at any negotiating table even if they are not physically present.

What may be the most disquieting challenge of this migration activism is that of the rebel priests who come from an ancient tradition of opting for the poor instead of succumbing to power. Mexico is a country that while moving toward secularism, remains very devoted to its religious heritage, especially among the poorest sectors, but also in the highest governmental levels where the Catholic religion is reaffirmed publicly and submission to its rules, even at the most personal level, is evident.[43] For the ruling elite, especially one sector led by Calderón Hinojosa and his wife Margarita Zavala[44] who clearly practice the Catholic faith, the criticism that comes from any of these groups takes on a special tone. How can they refuse to greet a priest blessed by all the rites of his faith that should earn him the highest respect? How do they disqualify a religious apostle spreading the creed of the charitable and supportive Christ and who is of the same faith as the one who calls himself a Catholic? How do you criticize denunciations, based on the purest tradition, of those with whom you share the same faith?[45] How do you reject a blessing from a representative of Christ although this blessing equalizes the powerful with the humblest? How do you not keep the promise to defend one of God's representatives on earth when from your position of power you can protect him?[46]

This places the activists who defend migrants, targets of the worst mafia and networks of power in an uneasy position, to say the least. Unfortunately, neither their followers' devotion nor the most powerful friends or officials can protect them completely. In some sense, the only thing that gives these priests and bishops a security blanket for their pastoral and comforting care to the hundreds of migrants who listen in several areas of the country is to be seen and recognized by society, not only nationally but also globally. The irony is that just as for the poorest, the greatest vulnerability is in invisibility, so it is necessary that they be seen to be a little more protected. What a paradox; these missionaries of God share the same fate as those who they protect and care passionately for, hence, their invisibility, like that of the humblest, is their greatest risk.[47]

BY WAY OF CONCLUSION: THERE IS ROOM FOR HOPE

As we have seen throughout these pages, we can say that in Mexico we are facing a new migration context, both because of a legal and sociological debate largely developed but yet to be made complete and binding, as well as a new social activism regarding the defense of migrants in the country. Both dimensions are intertwined but must be understood in several aspects:

1. The debate over immigration law in Mexico that was intended to cover various processes (immigration, emigration, transit, and return) was not actually achieved with the same degree of mastery on all points, and actually focused mainly on the issue of foreign residents in the country and transit migration.

2. The scenarios in Mexico of escalating violence and impunity in recent years is key to understanding why

there was a change in direction on the immigration debate in general to focus, in particular, on the issue of immigrants. This pushed to the background the theme of the Mexican diaspora. It remains as an outstanding issue to regulate and some even see the need of a separate law for the national social universe situated outside the country's borders.

3. The debate over the new law was not strictly technical but took place in an environment emerging from a common front in response to the critical situation facing migration in recent Mexican history. This front brings together diverse groups from very different paths: young professionals trained in the universal discourse of human rights; activists with a long presence and a fine and detailed knowledge of the uses and abuses of the law, and above all, closeness to the reality of migrants in the country; activists, humble in origin, but with forcefulness in their charitable and humanitarian work; political and social doers from national and international levels who have made visible the problem of human rights of migrants in Mexico (National Commission of Human Rights, Special Rapporteur on Migrants at the United Nations, Amnesty International, Human Rights Commission, and so on), and very importantly, as detailed in these pages, by the entrance of sectors of the Catholic Church in Mexico that while having done years of work with migrants, have become very relevant because they add strength and experience, and move the discourse of rights of migrants to one that has an impact on several sectors. It is worth mentioning that parallel to this more political process, there was a flowering of studies, reports, films, theater, graphic, and other art forms that focus on the situation of migration in Mexico, that shed light on the extreme cruelty and excruciating vulnerability of immigration in Mexico. Unquestionably, this will be critical in changing paradigms, discourse, and the collective images of the "others, the foreigners" in a country not very open to cosmopolitan diversity and plurality.

Thus, Mexican society learned from this process that it was not aware of its status as a country of migrants because it despised and avoided the issue of the missing and ignored the weight of that absence on the social, cultural, political, and economic dimensions of all involved. The current scenario takes on the subject from a very different place than the society might have imagined only a few years ago. At least for the experts, the intent was to make a law covering the entire migration process. Looking at the law that was enacted, it is obvious that we are facing new and multiple challenges, and a long list of pending issues on the need to resolve the juridical framework in a truly up-to-date dialogue on the universal themes of migration. But above all, and this is the most difficult and painful, it involves changing what in Mexico has resulted in the extreme situation in which we live today, and explains in large part how migration is lived, especially, but not only, for those passing through the country: Impunity as a rule, corruption as a profession, the permissibility of violence. If this changes, then and only then, will there be room for hope.

NOTES

1. Elena Zuñiga Herrera, Jesús Arroyo, Agustín Escobar, and Gustavo Verduzco, eds., *Migración México-Estados Unidos, Implicaciones y retos para ambos países* (México: CONAPO/UdeGuadalajara/CIESAS/Casa Juan Pablo/COLMEX, 2006).

2. "Mexico is the country with the largest migration in the world"—twelve million people living abroad, representing about 10 percent of the total population—in International Organization for Migration, World Migration Report 2011, Communicating Effectively about Migration, Geneva, 2001; http://publications.iom.int/bookstore/index.php?main_page=product_info&products_id=754 (accessed August 21, 2012).

3. Foreigners, in this case, are aliens residing in the country or persons in transit.

4. Foreign permanent residents in México account for 0.6 percent of the total national population according to the National Institute of Migration, Immigration Statistics, 2011. It is worrisome that while foreigners in Mexico constitute less than 1 percent of the population, 40 percent of Mexicans feel that too many live in the coun-

try and 45 percent believe that they "harm" it. Consejo Nacional para Prevenir la Discriminación, http://www.conapred.org.mx/index.php (accessed September 14, 2012).

5. Without forgetting the diplomatic episode of providing refuge to Guatemalans in the 1980s, another great national episode. See Katya Somohano and Pablo Yankelevich (coord.), *El refugio en México, entre la historia y los desafíos contemporáneos*, Comisión Mexicana de ayuda a Refugiados COMAR, México, 2011.

6. Among the historical communities there are Spanish, German, French, Arabs (mostly from Lebanon), Jews (from Syria and various European countries), Italians, Chinese, and Japanese. Product of the emblematic exile in the 1940s and 1970s were Spanish, Argentine, Chilean, Uruguayan, among others. Currently, the greatest presence of foreigners is made up of Americans, Cubans, Colombians, Ecuadorians, but especially many from Central America. Without ignoring the historical flow of Haitians that increased with the arrival of 350 who were welcomed as humanitarian refugees because of the 2010 earthquake. Other immigrant communities are small but their visibility is greater due to their racial features or culture, such as those from several African countries, as well as Asia. Some Brazilians and Russians are coming, too.

7. Paula Leite and Silvia Giorguli, eds., *Reflexiones en torno a la emigración mexicana como objeto de políticas públicas* (México: CONAPO, 2010).

8. Mónica Palma Mora, *De tierras extrañas, un estudio sobre la inmigración en México, 1950–1990*, México, Instituto Nacional de Migración, Colección Migración, 2006.

9. In the twentieth century, an immigration law was enacted in 1908, followed by another in 1926, in which the restrictive tone changed somewhat, and led to a more integrative attitude toward migration. But by 1936 the policy regarding foreigners entered into a new general law of population that maintained the need to populate the country as part of the state policy of the time. The emphasis, however, was placed on the fertility and mortality rates of the native population, and not on migration issues (both immigration and emigration).

10. Since the administrations of Ernesto Zedillo (1994–2000) and Vicente Fox (2000–2006), forums and consultations were held

with experts in the field, to discuss a reform of the juridical framework for migration and/or failing that, to generate a new population law.

11. For example, it imposed a penalty of up to two years imprisonment and a fine from 300 to 5,000 pesos, to whoever entered the country illegally.

12. Described in the report of the Joint Committee on Population and Development and Legislative Studies, Senate, Mexico, 2008.

13. Articles of the General Law of Population 118 and 125 were amended, and 19, 120, 121, 123, 124, and 127 were repealed.

14. For example, the reform established that sanctions against illegal entrance are now considered an administrative offense and require a fine of twenty to a hundred days of minimum wage.

15. For coverage of the promulgation see "Promulga Calderón Ley sobre Refugiados," *Noticias MVS*, January 26, 2011; http://ww2.noticiasmvs.com/noticias/capital/promulga-calderon-ley-sobre-refugiados-151.html (accessed September 4, 2012).

16. The human rights protected by international treaties ratified by Mexico are raised to the level of constitutionality. It establishes the obligation of all authorities to prevent, investigate, punish, and remedy human rights violations. It creates a catalog of rights which can never be suspended, such as the right to life, humane treatment of children, and the principle of legality and no retroactivity. The heads of organizations protecting human rights are selected from among the citizens; and the autonomy of the committees is strengthened. It establishes the authority of the National Human Rights Commission to declare as unconstituti onal local and federal laws that violate human rights contained in the Constitution and international treaties cosigned by Mexico.

17. Some examples are the different outreach and support programs from the state, such as the Mexican consular network (the largest in the world), economic investment programs (remittances), social programs, health/education, the projects representing the community through CCIME (Consejo Consultivo del Instituto de los Mexicanos en el Exterior) of the Ministry of Foreign Affairs, and Mexicans voting abroad for the second time in the elections of 2012.

18. Secretara de Gobernación Subsecretaria de Población, Migración y Asuntos Religiosos, Istituto Nacional de Migracion, Ley

de Migración, México, 2011; http://www.inm.gob.mx/index.php/page/Ley_Migracion.

19. Luisa Gabriela Morales Vega, *Migratory Categories in Mexico. Analysis of the Migration Act, México*, Biblioteca Jurídica Virtual del Instituto de Investigaciones Jurídicas, *UNAM, 2011.* http://biblio.juridicas.unam.mx/revista/pdf/DerechoInternacional/12/pim/pim25.pdf.

20. Sin Fronteras, *Informe sobre la Situación de los derechos humanos de las personas migrantes y solicitantes de asilo detenidas en las Estaciones Migratorias de México, 2007–2009* (México, 2010); http://www.sinfronteras.org.mx/index.php/es/publicaciones/informes-tematicos/ (accessed August 24, 2012).

21. This was an obvious aberration even if it were only in linguistic usage given the weight of the legal definition that criminalizes the act of migration. "No being is illegal" can be considered a universal principle in the advocacy for the rights of migrants.

22. From documents' analysis prepared by the Working Group for Migration Policy that were used in the elaboration of the Mandate for New Migration Law (mimeographs, September–October 2011).

23. Coined by the Rev. Alejandro Solalinde, activist and defender of migrants rights in Mexico.

24. Comisión Nacional de Derechos Humanos, *Informe especial sobre los casos de secuestro en contra de migrantes* (México: CNDH, 2009).

25. Tamaulipas; http://72migrantes.com/ (accessed August 21, 2012).

26. Comisión Nacional de Derechos Humanos, *Informe especial sobre los casos de secuestro en contra de migrantes*; http://www.acnur.org/t3/fileadmin/scripts/doc.php?file=biblioteca/pdf/7932 (accessed August 21, 2012).

27. See the note about this at: http://www.eluniversal.com.mx/notas/736296.html (accessed August 21, 2012).

28. Although according to Parametría 87 percent of Mexicans know about the kidnapping of migrants in the country, this does not indicate openness and solidarity, but only knowledge of the problem.

29. A year after the discovery of mass clandestine graves of migrants killed in Tamaulipas (2010), there were other findings at almost at the same site and in nearby states, with traces of the same criminal motive. See note: http://observadorglobal.com/a-un-ano-de-

la-masacre-de-tamaulipas-aun-mueren-migrantes-n29349.html
(accessed August 21, 2012).

30. For example: Mesoamerican Migrant Movement (MMM), International Tribunal of Conscience of the People in Motion; Commission on Migration Axis, Mexican Chapter; Permanent People's Tribunal; and PRECADEM (Prevention, Training, and Advocacy for Migrants); AC; Graduate for the Defense and Promotion of Human Rights, UACM.

31. By way of showing some of the groups that constitute the Working Group on Migration Law and policy 2010–2012: National Alliance of Latin American and Caribbean Communities (NALACC); Human Rights Center Fray Matías de Córdova; Human Rights Center Miguel Agustín Pro Juárez (PRODH); Coalition for the Defense of Migrants in Baja California; Pastoral Dimension of Human Mobility (DPMH); FUNDAR Analysis and Research Center; Ideas; Human Rights Litigation Strategic Studies Institute on Migration and Diffusion (INEDIM); Institute for Women in Migration (IMUMI); Network for the Rights of Children in Mexico (REDIM); Mexico Jesuit Migrant Service (SJM-MEX).

32. As noted by Gerardo Escareño Arciniega, general vicar of the Diocese of Saltillo, Bishop Vera's pastoral style, committed to the most vulnerable groups of society, has angered some sectors that think that the ecclesiastical work should have "less scope and significance," but despite that, the religious will continue to work with "courage, determination, and responsibility."

33. For example, one year after the tragedy of the seventy-two found (2011) in clandestine graves in Tamaulipas, a press conference was convened with the purpose of not ignoring such heinous crime: Fr. Alejandro Solalinde, Coordinator of Pastoral on Human Mobility in the South Pacific region, Ixtepec, Oaxaca and of the Albergue Brothers on the Road; Miguel Concha Malo, Director of Human Rights Center "Fray Francisco de Vitoria"; Miguel Alvarez Gandara, President, Serapaz; Fr. José Rosario Marroquin, Director Human Rights, Center Miguel Agustín Pro; Ana Lorena Delgadillo, Foundation for Justice and a Democratic State of Laws; Fr. Pedro Pantoja, Director "Bethlehem, Casa del Migrante," Diocese of Saltillo, Coahuila; Clemencia Correa, Graduate for Defense and Promotion of Human Rights, UACM; Camilo Pérez Bustillo and José Antonio Foronda,

Secretariat of the International Tribunal of Conscience of the People in Motion; Commission on the Migratory Axis, Mexico chapter; Permanent People's Tribunal; and PRECADEM (Prevention, Training and Advocacy for Migrants); AC Representatives of Caravan Paso a Paso SERAPAZ, located in Patricio Sanz 449, Col. del Valle, México D.F.

34. The pastoral work of the Mexican Catholic Church is widely known. For the most part, the Church has maintained the migrant shelters for years. Its work had been isolated, bound within its circles and without connection to a broader political context, as it occurred beginning in 2009.

35. Emiliano Ruiz Parra, "Solalinde," *Gatorpado* (September 2011); http://www.gatopardo.com/ReportajesGP.php?R=104&pagina =18 (accessed August 24, 2012).

36. As an example, the campaign "In Another's Shoes" organized by the Collective "The Loudest Scream" in partnership with the "Movement for Peace with Justice and Dignity"; http://www.youtube.com/watch? v = WRvWx0fNvxE (accessed August 21, 2012).

37. The international campaign to raise awareness of the attacks being hurled at the advocates of human rights can be seen here: http://www.yomedeclaro.org (accessed August 21, 2012).

38. One of several reports on the subject is that of Amnesty International 2010. See *Victimas Invisibles: Migrantes en Movimiento en México* (Madrid, Spain: Amnesty International, 2010); http://amnesty.org/es/library/asset/AMR41/014/2010/en/1345cec1-2d36-4da6-b9c0-e607e408b203/amr410142010es.pdf (accessed August 21, 2012).

39. Lawyers, communications specialists, sociologists, educators, psychologists, linguists, planners, artists, filmmakers, photographers, etc.

40. Sin Fronteras, *Perspectiva Jurídica y Social de la Detención de Migrantes en Iztapalapa, D.F. and Tenosique, Tabasco, México* (2011); http://www.sinfronteras.org.mx/index.php/es/publicaciones/informes-tematicos/ (accessed August 21, 2012).

41. Names that must be mentioned are Elvira Arellano and Martha Sanchez, representing the Mesoamerican Migrant Movement (MMM).

42. See: http://www.youtube.com/watch?v=cU8BVIMUGoA& feature=related (accessed August 21, 2012).

43. Since the time of Vicente Fox, president (2000–2006), there has been a rearrangement of the participation in religious acts by the powerful elite at the social level, especially in matters of personal interest, where he made sure that the papal blessing was seen by millions. Calderon (2006–2012) and his wife boasted about their religious ties and promoted that image by visiting the pope in a clear gesture that endorsed their religious practice. Even the PRI candidate Peña Nieto published his appeal to the pope for handling the personal paperwork for his marriage and sought the endorsement of the Catholic hierarchy. Interestingly, their intentions seem to promote the image of wanting to be recognized as being subordinate to religious rule.

44. Zavala Gómez del Campo, wife of President Calderón, was the chief officer of the National System for Integral Family Development (DIF), and its central theme was that of migrant children, a topic that, ironically, had an unparalleled increase during his tenure (2006–2012).

45. An example is the meeting called by The Mesoamerican Migrant Movement during Holy Week, 2012, the lodge's 72, and Shelter Home for Migrants, to hold a Migrant's Stations of the Cross, in Tabasco, Mexico. "Thorns are on your path, my hands' task is to remove them" was the title of the event that walked through key sites of the journey known as "The Path of the Migrant." The event sought to report crimes, harassment, and human rights violations perpetrated against migrants. Activists, transit migrants, and people from the community took part in representing the scenes of the Stations of the Cross; http://www.barriozona.com/inmigracion_migrantes_mexico_centroamerica_via_crucis_abusos_tabasco_guatemala.html (accessed August 21, 2012).

46. Paradoxes of the story: If on one hand a segment of the Church showed its most humble and charitable side toward the issue of migration, the religious hierarchy of Mexico did not even mention the subject and in spite of its possibilities did not support in any way the defense of the rights of migrants.

47. Even Fr. Solalinde left the country in May 2012 because of threats to his life for what he called "collusion" between officials and "narcos." He returned to his pastoral mission in Oaxaca, protected by bodyguards. See: http:// internacional.elpais.com/internacional/2012/05/16/actualidad/1337134142_530284.html (accessed August 21, 2012).

PART III

SPECIAL POPULATIONS

CHAPTER 8

The Catholic Church Confronts the Scourge of Human Trafficking

Terry Coonan

It was in recognition of a new and sobering "sign of the times" that the U.S. and Mexican bishops' conferences addressed the topic of human trafficking as a part of their 2003 joint pastoral letter *Strangers No Longer: Together on the Journey of Hope*. Recounting the varied abuses to which migrants crossing the U.S. border are subjected, the bishops described human trafficking as "a scourge" and noted that "[t]rafficking in persons—in which men, women, and children from all over the globe are transported to other countries for the purposes of forced prostitution or labor—inherently rejects the dignity of the human person and exploits conditions of global poverty" (SNL 90). More than a passing reference to yet another hardship suffered by migrants traversing the U.S. southwestern border, the statement was rather an explicit recognition on the part of the bishops of one of the most widespread and systematic human rights abuses of the modern world. It likewise augured what in recent years has become a leading role played by the Catholic Church in the twenty-first-century abolitionist movement.

In the decade that has followed the issuance of *Strangers No Longer*, human trafficking has come to be recognized as one of the grave moral crises facing the global community. The specter of human trafficking has become clearer with each passing year. Modern slavery expert Kevin Bales posits that as many as twenty-seven million people worldwide may now live in conditions approximating slavery.[1] The moral and humanitarian consequences of this reality cannot be under-estimated: there are now arguably more slaves in the world than at any time in human history, at the very moment in history that slavery is proscribed by law in every country in the world.[2] This anomaly consti-tutes far more than a challenge to the rule of law; it denotes a human-itarian crisis of epic proportions. In the face of this systemic evil, the Catholic Church has emerged as a vital voice and global actor.

Catholic leadership has been crucial to the modern abolitionist movement at a number of different levels. As a global faith community, Catholic service providers and organizations offer critical direct care to those victimized by modern slavery. This chapter will survey such efforts, noting in particular the ecumenical and collaborative role that the Catholic community continues to play in the direct care of those broken by the scourge of trafficking in persons. But in addition to its pastoral role in binding up the wounds inflicted by modern slavery, the Catholic Church plays an equally important role in articulating a com-prehensive approach to the larger moral issues raised by trafficking. The centuries-old tenets of Catholic moral theology—and in particu-lar their modern expression in Catholic social teaching—comprise a framework for analysis that is unrivalled by any other actor in the mod-ern anti-trafficking movement. This chapter likewise examines the contributions of Catholic teachings to the foundations of an ethically consistent response to trafficking.

THE DEEP MEMORY OF BONDAGE

The communal memory of slavery informs the very fabric of Catholic thinking. Human trafficking, roughly defined in modern par-lance as slavery and slavery-like practices, is not a dynamic new to the annals of human history. It is rather an age-old evil whose contours have shaped the historic identity of the Judeo-Christian community.[3] The particular vulnerability of persons far from the safety and familiarity of their native lands is etched at a primal level in the Judeo-Christian Scriptures and consciousness.[4] The pages of the Hebrew Scriptures are themselves replete with accounts that would now be identified as human trafficking offenses. Such scriptural stories are archetypes of the very kinds of exploitation that now appear nightly on CNN reports and investigative journalism programs. There is the plight of Joseph, sold into slavery by family members he trusted; the anguished isolation of the inhabitants of Jerusalem transported for forced labor to Babylon; and the wartime exile and enslavement of Northern Kingdom Israelites at the hands of a conquering Assyrian army. And of course, the defining event of the Hebrew Scriptures—the Exodus story—constitutes a deep memory of bondage suffered in a foreign land. From such deep memories came one of the bedrock ethical injunctions of the Hebrew people: "You shall not oppress a resident alien you know the heart of an alien, for you were aliens in the land of Egypt" (Exod 23:9).

THE SCOPE OF MODERN SLAVERY

Issued annually by the U.S. State Department, the Trafficking in Persons ("TIP") Report assesses both the scope of human trafficking worldwide and the effectiveness of responses by each nation during the previous year. The June 2012 TIP Report noted that a study conducted that same year by the International Labor Association conservatively places the number of modern slavery victims at almost twenty-one million persons.[5] Of this total, approximately 11.7 million victims are exploited in the Asia and Pacific region, another 3.7 million in Africa, 1.8 million in Latin America and the Caribbean, 1.6 million in central and southeastern Europe, and 1.5 million in Western Europe and North America.[6] The ILO study cited by the State Department further underscores the particular vulnerability of women and children to exploitation by human traffickers: the ILO estimates that women and girls constitute 55 percent of all forced labor victims throughout the world and 98 percent of all sex trafficking victims.[7] For its own part, the U.S. government since 2005 has consistently estimated that as many as fourteen thousand five hundred to seventeen thousand five hundred international victims cross U.S. borders every year and encounter a variety of modern slavery conditions.[8] Even allowing for statistical variations in different estimates, the dimensions of the modern slavery crisis are staggering.

VARIED WORLD RESPONSES

At the time that the bishops issued *Strangers No Longer* in 2003, there was growing recognition of this modern human rights crisis. The United Nations had in 2000 adopted the "Protocol to Prevent, Suppress, and Punish Trafficking in Persons, Especially Women and Children" (often referred to as the Palermo Protocol). That same year, the United States enacted landmark legislation—The Trafficking Victim Protection Act—that proved to be a sea change in how trafficking would be defined and prosecuted within the U.S. legal system and how the rights of victims of modern slavery would be protected under U.S. law. By 2003, trafficking as a "sign of the times" had already begun to lay claim to the legal and moral attention of the world community.

But even as trafficking was increasingly recognized as a worldwide pandemic, the responses by the international community proved greatly varied in both scope and effectiveness. International law that evolved regarding trafficking—the Palermo Protocol—addressed trafficking as a transnational criminal issue.[9] Formulated in the decade after the fall of the Berlin Wall, the Palermo Protocol recognized the confluence of trafficking in persons with a global rise in organized crime. International leaders accurately perceived that transnational smuggling of persons was increasingly becoming the purview of organized crime rings as well as the context in which much human trafficking was flourishing. The United Nations therefore focused its initial anti-trafficking efforts on the goal of effecting the worldwide criminalization of human trafficking, eliminating national "safe harbors" where traffickers could operate with impunity or launder the financial proceeds of trafficking conspiracies.[10]

Drafted as an addition to the broader UN "Convention on Transnational Organized Crime," the Palermo Protocol sought to elicit the support of as broad a coalition of sovereign nations as possible. Achieving such international consensus necessitated an approach that would entail a relatively low threshold of legal obligation on the part of signatory countries. The result was an international legal instrument that obligated countries to criminalize trafficking but merely recommended that countries provide protection and services to victims.[11]

This approach by the international community was not without logic or effectiveness: the UN Protocol quickly garnered the support of the requisite forty nations and by 2002 had entered into force. Among its considerable achievements, the Palermo Protocol established an internationally accepted definition of trafficking and largely achieved its goal of criminalizing trafficking worldwide. Important as it is, the Palermo Protocol nonetheless contains inherent limitations as a legal paradigm because it characterizes trafficking primarily as an issue of criminality and border security. The failure of the Protocol to obligate signatory countries to provide victim care or protection remains a significant gap in the international legal model.

The Trafficking Victim Protection Act ("TVPA") of 2000 incorporated a more comprehensive approach on the part of the United States toward combating the modern trafficking of persons. The TVPA not only greatly enhanced U.S. criminal penalties for trafficking, but furthermore established a new range of rights and remedies under U.S. law for trafficking victims.[12] In so doing, the United States created a legal model that over a decade later still sets the standard for integrating prosecutorial tools with victim remedies. Since the enactment of the TVPA, immigrant survivors of trafficking have been accorded victim status under U.S. law, even when they have engaged in unlawful activities such as prostitution or are illegally present in the United States. Moreover, immigrants certified as "victims of a severe form of trafficking" are eligible for the same benefits given refugees, including social services, job training, and a new "T" visa designed for foreign national trafficking victims who are undocumented.

Notwithstanding the fact that the TVPA establishes a "victim-centered" legal approach, it nonetheless still operates from a prosecutorial framework. Federal law enforcement officials control the issuance of temporary legal status ("Continued Presence") to victims when they are initially encountered, and likewise provide the endorsement that is the standard route to ultimately obtaining the T visa. Federal benefits and immigration relief remain largely contingent upon a victim's willingness to cooperate with law enforcement officials. The sole exception allowed is for minors, who are eligible for victim designation and benefits without the obligation of cooperating with law enforcement. Though the TVPA clearly evinces strong human rights sensibilities, it ultimately retains a prosecutorial framework. It would be most accurate to characterize it as a legal approach that is law

197

enforcement-focused while providing incidental human rights benefits to a select number of victims.

A DISTINCTLY CATHOLIC CONTRIBUTION

In contrast to both international and U.S. law, the approach of the Catholic Church to human trafficking is one in which human rights and victim concerns predominate. The Church's response to human trafficking is grounded in its article of faith which holds that all human beings are created in the image and likeness of God and are therefore imbued with fundamental dignity. Human trafficking, as the bishops emphasized in *Strangers No Longer*, "inherently rejects the dignity of the human person" (SNL 90).

The Church's pronouncements on the evil of human trafficking constantly underscore that modern slavery constitutes an affront to human dignity—and to the God who is the very source and guarantor of that dignity:

> The seventh commandment forbids acts or enterprises that for any reason—selfish or ideological, commercial, or totalitarian—lead to the enslavement of human beings, to their being bought, sold and exchanged like merchandise, in disregard for their personal dignity. It is a sin against the dignity of persons and their fundamental rights to reduce them by violence to their productive value or to a source of profit. (CCC 2414)

> [W]hatever insults human dignity, such as subhuman living conditions, arbitrary imprisonment, deportation, slavery, prostitution, the selling of women and children; as well as disgraceful working conditions, where men are treated as mere tools for profit, rather than as free and responsible persons; all these things others of their like are infamies indeed. They poison human society, but they do more harm to those who practice them than those who suffer from the injury. Moreover, they are a supreme dishonor to the Creator. (GS 27)

The trade in human persons constitutes a shocking offense against human dignity and a grave violation of fundamental human rights....Such situations are an affront to fundamental values which are shared by all cultures and peoples, values rooted in the very nature of the human person.[13]

Human trafficking is a horrific crime against the basic dignity and rights of the human person. All efforts must be expended to end it. In the end, we must work together—Church, state, and community—to eliminate the root causes and markets that permit traffickers to flourish; to make whole the survivors of this crime; and to ensure that, one day soon, trafficking in human persons vanishes from the face of the earth. (OHT)

The response of the Church to human trafficking has been critical in numerous respects. The theological framework of the Church's approach is at once both broader and deeper than those employed in international law or domestic U.S. law. Distinct from international law, the Church does not narrowly define trafficking as an organized crime problem or a border security issue. Repeatedly the Church has insisted that trafficking must be eradicated by eliminating the root causes that engender it. The U.S. Catholic bishops have noted:

Survivors of human trafficking are commonly linked by poverty and lack of opportunity. They are also connected by their desperation and their perception of migration as an accessible escape route. Often they seek to escape life in an oppressive slum, with the hope of finding opportunity and a brighter future elsewhere. (OHT)

The analysis of the Church likewise addresses both elements of the "push-pull" dynamic that accounts for modern slavery. In addition to a critique of the "push" factors that lead to trafficking (the circumstances that persuade persons to undertake risky immigration options), Catholic teachings also decry the "pull" factor of demand—the markets that allow trafficking to flourish. The U.S. Catholic bishops have reiterated:

199

Combined with...economic root causes is a demand in developed nations for the services of the sex trade and forced labor. Human trafficking will never be truly defeated without eliminating the consumerism which feeds it, and prosecuting those actors in receiving countries, including our own, that benefit because of the exploitation of vulnerable human beings. (OHT)

The Church's approach to combating human trafficking draws not only on its foundational belief in the sacredness of the human being, but also on the traditional tenet of Catholic social teaching that poverty and inequality must be eradicated for there to be genuine justice. Human trafficking, in the analysis and teaching of the Church, is not merely a crime or a threat to the sovereignty of national borders. It is rather a symptom of more profound causational evils. This analysis of human trafficking offers a depth and consistency that international law cannot match.

Neither does the Church prioritize criminal prosecution over victim care, as U.S. law still does by legislative design. Concern for victims has been the hallmark of the Church's response to modern trafficking. While a strong supporter of the Trafficking Victims Protection Act of 2000, the U.S. Conference of Catholic Bishops has nonetheless repeatedly advocated for changes to U.S. law that will remedy the gaps inherent in the TVPA's prosecutorial emphasis.

In this respect, the Church has exercised special concern for child trafficking victims. Congressional testimony in 2004 by Sister Mary Ellen Dougherty, a member of the Bishops' Office for Migration and Refugee Services, underscored the need for U.S. law to better recognize the particular vulnerabilities of child victims. The decision making process regarding child victims, declared Sister Dougherty, should always include the use of the "best interest of the child" standard, should offer an immediate safe haven, in the least restrictive setting possible, and should provide special care for the child's physical and emotional needs.[14]

Other concerns of the Church regarding the U.S. anti-trafficking statutory model include issues of victim identification, victim care, and better training of both federal and local law enforcement.[15] The USCCB has noted how current U.S. methods of victim identification and referral are unrealistically restrictive, vesting exclusive authority in the hands of law enforcement officials. Observing that relatively few victims of trafficking have been identified under this legal scheme, the bishops have urged that non-governmental child welfare agencies and social service providers also be empowered to officially refer victims to the U.S. Department of Health and Human Services (HHS) for help.[16] The bishops have likewise recommended that greater education and guidance be provided to federal and local law enforcement agencies so that victims do not go unrecognized, or worse, are detained as criminals or deported.[17]

Finally, the relatively short window of federally funded victim care has also claimed the attention of the Church. Noting the extended effects of trauma upon survivors of trafficking, the USCCB has called for more funding to be allocated for long-term victim care. The bishops have declared: "[t]rafficking victims, traumatized by their experience, require comprehensive care, not just emergency assistance and help in finding a job."[18]

The public witness of the Church on behalf of trafficking victims has been comprehensive and steadfast. USCCB testimony before Congress has underscored this foundational concern: "It is important to note...that all of our training and education is directed toward one end: the best interest of the victims."[19] In this regard, Catholic teachings offer a vital corrective to U.S. law, which ultimately embodies a decidedly instrumental approach to victim care: U.S. trafficking remedies and benefits are chiefly reserved for victims willing to assist law enforcement in the prosecution of traffickers. The approach of the Church is fundamentally different, centered as it is upon the well-being and recovery of all those exploited by modern slavery. Insistent that a society is measured by the manner in which it treats its most vulnerable members, Catholic teachings comprise a "victim-centered approach" toward human trafficking that surpasses even claims of the U.S. legal system to the same.

THE CHURCH IN THE WORLD: A CATHOLIC CALL TO ACTION

The commitment of the Church to eradicating trafficking has not been confined to theological pronouncements or to public testimony before Congress—it has been embraced as a constitutive element of the

Church's mission in the world. A "Coalition of Catholic Organizations Against Human Trafficking" has emerged to meet the needs of trafficking victims worldwide, to foster an empowerment approach to victim care, and to promote dialogue with the government officials tasked with addressing trafficking as a public policy issue. More than twenty Catholic organizations currently make up the coalition, including Catholic Relief Services, the Catholic Health Association, the Conference of Major Superiors of Men, the Leadership Conference of Women Religious, Jesuit Refugee Services, the National Council of Catholic Women, Covenant House, and many others. This coalition not only makes the resources of the Catholic Church directly available to victims of trafficking, but also brings Catholic international leadership to the twenty-first-century abolition movement.

Much as they have done on countless other peace and justice issues, Catholic women religious have assumed a leading role in the anti-trafficking movement. In 2009, representatives from over two hundred fifty orders of women religious met in Rome at the invitation of the International Union of Superiors General and the International Organization for Migration (IOM). The women religious established a new international network called "Talita Kum" (Aramaic for "Get Up") to coordinate and support the anti-trafficking work pursued by their respective orders throughout the world.[20] The grassroots work of this coalition includes not only direct victim care, but also broad-based educational and advocacy efforts. Sister Eugenia Bonetti, one of the leaders of women religious in Italy, noted that "traffickers are organized on a transnational level and we must do the same in order to fight them."[21] The Vatican hailed the efforts of the women religious, describing them as not only important, but prophetic.[22]

U.S. women religious have done groundbreaking work of their own to combat trafficking. The Sisters of the Divine Savior distribute an electronic newsletter entitled "Stop Trafficking." Co-sponsored by over sixty women's religious communities, the newsletter provides updates on international trafficking trends, exchanges best practices in advocacy and victim empowerment care models, and highlights the collaborative anti-trafficking work being undertaken worldwide by Catholic religious women.[23] Importantly, it also explores ways in which religious congregations and collaborators can take a corporate stance as investors against human trafficking.[24]

Catholic women's religious communities have played an especially vital role in countering sex trafficking. Numerous congregations have opened shelters to provide safety and care to women and children exploited in commercial sex conspiracies.[25] Yet other congregations have engaged in public advocacy to ensure that international sporting events such as the Olympic Games and World Cup do not become lucrative venues for pimps and sex traffickers.[26] Aware that such sexual exploitation is not endemic to international sports events alone, women's religious orders from Indiana and Michigan joined together to combat sex trafficking at the 2012 Super Bowl in Indianapolis. Working to help the hospitality industry recognize potential indicators of forced prostitution, the women religious delivered trafficking awareness materials to over two hundred hotels within a fifty-mile radius of the Super Bowl.[27] Clearly, no small part of the Catholic mission to abolish modern slavery has been undertaken by the Church's women religious.

For its part, the institutional Catholic Church in the United States has played its own critical role in combating human trafficking. Positioned as few other faith communities might be by virtue of its organizational structure and geographical reach, the U.S. Catholic Church early on assumed a strong leadership role in the American anti-trafficking movement. In 2006, the U.S. Department of Health and Human Services (HHS) awarded a five-year, $33.9 million contract to the U.S. Catholic Conference of Bishops/Migration and Refugee Services to administer social services to foreign-born victims of human trafficking identified in the United States.

The work that USCCB/MRS undertook on this grant was lauded for both the comprehensive victim care it provided and the ecumenical, collaborative nature of the program's administration. Since 2002, MRS provided care to nearly two thousand seven hundred victims of trafficking, from multiple foreign countries. MRS did so by subcontracting with a host of service providers, public and private, Catholic and non-Catholic alike, from a wide spectrum of U.S. civil society. Subcontractor partners included faith-based groups; refugee resettlement and immigrant advocacy groups; organizations serving survivors of domestic violence, sexual assault, and torture; and numerous community-based social service agencies.[28] The program established by USCCB/MRS proved a model not only of broad-based human rights collaboration, but also of tremendously effective partnering between faith-based groups and government in serving the needs of modern slavery victims.

An especially key subcontractor was Catholic Charities USA, whose 140 local U.S. offices provided an important point of contact with victims nationwide. With a well-established history of service to immigrants and other at-risk populations, Catholic Charities was ideally situated to offer intensive case management and legal assistance to foreign national survivors of trafficking. The model of care promoted by USCCB/MRS was a holistic one, and sought to aid trafficking survivors as they navigated the complex U.S. legal and social service systems. Support made available to survivors in this case management model included assistance with safe housing, provision of food and clothing, as well as medical and mental health services, and job skills training.

In what proved to be a very controversial decision, political appointees in the Department of Health and Human Services elected not to renew the USCCB/MRS grant when it expired in 2011, on the grounds that the Church refused to offer referrals for contraception or abortions.[29] Shortly thereafter, a federal district court ruled that the Catholic bishops could not use taxpayer money to impose their beliefs on others who might or might not share such beliefs.[30] Curiously, the lawsuit was not brought by survivors of trafficking, and service providers nationwide have reported very few requests by trafficking victims for abortion referrals. Regrettably then, the U.S. politics of abortion sufficed to displace a grantee that had achieved a "superior track record" of trafficking victim care.[31]

Church efforts to combat human trafficking are of course not confined to federal grant-funded work. In testimony to long-standing Catholic support for the principle of subsidiarity, local U.S. dioceses and state bishops' conferences have sponsored a host of anti-trafficking initiatives. One such signature initiative was undertaken by the Florida Catholic Conference of Bishops in 2009. Under the leadership of then Bishop Thomas Wenski of the Diocese of Orlando and Bishop Frank Dewane of the Diocese of Venice, the Florida Catholic Conference launched a statewide Catholic anti-trafficking program.[32]

Centering their efforts on a public awareness campaign, the Conference designed and piloted a Catholic human trafficking curriculum that was distributed to Florida's more than five hundred parish communities. The Conference also created a short video entitled "Invisible Chains" meant to engage the Catholic community in victim identification as well as prevention efforts. Finally, the bishops convened Catholic leaders statewide, forming an Ad Hoc Committee on Human Trafficking Awareness to begin outreach to Mass-going Catholics, Catholic health care organizations, and Catholic educators. Florida Catholics engaged in this faith-based initiative went on to work with state law enforcement officials, assisted the Florida Legislature in drafting new anti-trafficking laws, and swelled the ranks of a growing number of anti-trafficking coalitions statewide.

NEXT STEPS

A decade after the issuance of *Strangers No Longer*, and a dozen years after the adoption of the Palermo Protocol and the enactment of the Trafficking Victim Protection Act, the Catholic Church remains a key stakeholder in the anti-trafficking field. Pre-eminent among U.S. faith-based communities for its direct victim care, the American Church continues to place a very high priority on its anti-trafficking social justice mission.

The public witness of the Church likewise remains more essential than ever on this twenty-first–century human rights issue. Recent years have witnessed the emergence of a host of competing ideologies regarding the phenomenon of human trafficking. The faith-based, human rights framework of the Church's response constitutes a much-needed corrective to excesses and biases inherent in a number of the emerging anti-trafficking ideologies. As mentioned previously, the Church's response far transcends the organized crime and border security paradigm embodied by international law and the Palermo Protocol. So too does it offer a more consistent and less instrumental protection model for trafficking survivors than that established under the TVPA.

In an era of heightened xenophobia and increasingly anti-immigrant state laws such as Arizona's SB 1070, the immigration context of the Church's response to trafficking has also assumed renewed importance. Concern for the immigrant and for the vulnerabilities of immigrant populations are traditional core values of Catholic social teaching. So too is the Church's longstanding insistence that all people of good will "welcome the stranger" in their midst. One of the anomalies of the current wave of legislative restrictionism toward immigrants—and in particular the host of new anti-immigrant state laws—is that such laws represent the very antithesis of lessons learned by the anti-trafficking movement. At the same time that U.S. federal law has ushered in groundbreaking change by mandating that undocumented trafficking victims not be treated as lawbreakers, individual states increasingly characterize undocumented immigrants as "criminals." As the Church reminds us in *Strangers No Longer*,

> Part of the process of conversion of mind and heart deals with confronting attitudes of cultural superiority, indifference, and racism; accepting migrants not as foreboding aliens, terrorists, or economic threats, but rather as persons with dignity and rights, revealing the presence of Christ. (40)

The immigrant advocacy so central to the Catholic mission in the world will remain a vital dimension of the Church's contribution to global anti-trafficking efforts. But it will be equally incumbent upon the Church to more explicitly note in its teachings that human trafficking is not endemic to the world of immigration, nor does it require border crossings. While smuggling is defined under law as a crime against the borders of sovereign nations, human trafficking is a far more basic crime perpetrated against an individual that requires no movement of any kind. The insistence of the Trafficking Victim Protection Act on this point would be a useful and indeed much-needed addition to the Church's immigration-oriented approach.

Needless to say, Church teachings on human trafficking have not been confined to its international or immigrant dimension, and neither has the pastoral care of the Church been limited to foreign national victims.[33] Recent years have been marked by a growing awareness that the largest group of trafficking victims in the United States is comprised not of foreign nationals but rather of U.S. citizens—the vast majority of them U.S. minors caught up in the commercial sex industry. Shared Hope International estimates that as many as a hundred thousand U.S. citizen children—primarily runaway and "throwaway" children—are induced to participate in commercial sex annually.[34]

Equally sobering is the fact that such children are typically "groomed" by pimps for commercial sexual exploitation. The non-governmental Polaris Project estimates that the average age of entry into prostitution in the United States is now between twelve and fourteen years of age.[35]

This aspect of human trafficking alone constitutes a grave moral crisis of epidemic proportions. Here too Church expertise on empowerment models of victim care has an important role to play in this newest chapter of anti-trafficking work. Once again, Catholic women's religious communities have stepped forward to open shelters for girls and women exploited for prostitution.[36] Catholic Charities has also initiated residential-based programs meant to offer women the opportunity to exit "the life" of prostitution. As non-judgmental caregivers, Catholic advocates have important work ahead of them.

At an even more basic level, Catholic moral theology has renewed relevance in a contentious debate that has come to divide the anti-trafficking movement. Strongly held and diametrically opposed opinions have emerged regarding the question of whether all prostitution should in fact be defined as sex trafficking. This debate centers around the issue of consent that in legal terms distinguishes voluntary prostitution from involuntary sex trafficking. One school of thought, termed the abolitionist school, contends that all prostitution is inherently exploitative and is something to which few women can give meaningful consent.[37] As one abolitionist advocate emphasizes, "[i]nstead of the question 'did [a woman] voluntarily consent to prostitution?' the more relevant question would be 'did she have real alternatives to prostitution for survival?' "[38] Such an approach accurately captures the reality that an overwhelming majority of women engaged in commercial sex wish to leave it and yet are unable to do so. It also recognizes the myriad abuses and dehumanizing violence typically suffered by women participating in prostitution. Where the approach is on less certain ground is in its corollary insistence that consent to prostitution by women is not truly possible, the implication being that all prostitution therefore comprises sex trafficking.[39]

It is this corollary of the abolitionist argument that most deeply offends what has been termed the autonomy or "prostitution as labor" school of thought. This competing ideology, consistent with liberal feminist thinking, insists that the abolitionist approach infantilizes women with its core claim that women as responsible adults are inca-

pable of consenting to commercial sex. The autonomy school of thinking holds that prostitution represents not only a choice but even a valid
choice for adult women.[40] To decree that women cannot make such a
choice, the autonomy school holds, necessarily reduces women to a
condition of objects rather than agents. Prostitution, according to this
line of thinking, is an exercise of agency on the part of women and
comprises a right that cannot be denied them. The debate engendered
by these two competing schools of thinking has proved acrimonious,
engendering far more heat than light. It has furthermore served to
divide advocates in the anti-trafficking movement worldwide, at the
very moment that human trafficking continues to proliferate.

The time-honed sensibilities of Catholic ethics teachings have an
important role to play in restoring moral perspective to this debate.
While regarding prostitution and forced prostitution as grave moral
disorders, the Church does not become lost in the quagmire of the
consent issue. Rejecting a completely deterministic sense of human
existence, the Catholic worldview begins with the foundational notion
that humans are agents with free will. Church teachings recognize that
at times, the human exercise of free will may lead to sin. People can,
and do, make poor choices; prostitution is arguably one such choice.
But Catholic teachings, while recognizing agency on the part of
women, would nonetheless find the "right" to engage in prostitution to
be an impoverished and dubious one at best. Yet if there is condemnation therein, Catholic teachings reserve such for the sin rather than the
sinner.

Neither does the Church place the blame for the commercial sex
trade on the shoulders of women engaged in it. Quite the opposite is
true: Catholic ethics decry the demand side of prostitution and the culture of sexual permissiveness that informs it. Church teachings have
always been clear that those who purchase sex are equally degraded by
the transaction and equally responsible for it as a moral offense. And it
is the Catholic Christian notion of sin and redemption—and the constant call for human conversion—that allows the Church to oppose
prostitution not only as personal sin but social sin as well. The individuals who are party to commercial sex, and the larger society that
enables their sin, all stand in need of conversion.

Here the consistency and the time-tested instincts of Catholic
moral theology bring an important balance to a debate that continues

to balkanize the anti-trafficking movement. The strength of the Catholic ethics model is that it does not privilege consent but neither does it eradicate it entirely. This "moral balancing" is much needed in the modern anti-trafficking field, divided as it has been by certain ideological extremes.

Catholic moral sensibilities are equally important to other areas of the modern anti-trafficking agenda. The Church has been emphatic that labor trafficking as well as sex trafficking must be vigorously opposed, even while the media evinces a predilection for more sensationalist sex trafficking cases. Catholic championing of the rights and dignity of immigrant trafficking victims will also be increasingly important in an era of anti-immigrant public discourse. Church attention to the vulnerability of unaccompanied migrant children to human trafficking is particularly important, and continues to be a hallmark of Catholic teaching and pastoral ministry.[41]

So too should the Church continue its advocacy and outreach to U.S. citizen trafficking victims, especially American children exploited in domestic minor sex trafficking. Finally, the Catholic critique of the systemic roots of human trafficking—poverty, institutionalized violence, lack of educational opportunities for girls and women—is likewise important for continuing to target the underlying causes of trafficking that even vigorous prosecutions and empathetic victim care cannot hope to redress.

CONCLUSION

The significance of *Strangers No Longer* remains ongoing a decade after its landmark publication. The decision of the Catholic bishops of Mexico and the United States at that time to jointly address urgent common social issues still constitutes an important precedent. Such a precedent could be repeated and even expanded to now address international human trafficking. Drawing on the collaborative model of *Strangers No Longer*, bishops' conferences of both source and destination countries for human trafficking worldwide should consider convening in order to coordinate the education and advocacy efforts of their respective sees. If human trafficking is indeed the dark underside of globalization, the united efforts of the global Catholic community will be an important countervailing force.

Such efforts on the part of the Catholic community transcend mere obligations of charity. Pope Benedict XVI, in his first encyclical *God Is Love* (*Deus Caritas Est*) reiterated that welcoming the stranger is indeed welcoming Christ himself. Benedict reminded the faithful that "love of God and love of neighbor have become one; in the least of the brethren we find Jesus himself, and in Jesus we find God (DCE 15). As Church teachings make clear, twenty-first–century Catholics may well encounter the living God in the faces of brothers and sisters exploited by human trafficking.

NOTES

1. Kevin Bales, *Disposable People: New Slavery in the Global Economy* (Berkeley, CA: University of California Press, 2004), 8.

2. Benjamin Skinner, *A Crime So Monstrous: Face to Face with Modern Day Slavery* (New York: Free Press, 2008), xv.

3. It was the memory of enslavement that informed the core ethical prescriptions of the Hebrew people: "You shall not deprive a resident alien or an orphan of justice; you shall not take a widow's garment in pledge. Remember that you were a slave in Egypt and the Lord your God redeemed you from there; therefore I command you to do this. When you reap your harvest in your field and forget a sheaf in the field, you shall not go back to get it; it shall be left for the alien, the orphan, and the widow, so that the Lord your God may bless you in all your undertakings. When you beat your olive trees, do not strip what is left; it shall be for the alien, the orphan, and the widow. When you gather the grapes of your vineyard, do not glean what is left; it shall be for the alien, the orphan, and the widow. Remember that you were a slave in the land of Egypt; therefore I am commanding you to do this" (Deut 24:17–22).

4. Scripture scholars have noted that even the original connotation of the term *Israelite* may have referred to persons rendered vulnerable as a result of being "aliens" living far from any homeland: "The word 'Israelite'…has various meanings in the Bible, but originally it stood somewhat vaguely for a blending of various peoples whose only common bond consisted in their status (of lack of status) as refugees,

resident aliens, and dispossessed people uprooted from their homeland and frequently at the mercy of the local residents or landlords," Donald Senior and Carroll Stuhlmueller, *The Biblical Foundations For Mission* (Maryknoll, NY: Orbis Books, 1983), 56.

5. U.S. State Department, *2012 Trafficking in Persons Report* (Washington, DC: U.S. State Department), 45.

6. Ibid.

7. Ibid.

8. Heather Clausen, Mary Lane and Kevonne Small, "Estimating Human Trafficking into the United States: Development of a Methodology" (Washington, DC: U.S. Department of Justice, 2006), 3.

9. For an overview of the Palermo Protocol and its parent treaty, the Convention Against Transnational Organized Crime, see Anne Gallagher, "Human Rights and the New UN Protocols on Trafficking and Migrant Smuggling: A Preliminary Analysis," *Human Rights Quarterly* 23 (2001): 975–1004.

10. Ibid., 978.

11. Ibid., 990.

12. See Victims of Trafficking and Violence Protection Act of 2000, Pub. L. No. 106–386, 114 Stat. 1464 (Division A). The TVPA also established anti-trafficking efforts as a major foreign policy objective.

13. Pope John Paul II, Letter to Archbishop Jean-Louis Tauran on the Occasion of the International Conference on Twenty-first Century Slavery, May 15, 2002.

14. Testimony of Sister Mary Ellen Dougherty, Migration and Refugee Services/U.S. Conference of Catholic Bishops, before the Senate Subcommittee on the Constitution, Civil Rights, and Property Rights, July 7, 2004.

15. Testimony of Anastasia K. Brown, Migration and Refugee Services/U.S. Conference of Catholic Bishops, before the House Committee on the Judiciary, October 31, 2007.

16. Ibid.

17. Ibid.

18. Ibid.

19. Ibid.

20. Cindy Wooden, "Women Religious to Combat Human Trafficking," *Catholic News Service* (June 19, 2009).

21. Ibid.

22. Ibid.

23. See http://www.stopenslavement.org.

24. Ibid., "Corporate Stance," listing religious congregations that have utilized their power as investors to combat human trafficking.

25. See Zoe Ryan, "Visibility Aids the Fight Against Human Trafficking," *National Catholic Reporter* (July 11, 2011).

26. Cindy Wooden, "Women Religious to Combat Human Trafficking for 2010 Sporting Events," *Catholic News Service*, June 19, 2009 (describing efforts of Catholic women religious to combat sex trafficking at the 2010 Winter Olympic Games in Vancouver and the 2010 World Cup in South Africa).

27. Mark Pattison, "Women Religious Work to Ward Off Sex Trafficking at Super Bowl," *Catholic Free Press* (January 19, 2012).

28. Migration and Refugee Services/United States Conference of Catholic Bishops, "Reflections: HHS Service Mechanism for Foreign National Survivors of Human Trafficking" (Washington, DC: USCCB, 2010), 2–5.

29. Jerry Markon, "Abortion, Birth Control Access At Issue in Dispute Over Denial of Grant to Catholic Group," *Washington Post* (November 11, 2011).

30. American Civil Liberties Union of Massachusetts v. Kathleen Sebelius, U.S. District Court, District of Massachusetts (March 23, 2012).

31. Comments of Representative Christopher Smith, author of the TVPA, quoted in "Catholic Human Trafficking Outreach Lost," *Catholic News Agency* (November 11, 2011).

32. http://www.flaccb.org/HumanTrafficking; see also "Florida Catholics United Against Human Trafficking," *Catholic Health World* (February 1, 2011).

33. It was rather limitations imposed by U.S. federal funding sources that were responsible for the focus on immigrant victim care in the HHS grant to USCCB/MRS from 2006 to 2011.

34. Linda Smith, Samantha Healy Vardaman and Melissa Snow, *The National Report on Domestic Minor Sex Trafficking: America's*

Prostituted Children (Vancouver, WA: Shared Hope International, 2009), 4.

35. Statistics Snapshot, Polaris Project website on Human Trafficking, http://www.polarisproject.org/human-trafficking/sex-trafficking-in-the-us/street-prostitution.

36. One example of this anti-trafficking ministry is a shelter for U.S. citizen survivors of sex trafficking that was established by Franciscan Sisters in Tiffin, Ohio in 2008. The shelter offers survivors not only a secure residence but also health care services, social services, GED assistance, and child care help. Zoe Ryan, "Visibility Aids the Fight Against Human Trafficking," *National Catholic Reporter* (July 11, 2011).

37. See Jayashri Srikantiah, "Perfect Victims and Real Survivors: The Iconic Victim in Domestic Human Trafficking Law," 87 *B.U.L. Rev.* 194 (2007).

38. Melissa Farley, *Prostitution, Trafficking, and Traumatic Stress* (New York: Haworth Maltreatment and Trauma Press, 2003), 65.

39. See Terry Coonan, "Anatomy of A Sex Trafficking Case," *Intercultural Human Rights Law Review* 5 (2010), 349–55. U.S. law takes the position that not all prostitution is sex trafficking, but that prostitution becomes trafficking when a participant's consent is nullified through force, fraud, or coercion.

40. See Susan E. Thompson, "Prostitution: A Choice Ignored," *Women's Rts. L. Rep.* 21 (2001), 217 (summarizing arguments that prostitution represents a valid choice for women absent elements of force or coercion).

41. The Church has served as one of the leading voices in U.S. public discourse regarding the rights and vulnerabilities of child trafficking victims. See, e.g., *Unaccompanied Migrant Children and Victims of Human Trafficking on the US/Mexico Border*, USCCB, 2006 Report.

CHAPTER 9

Refugees: Working for More Generous, Just, and Humane Policies

Maryann Cusimano Love

MORE GENEROUS, JUST, AND HUMANE POLICY

Jesus, Mary, and Joseph were refugees, as noted in *Strangers No Longer: Together on the Journey of Hope.* The Holy Family left Palestine in the dead of night with nothing but the clothes on their backs. In the words of international law, they were fleeing a well-founded fear of persecution for reasons of religion, nationality, race, membership of a particular social group, or political opinion, were outside their country of origin and unable to return.[1] The oppressive regime was already killing infants in the region, and the Holy Family was lucky to escape with their lives across the border into neighboring Egypt. After the harrowing exodus, the Gospels offer no details of Christ's early years as a Palestinian Christian refugee in Egypt. But life in limbo could not have been easy, separated from family and friends, from Joseph's carpentry work in Nazareth, from their faith community, and the world they knew and loved, worrying when and if they ever would be able to return home.

This is the fate of modern holy families today. Recognizing Christ in the faces of people on the move, the Catholic Church takes a distinctive approach to issues of refugees, religious persecution, and migrants. Unlike many human rights and international refugee groups, the Church advocates and serves not only those who meet the international law criteria of refugees, but all types of people on the move (including internally displaced persons, climate change refugees, and other migrants), because of the imperative to protect the human life and dignity of all. As noted in *Strangers No Longer*, the Church takes a holistic approach marked by accompaniment and solidarity across time, distance, and a variety of issues affecting people on the move. The public policy of the Catholic Church is to advocate for, serve and protect migrants at origin, in transit, and at destinations; to develop collaborative responses among governments and intergovernmental organizations and local faith communities on both sides of borders; to address the underlying root causes of migration; to create legal avenues for migrants; to legalize those already undocumented persons; and to unite families, protecting women and minors.[2] Rather than only working reactively, to accompany and serve refugees and migrants after they are displaced, Catholic organizations work proactively, to build peace, end violence, protect the environment, and develop economic opportunities, so that people will not be pushed out of their home communities by political and economic strife. This end-to-end, holistic and humane approach is quite different than the much narrower advocacy, services, and issue area.

NEVER AGAIN, ONCE AGAIN

Current U.S. and international refugee policies were a reaction to the legacy of the Holocaust and the Second World War. On May 13, 1939, the *SS St. Louis* passenger ship set sail from Hamburg, Germany. Nine hundred of its 937 passengers were German Jews fleeing Hitler's Nazi regime to join relatives or start new lives in the Americas. But when the ship arrived in Havana, the Cuban government refused entry to the passengers. The captain then sailed the ship to Florida, but the U.S. government also refused to admit the refugees; the Coast Guard even fired a warning shot to turn the ship away from the U.S. coastline. The ship's passengers, dubbed "the Voyage of the Damned," then appealed to other countries to save them from the certain death awaiting should they be returned to Nazi Germany. Belgium, Holland, France, and England eventually admitted the refugees, but the first three countries were overrun by the Nazis within months. The St. Louis passengers died in the Holocaust along with other European Jews who were unable to escape. Only the few passengers admitted into England survived.

After the Nazi regime's ouster and the end of World War II, memory of the Holocaust galvanized international human rights groups. The establishment of the Universal Declaration of Human Rights, the International Convention to Prevent Genocide, and the United Nations High Commissioner for Refugees were all informed by the Holocaust and the motto "Never again."[3] The 1951 UN Convention on Refugees' definition of a refugee as any person who "owing to well-founded fear of being persecuted for reasons of race, religion, nationality, membership in a particular social group, or political opinion, is outside the country of his nationality, and is unable to return to it," becomes more understandable in the context of the Holocaust. Had this treaty been in force before World War II, the thinking went, countries would not have been allowed to turn away Jews fleeing Nazi persecution. People fleeing persecution, refugees, ought to be allowed protected status and not be forcibly returned to their home countries and the peril that awaits them there. In the United States, Eleanor Roosevelt led these post-war human rights reforms. The United States is one of 134 countries who are bound by this law to accept refugees and not forcibly return them. For years, the United States has been a leader in refugee resettlement, admitting 2.6 million refugees since 1975, and encouraging other countries to follow our example of promising to admit 70,000 refugees into the country each year.

Although the 1951 Convention has helped some, many more migrants are not covered by these norms. Women fleeing violence, people fleeing natural disasters and climate change, internally displaced persons, and people fleeing conflict who cannot claim asylum status because they are not part of a group protected by the 1951 Convention, are not recognized by current refugee law and international regimes. They are recognized by the Catholic Church, however, who works for all people on the move.

Unfortunately, despite pledges of "never again," war criminals have conducted genocides and crimes against humanity since 1951, in places as diverse as Sudan, the former Republic of Yugoslavia, Rwanda, and the Democratic Republic of Congo. Countries have often stood silent before genocide, and failed to prevent, block, or bring to justice genocidal leaders. And countries have closed borders, failing to allow people to flee across borders in search of greater safety and freedom. Of people who make it across an international border, most refugees stay in the neighborhood, just beyond the border; 75 percent of refugees live in neighboring countries. Pakistan, Syria, and Iran receive most of the world's refugees from neighboring conflicts. Eighty percent of receiving countries are developing countries, and in these poor countries, refugees face growing poverty, loss of culture, hopelessness, and despair.

Many more never make it across the border. IDPs (internally displaced persons, who have not crossed an international border) outnumber refugees about two to one. Originally with a mandate to serve only refugees, in 1992 the UN extended the UN High Commission on Refugees organization's mission to also serve IDPs in response to the war in Bosnia Herzegovina. Francis Deng (a Sudanese Catholic) was appointed as the Representative on Internally Displaced Persons. This decision heralded the beginning of a new era in which the UNHCR's mandate of assisting and protecting refugees was expanded to include IDPs. Most IDPs reside in Sudan, Colombia, Iraq, the Democratic Republic of Congo, and Somalia.[4]

Decisions concerning refugee and IDP policies are largely decided by individual states. Globalization has led to legal harmonization and liberalization of policies regarding the international movement of products, capital, ideas, and information across borders. And while globalization has made transportation and communication for the movement of people across borders easier than ever before in practice, globalization has not led to harmonized or liberalized legal policies allowing free movements of people across borders. The current form of globalization puts profits before people, creating better systems for products and cash to move across international borders than for people to make similar moves.

The Catholic Church instead advocates to put people before profits in global systems, using globalization to pursue more authentic and holistic human development. The Church ministers to the refugees, IDPs, and victims of violence in all those conflicts, but the Church has also not restricted itself to the narrow definitions of the 1951 refugee convention. The Catholic Church accompanies, serves, and advocates for all people on the move, whether or not they fit the 1951 refugee convention, and works to build peace and prosperity, to reduce the push factors that force people from their homes.

REFUGEES AND RELIGIOUS PERSECUTION

The top refugee-sending countries, Afghanistan, Iraq, Somalia, and Sudan, are also among the world's worst violators of religious freedom. People fleeing religious persecution and violence from these countries alone account for over half of all refugees in the world today. This should not be surprising. As Pope Benedict XVI noted in his 2011 "World Day of Peace" message, religious freedom is a security issue, and peace depends upon it. Refugees flee war, and a majority of the world's most deadly wars occur in repressive countries with the worst records of violating religious freedom.[5] Fifty years ago, Blessed John XXIII's encyclical *Pacem in Terris* set the international policy advocacy and ministry priorities for the Catholic Church, working to build a world of greater peace and justice, respecting religious freedom.[6]

The Church advocates and ministers to these vulnerable people. Cardinal Theodore McCarrick and Bishop Nicholas DiMarzio led a delegation from Catholic Relief Services, the U.S. Conference of Catholic Bishops, and the International Catholic Migration Commission, to visit Iraqi Christians fleeing Iraq at the height of the civil violence there. As Cardinal McCarrick recounted, "Imagine you are a Christian family living in the Dora neighborhood outside of Baghdad. In the middle of the night there is pounding on your door. You are visited by armed gangs of Islamic extremists who threaten you and your family. You are told you have three options: give up your faith and convert to Islam, or die, or leave your homes, businesses, possessions, and communities behind and flee. There is no doubt that you will be killed if you do not comply. Thousands have already been killed by similar death squads, and the Iraqi government is either unable or unwilling to protect you. Who among us would choose not to renounce our faith under such death threats? Yet these Christians do not renounce the faith. They do not convert. They choose to flee, to lose everything they own and risk their lives, rather than lose their faith. These are the true modern day martyrs."[7]

These Christians have been at home in Iraq for centuries. But of the two thousand Christian families that once lived in the neighborhood of Dora alone, fewer than perhaps three hundred remain. By 2007, more than two million Iraqis had fled the country. Another two million fled their homes but remained inside Iraq, unable to cross an international border. Minority communities, such as Iraqi Christians, are particularly hard hit. More than one and a half million Christians lived in Iraq prior to the war. Those communities are now depleted by more than three fourths: only some three hundred thousand remain.[8] The two million internally displaced Iraqis within the country continue to fear daily violence. In Mosul, Iraqi Christians today face death threats and similar ultimatums to leave, convert, or be killed.

The U.S. invasion of Iraq, and the "Jasmine Revolutions," have endangered Christians in the region, who have been forced to flee religious persecution. Of the two million Iraqi refugees outside the country, more than one million fled to Syria, where they now must flee for their lives again. As minority Christian groups and as foreigners, Iraqis are targeted by combatants in the Syrian civil war. In Syria, Iraqis are often seen as supportive of the Assad government given the protection they had been given under his regime, and are thus put at greater risk. An autumn 2012 delegation trip sponsored by the USCCB to the region confirmed these concerns, noting that opposition forces to the Assad regime located in the Damascus region have threatened Iraqis living there and at times told them to leave the area.[9]

As they flee the violence to Lebanon, Jordan, and Turkey, they continue to live in a permanent state of insecurity. They are not allowed to hold jobs, send their children to school, or access health care. Fearing arrest and deportation, they often live in hiding, continually indoors to avoid hostile authorities. Without work they cannot pay the rent, and most live in overcrowded conditions in poor housing, fearful of eviction. Host countries may have begrudgingly allowed temporary entry to refugees, but they do not want Iraqis to feel welcome or settle permanently in their countries. Host governments fear they cannot support the costly needs of vulnerable refugee populations, and they cannot risk increased ethnic and religious conflicts which the quickly changing demographics may entail. They do not want the Iraqis to become the new Palestinians, refugees who stay permanently because they can never go back.

The USCCB advocates consistently for these vulnerable populations. Prior to the Iraq War, the pope and the U.S. Catholic Bishops advocated against the U.S. invasion on the grounds that it did not meet the criteria of Just War Tradition, including the criteria of proportionality, that more harm than good would come from the war. After the invasion, the Catholic Church argued for religious freedom and the protection of civilians, including refugees and IDPs, whether or not they met the definition of the 1951 Refugee Convention.

Since the Second Vatican Council, the Catholic Church has changed its position to become a vigorous advocate for protecting religious freedom and has played an important role in changing U.S. foreign policy toward international religious freedom.[10] The Church worked to create an unprecedented coalition of people from all faith traditions and none, and secular human rights advocates and folks with regional concerns, to create the landmark 1998 International Religious Freedom Act. The law marked a sea change in U.S. foreign policy toward international religious freedom (IRF), creating an International Religious Freedom office at the Department of State and a position of Ambassador at large to advocate for international religious freedom. It mandated by law that every year the U.S. government produce a report documenting each country's record and abuses regarding international religious freedom. Countries would be graded on those records, and a list of actions were recommended be taken by those deemed the worst abusers of international religious freedom. In order to produce the legally mandated report, Department of State personnel around the world would have to be trained in international religious freedom, and have some basic competency in understanding world religions. And rather than keeping religious actors and factors at arm's length, the law mandates that U.S. State Department personnel reach out to religious actors around the world. How else would they get the information needed to document countries' records on IRF? The law also created the non-partisan watchdog group, the U.S. Commission on International Religious Freedom (USCIRF), which also works to promote IRF and sends its recommendations to the Secretary of State and the President.[11]

Working to protect religious freedom is one way the Catholic Church works to address the root causes of displacement around the world. Since violations of religious liberty cause violence, wars, and refugee flows as people flee persecution, advances in protecting religious freedom will also protect people in their home communities, and lessen the push factors driving people to flee.

Establishing the IRF law was a huge accomplishment. It created a legal basis for discussion and promotion of IRF issues, and created staff and a budget to do so, and it provides the informational base needed to protect migrants. These are very important policy steps. They provide the needed information base to make policy, and they provide leverage, to keep IRF issues on the policy radar screen, ensuring that the people who flee religious persecution each year will be documented and presented for consideration to U.S. foreign policymakers. These instruments do not alone make policy. The President and Secretary of State must still decide whether and how to pressure governments to improve their IRF policies, and often, as is the case with Saudi Arabia, the decision is made that other pressing policy concerns preempt IRF concerns. However, the law, the State Department office, and the USCIRF ensure that the United States will never be silent on IRF, and that policymakers will at least be forced to consider IRF in relation to policy. While reports alone do not change repressive policies, they do keep refugees of religious persecution in the limelight, and provide leverage for advocacy. Without the reporting functions, the United States and other governments would be operating blind, making policy in the dark without vetted, thorough, trusted information on religious freedom violations. Without the law, policymakers would not be forced, by law, to consider the effects of their policies on IRF and to justify it on the basis of IRF. These may seem meager gains to those persecuted, but policy needs an information base, and acknowledging the problems is the first step toward solving them. The U.S. International Religious Freedom Act was renewed in 2012. Other countries, such as Canada and Italy, are currently considering enacting similar laws. By these, the Church works to address the root causes of migration, and protect vulnerable people within their home communities.

POST-9/11 ADVOCACY

U.S. refugee and migration policy has become more difficult since the September 11, 2001, terrorist attacks on the United States. For example, most Iraqi refugees cannot return home to Iraq and permanent settlement in the countries where they have fled, such as Syria and Lebanon, are not options. That leaves resettlement in a third country, like the United States. Traditionally the United States has a generous record of refugee resettlement. Of the 1.5 million "boat people" refugees of the wars in Vietnam and surrounding areas, the United States resettled over a hundred sixty thousand, about ten percent. Catholic parishes and dioceses sponsored many of these refugee families. The United States took responsibility for the fate of the refugees our military intervention helped create. Unfortunately, during the early years of the Iraq war, the Bush administration admitted few Iraqi refugees, and the USA PATRIOT Act worked against Iraqi refugee resettlement in the United States.

The USCCB and other Catholic organizations effectively advocated for more generous, just, and humane policies toward Iraqi and other refugees. Ironically, although not one of the 9/11 bombers entered the United States as a refugee claiming asylum, the U.S. refugee admittance process was severely truncated after the terrorist attacks. After the 9/11 and other attacks, refugee and asylum and immigration programs came under increased scrutiny and anti-immigration platforms thrived in the politics of Western countries. The U.S. government initially placed a moratorium on refugee admissions while a comprehensive review of procedures was undertaken and new security measures were developed and implemented. As Arthur Dewey, then Assistant Secretary of State for Population, Refugees, and Migration, noted, "demented individuals" might use the U.S. refugee admissions program as "a soft underbelly for such entry."[12] Refugee admissions dropped precipitously. A decade ago, the United States typically allowed about a hundred thirty thousand refugees into the country each year. In 2001, the United States admitted 68,426. This fell to 27,110 in 2002 and 28,455 in 2003, even though the Presidential authorization for seventy thousand refugees had not changed.[13] Initially bureaucratic inertia seemed to be the stumbling block for resumption of the U.S. refugee resettlement program. Then the program was underfunded. Today, thanks to effective advocacy by Catholic and other civil society groups, refugee admissions are returning to pre-9/11 levels.

But today the USA PATRIOT anti-terrorism law itself is an obstacle to legitimate refugees. A provision of the Patriot Act excludes from refugee admission anyone who has provided "material support" to any organization involved in terrorist activities. Unfortunately this clause has been broadly interpreted without exceptions for "support" forced at gunpoint or under duress, or for minimal or unknowing support. This means that Colombian families forced to pay ransom for the return of kidnapped loved ones are deemed to be terrorist supporters rather than being recognized as victims of terrorism. Most Colombians identified by the UNHCR as in need of resettlement are thus excluded from resettlement to the United States, as extortion by paramilitary forces is routine.[14]

For example, Jesus, a young Colombian, was forced from his home by the decades-old civil war. He and others in his village were captured by the paramilitaries in 2005. They were massed into a forced death march. At gunpoint, they were made to dig graves for the dead. Jesus said, "I never knew when I would be digging my own grave," because often the paramilitaries shot the gravedigger and pushed him into the hole he had just finished digging. Along the way, Jesus was able to escape, and fled for his life into neighboring Ecuador.[15] International law protects people like Jesus, fleeing for their life from political persecution in their home country. Unfortunately current U.S. law does not. Under the 2001 USA PATRIOT Act and the 2005 REAL ID Act, Jesus' forced grave digging at gunpoint is classified as giving "material support" to terrorist groups. Rather than being recognized as victims of terrorists, Jesus and other refugees like him are falsely branded as terrorist sympathizers, and stripped of the protections due them by U.S. and international refugee law. Victims who have been raped, tortured, robbed, kidnaped, and extorted, and who have had family members harmed or killed by terrorist groups, are denied asylum and refugee status and are banned from the United States for giving "material support" to terrorist groups. In a cruel irony, the very information refugees themselves provide to show their refugee status is used against them to bar their entry to the United States.

Over five million Colombians have been internally displaced by the long-running civil war, and another 500,000 have fled outside Colombia. Many fear return to Colombia, yet third country resettlement is illusive, keeping many refugees from Colombia vulnerable to human trafficking and other violence. Colombians form the largest displacement crisis in the Western Hemisphere, and constitute the seventh largest refugee population in the world. Yet despite the need, the United States resettled only 123 Colombian refugees in 2010, and a paltry fifty-seven were admitted in 2009. While the U.S. government has sent more than $8 billion in aid to Colombia under a program called Plan Colombia over the past decade, until very recently, 80 percent of this aid was earmarked for arming and training the Colombian military, even though the Colombian military has committed gross human rights abuses. The Catholic Church advocates for the protection of Colombian refugees, including allocating more of U.S. aid to Colombia to protect victims of the violence, opposing the militarization of foreign aid.[16]

The Material Support Ban even precluded Iraqis who worked with U.S. forces to overthrow the government of Saddam Hussein from the United States; they were initially excluded by this law that was intended to catch terrorists. The USCCB and Catholic organizations have effectively advocated for reform, waivers, and exemptions to the Material Support Ban of the Patriot Act. Catholics, in coalition with others, have asked for and won waivers and exemptions from this law for groups, such as 100,000 Bhutanese refugees in Nepal. But none of these proposed waivers would help Jesus, or any of the Colombians hurt by the Material Support Ban. Limited exemptions can't fix a bad law, but the exemptions have helped hundreds of thousands of refugees, no small feat in the current anti-immigrant climate.

CLIMATE CHANGE MIGRANTS

Environmental refugees are the new refugee challenge. Our laws and institutions do not recognize them, yet due to global climate change, their numbers are growing quickly. The Intergovernmental Panel on Climate Change warns that we may face 150 million environmental refugees by 2050.[17] That would be five times the numbers of refugees and internally displaced persons we struggle to serve now.

The United Nations University's Institute for Environment and Human Security estimates there are already more environmental refugees than political refugees. Island countries such as the Republic of Kiribati, the Maldives, Tuvalu, and parts of Bangladesh and Papua New Guinea, are disappearing and are already relocating their people. Negotiations are underway to move islanders to New Zealand and Australia. Kiribati President Anote Tong calls it "migrating with dignity."[18]

The Maldivian President, Mohamed Nasheed, said his government was considering Australia as a possible new home. "It is increasingly becoming difficult to sustain the islands, in the natural manner that these islands have been."[19] Populous countries such as India and Indonesia are vulnerable.

The world's poorest people bear the brunt of the cost of climate change, while contributing the least to the problem. Of the twenty-six countries deemed by most to be the most vulnerable to climate change impacts, twenty-three are in Africa. From Sudan to Rwanda, the UN High Commissioner for Refugees, Antonio Guterres, notes that the combined impact of conflict, environmental, and economic factors challenges our existing categories for refugees.

Dr. Maryanne Loughry, RSM, Associate Director of Jesuit Refugee Services, Australia, counsels that, "protection mechanisms need to be put in place to ensure that people are not left struggling to survive in ever diminishing settings while the world debates the realities of climate change."[20] Catholic organizations have effectively advocated to include foreign aid for climate change adaptation programs into U.S. climate change legislative bills. Although none have passed so far, the Catholic Church has been effective in moving the climate change debate toward concern for the most vulnerable.

REFUGEES: THE FEMALE FACE

Eighty percent of refugees are women and children. There are a number of reasons for this. First, demographically men are much more likely to be combatants, either by force, conscription, or as volunteers. Women and children are often vulnerable when men are away fighting, particularly in the many areas of the world where government capacity is lacking, in failed and failing states. Where local systems of protection are lacking, women and children may be forced to flee violence. Secondly, even if male family members are not combatants, in many areas of the world property rights are poorly protected. Without papers to prove property rights and effective legal systems to enforce them, people are forced to remain in insecure areas in order to protect property rights. So women may flee with children and vulnerable family members, while men remain to try to protect and retain the family home and lands.

Women are also refugees because women are more religious than men.[21] When Boko Haram bombs Nigerian churches, when the Taliban and other militants bomb schools because "Western education is sacrilege, is a sin," who are in those churches and schools? Women and girls.

Social science and demographics tell us that women are more religious than men, by almost any benchmark. Whether you measure belief in God, in a supreme being, attendance at religious services, personal prayer and religious practices, teaching religious values to children, and raising children within a religious tradition, by any of these benchmarks, women consistently rank as more religious than men, across time and cultures. These results are so consistent and accepted that the academic debates have tended to focus on *why* women are more religious than men (Is this nature or nurture? Are women more relational?), not *whether* they are more religious than men.

Because women are more religious than men, religious repression, persecution, violence and the resulting refugee flows affect women most. When churches are bombed, who are the people praying in those churches, hurt and killed? Women. When people are forced to flee religious persecution as refugees, who are those refugees? Predominantly women and their children. When religious organizations that accompany refugees, like CRS, Caritas Internationalis, and Jesuit Refugee Services, find their service work curtailed or banned because of their religious affiliation, who is hurt most? The women who make up most of the bottom billion of the world's impoverished, who rely on the activities of those religious organizations: 70 percent of the bottom billion, the world's poorest, are women and girls and 70 percent of youth not in school are women and girls. Girls are three times more likely to be malnourished. When faith-based organizations are curtailed in their service work, women and girls are harmed. Women are the primary refugee victims of violations religious freedom.

Women are also on the front lines of those responding to refugees and violations of religious freedom. Women lead NGOs and women refugees advocate for other refugees, such as Caroline Woo, a former refugee now serving as President of Catholic Relief Services. Women teachers and health care workers work with victims, and women lawyers take up the cases in international venues. But the female face of refugees and religious persecution is often not seen. When victims of religious persecution or violence are counted, they are counted as Christian or Muslim, civilian vs. security forces. Women are not counted, because in too many parts of the world, women simply do not count as fully human.

The female face of refugees is important for understanding what the Catholic Church can contribute to U.S. and international policy on refugees. Women religious outnumber male clerics internationally nearly two to one. These female faith organizations provide fertile resources for ministering to women migrants. For example, women migrants who have been trafficked or are victims of sexual and gender-based violence are much more receptive to interacting with female rather than male social workers, doctors, and refugee advocates. Women's religious orders have been quite active in anti-human trafficking efforts, recognizing that women migrants and refugees are particularly vulnerable to fall prey to traffickers. Animated by the fundamental dignity of all, Catholic organizations involve refugees and migrants themselves in decision making, as teachers and service providers in the camps, working to restore their human dignity through work and education. Women's education and economic development training are natural programs for Catholic organizations, working from a more holistic and sacred view of the agency of refugees and migrants.

CONCLUSIONS: ADDRESSING ROOT CAUSES

The bishops in *Strangers No Longer* noted that "the Church is increasingly called to be sign and instrument both of a very closely knit union with God and of the unity of the whole human race" (LG 1). Solidarity means taking responsibility for those in trouble. The Church must, therefore, welcome all persons regardless of race, culture, language, and nation with joy, charity, and hope. It must do so with special care for those who find themselves—regardless of motive—in situations of poverty, marginalization, and exclusion, in order to create "a system that is more generous, just, and humane."

Catholic organizations work proactively to end violence and build peace, particularly in the fifty years since *Pacem in Terris* helped

227

organize and mobilize the Catholic Church in peacebuilding and justice work. The Church still works reactively to minister to victims of violence and poverty, as in Colombia, where the Catholic Church has been at the front lines in advocating for the rights of refugees and IDPs, including passage of new laws to restore property rights to those IDPs and refugees who lost their homes and property fleeing the violence. But unlike many other organizations, the Church can use its vast institutional networks and presence as both a local church and transnational advocacy network, to address both the root causes as well as the symptoms of political and economic dislocations that force people from their homes. The Catholic Church in the United States and Colombia minister to refugees and migrants, but also work to end the conflicts in Colombia causing refugee and IDP flows. We work in solidarity across borders to address root causes.

Two thousand years ago, Mary, Joseph, and Jesus themselves were refugees, fleeing into Egypt to escape Herod's attempts to kill the child Jesus. Today as Christians, we are called to speak for these modern "holy families," who flee their homes, yet who have no voice in the political process, no voice but ours.

NOTES

1. Dr. Maryann Cusimano Love, "Modern Day Exodus," *America* (February 4, 2008).

2. *Strangers No Longer: Together on the Journey of Hope.*

3. United Nations, "1951 Convention Related to the Status of Refugees," reprinted in *Convention and Protocol Relating to the Status of Refugees* (Geneva, Switzerland: UNHCR, 2011); http://www.unhcr.org/3b66c2aa10.html (accessed November 14, 2012).

4. For an interview with Francis Deng in which he highlighted this shift, see "Interview: Dr. Francis M. Deng, Advocate for the Uprooted," *Refugee* (March 1, 1996); http://www.unhcr.org/cgi-bin/texis/vtx/search?page=search&docid=3b5547444&query=francis deng (accessed November 14, 2012).

5. Dr. Maryann Cusimano Love, "The Female Face of Faith," speech at September 12, 2012, Conference on International Religious Freedom, The Catholic University of America; also, Maryann Cusimano Love, "Faith and Freedom," *America* (February 14, 2011);

and Maryann Cusimano Love, Chapter 7, "God and Global Governance," in *Beyond Sovereignty*, 4th edition (New York: Cengage, 2011).

6. *"Pacem in Terris* at 50: Peacebuilding 2013," conference at the Catholic University of America, April 9–10, 2013, www.cua.ipr; Dr. Maryann Cusimano Love, "Catholic Peacebuilding and Good Governance," book chapter for the Vatican Pontifical Council for Justice and Peace, presented at the Vatican May 30, 2012; Dr. Maryann Cusimano Love, "Peace and Change," Georgetown University Woodstock Theological Report on *Pacem in Terris*, October 2011.

7. Migration and Refugee Services/United States Conference of Catholic Bishops, "Escaping Mayhem and Murder: Iraqi Refugees in the Middle East" (Washington, DC: The United States Conference of Catholic Bishops, 2007). To request a copy of the report, please do so through the USCCB website: http://www.usccb.org/about/migration-and-refugee-services/; Love, "A Modern Day Exodus."

8. MRS/USCCB, "Escaping Mayhem and Murder," 3.

9. United States Conference of Catholic Bishops, "Mission to the Middle East: Report of the United States Conference of Catholic Bishops on Syrian Refugees," October 2012; http://www.usccb.org/about/migration-policy/fact-finding-mission-reports/ (last accessed November 14, 2012).

10. Love, "The Female Face of Faith"; "The Advocacy of the U.S. Catholic Bishops for International Religious Freedom" by Stephen Colecchi, USCCB Director of the Office of International Justice and Peace, speech delivered at the September 12, 2012, Conference on International Religious Freedom, The Catholic University of America, http://iprcua.com/2012/09/12/international-religious-liberty/. Dr. Colecchi's speech is also published in an article that explores the "bishops' history of championing religious freedom around the world, their understanding of religious freedom, and the advocacy strategies they employ in its defence." The article appears in *The Review of Faith and International Affairs*, vol. 10, no. 3, Fall 2012.

11. "International Religious Freedom Act of 1998," H.R. 2431, 105th Congress.

12. Arthur E. Dewey, "Immigration After 9/11: The View from the United States," Remarks to the American Society for International

Law (April 3, 2003); http://2001-2009.state.gov/g/prm/rls/2003/37906.htm (accessed November 12, 2012).

13. Erin Patrick, "The U.S. Refugee Resettlement Program," *U.S. In Focus*, Migration Policy Institute; http://www.migrationinformation.org/feature/display.cfm?ID=229#4 (accessed November 12, 2012).

14. Testimony of Bishop Thomas G. Wenski before the Senate Judiciary Committee Subcommittee on Human Rights and Law, Washington, DC, September 19, 2007.

15. Statement of the Most Reverend Thomas Wenski before the Subcommittee on Human Rights and Law, Subcommittee of the Senate Judiciary Committee, September 19, 2007; http://www.voiceofthepoor.org/poverty_news_files/BishopWenskiTestimony2007.pdf (accessed November 12, 2012). The name of the person involved was changed to protect his identity.

16. USCCB, "Colombia Refugee Crisis: No End in Sight"; http://www.usccb.org/issues-and-action/human-life-and-dignity/migrants-refugees-and-travelers/columbianrefugees.cfm.

17. Md Shamsuddoha and Rezaul Karim Chowdhury, "Climate Change Induced Forced Migrants: in need of dignified recognition under a new Protocol," Report for the Equity and Justice Working Group Bangladesh (April 2009); http://www.glogov.org/images/doc/equitybd.pdf.

18. Salvatore Cardoni, "As Kiribati Sinks, 'Migrating With Dignity' Is Looming Option," *TakePart* (February 7, 2011); http://www.takepart.com/article/2011/02/17/kiribati-sinks-migrating-dignity-looming-option (accessed November 14, 2012).

19. Ben Doherty, "Climate Change Castaways Consider Move to Australia," *Sydney Morning Herald* (January 7, 2012); http://www.smh.com.au/environment/climate-change/climate-change-castaways-consider-move-to-australia-20120106-1pobf.html (accessed November 12, 2012).

20. Maryann Cusimano Love, "Shelter from the Storms," *America* (January 4, 2010); http://www.americamagazine.org/content/article.cfm?article_id=12074 (accessed November 14, 2012).

21. Love, "The Female Face of Faith."

CHAPTER 10

Achieving the DREAM

Catholic Support for Immigrant Youth

Colleen Cross

MAMADOU'S STORY

My story begins eighteen years ago. I was born in the Republic of Mali but my family migrated to the United States when I was one year old. Coming here to the United States at a young age introduced me to the culture, the lifestyle and the vitality of America. But my favorite was going to school. School was my specialty and there was the place I shined. Only in America could I have been an honor roll student. America is the best country for educational liberty and I was completely immersed in this freedom. I grew up as an American, I went to school as an American and, in essence, I am American—but it ends there. You see, I am not a citizen nor am I green card holder. I did not ask to come here, yet ten out of ten times I do not regret being here.

Right now I am disabled from continuing college because I am unable to receive the scholarship I was rewarded, since I cannot receive federal aid. I want to go to school. I want to learn and it's unbelievable to think my journey ends now.[1]

In 1971, the Synod of Bishops released the document *Justice in the World*. Addressing one of the major features of the Church's mission—to advance justice in the world—the bishops stated that "action on

231

behalf of justice and participation in the transformation of the world fully appear to us as a constitutive dimension of the preaching of the Gospel...of the Church's mission for the redemption of the human race and its liberation from every oppressive situation" (JIW 6). A particular responsibility of the Church, rooted in her mission of witness, is to draw the world's attention to the need for justice and love that is present within the gospel message. This witness must not only be carried out in the Church as institution, but in the lives and commitments of the members of the Body of Christ (JIW 36). This is an essential aspect of the Christian task and, to do this effectively, it is important to evaluate the "signs of the times"—those issues that are of pressing importance at a given historical period.

Following in this tradition, the bishops of the United States and Mexico issued the pastoral letter *Strangers No Longer* in 2003 as a way to respond to the ongoing migration phenomenon between their two countries. As *Justice in the World* provided a broader and more theoretical account of the importance of action on behalf of justice, *Strangers No Longer* roots this call within the specific context of immigration. As such, the bishops emphasize that immigration must remain a central concern for American Catholics.

An important segment of migrant populations that deserve particular attention in light of the Catholic Church's teaching on justice are undocumented immigrant youth living in the United States. Brought to the United States illegally, albeit through no fault of their own, students like Mamadou face the risk of becoming a permanent underclass in society. Many times forced to hide in the shadows and lacking the educational and other professional opportunities to develop their God-given gifts, these young people are often stifled in their attempts to attain true human development. Although they possess significant potential, the door remains closed to them. The Church believes that the situation confronting hundreds of thousands of undocumented, immigrant young signifies an injustice where "changing the status quo is an issue of moral gravity."[2] The Development, Relief, and Education for Alien Minors (DREAM) Act is one aspect of this reform that seeks to rectify this situation by providing educational opportunities and creating an earned path to citizenship for qualified immigrant youth. Analyzing the DREAM Act in light of a faith that seeks justice, this chapter will examine the commitment of the Church to immigrant youth through the key moral principles of human dignity, solidarity, and integral human development.

WHAT IS THE DREAM ACT?

The DREAM Act has a long and tumultuous history. Presented in its earliest form in 2001, the legislation seeks to provide undocumented immigrant youth educational opportunities and a pathway toward earned citizenship. In a word, the DREAM Act is about *opportunity*; it seeks to correct an injustice present in today's society: "They didn't decide, when they were six, seven or eight years old, to come here [illegally]....Should we hold children responsible for the actions of their parents?...They're all American except for that little paper. Culturally, linguistically, socially, American is who they are. We've educated them, so let's let them join the military, let them go to college. Let them give this country a lot in return for what we've given them."[3]

The origins of the DREAM Act are apparent in the Immigrant Children's Educational Advancement and Dropout Prevention Act of 2001, HR 1582.[4] Authored by Representative Luis Gutierrez (D-IL), and introduced in April of that year, the bill was designed to limit the high school drop-out rate among immigrant youth and provide an adjustment in legal status to minors who pursued higher education.[5] The bill recognized that these youth were not brought to the United States of their own volition. They often self-identify with the United States and consider it to be their home, and yet their irregular status and the inability to attend institutions of higher education make it less likely that they will achieve success in life and be able to contribute to society.[6]

However, this raises an important question: Why was it necessary to draft legislation of this sort in the early years of the twenty-first century? The 1982 *Plyler v. Doe* case set a precedent for allowing undocumented youth to attend public schools within the United States.[7] While the decision emphasized that "education has a fundamental role in maintaining the fabric of our society,"[8] it focused on primary and secondary schools, allowing states to contest the essential nature of postsecondary education.[9] Although the practice of excluding immigrant youth from higher education benefits was common, it was not enacted into federal law until the Illegal Immigration Reform and Immigrant Responsibility Act (IIRIRA) of 1996.[10] Section 505 of IIRIRA mandated that "an alien who is not lawfully present in the United States shall not be eligible on the basis of residence within a State (or a political subdivision) for any postsecondary education benefit unless a citizen or national of the United States is eligible for such a benefit (in no less an amount, duration, and scope) without regard to whether the citizen or national is such a resident."[11] While this statute did not explicitly prohibit undocumented youth from receiving higher education benefits altogether, the financial costs to individual states seeking to grant in-state benefits to these youth effectively closed the door on higher education for millions. As a result, a new generation of unauthorized immigrant youth spent the majority of their lives in the United States, living as Americans and considering the United States to be their home, only to find that they were in practice unable to attend college. Recognizing that these youth had much to contribute and should not be held accountable for the actions of those who brought them into the United States, legislation attempting to fix this problem arose.

Shortly after Representative Gutierrez released his bill, the first Development, Relief, and Education for Alien Minors (DREAM) Act was introduced on August 1, 2001, by Senator Orrin Hatch (R-UT).[12] This Act, S. 1291, had a twofold purpose: first, to cancel removal proceedings and adjust the residency status of certain eligible undocumented youth who were long term residents of the United States and had graduated from a U.S. high school;[13] and second, to repeal section 505 of the IIRIRA of 1996 in order to restore the state option of determination of residency for the purpose of in-state tuition.[14] In order to be eligible for the act, the students had to: (1) have reached the age of twelve before the enactment of S. 1291; (2) be under the age of twenty-one; (3) have graduated high school or received a recognized equivalent; (4) have been continuously present in the United States for not less than five years before the enactment of S. 1291; (5) be of good moral character; and (6) not be convicted of certain crimes and not pose a risk to national security.[15] Although S. 1291 was placed on the Senate legislative calendar, it never proceeded to a floor vote.[16]

From 2001 to 2012, DREAM legislation was proposed at least six times. In each case, Congress was unable to pass the legislation due to insufficient support. Although versions of the DREAM Act proceeded to a floor vote, they either failed to reach cloture and were effectively rendered dead in the water, did not receive a sufficient number of votes to pass, or both chambers of Congress were unable to reach a consensus on provisions in the bill.[17]

There was a significant amount of DREAM-related activity in 2010. During the 111th Congress (January 3, 2009–January 3, 2011) H.R. 5281, the Removal Clarification Act of 2010, was introduced into the House of Representatives.[18] However, due to significant amendments to the bill, including the addition of DREAM legislation is sections 4–16, the bill came to be known as the DREAM Act of 2010.[19] Complications arose when the two chambers sought to resolve differences in legislation surrounding the DREAM Act. Although the bill, with certain amendments, passed the House with a vote of 216–198, Senate consideration of the amendments the House had made failed to reach cloture by five votes.[20] Unable to prevent filibuster, the bill could not proceed. This was the last major attempt to pass DREAM legislation.

Although the original DREAM Act did not pass Congress, successive versions continued to be introduced. While the intent of the DREAM Act remained the same, changes to its eligibility requirements and implementation also occurred. Notable developments included the addition of a provision for those in qualified institutions of higher learning and a provision for military service. In this manner, the DREAM Act developed into the form it is known for today: an earned path to citizenship for qualified youth who serve a minimum of two years in the U.S. Armed Forces or complete a minimum of two years of postsecondary education. The current version of the DREAM Act, S 952[21] and HR 1842[22], continues the legacy of its predecessors with the same twofold purpose as the DREAM Act of 2001.[23]

The first major provision of the DREAM Act would allow unauthorized immigrant youth to adjust their status to conditional lawful permanent resident (LPR) for an initial period of six years. If certain criteria have been met, the DREAMer would then be allowed to file for the removal of conditional status, thereby becoming an LPR and potentially providing a pathway to eventual citizenship. In order to qualify under the Act, the unauthorized immigrant must (1) have come to the United States before the age of sixteen and be under the age of thirty-six (S 952)[24] or thirty-three (HR 1842);[25] (2) have retained residency in the United States for a minimum of five years;[26] (3) have earned a diploma from a U.S. high school, received a G.E.D., or been admitted to a U.S. institution of higher learning;[27] (4) have been a person of good moral character since entering the United States;[28] (5) have not committed certain crimes or offenses;[29] (6) not pose a danger to national security or public safety;[30] and (7) submit both biometric and biographic data and undergo a medical examination.[31]

The provision for adjustment of status within the DREAM Act stipulates that the conditional basis for LPR may be removed and the status of the individual adjusted to that of LPR if one of the two requirements is met within the initial six-year period of conditional status: either the individual earns a two-year degree from an institution of higher learning located within the United States or completes two years, in good standing, toward a bachelor's degree or higher in the United States; or the individual serves a minimum of two years in the U.S. Armed Forces and receives an honorable discharge if discharged. This provision, rather than being a form of amnesty, allows unauthorized youth to earn their citizenship through higher education or military service and thereby contribute to their communities.

The second major purpose of the DREAM Act is to repeal section 505 of IIRIRA that prohibited states from providing access to in-state tuition to unauthorized immigrants who reside in-state.[32] By repealing this law, states would regain the authority to determine eligibility for in-state tuition. The higher education assistance provisions in these Acts would also grant unauthorized immigrant students access to other forms of Federal assistance including student loans and the ability to participate in work-study programs.[33] Neither of these bills has come to a vote as of the 112th Congress.

Particularly worthy of note is that contrary to popular belief, the DREAM Act was not in its origin a single-party issue; released by a Republican, the earliest version of the DREAM Act and subsequent versions received strong bipartisan support.[34] While the bipartisan support that the DREAM Act enjoyed may have disintegrated, and those who originally introduced and co-sponsored the legislation may have rescinded their support, the original purpose of the DREAM Act has not changed substantially: it seeks to provide educational opportunities and an earned pathway to citizenship for qualified youth.

Although the DREAM Act has not yet been able to help students like Mamadou achieve their dreams of higher education, the policy of deferred action announced by President Obama on June 15, 2012, and effective on August 15 was a step in the right direction. Essentially an act of prosecutorial discretion on the part of the Department of Homeland Security, the policy defers the removal proceedings of qualified youth. In the memorandum announcing this action, Secretary of Homeland Security Janet Napolitano acknowledged that certain immigrant youth were brought to the United States as children, not of their own volition, and have come to know the United States as their only home.[35] Recognizing that they did not actively intend to violate U.S. immigration laws, the policy would defer the removal proceedings of eligible individuals for a period of two years. In order to qualify the individual must (1) have entered the United States before the age of sixteen and not be above the age of thirty; (2) have maintained continuous residency in the United States for a minimum of five years before June 15, 2012, and have been present in the United States on this same date; (3) be a current student, have graduated from high school, received a G.E.D., or be an honorably discharged veteran of the U.S. Armed Forces or Coast Guard; and (4) not be convicted of a felony, significant misdemeanor, or multiple misdemeanors, and not pose a threat to national security or public safety.[36] According to certain estimates, there are close to one million individuals who would immediately qualify for deferred action and another 400,000 who would eventually meet the requirements if the policy were to remain in effect.[37]

President Obama's policy has drawn critiques from both sides of the aisle, yet it is the first federal action of tangible relief for DREAM eligible youth. As such, the Catholic Church welcomes the initiative but recognizes that it is only a first step, not a substitute for further action. In the words of Archbishop José Gomez,

> The action by the President today is no substitute for enactment of the DREAM Act in Congress. We encourage our elected officials of both parties to take this opportunity to work together to enact this important law, which would give these youth a path to citizenship and a chance to become Americans. We also renew our call for bipartisan efforts to enact comprehensive and humane reform our nation's broken immigration system.[38]

237

CATHOLIC SUPPORT OF THE DREAM ACT

Written in 1999, the Apostolic Exhortation of Pope John Paul II, *Ecclesia in America*, sought to foster a commitment to justice and solidarity in America[39] Appealing to the centrality of Christ in the Christian message, which calls for both the conversion of mind and heart, Pope John Paul II declared that

> the Way to Conversion, Communion and Solidarity in America... makes clear the centrality of the person of the Risen Christ, present in the life of the Church and calling people to conversion, communion and solidarity. The starting-point of such a program of evangelization is in fact the encounter with the Lord. Given by Christ in the Paschal Mystery, the Holy Spirit guides us towards those pastoral goals which the Church in America must attain in the third Christian millennium. (EA 3)

An integral part of this mission of evangelization is the transformation of the world through the struggle against injustice (SRS 41). The encounter with Christ must lead one to be concerned with the signs of the times and the restoration of justice in the world. Speaking to this reality, Pope Paul VI addressed the need for affective evangelization in *Evangelii Nuntiandi*:

> How in fact can one proclaim the new commandment without promoting in justice and in peace the true, authentic advancement of man? ...It is impossible to accept "that in evangelization one could or should ignore the importance of the problems so much discussed today, concerning justice, liberation, development and peace in the world. This would be to forget the lesson which comes to us from the Gospel concerning love of our neighbor who is suffering and in need." (31)

Reflecting this vision, the bishops of Mexico and the United States authored the pastoral letter *Strangers No Longer* to address the migration concerns present within their two countries. *Strangers No Longer* ultimately provides a challenge to all Christians to see the crucified and risen Christ in the face of the stranger (SNL 40). On this point, the bishops write that "Faith in the presence of Christ in the migrant leads to a conversion of mind and heart, which leads to a renewed spirit of communion and to the building of structures of solidarity to accompany the migrant."[40] Grounded in Catholic social teaching, the letter calls attention to the struggles and injustices present within the migrant experience, challenging both inadequate pastoral responses and failed public policies connected to migration that dismiss the inherent dignity of all human beings as they are created in *imago Dei*.

The parable of the sheep and the goats (Matt 25:31–46) makes clear that our Christian faith is inextricably linked to how we treat the least of those in our midst: the poor, the oppressed, and the vulnerable. Echoing this command, *Strangers No Longer* states, "We judge ourselves as a community of faith by the way we treat the most vulnerable among us" (SNL 6). Not surprisingly then, a central theme in *Strangers No Longer* is its commitment to solidarity with the migrant. One consequence of this commitment is apparent in the bishops' support for comprehensive immigration reform (CIR) and the legalization of unauthorized populations currently present in the United States (SNL 68–71). In this respect, the DREAMer is a specific instance of this larger population. However, the text itself of *Strangers No Longer* does not contain a reference to DREAM legislation. The decision to exclude the DREAM Act from the text is particularly curious, as the Church has supported the legislation since its inception in 2001. Writing in support of the Student Adjustment Act of 2001,[41] an immediate predecessor of the DREAM Act, Bishop DiMarzio, then chairman of the National Conference of Catholic Bishops Committee on Migration, said,

> H.R. 1918 is much needed to assist young persons who have completed high school but, because of their lack of immigration status, are unable to access certain educational benefits which would allow them to attend college. These young people are bright and eager to receive a college education, yet often are unable to reach their full potential because they cannot obtain in-state tuition or federal tuition assistance....Perhaps the most important aspect of the Student Adjustment Act is that it invests in young persons

who will contribute to the future of our nation as they grow and mature.[42]

One explanation for its absence in *Strangers* is that the Church's support of the DREAM Act was originally rooted in a larger commitment to comprehensive immigration reform and not as an individual piece of legislation. The situation of DREAM eligible youth is only one injustice present in the plight of migrants in the United States. As a result, many of the efforts of the Church to advocate for DREAM legislation are directly tied to CIR. Testifying before the U.S. House of Representatives Subcommittee on Immigration, Citizenship, Refugees, Border Security, and International Law in May of 2007, Archbishop Thomas Wenski[43] urged the enactment of the DREAM Act through inclusion in a CIR measure.[44] In the same vein, speaking at a press conference held by Christian and Jewish leaders detailing the need for CIR, Cardinal Theodore McCarrick stated, "We also ask that…the DREAM Act, which assists undocumented students who came to our nation through no fault of their own,…[is] included in any final legislative package…In our view, only a comprehensive approach to immigration reform will effectively address our nation's immigration crisis."[45] However, it is important to note that there are practical considerations at play. While the bishops strongly desire CIR, and continue to advocate for the DREAM Act within the context of CIR, their growing willingness to support the passage of the DREAM Act as a separate piece of legislation reflects the climate in which we find ourselves. Given the lack of political support in Congress for comprehensive reform and in light of prevailing popular public opinion, it has in recent years been more likely that DREAM legislation would pass on its own than in the context of a more comprehensive bill.

In addition to concerns related to the political climate noted above, other practical considerations play a role in weighing the legitimacy of the DREAM Act. For example, given that the United States has spent a significant amount of money educating the DREAMer population, it would seem a shame to let this investment go to waste. DREAMers have the ability to contribute to our nation in a multitude of ways, including in science, technology, engineering, and math, fields currently facing a growing shortage of Americans to fill these jobs.[46] In a 2009 strategic issues panel, the University of Denver examined the economic advantage of immigrant talent to the U.S. economy and workforce:

> It is difficult to overstate the importance of immigrant talent to maintaining U.S. leadership in a highly competitive global economy. Traditionally, our excellent higher education system, political freedoms and business-friendly environment have helped the United States maintain a competitive edge. For example, over the past 15 years immigrants have started 25 percent of all U.S. public companies that were backed by venture capital. These companies employ hundreds of thousands of American workers, often in high-tech, high-paying fields such as software, semiconductors and biotechnology. Companies started by immigrants read like a who's who of high-tech leaders: Intel, Sun Microsystems, eBay, Yahoo! and Google.[47]

Although this report suggests recruiting global talent to the United States, if this is true of individuals educated elsewhere, it would also seem to be true of immigrant youth who received their education here. The American community has supported their growth and development and we should seek to utilize their abilities and skills for the good of the country. They possess significant potential, a potential that cannot be fully realized unless they are allowed to advance their capabilities through the completion of postsecondary education or through providing another contribution to the nation such as through services in the military.

While the Church supports the DREAM Act and allies herself with immigrant youth for practical reasons its support is, at its core, given for moral considerations. In a letter to Congress on December 2, 2010, Archbishop Gomez expressed the support of the Church for the DREAM Act stating, "There are times when a proposal should be enacted because, simply put, it is the right thing to do. This is one of them...The DREAM Act represents a practical, fair, and compassionate solution for thousands of young persons in our nation who simply want to reach their God-given potential and contribute to the well-being of our nation."[48] The institutional Church's support for the

DREAM Act, not to mention efforts in support of CIR, is not motivated by politics but is fundamentally

> about preaching the good news of God's love for all peoples.
> It is about transforming the city of man into the family of
> God. In her social teaching the church is not trying to dictate politics or run society. Instead, the church, through
> prayer and reflection on the Gospel, and through study of
> the signs of the times, tries to translate Christ's love into
> principles for Christian witness and action.[49]

It is a call of our faith to be in solidarity with the most vulnerable among us. For the Church, solidarity with the migrant has come to mean a journey of accompaniment and a commitment to biblical visions of justice and hospitality. This is attained particularly through the recognition of the *imago Dei* in those society deems "other," less than, or forgotten.

The bishops are cognizant that "this is clearly a difficult and complex issue from the civil and political, as well as the social and economic, but above all from the human point of view."[50] The DREAM Act raises questions that still need to be explored further, including issues of scholarship, legal aid, and distributive justice. However, "as a Christian, there are no prior commitments that can overrule or trump this biblical tradition of compassion for the stranger, the alien and the worker. Whatever economic, political or social policies we discuss—and whatever discussion of constitutional rights and liberties—we cannot turn our backs to this biblical legacy of hope."[51] Such is the commitment of the Church to immigration reform.

WHY SHOULD WE CARE?

The DREAM Act plays an essential role within our Catholic communities. On the one hand, many of these DREAMers are Catholic—they are the future of the Church, and as such, the Church should support them. While pastoral concerns are important, DREAM legislation also touches on deeper issues dealing with human dignity, commitment to the vulnerable, and the responsibility to work toward human development. As Pope Paul VI noted in his encyclical *Populorum Progressio*, "in order to be authentic, it [development] must be complete: integral, that is, it has to promote the good of every man and of the whole man" (14). Working toward the fullness of human flourishing for every person requires work on behalf of the disenfranchised. In the context of DREAM eligible youth, this manifests itself in a commitment to education. As the verdict in *Plyler v. Doe* stated, "education has a fundamental role in maintaining the fabric of our society."[52] However, while the Supreme Court did not recognize this fundamental role within the context of higher education, our faith calls us to consider its importance. If DREAMers are denied the opportunity to develop their God-given potential and capabilities through postsecondary education, they are in effect prohibited from contributing to a society in which their identity and worldview had been largely formed, thus weakening it in the long run.

The commitment to the DREAM Act is not simply rooted in economic efficiencies or pragmatic reasoning; rather it is a vision of our faith, a faith that acts on behalf of justice for the good of all. Speaking on the Ninety-Seventh World Day of Migrants, Pope Benedict XVI stated, "Human brotherhood is the...experience of a relationship that unites, of a profound bond with the other, different from me, based on the simple fact of being human beings. Assumed and lived responsibly, it fosters a life of communion and sharing with all and in particular with migrants; it supports the gift of self to others, for their good, for the good of all, in the local, national and world political communities."[53] The Development, Relief, and Education for Minors Act, like *Strangers No Longer*, ultimately poses a challenge to "see the face of Christ, crucified and risen, in the stranger" and enter into a relationship of communion with the migrant (SNL 40).

NOTES

1. *Mamadou.* Taken with minimal editing from Dream Activist: Undocumented Students Action & Resource Network; http://www.dreamactivist.org/about/our-stories/mamadou/ (accessed September 1, 2012).

2. "Statement of Cardinal Theodore E. McCarrick," Archbishop Emeritus of Washington. Comprehensive Immigration Reform.

March 1, 2006; http://old.usccb.org/comm/archives/2006/06-039.shtml (accessed September 3, 2012). Although this quote specifically deals with the larger context of comprehensive immigration reform, it is particularly relevant as the bishops consider DREAM one aspect of this platform.

    3. Statements of Representative Luis Gutierrez and Elizabeth Llorente, "Gutiérrez Dreams the Impossible DREAM Act," Fox News Latino, November 29, 2010; http://latino.foxnews.com/latino/poli tics/2010/11/29/luis-gutierrez-immigration-reform-personal-mis sion/ (accessed September 3, 2012).

    4. United States House of Representatives, *Children's Educational Advancement and Dropout Prevention Act of 2001*, HR 1582, 107th Congress, 1st sess. (Washington, DC: Library of Congress, April 25, 2001). Hereafter referred to as HR 1582. In describing his work with the DREAM Act, Representative Luis Gutierrez, considers HR 1582 to be the official predecessor to the DREAM Act. Rep. Luis Gutierrez, *Issues: Immigration—DREAM Act;* http://www.gutierrez. house.gov/index.php?option=com_content&view=article&id=710&It emid=75 (accessed August 26, 2012).

    5. Found in the text of the legislation, HR 1582 sought to lower high school dropout rates through the adjustment of legal status for these immigrant youth and changes in state admissibility and tuition guidelines for college and universities. HR 1582, 2.b.

    6. HR 1582, 2.a.

    7. *Plyler v. Doe*, 457 U.S. 202 (1982); Joey Feder, "Unauthorized Alien Students, Higher Education, and In-State Tuition Rates: A Legal Analysis," Congressional Research Service. (December 22, 2011), 1–2.

    8. 457 U.S. 202 at 221.

    9. Feder, 2.

    10. Division C of Public Law 104–208. Hereafter referred to as IIRIRA.

    11. IIRIRA, § 505.

    12. United States Senate, *Development, Relief, and Education for Alien Minors Act*, S 1291, 107th Congress, 1st sess. (Washington, DC: Library of Congress, August 1, 2001); hereafter referred to as S 1291. It is important to note that an amended version of the DREAM Act was introduced to the Senate on June 20, 2002. For the purposes of this

discussion, the terms of the amended bill will be discussed when referring to S 1291.

13. S 1291, 3.

14. S 1291, 2.

15. S 1291, 3.a.1.

16. United States Congress, Committee Reports, 108th Congress, Senate Report 108–224, *Amending the Illegal Immigration Reform Act of 1996. II. Legislative History.* Washington, DC: Library of Congress. Print.

17. The DREAM Act of 2003, S. 1545; The DREAM Act of 2005, S. 2075; in 2006, the DREAM Act was included in the Comprehensive Immigration Reform Act (CIRA) S 2611 (The DREAM Act was contained under Subtitle C—The DREAM Act (of 2006), Sections 621–32. The companion bill to S 2611 was HR 4437); The DREAM Act of 2007, S. 2205; In 2010, the National Defense Authorization Act for Fiscal Year 2011 was released, containing a version of the DREAM Act, S. 3454.

18. United States House of Representatives, *Removal Clarification Act of 2010* HR 5281, 111th Congress, 2nd sess. (Washington, DC: Library of Congress, May 12, 2010); hereafter referred to as HR 5281. For the purposes of this discussion, the DREAM Act of 2010 will be discussed when mentioning HR 5281.

19. HR 5281, 4.

20. HR 5281, Bill Summary & Status.

21. United States Senate, *Development, Relief, and Education for Alien Minors Act of 2011*, S 952, 112th Congress, 1st sess. (Washington, DC: Library of Congress, May 11, 2011); hereafter referred to as S 952.

22. United States House of Representatives, *Development, Relief, and Education for Alien Minors Act of 2011*, HR 1842, 112th Congress, 1st sess. (Washington, DC: Library of Congress, May 11, 2011); hereafter referred to as HR 1842. These two Acts were introduced as companion bills and therefore have only slight variations.

23. United States Conference of Catholic Bishops, "Update: The Development, Relief, and Education for Alien Minors Act (DREAM Act)" (Washington, DC: The United States Conference of Catholic Bishops. June 2012); http://www.justiceforimmigrants.org/documents

/Backgrounder-DREAM-Act-Update-Final2.pdf (accessed September 3, 2012).

24. Ibid., 3.b.1.B and F.

25. Ibid., 3.a.E.

26. S 952, 3.b.1.A. and HR 1842, 3.a.1.A.

27. S 952, 3.b.1.E. and HR 1842, 3.a.1.D.

28. S 952, 3.b.1.C. and HR 1842, 3.a.1.B.

29. S 952, 3.b.1.D. and HR 1842, 3.a.1.C.

30. S 952, 3.b.4. and HR 1842, 3.a.4.

31. S 952, 3.b.3 and 5. and HR 1842, 3.a.3 and 5.

32. S 952, 9.b. and HR 1842, 8.b.

33. S 952, 9 and HR 1842, 8.

34. The DREAM Act was introduced by Senator Orrin Hatch and cosponsored by eighteen other Senators. Of this group, seven were Republicans and nine were Democrats. S 1291, List of Sponsors.

35. Janet Napolitano, Secretary, United States Department of Homeland Security, *Exercising Prosecutorial Discretion with Respect to Individuals Who Came to the United States as Children* (Memorandum, June 15, 2012).

36. Ibid.

37. Immigration Policy Center, *Who and Where the DREAMers Are: A Demographic*, August 18, 2012; http://www.immigrationpolicy. org/just-facts/who-and-where-dreamers-are (accessed September 3, 2012).

38. Statement of Most Reverend José H. Gomez, Archbishop of Los Angeles, *The Announcement of Deferred Action for DREAM Eligible Youth* (Washington, DC: United States Conference of Catholic Bishops, June 15, 2012); http://justiceforimmigrants.org/documents/ DREAM-Statement-6-15-2012.pdf (accessed September 8, 2012).

39. America is used in the unitive sense to refer to both the North and South American continents.

40. Ibid.

41. United States Congress, House of Representatives. *The Student Adjustment Act of 2001*. 107th Congress, 1st sess. May 21, 2001. H.R. 1918. Washington: The Library of Congress. Print.

42. Bishop Nicholas DiMarzio, Chairman, NCCB Committee on Migration. Letter to Representative Christopher Cannon, June 4,

2001, provided by the Department of Migration and Refugee Services, United States Conference of Catholic Bishops.

43. During the time of his testimony, Archbishop Wenski had not yet been elevated to the status of archbishop and was serving as a bishop.

44. Archbishop Thomas Wenski, "Congressional Testimony on Immigration," transcript of testimony given before the U.S. House of Representatives Subcommittee on Immigration, Citizenship, Refugees, Border Security, and International Law on May 22, 2007, *Origins* 37, no. 4 (June 7, 2007).

45. Cardinal Theodore McCarrick, "Which Immigration Bill is Needed?" Transcript of address given during a press conference on March 1, 2006, *Origins* 35, no. 38 (March 9, 2006): 638.

46. Shelley DuBois, "America's Science Job Conundrum," Cable News Network, July 15, 2011; http://management.fortune.cnn.com/ 2011/07/15/america-science-job-conundrum/ (accessed September 6, 2012); Amy Kaslow, "How to Secure America's Future in Manufacturing," Cable News Network, July 25, 2012; http://management. fortune.cnn.com/2012/07/25/american-manufacturing-future-jobs/ (accessed September 6, 2012).

47. *Architecture for Immigration Reform: Fitting the Pieces of Public Policy*, The University of Denver, Strategic Issues Program, 2009 Immigration Panel, Final Report, 36; http://www.du.edu/issues/ media/documents/2009IMMIGRATIONREPORT.pdf (accessed September 3, 2012).

48. Archbishop José Gomez, Archbishop of Los Angeles, "Letter to the U.S. House of Representatives," December 2, 2010; http://old.usccb.org/comm/archives/2010/10-227.shtml (accessed September 3, 2012).

49. Archbishop José Gomez, "The Immigration Crisis and the Duty of Catholic Witness," *Origins* 40, no. 37 (February 24, 2011).

50. Pope Benedict XVI, *Address of His Holiness Pope Benedict XVI to the Bishops of the United States* (May 18, 2012); http://www.vati can.va/holy_father/benedict_xvi/speeches/2012/may/documents/hf_b en-xvi_spe_20120518_bishops-us-fourteen_en.html (accessed August 26, 2012).

51. Cardinal Roger Mahony, "For Goodness' Sake: Why America Needs Immigration Reform," Transcript of speech given at

the University of North Carolina in Chapel Hill, February 2, 2011, *Origins* 40, no. 37 (February 24, 2011).

52. 457 U.S. 202 at 221.

53. Pope Benedict XVI *Message of His Holiness Benedict XVI for the 97th World Day of Migrants and Refugees (2011)*; http://www.vati can.va/holy_father/benedict_xvi/messages/migration/documents/hf_b en-xvi_mes_20100927_world-migrants-day_en.html (accessed September 5, 2012).

PART IV

LOOKING BACK, LOOKING AHEAD

CHAPTER 11

Illegal Immigration, the Bishops, and the Laity: "Strangers No Longer"

Mark Ensalaco

INTRODUCTION

A decade later, the American bishops' pastoral letter on immigration, *Strangers No Longer* (*Strangers*) reads like a parable about the Church's influence over public opinion and policy—and the laity. SNL was a bold and therefore inevitably controversial letter. In it the bishops transcribed the Church's moral and social doctrine into a set of reasonable policy proposals. *Strangers* was, and is, an appeal to reason as well as conscience, but once Congress took up the issue the debate about comprehensive immigration reform became shrill and a bipartisan bill went down to defeat. In the decade since *Strangers* the mood toward migrants has become implacably hostile among broad swaths of the American public and a number of states have enacted draconian anti-immigrant measures that the federal government has challenged in court. The bishops appealed for a civil debate about this urgent matter to no avail. It was as if their words fell mainly on flinty ground or among thorns where they withered in the white heat of politics or were strangled by politicians' worldly concerns about their electoral prospects.

Many—probably most Catholics—were either ignorant of *Strangers'* existence or ignored it altogether so it influenced their thinking, and voting, not at all. Still, and this may be the single most important aspect of *Strangers*, many Catholics heard its message and responded in myriad ways to create in their communities, as the bishops had asked, a climate of hospitality rather than hostility. *Strangers*, published four full years before President Bush called on Congress to create an immigration system "worthy of America" in his 2007 State of the Union Address, was an early expression of a growing sense that the immigration system was broken.[1] When it appeared, the bishops thought they perceived signs of a "growing consciousness of migrants and bearers of faith and culture," leading them to believe in the possibility of a dialogue about ways to "humanize the immigration phenomenon" and to build a more "just and generous immigration system." The bishops had already reached the conclusion that migration between Mexico and the United States was "necessary and beneficial" and hoped to persuade American society this was so (SNL 2, 8, 10, 12). But the bishops badly misread the mood in the country.

A year after *Strangers'* publication, one of America's most prominent conservative political scientists warned of the threat to America's national and cultural identity posed by a the new wave of migrants from Latin America. So, although Latin American migrants may be bearers of faith and culture, many Americans consider that culture to be alien and share this political scientist's conclusion that "cultural America is under siege."[2] Thus many Americans categorically reject the very premise of *Strangers*. But many Catholics, including those who actually responded to the bishops' appeal to welcome migrants into their communities, sincerely expressed reservations, doubts, and even objections to the bishops' policy positions on illegal immigration. As an advocate of migrants' rights who has spoken on *Strangers*, I often hear variations of three objections from Catholic audiences.

One objection to the bishops' pronouncements in *Strangers* reflects the conviction of many Catholics that when making public statements the bishops should limit themselves to abortion, euthanasia, gay marriage, and other matters of sexual morality. There are many Catholics who obediently heed the bishops' teachings on matters of faith and morals, but openly question the bishops' competence to speak authoritatively on such a complex policy matter as illegal immigration. In *Strangers* the bishops lay out specific policy proposals aimed at a comprehensive reform of U.S. immigration law and policy. So,

American Catholics, be they citizens or public officials, liberals or con-servatives, may conclude that the bishops' message clashes with their prudential judgment and choose to ignore *Strangers* for that reason.

A second objection turns on the credibility of bishops' policy positions insofar as they are founded on abstractions of Catholic moral theology. In *Strangers* the bishops make an astonishing statement derived from the principle of the universal destination of goods: undocumented migrants have an almost absolute right to seek work in foreign lands and wealthy states have a corresponding obligation to accommodate migration flows that supersedes their sovereign right to control their borders. Many find these assertions to be incredible in the sense they provide no realistic and therefore credible foundation for public policy, because they clash with consensus norms of the interna-tional community consisting of sovereign states.

Finally, there is the objection to the bishops' misplacement of the moral burden (as well as the political, economic, and budgetary burdens) to resolve the immigration crisis squarely on the United States. In *Strangers* the bishops call for quite specific reforms of U.S. immigration law and enforcement policies but only vaguely appeal to the United States and Mexico to address the root causes of migration. Therefore the bishops implicitly absolve the Mexican government of its moral duties toward its own population, and, more worrisome, absolve Mexican Catholics of the moral obligation to construct a more just Mexican soci-ety. If the bishops choose to stand in solidarity with migrants, perhaps it is better to stand with them in an authentic struggle for justice in Mexico, a struggle guided by the very social teaching that the bishops invoke in their appeal for comprehensive immigration reform.

In retrospect, none of these objections obviates the cogency of the bishops' message in *Strangers*. Nonetheless, as the American bishops renew the campaign to achieve justice for migrants, they would do well to take these objections into consideration; a coherent response to these and other concerns may persuade Catholics, as faithful citizens or perhaps as public officials, to help turn the tide of public and political opinion in favor of a more just and humane immigration system.

THE BISHOPS' COMPETENCE AND THE LAITY

At its core, *Strangers* was an expression of the Church's solidarity with migrants and a pledge to advocate on their behalf for just and fair migration policies (SNL 105, 106). Whatever else just and fair migration policies may entail, the bishops reckoned that justice demanded the legalization of the nearly eleven million undocumented migrants already in the United States. This is the single most controversial aspect of *Strangers*. Catholics who oppose the very idea of comprehensive immigration reform as a form of amnesty that rewards violation of the law may regard the policy proposals the bishop laid out in *Strangers* as misguided. But there is a more fundamental criticism: the bishops' intervention in the policy debate took them far beyond their competence and perilously close to trespassing on the rightful prerogatives of civil authorities who are called upon to exercise prudential judgment in making decisions for the common good.

The bishops offered a compelling pastoral reason for venturing into the immigration debate in *Strangers*. "Migrants and immigrants are in our parishes," they wrote, and in both Mexico and the United States, there is "much injustice and violence against them and much suffering and despair among them." Thus the Church could not remain silent because Catholics "judge ourselves as a community of faith by the way we treat the most vulnerable among us" (SNL 5, 6). This is well and good. A Catholic with deep concerns about immigration might commend the Church's pastoral concern for suffering migrants, but nonetheless insist that the Church confine itself to simple acts of charity toward migrants. But silence on matters of injustice is not an option. *Strangers* not only reflects the American bishops' pastoral concerns, it flows from the Church's prophetic duty to proclaim the justice of kingdom of God and to denounce injustice rooted in sin.

Vatican II forcefully reaffirmed the Church's responsibility to speak on social matters as an aspect of its dialogue with the modern world and thereby the validity of the Church's social doctrine as it has evolved since *Rerum Novarum*. So, while Vatican II was careful to acknowledge the autonomy and independence of the political community and the Church, it resolutely declared the Church's freedom, right, and responsibility "to pass moral judgments even in matters relating to politics, whenever the fundamental rights of man or the salvation of souls requires it" (GS 76). Paul VI derived the "public relevance of the Gospel" from that fact that social injustice is rooted in sin and therefore insisted that the Church cannot remain silent on social matters (EN 34). John Paul II similarly warned that Church would relegate "the Christian message to a purely other-worldly salvation incapable of shedding light on our worldly existence," if it were to ignore social injustice (CA 5). The Pontifical Council on Justice and Peace has summarized the Church's affirmation of its social doctrine in all-encompassing terms: the Church has the "right to proclaim the Gospel in the context of society, to make the liberating word of the Gospel resound in the complex worlds of production, labor, business, finance, trade, politics, law, culture, social communications, where men and women live" (CSDC 70).

The American bishops have restated this teaching in their instruction on faithful citizenship. To those who might question whether "it is appropriate for the Church to play a role in political life," the bishops responded firmly that "the Church's obligation to participate in shaping the moral character of society is a requirement of our faith." In fact the Church's moral convictions are assets the Church brings to the political dialogue in a pluralistic society and the Church's social teachings accord with America's foundational "life, liberty and pursuit of happiness" (FCFC 9, 11, 12). This includes the bishops' views on immigration, which *Faithful Citizenship* (FCFC) mentions no fewer than three times (2, 5, 90).[3]

Despite all this some Catholics may still question the bishops' competence to venture into the specific details of immigration law and policy, where, as the adage goes, the devil lives. For one thing, the Church's writ to proclaim the gin the context of society is inherently limited because of the differing natures of the Church and the political order: "Christ, to be sure, gave His Church no proper mission in the political, economic, or social order" (GS 42). The Church's mission has real relevance to the human community, but when the Church feels compelled to initiate activities on behalf of humankind, these are most appropriately acts of mercy. Or, as John Paul II cautioned, because the Church must respect the "legitimate autonomy of the democratic order," it is not entitled to express "preferences about institutional or constitutional solutions" to even the most serious issues facing democratic governments, including the "scandal of abortion" (CA 47). The

Pontifical Council for Justice and Peace took John Paul II's statement farther stating that it does not belong to the Church to question "the merit of political programmes, except as concerns their religious or moral implications" (CSDC 24). Pope Benedict XVI adopted a similar tone is his very first encyclical: "the formation of just structures is not directly the duty of the Church, but belongs to the world of politics, the sphere of the autonomous use of reason." The direct duty to work for a more just society, he observed, "is proper to the lay faithful" (DCE 29).[4]

Indeed, Vatican II is forthright about the special competence of the laity in the public realm. The Council affirmed that the duty to engage in temporal affairs "belongs to the laity" who are to direct them toward "God's will" and thereby "remedy the customs and conditions of the world" (LG 31, 36). *The Pastoral Constitution on the Church*, perhaps the most important pronouncement of Vatican II, is even more forceful: "Secular duties and activities belong properly although not exclusively to laymen." So, although the lay Catholic is to pay close attention to the "teaching authority of the Church" as she or he cultivates a "well-formed Christian conscience," those who have "genuine expertise" in secular matters must "take on his own distinctive role" in the earthly city and "not imagine that his pastors are always such experts, that to every problem which arises, however complicated, they can readily give him a concrete solution, or even that such is their mission" (GS 43). *The Decree on the Apostolate of the Laity* (AA), perhaps the least appreciated document of the Second Vatican Council, likewise notes that complex social issues, presumably like immigration, demand "intelligent attention and examination" from the laity. As citizens among citizens, lay Catholics are to bring their own "special competence" to bear on worldly affairs and to "act on their own responsibility" as they seek to renew the temporal order (AA 1, 7).

These pronouncements speak directly to the prudential judgment of the laity. It is the direct duty of the laity to engage in worldly affairs and to "act in accordance with the dictates of prudence" (CSDC 547–48; GS 34).[5] Prudence is demanding. But there are Catholic voters and public officials with the attributes the Church expects from them—a properly formed conscience, the virtues of prudence, a sense of realism and responsibility, wisdom, courage, and a correct will—who have arrived at an objective understanding of the immigration crisis that differs programmatically from the bishops'. After reflection, consultation, and analysis many Catholics have decided that the bishops' specific policy proposals are not the best policy alternatives and are not what is most fitting in the specific context of American society. Therefore, after thoughtful and even prayerful reflection, they have in good conscience decided it is their duty to oppose enactment of comprehensive immigration reform as a matter of prudential judgment. The argument goes something like this: It principally is the task of the laity, as Vatican II teaches, to apply the moral precepts of Catholicism in the complex world of politics and economics where men and women live; lay Catholics, with real-world experience in temporal affairs, bring a special competence to this task, a competence the bishops' are not likely to possess; therefore, lay Catholics will almost inevitably arrive at differing prudential judgments about matters of policy because the abstractions of Catholic moral theology provide little in the way of practical policy guidance.

The dialogue between the bishops and the laity is almost inevitably infused with the tension between the bishops' authority to teach the eternal truths of the faith and the laity's prudential judgment about complex worlds of economics and politics. The bishops have seen this before, most notoriously in response to the pastoral letter *Economic Justice for All*. In that letter, as in *Strangers*, the bishops framed a set of policy recommendations that they believed to be "reasonable and balanced" albeit in some instances "controversial." Then the bishops' added a proviso that the letter's critics would seize upon: As bishops, "we do not claim to make these prudential judgments with the same kind of authority that marks our declarations of principle." Nonetheless, the bishops concluded it was important to offer specific judgments on the complex challenges confronting the American economy lest the Church teachings "be left at the level of appealing generalities" (EJA 20). But even before *Economic Justice for All* appeared, a group of dissident lay Catholics with vast experience in government and business objected to what they saw as the Church's intrusion into matters in which it did not have expertise, insisting that Catholic social teaching displays a serious misunderstanding of the dynamics of wealth creation and that the bishops failed to discern the superior moral virtues of "democratic capitalism."[6] Critics of *Strangers* are likely to recognize a similar misunderstanding of the workings of the modern economy in the bishops' vague criticism of the North American Free Trade Agreement (NAFTA) as a cause of economic dislocation of individual proprietors in rural Mexico and therefore the first cause of the immigration crisis (SNL 60). This is simply a failure to grasp that a market economy, "like God's creation itself," is marked by "creative destruction" and that sudden change in patterns of world trade inevitably cause dislocation in the labor force.[7]

More recently, the chairman of the House budget committee, a Catholic, objected to the bishops' criticisms of his budget plan by invoking the rightful prerogatives of Catholics in public office. "The Church," the chairman wrote, "normally and rightfully refrains from pronouncing directly on specific legislation—the subject of prudence about which there is legitimate diversity of choice and judgment—but properly brings to light the moral principles that inform legislative deliberation."[8] The unmistakable insinuation of the chairman's letter was that the bishops had made direct pronouncement on a specific piece of legislation and strayed too far into the world of politics where there is legitimate diversity of choice and (prudential) judgment.[9]

There is a straightforward defense against this objection to the bishops' competence to propose policy: the bishops did not spin the policy proposals in *Strangers* out of thin neo-scholastic air. The bishops conducted extensive consultations both in Mexico and the United States with public officials, and law enforcement officers, as well as migrants' rights advocates and most important, migrants themselves (SNL 7). The proposals were drafted by the professional staff of the USCCB's Department Migration and Refugee Services, the Office of Migration and Refugee Policy, the Catholic Legal Immigration Network, and others. Moreover, the bishops' recommendations were substantially similar to proposals put forward by many advocacy organizations, both faith-based and secular. President Bush later endorsed comprehensive immigration reform; indeed, his appeal to bring illegal immigrants "out of the shadows" by creating a path to citizenship was in some ways bolder than the bishops' call merely for legal residency. Multiple business associations, including the U.S. Chamber of Commerce, supported the president's position. Elected officials from both parties, including Senator Ted Kennedy (D-MA), a Catholic, and Senator John McCain (R-AZ), drafted a bipartisan comprehensive immigration reform bill. The bishops had the policy right; what they had not anticipated, and what they never effectively countered, was a concerted campaign to vilify migrants and to pressure lawmakers, including Senator McCain, to jettison reasonable reforms for fear of the electoral consequences of enacting them into law. *Strangers* was an appeal to reason as well as conscience and the specific proposals withstand rational scrutiny and the test of time.

THE RIGHTS OF MIGRANTS AND THE OBLIGATIONS OF SOVEREIGN STATES

In defense of their appeal for the legalization of the undocumented the bishops cite the cold hard economic realities of illegal immigration. Despite the rhetoric about illegal immigration, they noted, illegal migrants "labor with the quiet acquiescence of both government and industry." Legalization would benefit both Mexico and the United States by stabilizing the U.S. labor market and maintaining the flow of remittances to Mexico, among other benefits (SNL 68–70). But behind the bishops' pragmatic argument for the legalization of the undocumented is a moral argument framed around the principle of the universal destination of goods that posits categorically that "all the goods of the earth belong to all people" (SNL 35).[10] Guided by this principal the bishops make two astonishing statements. The first statement concerns basic economic (human) rights of individuals: "When persons cannot find employment in their country of origin to support themselves and their families, they have a right to find work elsewhere in order to survive. Sovereign states should find ways to support this right" (SNL 35).

In making this pronouncement, the bishops are faithful to papal statements on immigration reaching back to Pius XII, whose teaching was repeated and amplified in the encyclicals and apostolic exhortations of John XXIII and John Paul II, who extended the right "even in cases of non-legal immigration" (EF; PT 25; SRS 24; EA 65). But there is history behind these papal statements. Pius XII wrote *Exsul Familia* at a time when Europe was still coping with the refugee crisis resulting from the Second World War and soon after the United Nations adopted a refugee convention to address the plight of those who fled the Soviet Bloc, due to well-founded fears of persecution. John XXIII's pronouncement on migration in *Pacem in Terris* came while the Soviets were actually reinforcing the Berlin Wall in an effort to prevent the mass exodus of East Germans to the West. So John XXIII's categorical statement—"every human being has the right to freedom of movement and of residence within the confines of his own country; and, when there are just reasons for it, the right to emigrate to other countries and take up residence there" (PT 25)[11]—has to be read as a rebuke of the Soviet Union's practice denying freedom of internal movement as well as the freedom to emigrate.

Nonetheless, the Church now interprets John XXIII's statement that every human person has the right to emigrate to other countries, where there is a just reason for it, to include the right to migrate for economic reasons. This is a strong moral claim that demands equally strong criteria for prudential judgment. In this regard the conditional clause—"where there is just reason for it"—begs the question: what sorts of conditions justify illegal migration? The bishops' language in *Strangers* is ambiguous: "When persons cannot find employment in their country of origin to support themselves and their families, they have a right to find work elsewhere in order to survive" (SNL 35). Few question the right to migrate as a matter of survival: international agencies and NGOs, including Catholic Relief Services, respond to humanitarian emergencies which threaten the very survival of refugees and migrants every day all around the world. But it is hardly credible to equate migration from Mexico with the sort of humanitarian emergency that existed in post-war Europe when Pius XII wrote *Exul Familia* or that exists in many parts of the global south today.[12]

The claim to a right to migrate without authorization simply when one cannot find employment to support oneself and one's family is far more tenuous. The bishops attempt to defend that claim this way: "In the current conditions of the world, in which global poverty and persecution are rampant, the presumption is that persons must migrate in order to support and protect themselves and that nations who are able to receive them should do so whenever possible" (SNL 39). This is fundamentally the bishops' stark assessment of the current migration reality between the United States and Mexico. The bishops make no attempt to justify the presumption that Mexican citizens must migrate to support and protect themselves much less simply to survive. To be sure, as the bishops correctly note, economic inequality between the United States and Mexico helps drive the migration phenomenon (SNL 60). But the bishops do not credibly establish that Mexicans cannot support themselves, or survive, without migrating to the United States. It is entirely conceivable that many, perhaps even most, Mexican migrants enter the United States in search of higher wages than they could earn in Mexico. This is an entirely comprehensible motivation, but it may not qualify as one of the "just reasons" for migration that John XXIII spoke of in *Pacem in Terris*. At issue here is the credibility of the bishops' assertions about human rights of migrants vis-à-vis the rights and obligations of sovereign states. In fact, the bishops' assertions clash with the consensus norms of the international community regarding immigration as reflected in international human rights law.

John Paul II, who extolled the adoption of the United Nations Universal Declaration of Human Rights as "a true milestone on the path of humanity's moral progress," essentially framed "non-legal immigration" as a human rights issue.[13] Accordingly the bishops make multiple references to migrants' human rights in *Strangers*. Admittedly, John Paul II and the bishops view the question of human rights in light of the natural law tradition which informs Catholic social teaching rather than as a reflection of the consensus norms of the international community. Nonetheless the bishops make an allusion to one international human rights convention, the 1951 Convention on the Status of Refugees, and make a specific reference to another, the 1990 United Nations Convention on the Protection of the Rights of All Migrant Workers and Members of Their Families (CMW). However, neither these conventions, nor indeed any other international human rights treaty, lend support to the bishops' position with respect to either the right of migrants to cross borders without authorization or the obligation of states, particularly more economically powerful states, to accommodate migration flows.

The allusion to the Convention on the Status of Refugees comes in the context of the bishops' insistence that "those who flee wars and persecution should be protected by the global community," to which they add, "migrants have a right to claim refugee status without incarceration and to have their claims fully considered by a competent authority" (SNL 37). There is nothing controversial about the statement that those who flee war and persecution deserve the protections of the international community: the international community developed those protections in the 1951 refugee convention. But, just as voluntary migration from Mexico is not forced migration in the strict sense, Mexican migrants are not refugees according to the refugee convention which applies only to those who are compelled to flee their homelands "owing to well-founded fear of being persecuted for reasons of race, religion, nationality, membership of a particular social group, or political opinion."[14] Indeed the bishops' statement that migrants have a right to claim refugee status without incarceration and to have their claims fully considered by a competent authority is virtually irrelevant to the situation along the U.S.-Mexico border. Not a single Mexican or Central American citizen even applied for refugee or asylum status in 2003, the year *Strangers* was published.[15]

The bishops' specific reference to the 1990 United Nations "Convention on the Protection of the Rights of All Migrant Workers and Members of Their Families" (CMW) comes in the context of their appeal for the United States to sign the convention.[16] The bishops' endorsement of the CMW is understandable: its implementation would, in their words, serve "to honor the labor rights of foreign born workers" in the United States (SNL 77). Nonetheless, the CMW itself is controversial. More than two decades after it was drafted, the Convention has yet to enter into force, principally because only sending nations like Mexico which benefit from the foreign remittances of migrant workers have ratified it; receiving states, like the United States, have shunned the convention. Moreover, the only provision of the CMW that accommodates the bishops' appeal for justice for migrants is found in article 69 which calls on states only to "consider the possibility of regularizing the situation of [undocumented migrant workers] in accordance with applicable national legislation and bilateral or multilateral agreements." Obviously, the bishops' appeal in *Strangers* is for the United States to reform the applicable national legislation to regularize (legalize) the status of Mexican migrant workers. Otherwise, there is nothing in the convention that remotely supports the bishops' categorical assertions about the rights to search for work in a foreign land without authorization.

Notably the CMW, like earlier International Labor Organization conventions concerning migrant workers, principally concerns the rights of documented workers.[17] Therefore it does recognize both the "right" of undocumented workers to cross national frontiers without authorization and the "obligation" of any state to accommodate migration flows. To the contrary, the convention specifically justifies United States enforcement efforts to halt illegal immigration. Indeed, the CMW very specifically stipulates that states have an obligation to take measures to prevent and eliminate the clandestine movement and employment of undocumented migrants and to impose effective sanctions on both smugglers and the employers of undocumented workers, and more generally to ensure that irregular situations of undocumented workers do not persist.[18] But the bishops in *Strangers* do not call upon the United States, much less Mexico (which, unlike the United States, is a signatory to the CMW) to meet their obligations to eliminate clandestine human smuggling. Instead, they actually call on the United States and Mexico to abandon enforcement strategies that, in the bishops' estimation, give rise to smuggling operations (SNL 88–91).[19]

The critical issue here is that international human rights law is relevant to the migration reality between Mexico and the United States only insofar as human rights law demands that the Mexican government fulfill its state obligations to promote the economic rights of its own population. The International Covenant on Economic and Social Rights recognizes that everyone has the inalienable right to work (article 6), provide an adequate standard of living for himself and his family (article 11), and a host of other economic rights.[20] Under the Covenant, individual states have the obligation to devote the maximum of available resources to the progressive realization of those rights (article 1). But this obligation falls solely on states like Mexico, where work is scarce and the standard of living is inadequate. The Covenant does not recognize the right of anyone to migrate illegally in search of work or a better standard of living, nor does it obligate prosperous states, like the United States, to assume the burden of providing work to migrants.

The bishops' assertions about the right to migrate directly translate into their assertions about the limitation on sovereign states' right to control their borders and the obligation of prosperous states to accommodate migrants. In this regard the bishops make a second astonishing statement: "The Church recognizes the right of sovereign nations to control their borders but rejects such control when it is exerted merely for the purpose of acquiring additional wealth" (SNL 36). In the decade since *Strangers*, there has been a groundswell of popular demand for stricter border enforcement to slow the rate of illegal immigration into the United States. The reasons are fairly obvious: American citizens, especially in border states, have legitimate concerns about the impact of illegal immigration on their communities. The concerns may well be exaggerated: there are ongoing contentious debates about the net economic costs or benefits of illegal immigration. But it is not credible to imply that the demands for stricter enforcement of immigration law are motivated by a desire to acquire additional wealth. In fact, it is difficult to imagine how any sovereign nation could amass additional wealth by controlling its borders, except insofar as preventing illegal immigration spares the expenditure of tax dollars on services for non-citizens. The fact is that there are millions of Americans who view illegal immigration strictly as a question of the rule of law, not national treasure. The autonomy of the democratic order, which the Church rightly acknowledges, obligates elected officials to comply with the legitimate demands of the electorate to curb illegal immigration.

Then there is the bishops' assertion that more prosperous nations have a stronger moral obligation to accommodate migration flows. Human rights conventions and other multilateral treaties are exceedingly specific about obligations. But the bishops, having asserted that more economically powerful states have an (implied) obligation to accommodate migration flows, make no attempt to explicitly define the parameters of an obligation to accommodate. Instead they appeal for three actions—the creation of legal avenues for migration, increasing the number of family visas, and the legalization of the undocumented—that are presumably aimed at accommodating migrants' needs (SNL 63, 68–70). The creation of legal avenues for migration would accommodate the need for migrants to find work in the United States to support themselves and their families. An increase in the number of visas would promote family reunification. The legalization of the undocumented would allow migrants to continue sending a portion of their earnings to their families in Mexico.

However, critics of the bishops' proposals warn that, if the United States were to take these actions to meet an implied obligation to accommodate migrants, there would be serious ramifications. Increasing the number of family visas to promote family reunification would substantially increase the number of Mexican families living in American communities with all the social and economic impacts that would entail. The call for the legalization of migrants who entered the country illegally is effectively a call for amnesty, an outcome that would undermine the rule of law in the minds of many. And, although the bishops' call for legalization is not an explicit call for the creation of a pathway to citizenship, that is the obvious logical trajectory of legalization. Here the implications for American democracy are tremendous. The grant of citizenship to some substantial percentage of more than eleven million illegal immigrants would transform the American electorate. Given the concentration of the Hispanic population in critical electoral states, these new American citizens could have a decisive impact on elections at the national as well as state and local levels. Thus, ironically those who had once broken American laws would have the democratic power to influence the enactment of law.

The Church's doctrine of rights and obligations creates a serious dilemma for the prudent Catholic public official living in the modern world composed of sovereign states. Insofar as moral considerations factor in policymaking at all, those considerations are framed in the language of human rights law. But human rights law reflects the minimal consensus of the international community, a consensus that would not exist if rights claims were founded on religious doctrine. Catholics played an important role in the drafting of the Universal Declaration of Human Rights, but as one of them, Jacques Maritain, once observed "yes we agree on rights but on the condition no one asks us why."[21] By invoking a natural law principle like the universal destination of goods, the bishops weaken the credibility of the secular human rights arguments for comprehensive immigration reform. This is important because there are many Catholics who prefer the secular language of human rights law over natural law theory because natural law provides no clear guidance on complex matters like migration in the murky world of politics. In fact, one can actually invoke natural law theory to oppose the bishops' position in *Strangers*. As one prominent Catholic intellectual put it, the personalist principle, the bedrock for all Catholic thinking about public policy, "does not confer an absolute right on anyone to live wherever he or she chooses." To the contrary, a "proper

Catholic understanding of limited and constitutional government grasps that the state…has the right to enforce its citizenship laws."[22]

The bishops can answer this objection about the credibility of their assertions about the rights of migrants and the obligations of sovereign states. First, prosperous states, like the United States, publically acknowledge their responsibilities toward impoverished ones even though they refuse to define those responsibilities in the legal terms of international treaty obligations. The United States and other advanced industrialized states acknowledged their responsibilities for the survival, protection, and development of children in the declarations and plans of action of the 1990 World Summit for Children and the 2002 United Nations General Assembly special session on children.[23] The developed industrial states have pledged assistance to poor states under the auspices of the United Nations Millennium Development Goals. And, independently of these multilateral initiatives, prosperous states provide development, humanitarian, and other forms of assistance to the nations of the global south in an implicit acknowledgment of their responsibilities toward the poor. The bishops' statement that the prosperous have a responsibility to accommodate migration flows is perfectly consistent with the international community's growing sense of the humanitarian responsibility of the more prosperous states.

Moreover, the objection that the bishops' doctrine of rights and obligations clashes with international human rights law ignores an important fact: international human rights law is not set in stone, rather it is constantly evolving and its evolution reflects the struggle for justice of those who are poor or afflicted in anyway (GS 1). Thus when the bishops urge states to assume moral obligations that surpass those presently codified in international human rights law, they give powerful impetus to the evolution of the consensus norms of the international community. The bishops proclaim the Gospel, not the Universal Declaration of Human Rights. To insist that the bishops confine themselves to a secular view of rights and duties would be to ask them, as John Paul II expressed it, to relegate "the Christian message to a purely other-worldly salvation incapable of shedding light on our worldly existence" (CA 5). Instead the bishops in *Strangers* boldly address the moral dimensions of the global reality of immigration. The migration of millions of Mexicans and Latin Americans over the past three decades is the manifestation of a global phenomenon with roots in poverty, underdevelopment, and globalization. In its current state, international law provides inadequate protections of the human rights of migrants, no doubt because the consensus norms of the international community unduly reflect the interests of the powerful. For this reason the Church has consistently challenged the injustices of the global economy. As Benedict XVI aptly observed, "In today's complex situation, not least because of the growth of a globalized economy, the Church's social doctrine has become a set of fundamental guidelines offering approaches that are valid even beyond the confines of the Church; in the face of ongoing development these guidelines need to be addressed in the context of dialogue with all those seriously concerned for humanity and for the world in which we live" (DCE 26). The bishops' pastoral letter on migration draws from this legacy. Just as "the poor do not need charity but justice" (DCE 26), migrants need a more just and humane immigration system that reflects the economic realities of migrant labor in the global economy. The objection to the bishops' appeal to a moral law above international law is really no objection at all.

THE MORAL BURDEN OF REFORM

The bishops felt compelled to draft *Strangers* because of migrants' suffering and despair in the face of injustice and violence both in Mexico and the United States (SNL 5). This stirred their consciences to exercise their pastoral responsibilities: "The bishop as pastor of the local church should lead the priests, deacons, religious, and faithful in promoting justice and in denouncing injustice towards migrants and immigrants, courageously defending their basic human rights" (SNL 43). But the bishops' denunciation of injustice in the defense of migrants' human rights is directed mainly at the supposed injustices of America's broken immigration system. Accordingly, their policy recommendations are directed almost entirely at the United States. This is one aspect of *Strangers* that especially perplexes liberal Catholics. There is precious little in *Strangers* about the Mexican state's failures of due diligence, or, for that matter, the responsibility of the Mexican bishops' to denounce injustice and defend the human rights of Mexicans.

In 2003 when the bishops published *Strangers* more than three-quarters of a million migrants were entering the United States without authorization each year. The overwhelming majority of them came from Latin America, more than half of them from Mexico. Illegal immigration across the United States-Mexico border had become, in John Paul II's words, "a social emergency."[24] But the American bishops' response, like the response of John Paul II, was to focus on the responsibilities of host countries.[25] The sole exception in *Strangers* is the bishops' call to address the root causes of migration. For critics of *Strangers* the single most important cause of migration is the Mexican state's abject failure to care for its poor. Here the bishops are almost entirely silent.

The bishops speak out forcefully against xenophobic and racist attitudes that lead to the mistreatment of migrants as criminals in the United States, alleged abuse of migrants by U.S. Border Patrol, the "shameful" treatment of unaccompanied minors, and border enforcement policies that contribute to the deaths of migrants in both Mexico and the United States (SNL 80–82, 86–87). Admittedly, the bishops direct their most severe language at the corruption, brutality, and "systematic abuses of basic human rights" of Mexican law enforcement officials as well at the "bandits" who extort and abuse migrants attempting to reach the United States (SNL 83). But the denunciation virtually ends there. There is nothing about the Mexican state's failure to fulfill its duty to protect its population, in the words of Pope Benedict XVI, or to make a positive contribution to the creation of an overall climate in which the individual can both safeguard his own rights and fulfill his duties, in the language of John XXIII in *Pacem in Terris*. *Strangers* issues a vague call for the creation of economic opportunities in Mexico to reduce poverty and thereby reduce the incentives of Mexicans to seek work across the border. But even here the bishops attribute migration primarily to the economic inequality between Mexico and the United States resulting, in part, from the implementation of the North American Free Trade Agreement (SNL 59–61). Here the bishops missed an important opportunity to criticize the endemic and oppressive economic inequalities within Mexico, inequalities that existed long before NAFTA.

In fairness, the tone in *Strangers* is generally one of pastoral compassion rather than prophetic denunciation. But many American Catholics may wonder why the bishops chose not to scrutinize Mexico's governance failures with the same force as they speak of xenophobic and racist attitudes in the United States, Border Patrol agents' abuses of migrants, or the shameful treatment of unaccompanied minors in the United States. The bishops' remark about the shameful treatment of unaccompanied minors is especially irksome to some Americans. The fact that children perish in the desert is absolutely shameful. But the real shame belongs to Mexican families who permit their children to undertake a dangerous journey through the desert, or with Mexican authorities who fail to police their own northern border in order to protect children from abuse by "bandits." If as John Paul II aptly noted, "illegal immigration should be prevented" and it is imperative to "combat vigorously the criminal activities which exploit illegal immigrants,"[26] many Catholics believe that this responsibility falls primarily on the Mexican authorities.

Strangers, then, is inconsistent in its invocation of the Church's social doctrine. *Pacem in Terris*—which contains the categorical statement about the rights to emigrate to other countries and take up residence there when there are just reasons for emigration—is equally forceful in its teachings about the duties of governments to create a climate in which citizens may safeguard their rights and fulfill their duties: "In the modern world especially, political, economic, and cultural inequities among citizens become more and more widespread when public authorities fail to take appropriate action in these spheres (PT 25)." John XXIII rightly warned that this official failure is an affront to human dignity and rights. Indeed, *Pacem in Terris*, much like the Universal Declaration of Human Rights, specifies a comprehensive set of actions the state must implement to enable citizens to maintain a decent standard of living (PT 64).[27] Had the bishops applied John XXIII's moral standard to Mexico, *Strangers* might have been a more cogent and more convincing document. It is basically unfair for the bishops to ask the United States to assume moral burdens but refrain from asking the Mexican authorities to assume those same moral burdens.

The problem with *Strangers* is not only that it shies away from forceful criticism of the Mexican authorities' grave failures, but additionally that virtually all the reforms the bishops proposed concern legislative action to be undertaken by the United States (SNL 63–92).[28] In this regard the bishops' misplacement of the moral burden for reform on the United States tacitly absolves Mexican authorities of their economic and social responsibilities toward the Mexican population. The implementation of the bishops' specific recommendations—an employment based immigration policy, a guest worker program, and legalization of undocumented migrants in the United States—would resolve social problems that the Mexican state ought to solve. Each job a Mexican migrant finds in the United States is one less job the Mexican society must generate in Mexico. Every dollar Mexicans send home in remittances, which the bishops rightly call the lifeblood of Mexican families (SNL 72), is one less dollar the Mexican state must direct toward the social welfare of its citizens. Each Mexican student who attends school in the United States is one less student the Mexican authorities must educate. The objection can be put more forcefully. If, as the bishops urge, the United States were to accommodate the flow of migrants from Mexico, there would be no urgent reason for Mexican authorities to care for the least of their brothers and sisters; and if the existence of widespread poverty in Mexico is a social injustice, then the implementation of the bishops' proposals, by relieving the pressure on the Mexican state to enact systemic reforms, would inadvertently serve to perpetuate that injustice.

This objection can be extended to the Mexican Church, including the lay faithful, who have the same duty as American Catholics to work for justice as a requirement of faith. It is incomprehensible that the bishops would call on American Catholics to fulfill the duties of faithful citizenship and to summon "the courage to act in defense of moral principles when making decisions about how to build a society of justice and peace" (FCFC 19), and yet absolve Mexican citizens, the overwhelming majority of whom are Catholic, of that same duty.

The Second Vatican Council could not have been more forceful about the social duty of the laity: "The Christian who neglects his temporal duties, neglects his duties toward his neighbor and even God, and jeopardizes his eternal salvation" (GS 43) So not only is it legitimate for Catholics to defend their own human rights and the rights of their fellow citizens, Catholics, especially those called to a vocation in politics, "must take action against any form of injustice and tyranny," and "dedicate themselves to the service of all with sincerity and fairness, indeed, with the charity and fortitude demanded by political life" (GS 74–75). John Paul II spoke the truth plainly, "America needs lay Christians able to assume role of leadership in society":

It is urgent to train men and women who, in keeping with their vocation, can influence public life, and direct it to the common good. In political life, understood in its truest and noblest sense as the administration of the common good, they can find the path of their own sanctification. For this, they must be formed in the truths and values of the Church's social teaching, and in the basic notions of a theology of the laity. A deeper knowledge of Christian ethical principles and moral values will enable them to be exponents of these in their own particular setting.... (EA 44)[29]

The Church instructs the laity to defend human rights and oppose injustice and tyranny. The laity is to act with prudence. Lay Catholics are also to display fortitude, the virtue that enables one to "conquer fear, even fear of death, and to face trials and persecution," and "disposes one even to renounce and sacrifice his life in defense of a just cause" (CCC 1808). But *Strangers* makes no demands on Mexican Catholics to take action against tyranny and oppression in their own society, much less to sacrifice their lives in defense of a just cause like systemic reform of the injustices of Mexican society that have forced millions of Mexicans to abandon their country in recent decades. Instead, *Strangers* is oriented almost entirely toward pastoral accompaniment of migrants involving the provision of social and legal services, the opening of migrant shelters, and the integration of migrants in American society (SNL 42). In this regard the bishops tacitly limit the involvement of the laity to action north of the U.S.-Mexico border. Thus the bishops note that the laity, along with the clergy and religious, can become "pastoral agents working for peace, justice, and systemic social change to benefit the most vulnerable members of the community" (SNL 43).[30] But the context of this statement indicates that what the bishops have in mind is the systemic change in American society's attitude toward migrants rather than systemic change in Mexico or Latin America.

For many Catholics who resolutely affirm the public relevance of the Gospel, this orientation toward migrant resettlement rather than social justice advocacy comes as a disappointment. It is a far cry from the spirit of the Latin American Church that emerged after Medellín and produced an Oscar Romero. In 1968, when the Latin American bishops assembled in Colombia, widespread poverty and persecution were facts of life, not a presumption. Yet the Latin American bishops called on lay Catholics to interpret poverty and persecution as signs of the times in light of the Gospel and the Church's social teachings, rise in defense of their legitimate rights, and take action against tyranny and oppression: "The church—the People of God—will lend its support to the downtrodden of every social class so that they might come to know their rights and how to use them."[31] The Latin American Church in that epoch was an inspiration to so many American Catholics because their Latin American brothers and sisters displayed "the charity and fortitude" that the struggle for social justice demanded and because so many were willing to renounce and sacrifice their lives in defense of that just cause.

Strangers is nearly entirely devoid of this sort of exhortation. Instead, *Strangers* almost has a tone of fatalism about the poverty and persecution that compel migrants to flee their homes and communities: apparently the most the Church can do is assist migrants on their journey of hope to a life of dignity elsewhere. Virtually all of the pastoral challenges and responses the bishops lay out concern the pastoral accompaniment of migrants coming to America rather than the solidarity with Catholics struggling for justice in Latin America. So, in one important example, the bishops call for representatives from both the American and Mexican episcopal conferences to study ways to "help migrants themselves to continue an active role as lay leaders in new settings" (viz. their new settings in the United States, as opposed to their own particular settings, as John Paul II urged) (SNL 51). As important as this may be, the bishops could just as well have called for a study of ways to help Latin American Catholics return to their own communities as active lay leaders capable of making the "liberating word of the Gospel" resound in them (CSDC 70). Instead, in one isolated passage the bishops pledge merely to "support the creation of the necessary conditions so that all may enjoy full fruit of their work and life in their homeland, if they so wish" (SNL 105). Ardent Catholic advocates of social justice in Latin America might have wished that the bishops message of solidarity with the migrants—"we stand in solidarity with you" (SNL 9)—had been a pledge to stand in solidarity in the struggle for justice in the migrants' native lands.

For these Catholics, then, it comes as an irony that bishops published *Strangers* in response to John Paul II's exhortation in *Ecclesia in America*, an exhortation the Holy Father chose to deliver in the Basilica of Our Lady of Guadalupe in the heart of the Mexican capital. It is ironic because John Paul's solicitude for those who are "abandoned or rejected by society" led him to call for action against exploitation and oppression:

> This constant dedication to the poor and disadvantaged emerges in the Church's social teaching, which ceaselessly invites the Christian community to a commitment to overcome every form of exploitation and oppression. It is a question not only of alleviating the most serious and urgent needs through individual actions here and there, but of uncovering the roots of evil and proposing initiatives to make social, political, and economic structures more just and fraternal. (EA 18)

There is only a faint echo of John Paul II's invitation to the Christian community to propose initiatives to make social, political, and economic structures simply more just in *Strangers*.

This objection to *Strangers* is in some ways the most cogent: it correctly challenges the bishops, particularly the Mexican bishops, to speak out in the future on the grave injustices that drive migration. But in a deeper sense this objection does not negate the veracity of the bishops' claims that the U.S. immigration system is badly in need of reform or that the United States bears important moral responsibilities toward its southern neighbors. The American bishops were compelled to speak out on the immigration crisis because of the suffering and despair of migrants in their parishes. That fact demanded a pastoral response that could not shun complex policy matters.

The objection to the misplacement of the moral burden of reform misses a crucial fact. To be sure, the Mexican authorities bear a heavy moral burden to enact systemic economic reforms that would enable Mexicans to support themselves and their families. But that fact in no way eliminates the United States' responsibility to reform a broken immigration system that ignores the economic realities and the moral dimension of migration. The current immigration system renders migrants who come to the United States vulnerable to exploitation of all kinds once they arrive. Current border enforcement strategies compel migrants to risk death by exposure in the desert and to place themselves at the mercy of human smugglers. The bishops' proposals directly address these grave moral concerns. The bishops call for specific actions that the United States can and therefore must take; indeed they are actions that only the United States can take. The bishops' call for the United States to implement comprehensive immigration reform does not absolve the Mexican authorities of their responsibilities; rather it is a call on the United States to acknowledge a moral burden it already bears.

The same holds true for the objection that the bishops implicitly absolve Mexican Catholics of their duties to work for social justice in Mexico. The bishops rightly presume that the Church in Mexico—the bishops, priests, and the laity, the entire people of God—have embraced John Paul II's invitation to "overcome every form of exploitation and oppression" in a manner that goes beyond merely "alleviating the most serious and urgent needs through individual actions here and there." But *Strangers* is a pastoral letter that addresses the reality of migration *to* the United States and the situation of migrants *in* the United States. So *Strangers* first and foremost is a call for American Catholics to stand in solidarity with the migrants already in their communities. Solidarity with the most vulnerable, like the obligation to make the liberating word of the Gospel resound in the complex world where men and women live, is also a requirement of the faith. Yes, John Paul II delivered *Ecclesia in America* in a basilica in the Mexican capital, but he opened his exhortation with a passage from Scripture: "From everyone to whom much has been given, much will be required; and from one to whom much has been entrusted, even more will be demanded" (Luke 12:48). In *Strangers* the bishops applied that admonition to the United States and to the American Catholics who have received the blessings of liberty and prosperity.

CONCLUSION

In *Strangers* the bishops adopted an approach taken decades earlier in the pastoral letters on the U.S. economy and the challenge of peace. On the one hand they addressed their specific policy proposals to the American public and invoked the familiar language of human rights in the hope of creating a moral consensus about the need for immigration reform. On the other hand they addressed the Catholic faithful, invoking the language of the Gospel and the Church's social teaching in the hope of stirring a sense of the laity's responsibilities in the society in which they live.[32] A decade later *Strangers*, as an effort to influence public opinion, policy, and the laity, reads like a parable. The failure of comprehensive immigration reform legislation in Congress highlighted limitations of the bishops' ability to sway public opinion with the weight of its pragmatic arguments about the benefits of immigration and its moral discourse about migrants' human rights. Reason had its limits in the politically charged atmosphere in the nation. But the fact remains that, despite any objections to the bishops' specific policy proposals, Catholics throughout the United States heeded the bishops' message of solidarity. The bishops' call to conversion, communion, and solidarity, inspired many Catholics to provide social and legal services to migrants, open migrant shelters, persuade city councils to establish "sanctuary cities," and otherwise defend migrants' fundamental human rights. In this they may have found, in John Paul's words, their own "path to sanctification" (EA 44). The fact that so many Catholics heeded the bishops' message, especially in communities where anti-migrant sentiments run high, attests to the dynamism of the Church. In this regard, there was no contradiction between the bishops' teaching on immigration and the laity's prudential judgment. At the same time, the fact that many Catholics expressed objections to the bishops' specific policy proposals also attests to the dynamism of the Church. The Church's dialogue with the modern world must begin with a dialogue between its own hierarchy and laity.

NOTES

1. President Bush, State of the Union Address, January 23, 2007, available at georgebush-whitehouse.archives.gov.

2. Samuel P. Huntington, *Who We Are: The Challenges to American National Identity* (New York: Simon and Schuster, 2004), 12.

3. Immigration is mentioned consecutively in connection with the challenges facing the nation, in connection with solidarity, love of

neighbor, and the scriptural call to welcome the stranger, and as a goal for political life.

4. "The direct duty to work for a just ordering of society, on the other hand, is proper to the lay faithful. As citizens of the State, they are called to take part in public life in a personal capacity. So they cannot relinquish their participation 'in the many different economic, social, legislative, administrative and cultural areas, which are intended to promote organically and institutionally the common good.' The mission of the lay faithful is therefore to configure social life correctly, respecting its legitimate autonomy and cooperating with other citizens according to their respective competences and fulfilling their own responsibility."

5. The American bishops in the instruction on faithful citizenship typically express this in simpler language: "prudence shapes and informs our ability to deliberate over available alternatives, to determine what is most fitting to a specific context, and to act decisively." To this the American bishops add, "Exercising this virtue often requires the courage to act in defense of moral principles when making decisions about how to build a society of justice and peace," FCFC, 19.

6. Lay Commission on Catholic Social Teaching and the U.S. Economy, "Towards the Future: Catholic Social Teaching and the U.S. Economy. A Lay Letter" (1984), 10 and 37.

7. "Towards the Future," 19, 74.

8. Representative Paul Ryan, letter to Archbishop Dolan (April 29, 2011), http://budget.house.gov/fy2012budget/dolandialogue.htm (accessed August 24, 2012).

9. In his response, Cardinal Dolan, while acknowledging that Vatican II reminds us "it is the lay faithful who have the specific charism of political leadership and decision," emphasized the imperative to adhere to the Church's teaching. "The principles of Catholic social teaching contains truths that need to be applied. Thus one must always exercise prudential judgments in applying these principles while never contradicting the intrinsic values that they protect." Cardinal Dolan, letter to Rep. Ryan (May 18, 2011); http://budget.house.gov/fy2012budget/dolandialogue.htm (accessed August 24, 2012).

10. The Catechism is more expansive on the point: "The more prosperous nations are obliged, to the extent they are able, to welcome the foreigner in search of the security and the means of livelihood

which he cannot find in his country of origin. Public authorities should see to it that the natural right is respected that places a guest under the protection of those who receive him. Political authorities, for the sake of the common good for which they are responsible, may make the exercise of the right to immigrate subject to various juridical conditions, especially with regard to the immigrants' duties toward their country of adoption. Immigrants are obliged to respect with gratitude the material and spiritual heritage of the country that receives them, to obey its laws, and assist in carrying civic burdens." United States Catholic Conference, *English Translation of the Catechism of the Catholic Church for the United States of America* (Rome: Liberia Editrice Vaticana, 1997), no. 2241. Hereafter, Catechism.

11. Notably, the very next section of *Pacem in Terris* concerns political rights. Indeed, it reads like an indictment of regimes, like the Soviet Bloc regimes "which govern solely or mainly by means of threats and intimidation, or promises of reward, and refuse to recognize human rights or act in violation of them...."

12. In one passage (SNL 106) the bishops refer to those who "are forced to migrate" but they make no attempt to equate the migration phenomenon along the U.S.-Mexico border with "forced migration." Nor would this be defensible, since the phenomenon does not meet the International Migration Organization's criteria for forced (or involuntary) migration, which encompasses refugees and internally displaced persons who flee conflict, man-made or natural disasters, famine, infectious diseases, or who are forcibly displaced by government action.

13. John Paul II, Address to the 34th General Assembly of the United Nations (2 October 1979), 7; http://www.vatican.va/holy_father/john_paul_ii/speeches/1979/october/documents/hf_jp-ii_spe_19791002_general-assembly-onu_en.html (accessed August 24, 2012).

14. "Convention Relating to the Status of Refugees." Adopted on July 28, 1951 by the United Nations Conference of Plenipotentiaries on the Status of Refugees and Stateless Persons convened under General Assembly resolution 429 (V) of December 14, 1950. Entry into force: April 22, 1954, in accordance with article 43. Article 1.

15. According to the U.S. Department of State's report to Congress in 2004, the United States and received no refugee or asylum petitions from any Mexican or Central American national. Those peti-

tions came almost entirely from Colombians fleeing a brutal civil conflict and Cubans who claimed the very right to emigrate for the reasons John XXIII specifically mentioned in *Pacem in Terris*. See Department of State, Department of Homeland Security, Department of Health and Human Services, "Report to the Committees on the Judiciary United States Senate and United States house of Representatives in Fulfillment of the Requirements of Section 207 (e) (1)–(7) of the Immigration and Nationality Act," 2004.

16. "International Convention on the Protection of the Rights of All Migrant Workers and Members of Their Families." Adopted by General Assembly resolution 45/158 of December 18, 1990.

17. See, for example, "Convention concerning Migrations in Abusive Conditions and the Promotion of Equality of Opportunity and Treatment of Migrant Workers" (no. 143). Entry into force: December 9, 1978. Adoption: Geneva, 60th ILC session (June 24, 1975); "Convention concerning Discrimination in Respect of Employment and Occupation" (no. 111). Entry into force: June 15, 1960. Adoption: Geneva, 42nd ILC session (June 25, 1958).

18. CMW, articles 68–69.

19. However, the bishops do call for vigorous enforcement of laws that criminalize and punish human trafficking.

20. "International Covenant on Economic, Social, and Cultural Rights." Adopted and opened for signature, ratification, and accession by General Assembly resolution 2200A (XXI) of December 16, 1966; entry into force January 3, 1976, in accordance with article 27.

21. Quoted in Mary Ann Glendon, *A World Made New: Eleanor Roosevelt and the Universal Declaration of Human Rights* (New York: Random House, 2001), 77.

22. "The laws we make through our elected representatives are under the scrutiny of the natural moral law we can know by reason, which means our political judgments should be rational...The inalienable dignity and value of every human being from conception until natural death is the bedrock personalist principle from which Catholic thinking about public policy begins. The dignity does not confer an absolute right on anyone to live wherever he or she chooses. A proper Catholic understanding of limited and constitutional government grasps that the state...has a right to enforce its citizenship laws..."

George Weigel, "An Immigration Debate Primer," *Denver Catholic Register* (May 19, 2010).

23. See, Mark Ensalaco, "The Right of the Child to Development," in Mark Ensalaco and Linda Majka eds., *Children's Human Rights: Progress and Challenges for Children World Wide* (Lanham, MD: Roman and Littlefield, 2005), 18–20.

24. Pope John Paul II, "Undocumented Migrants," Annual Message for World Migration Day 1996, given July 25 1995, 1; http://www.vatican.va/holy_father/john_paul_ii/messages/migration/documents/hf_jp-ii_mes_25071995_undocumented_migrants_en.html (accessed August 24, 2012).

25. Ibid., 4.

26. Ibid., 2.

27. "The public administration must therefore give considerable care and thought to the question of social as well as economic progress, and to the development of essential services in keeping with the expansion of the productive system. Such services include road-building, transportation, communications, drinking-water, housing, medical care, ample facilities for the practice of religion, and aids to recreation. The government must also see to the provision of insurance facilities, to obviate any likelihood of a citizen's being unable to maintain a decent standard of living in the event of some misfortune, or greatly increased family responsibilities."

28. The proposals include the creation of legal avenues for migration; legalization of the undocumented; employment based migration; humane enforcement policies in Mexico and the United States; reform of border enforcement tactics; and respect for migrants' due process.

29. Similarly Benedict XVI, in his first encyclical, repeated that the laity has the duty to work for a "just ordering of society" and therefore to become personally engaged in public life (DCE 29).

30. "As leaven in the society, pastoral agents can be instruments for peace and justice to promote systemic change by making legislators and other government officials aware of what they see in the community. Working closely with other advocates for workers and with nongovernmental organizations, the Church can be instrumental in developing initiatives for social change that benefit the most vulnerable members of the community."

31. Cited in Marvin L. Krier Mich, *Catholic Social Teaching and Movements* (Mystic, CT: Twenty-Third Publications, 2006), 243.

32. Here I am indebted to David O'Brien, who described these two complementary styles of teaching. See, David O'Brien, *Public Catholicism* (Maryknoll, NY: Orbis Books, 1996), 249.

CHAPTER 12

Moving Forward: Next Steps toward Immigration Reform

J. Kevin Appleby

On September 6, 2001, Vicente Fox, President of Mexico, addressed a joint session of the U.S. Congress, calling for a "regularization" of undocumented immigrants in the United States. At the end of his speech, he received a standing ovation.[1] Experts and immigration advocates expected the passage of a comprehensive immigration reform[2] bill by the end of the year.[3]

Five days later, the terrorist attacks of September 11, 2001, set back the issue of immigration reform indefinitely as national security concerns became a priority for Congress and the Bush administration. To date, Congress has yet to pass meaningful immigration reform legislation despite several attempts to do so.[4]

Since that tragic day in 2001, the U.S. Catholic bishops, through the U.S. Conference of Catholic Bishops (USCCB), have continued to push for immigration reform legislation. In their 2003 joint pastoral letter with the Mexican bishops entitled, *Strangers No Longer: Together on the Journey of Hope*, the U.S. bishops make the case that reform of our nation's immigration system remains in the best interests of our nation, as it would keep U.S. based immigrant families together, end the exploitation of undocumented migrants, and uphold and restore the rule of law.

As the pastoral letter celebrates its first decade, it is important to look back at the immigration debate over the past ten years, note the lessons learned, and develop a strategy for moving forward on the issue in the years ahead. As before, the Church will play an important role in any future national discussion of comprehensive immigration reform.

UNDERSTANDING THE CHURCH POSITION ON IMMIGRATION REFORM

The public policy position of the U.S. Catholic bishops on immigration reform has been misunderstood by some and misrepresented by others. As detailed in *Strangers No Longer*, the bishops view immigration reform as a way to repair a flawed immigration system in a humanitarian manner, but also to help end—or at least significantly reduce—irregular, or undocumented migration to the United States (SNL 2).

Contrary to some assertions,[5] the Catholic Church is not supportive of "open borders" or primarily interested in "filling the pews" with Catholic immigrants. As the bishops have pointed out, immigrants are already present in parishes and Church-sponsored social welfare agencies around the country. Without a change in the law, the Church is unable to help migrants separated from their families by detention or deportation or prevent their exploitation and death.[6]

The central, and most controversial, part of the USCCB position is the support of a program to provide a path to citizenship for eleven million undocumented persons residing in the United States. As more than four million U.S. citizen children live in families with one or more undocumented persons, a program which allows these family members—typically parents—to come out of the shadows and earn their citizenship would ensure that children are not separated from their deported parents. Providing legal status and a path to citizenship to this population also would reduce their exploitation and abuse in the workplace and community, as they would be better able to assert their rights. A legalization program with a path to citizenship is a central component of any immigration reform bill and also a main feature of the position outlined in *Strangers No Longer* (SNL 68–71).

Other reforms recommended by the bishops include a "future flow" worker program[7] that would allow migrant workers to enter the country and work legally, and changes to the family-based immigration system to reduce lengthy waiting times for family reunification (SNL 74–76). A "future flow" worker program, equipped with the proper worker protections, would prevent migrant workers, seeking to support their families, from crossing the desert at the risk of their lives (SNL

72–75). Reforms to the family-based immigration system would ensure that families are able to join their loved ones in a more timely fashion, thus discouraging them from attempting to enter the country illegally. Both these programs would serve the cause of family unity (SNL 64–66).

In recommending these changes to the legal immigration system, the U.S. bishops argue that illegal behavior would be replaced with legal behavior, both protecting the migrants from exploitation and abuse and restoring the rule of law. Under the current system, illegality is the norm, as there are insufficient legal avenues for persons to enter our nation to work or to join their families (SNL 76).

Enforcement of the law and national security are served, not undermined, by these reforms to the legal immigration system. By bringing the undocumented out of the shadows and creating legal avenues for migration, the bishops argue, those who are no threat to our communities and simply want to work would register with the government and become known to law enforcement, thus allowing law enforcement resources to be focused upon those who seek to harm us—criminals, smugglers, and human traffickers (SNL 70). As then Department of Homeland Security (DHS) Secretary Michael Chertoff testified before Congress in 2005, a program that permits workers to enter legally would assist the Border Patrol in defending the nation's borders.[8]

Instead of embracing this argument, Congress has spent an unprecedented amount of funds on immigration enforcement—as much as $150 billion since 2000—to reduce illegal immigration.[9] The opposite has happened. Since 2000, the number of undocumented immigrants in the nation has grown by 50 percent.[10]

To be sure, as they state in *Strangers No Longer*, the U.S. Catholic bishops support the right of a sovereign nation to secure its borders in order to protect the common good of its citizenry. However, this must not be achieved without respecting the basic human rights and dignity of the individual, a tenet of the document which current border and interior enforcement policies fail to meet (SNL 78–80).

From the bishops' perspective, and consistent with the right of a sovereign nation to control its borders, enforcement policies are best employed within the context of other legal immigration reforms outlined, thus creating a system with clear legal markers for migrants to follow. The combination of legal reforms with humane enforcement would help minimize illegal immigration and protect the basic human rights of migrants, the bishops conclude.

While immigration reform would help minimize illegal immigration, it would not end it. As long as gaps in economic development exist in the world, humans will move to areas and countries where they are able to not only survive but where the potential to improve their quality of life exists. Accordingly, the bishops state that the development of sustainable economies in sending countries represents the best long-term solution to the challenge of illegal immigration, as persons would be able to find jobs in their home countries to support their families in dignity (SNL 59–61). In other words, sustainable economic development is the Church's answer to a border wall.

From a broader perspective, the bishops make a larger moral point with regard to the U.S. immigration system. As a moral matter, they argue, our nation cannot use the labor of the undocumented to our benefit without extending to them the protections of our laws. In other words, we cannot use undocumented workers to pick our food, clean our houses, and take care of our children and our elderly while also violating their basic God-given rights. Such an immoral system must be changed.[11]

LESSONS LEARNED IN THE TEN YEARS OF *STRANGERS NO LONGER*

A SHORT HISTORY

Clearly, the 9/11 attacks produced a new and powerful dynamic within the immigration discussion, shelving any consideration of immigration reform for years. By the time the U.S. and Mexican bishops issued their pastoral letter in early 2003, the Congress and the Bush administration had already moved forward with an array of new policies designed to increase security within the nation's immigration system. Such laws and policies included the USA PATRIOT Act, the creation of the Department of Homeland Security, a new visa security system, and terrorist-related bars to admissibility, to name a few. Much has been discussed about the utility (and humanity) of these new policies, but the political environment during this period (2001–2006) was conducive to their adoption, regardless of their effectiveness against terrorist attacks. In fact, many have argued that Congress and the administration overreached, leaving millions of innocent persons to pay the price.[12]

During this period, the U.S. bishops delivered a message, unpopular at the time, that all immigrants cannot be blamed for the actions of a few, and that security policies should balance, to the greatest extent possible, immigrant rights with anti-terrorism goals (SNL 100).[13] In testimony before Congress in 2007, Bishop Thomas Wenski, then Bishop of Orlando, told the House Judiciary Committee that enforcement priorities should uphold, not undermine, basic human rights. [14]

As the bishops promoted their pastoral letter, however, it became clear that many in the nation were not disposed to a pro-immigrant message, and that further education on the issue was needed. As such, the U.S. Catholic bishops launched the Justice for Immigrants campaign in May 2005 to educate Catholics about immigration.[15]

It was not until 2006, five years after the 9/11 attacks, that Congress once again turned to the issue of immigration reform, but only in reaction to harsh enforcement legislation passed in the House of Representatives. On December 16, 2005, the House of Representatives passed the "Border Protection, Antiterrorism, and Illegal Immigration Control Act" (HR 4437), sponsored by Representative James Sensenbrenner (R-WI) and Representative Peter King (R-NY). The legislation contained many harsh enforcement provisions, most notably the criminalization of undocumented presence and of assisting undocumented persons with basic necessities. The latter provision would have placed at risk of criminal prosecution priests, nuns, and other Good Samaritans who minister to and provide social services to immigrants.[16]

During 2006, HR 4437 sparked outrage among immigrant communities and generated a series of marches and protests across the nation.[17] The U.S. bishops strongly opposed HR 4437 and helped push for the adoption of a more humane, comprehensive immigration package in the U.S. Senate. The resulting Senate bill,[18] which included a three-tier legalization system and a "future flow" worker program, passed the U.S. Senate by a 62–36 vote on May 25, 2006. The USCCB supported passage of the legislation, which did not include the harsh provisions of the House legislation. In retrospect, this successful vote represented the high-water mark for immigration advocates in the post-9/11 period.

At that point, the ill repute of the House bill across the nation caused Senate leaders to delay appointing conferees to join the two bills. Representative Sensenbrenner publicly declared the Senate bill dead in the House. Behind the scenes, however, he urged the Senate leadership to appoint conferees, as he and other House leaders were prepared to negotiate a compromise. Because of concerns in the immigrant community, including among the U.S. bishops, that any final bill could contain many, or at least some, of the harsh immigration provisions of the House legislation, the Senate leadership did not appoint conferees and the issue died for the year.[19]

Another opportunity for a comprehensive bill came in 2007, when Senator Edward M. Kennedy (D-MA), chairman of the Senate Subcommittee on Immigration, worked with the Bush administration on bipartisan legislation. Negotiations with Senate Republicans, led by Arizona Senator Jon Kyl (R-AZ), proved difficult, as they, along with the Bush administration, demanded an overhaul of the legal immigration system from the current family and employment-based quota system to a point system, similar to the Canadian model.[20] Senator Kyl also wanted a more "streamlined" legalization program which limited the eligibility requirements,[21] potentially eliminating a significant portion of the undocumented population.

Senator Kennedy heroically tried to forge a compromise acceptable to both the Republican side and Democrats aligned with pro-immigration groups, arguing that any deficiencies in the legislation could be corrected in the House of Representatives. In the end, such efforts failed, as Senate majority leader Harry Reid (D-NV), deferring to Senator Kennedy, brought to the Senate floor legislation which included a point-based system and the removal of certain family-based immigration categories. Because of this and limitations on the legalization program, the U.S. Catholic bishops issued a "flyer" to all Senators urging a vote against cloture and requesting that the legislation be sent back to committee for further revision. As a result of this intervention, lukewarm support from immigrant rights groups, and opposition from anti-immigrant forces, on June 28th the legislation failed, by fourteen votes, to garner the sixty votes needed for cloture.[22]

The decision by the U.S. Bishop's Committee on Migration to oppose cloture, instead of urging that the 2007 legislation move forward, was carefully considered and based on several factors. First, the legislation marked a significant departure from the current legal immigration system, basing legal entry mainly upon education and high-skilled labor, not family ties, a system which historically had served our nation well. Family unity is a core principle which the Church, and our nation, has honored for centuries, to our benefit. The 2007 legislation would have shifted the U.S. immigration system to a merit-based system, leaving the poor and their families with little opportunity to participate. It also would have favored the wealthy immigrant at the expense of the poor one.[23]

Second, there was no guarantee, despite Senator Kennedy's assurances, that the House of Representatives would have been able to produce a substantially improved bill. Although governed by a slim Democratic majority, conservative Democrats, combined with a strong Republican minority, would have likely opposed a more generous measure. It was unclear at the time whether the new point system, supported by the President, would have survived in any final legislation. Since it was supported by the Republicans, big business, and the administration, it likely would have been included in some form.

Perhaps Senator Kennedy, with decades of legislative experience, knew that the 2007 legislation had to reach a low mark before any improvements could be made, and maybe the House of Representatives could have passed a stronger and more just version of the measure. In any case, the USCCB could not support the 2007 legislation in the U.S. Senate on policy grounds. Given the bishops' public involvement in the issue, the USCCB also could not remain neutral. In fact, many Senate offices contacted the USCCB for advice on the bill. It became clear that the Catholic bishops could not remain silent on such a drastic—and damaging, in their view—change to our national immigration system.

The 2006 and 2007 bills marked the last opportunities for comprehensive legislation for a while, as the economic recession began in 2008 and, according to many economists, continues today. With unemployment leaping to 9 percent nationwide, momentum toward reform had stalled. The DREAM Act, a smaller legalization program for young immigrants, fell five votes short of passage in December,

2010.[24] Since then, states and localities have attempted to fill the void, passing their own measures related to illegal immigration, culminating in the recent Supreme Court decision in *Arizona v. United States.*

LESSONS LEARNED

Many lessons can be learned from the 2006 and 2007 debates which can be used in future legislative battles. The most apparent lesson is that opportunities to enact immigration reform legislation come rarely and depend upon a variety of variables, such as the national economic situation, national security concerns, and election cycles. When an opportunity comes, as it did in those years, pro-immigrant advocates must fully prepare for the inevitable trade-offs and not abandon the process prematurely. In other words, pro-reform advocates should better coordinate strategy, knowing in advance the contours of any possible agreement and working for the best compromise possible. As the saying goes, the perfect should not be the enemy of the good.

A second hard lesson learned is that immigration reform proponents must work harder to generate grassroots support for passage of the legislation. In 2007, opponents of the legislation wrote and called their Senators at least ten times more than proponents, giving the minority more power in negotiations. The loss of the cloture vote by such a substantial margin was due in part to the power demonstrated by the opponents of the bill.[25] Pro-reform advocates have worked since that time to bolster support across the nation, but much more work needs to be done.

A third lesson is that strong emotions exist on both sides of the immigration issue. While this observation may seem obvious, in 2006 and 2007 both supporters and opponents of immigration reform underestimated the strong feelings on the other side of the issue. In 2006, immigration reform opponents (and enforcement proponents) did not expect the national opposition to HR 4437. Similarly, supporters failed to anticipate the strong grassroots opposition to the legalization program in the 2007 bill.

Why is immigration such an explosive issue and why should pro-reform advocates take this into account? One main consideration is because the national immigration debate is not merely about how we determine who enters the country and under what rules; it also is about the identity and future of our nation. As such, the divisiveness of the issue has increased, and has become perhaps the most emotional domestic issue our nation faces, outside abortion.

In order to bridge this divide, more dialogue between pro-immigrant groups and individuals and immigration opponents must occur at the same time education of the American public continues. In the end, any solution to this national challenge will involve compromise and political courage, bolstered by an American public aware of the consequences of not fixing a broken system. In order to reach this point and to break the current stalemate on immigration policy in this country, several preparatory steps must be taken.

MOVING FORWARD: SOLVING THE IMMIGRATION CHALLENGE

Before the nation is ready to solve the immigration challenge, several necessary steps must be taken to prepare for it—in other words, to make the ground politically fertile for reform legislation. Some are policies which had not been in place during the 2006 and 2007 debates and had an unmeasured but real impact upon their outcomes; others are environmental factors that must improve.

THE DEVELOPMENT OF A NATIONAL IMMIGRANT INTEGRATION POLICY

One of the underreported factors undermining immigration reform—especially a program providing legal status to the undocumented—is the perception held by some Americans that newly arrived immigrants do not want to become Americans, but would rather maintain their culture, language, and national allegiances while inhabiting our nation. Of course, this perception is based upon messages developed by anti-immigrant organizations,[26] which are adept at scapegoating immigrants for our nation's social ills. In fact, immigrants today integrate at the same rate as immigrants who came several generations ago. The United States continues to rank among the top nations in successfully integrating immigrants, despite the absence of a national immigrant integration policy.[27]

Historically, churches and local communities have played a large role in welcoming and integrating immigrants to the United States, with federal and state governments playing a more limited role. But many Americans want to be reassured by their government that newcomers are playing by the same rules as they are and are loyal to the nation and its culture prior to further changes being made to the nation's immigration system. In this regard, political leaders and government officials should focus more attention on policies which assist immigrants to become Americans, such as English and civics instruction.

While the Obama administration has recommended and Congress has appropriated some funding for these purposes in recent years, the amount has been miniscule compared to other programs.[28] Moreover, neither Congressional leaders nor the President have spoken consistently to the need for integration initiatives in the context of overall immigration reform.

Why is it important that integration be included as a component of immigration reform? Because it is part of the response to the cultural fear that some Americans have toward immigration—the fear that they are losing the American culture they grew up with and know well. Polling and focus groups have shown that Americans believe that immigrants should become integrated and learn English as soon as possible.[29]

When immigrants marched in several cities around the nation in 2006, for example, many Americans reacted negatively to the Mexican flags and Spanish messages which were a prominent part of the marches, thus negating their effectiveness.[30] If our elected officials, by both word and deed, are able to show the American public that integration is an important aspect of our immigration policies, it would help reduce the cultural fear undermining progress on immigration reform.[31]

Another unfounded fear many Americans have is that immigrants—especially those without legal status—are benefitting from the United States economically and in other ways without abiding by the requirements of being a U.S. citizen, including the payment of taxes, service in the military, and other obligations.

While the facts show this not to be true[32]—as undocumented persons do pay taxes and serve in the military—the perception among many Americans is to the contrary. A robust integration policy would help correct this misperception. Ironically, a program which provides legal status to the undocumented population that requires them to pay back taxes and get in the back of the line for citizenship also would counter this perception.[33] In reality, a legalization program is the ultimate immigrant integration program.

RESTORING FAITH IN GOVERNMENT

In recent years, the U.S. government has focused upon a build-up of enforcement resources, both along the border and in the interior of the nation. This has been one of several factors that have led to the decrease in migration over the past five years.[34] However, little attention and scant resources have been directed toward the benefit side of the immigration system—citizenship, permanent residency, asylum, and refugee adjudications—in an effort to shorten waiting times and clear backlogs. If the government cannot efficiently process current applications for benefits, how can it handle a legalization program for eleven million persons?[35]

Part of the problem is that the U.S. Citizenship and Immigration Service (USCIS), the agency within the Department of Homeland Security (DHS) tasked with discharging these responsibilities, is primarily funded by user fees. Any reform legislation would have to be accompanied by a commitment of more resources to this agency, or, in the alternative, to a newly created and separate office charged with implementation. User fees charged to those applying for any new legalization program would be insufficient to cover all the costs associated with such a large program.

To make matters worse, in recent years the American public's confidence in the performance and efficiency of the U.S. government has reached new lows. The humanitarian responses to natural disasters, highlighted by the lackluster response to Hurricane Katrina in 2007, combined with a general dissatisfaction with the government's ability to revive the nation's economy, has led to some disillusionment with government as the antidote to the nation's ills.[36] The inability of Congress to pass meaningful legislation on a range of topics certainly has not helped matters.

In this context, the American public must be shown that government can implement a massive immigration reform program, first, and then can guarantee that such a program would be effective in reducing, if not ending, illegal immigration in the future.

"SECURING" THE BORDER

Some elected officials have argued that "securing" U.S. borders is the only way to end illegal immigration. They also claim that it is the only way to convince the American public that illegal immigration will be reduced, if not ended. As such, proposals have been discussed which would require border security measures in advance of the implementation of any legalization program.

During the post-9/11 era, there have been many immigration policies adopted in the name of border security, including an unprecedented enforcement build-up along the nation's southern border.[37] Despite recent evidence that illegal immigration from Mexico and Latin American has virtually stopped,[38] some immigration opponents still claim that the U.S.-Mexico border is not secure. This is often used by some in Congress to hold off any real discussion of a major overhaul of our nation's immigration laws.[39] Sadly, whether Congress can come to some agreement on immigration reform may depend upon whether they can agree upon the definition of a "secure" border.

Part of reaching an agreement on such a definition will depend on the comfort level of the American public regarding national security in the post-9/11 era. There already are signs that the country is moving away from the uneasiness of the 2001–2006 period, when many immigration policies were adopted in the name of national security. The absence of another successful terrorist attack since 9/11, the end of the Iraq war, and recent successes against the Al-Qaeda leadership (the death of Osama Bin Laden being primary), have helped ease the American psyche in this regard. However, it is safe to assume that national security will never be completely divorced from immigration policy, only that it will remain one of many factors to consider in fashioning it.

The U.S. Catholic bishops, following Catholic social teaching, support the right of a sovereign nation to control its borders. However, the definition of "control" is dependent upon other variables, including the right of an individual to migrate. In the Catholic tradition, neither the right to migrate nor the right to control one's borders is absolute. As a result, a balancing test emerges which calculates the obligation of nations to legally welcome immigrants against their right to control their borders to serve the common good of their citizens.

In *Strangers No Longer*, the U.S. and Mexican bishops address this issue by stating that no sovereign nation should control its borders at the expense of basic human rights: "While the sovereign state may impose reasonable limits on immigration, the common good is not served when the basic human rights of the individual are violated" (SNL 39) They conclude: "In the current condition of the world, in which global poverty and persecution are rampant, the presumption is that persons must migrate in order to support and protect themselves and that nations who are able to receive them do so whenever possible" (SNL 39).[40] As a result, the U.S. bishops have argued against an enforcement-only approach to "securing" the border, instead maintaining that immigration reform, which would help legalize flows of migrants into the United States, represents the more secure and humane approach. In addition, the bishops and others have stated that it is virtually impossible to "secure" a three thousand-mile border through enforcement.[41]

ECONOMIC RECOVERY

Of course, comprehensive immigration reform will not gain political traction without the nation's economy sufficiently recovering from the recession, which began as early as 2008. This is most important in terms of the national unemployment rate. Polls have shown that Americans want Congress to focus on job creation above other issues.[42]

In this political environment, it is vital that immigration reform supporters make the case that immigrants can assist in such a recovery, a notion counterintuitive to many Americans. American history has demonstrated that during depressed economic periods immigrants are often used as scapegoats for the nation's struggles, despite evidence that immigrants are the "first fired" during such periods.[43] However, research shows that immigrants, many of whom are undocumented, are necessary to keep important industries working, particularly the agriculture and the service industries. Further research finds that immigrants, who often start businesses or keep them going, help create jobs over the long term.[44]

Despite this evidence, elected officials of both parties remain extremely reluctant to discuss, much less vote on, immigration reform legislation during economic down periods. It is unlikely that this reality will change until the U.S. economy shows signs of improvement. With continued advocacy and education about the contributions of immigrants to economic growth, however, immigration reform supporters may be able to move up the timetable for congressional action.

ELEMENTS OF A NEW "GRAND BARGAIN"

Assuming some, if not all, of these preliminary steps occur, a viable blueprint for a bipartisan agreement on immigration reform could surface within the next few years. Such a blueprint would include the basic elements of past bills, including a legalization program for the undocumented and changes to the employment and family-based immigration systems. These reforms would be balanced with new enforcement measures, which would include further steps to "secure" the borders and some version of a mandatory nationwide employment verification system, otherwise known as E-verify.[45]

However, such a "grand bargain," as past attempts at bipartisan agreement have been called, is fraught with dangers and challenges. First would be attempts by opponents to weaken any legalization program, either by limiting the number eligible for a program, reducing the immigration benefits potential beneficiaries would receive, or both. The most troubling proposal would grant the undocumented population legal status without providing them a path to citizenship. This idea was most recently proposed by Senator Marco Rubio (R-FL) in his (unwritten) version of the DREAM Act.[46]

The U.S. bishops have opposed such a proposal, arguing that it would create a "permanent underclass" in U.S. society, a concept which has led to social unrest in the past and which undermines basic Constitutional principles. Moreover, the bishops have stated, it would exclude a segment of the permanent population from participating in the political process, thus disenfranchising them and leaving them without the ability to redress the government for grievances, a basic right of any citizen.[47]

A second challenge likely will surface in the debate over the legal immigration system, as pro-business political forces will attempt to increase the number of employment-based visas, particularly in the highly skilled categories, at the expense of the family-based immigration system. As discussed earlier, this occurred in 2007 with the proposed point-based system.

At a minimum, there will be attempts to eliminate the third and fourth preference categories[48] and limit family reunification categories to the nuclear family (spouses and children). The USCCB has opposed these changes, stating that the U.S. immigration system should remain a family-based system, a framework that has served our nation well since its inception. The USCCB would not oppose an increase in employment-based visas, but not at the expense of family visas and in addition to a reduction of waiting times in current family categories.[49]

Another flashpoint in any future debate will be the creation of a "future flow" program, which would allow migrant workers to enter and work in certain industries legally, rather than working illegally and crossing, at great peril, the U.S.-Mexico border. As mentioned earlier, in *Strangers No Longer* the U.S. and Mexican bishops outline basic requirements for such a program, including the enforcement of basic workplace protections and the ability, under certain conditions, for workers to apply for permanent residency. Such a program, they reason, would substantially improve the status quo, in which undocumented workers risk their lives in the desert to find work and, once having found it, are subject to exploitation and abuse (SNL 75).

To date, the fate of such a new program has depended upon discussions between U.S. labor organizations and business groups, which the U.S. bishops have encouraged. However, how such discussions are resolved in an agreement, and how that agreement is received by Congress, could determine whether immigration reform legislation moves forward.

Finally, the issues of both workplace and border enforcement will undoubtedly be a central part of any bipartisan agreement. In terms of workplace enforcement, a mandatory nationwide employment verification system has been debated for several years, but has not gained sufficient support as a stand-alone measure.

At this juncture, it is clear that politically such a massive program would have to be accompanied by other immigration reforms.[50] Notwithstanding its implementation problems, the U.S. bishops have not opposed such a program, provided it is accompanied by a national legalization program and by certain protections for workers. Before such a system is passed into law, they state, all undocumented workers should be legalized and become part of the new system in order to avoid the creation of an underground economy and further exploitation and abuse of the undocumented. In addition, a transparent appeals process for workers who are flagged in the system must be created.[51]

As for border enforcement, the argument that the southern border must be "secure" before the enactment of other reforms, including a legalization program, certainly will resurface in any future debate. Some elected officials, most notably Senator John McCain (R-AZ), have suggested that certain "benchmarks" for securing the border be reached before any legalization program commences.[52] Of course, the debate would center upon the definition of "benchmarks," whether reaching them would be time-limited, and whether the legalization program would be implemented if certain goals are not achieved. In 2010, Senator McCain and Senator Kyl introduced a ten-point plan for enhanced security of the border,[53] which could be used as a template in any future negotiations.

Despite these questions, such a framework could represent a workable compromise for moving legislation forward. In such a debate, the U.S. bishops would fight for humane and achievable benchmarks and would argue that implementation of the legalization program occur within a reasonable period and not be dependent upon whether all the benchmarks are achieved. The USCCB also would support a standard based upon "operational control" of the border, the term currently used by the Department of Homeland Security.

In short, the elements of a bipartisan immigration reform agreement exist, but the political will, at least at the moment, does not. The role of the faith community, particularly the Catholic community, could make a difference in moving the issue forward and achieving reform legislation in the not too distant future.

THE ROLE OF THE CATHOLIC COMMUNITY IN MOVING IMMIGRATION REFORM FORWARD

With a strong tradition of welcoming newcomers to the United States, the Catholic community could play a decisive role in pushing immigration reform forward. The Catholic Church in the United States is itself an immigrant Church, having grown as successive waves of immigrants reached U.S. shores. After their families, parishes often have served as a second home for many immigrants and have become the focal point of many immigrant communities.[54]

Given such an immigrant-rich history, combined with nearly seventy million Catholics nationwide, the Catholic Church is uniquely positioned to influence any future immigration reform debate. The challenge for the Church, however, is educating Catholics about the issue and mobilizing sufficient numbers to impact Congress. This has been an ongoing effort with still more to accomplish. As previously mentioned, 60 percent of Catholics support a legalization program, provided applicants are required to register with the government, pay a fine, and learn English.

The problem, as it is with all Americans, is motivating Catholics to become politically active in supporting the issue, that is, calling or writing their legislators. The Justice for Immigrants (JFI) campaign, begun by the U.S. bishops in 2005, has worked to achieve this end, with over fifty thousand Catholics and nearly twenty Catholic groups as partners in the campaign. With these individuals and groups working together, sufficient numbers could be generated to make a significant difference in any future debate.

In order to increase these numbers, however, the U.S. bishops must continue to speak out on the issue and respond to the concerns of Catholics who are ambivalent or who have legitimate concerns about the rule of law and the enforcement of immigration laws. Although the bishops support enforcement as one part of the immigration solution, too many Catholics believe that the Church does not speak enough about that aspect of the issue, particularly about the rule of law.[55]

To complicate matters, the emphasis on immigration as an issue varies from diocese to diocese and from parish to parish. Although understandable in such a big organization, there often are different priorities in different (arch)dioceses, as well as a lack of resources. As many Catholics do not agree with the discussion of immigration—considered a political issue—during Mass, additional avenues for discussing the issue must be found. For example, Archbishop Charles Chaput, then Archbishop of Denver, courageously held "town halls" around his archdiocese in 2006, and answered questions from Catholics on the issue.[56]

Additionally, the U.S. bishops must recruit Catholic fraternal orders such as the Knights of Columbus, the Knights of Malta, and Legatus, the Catholic business group, to assist in the effort. These groups have large (and influential) memberships, but do not consistently promote the Church's teaching on immigration. Archbishop José H. Gomez, Archbishop of Los Angeles, and current Chairman of the USCCB Committee on Migration, has specifically reached out to these groups, stating to them that welcoming immigrants is part of the pastoral mission of the Church, and, thus, part of their mission, too.[57]

The Catholic Church, perhaps more than any institution in the United States, has a vested interest in immigration reform. Each day, Catholic parishes, social service agencies, hospitals, and schools witness the consequences of a broken immigration system, as immigrants and their families ask for their help. Without immigration reform, the Church is limited in how she can help this growing population of Catholics, not to mention immigrants of other faiths.[58] And as a witness to the suffering brought about by a broken system, the Catholic community, led by the U.S. bishops, must continue to call for humane immigration reform, and use its resources, where possible, to achieve it. The role of the Catholic Church in any future immigration debate will be crucial to its outcome.

CONCLUSION

Since *Strangers No Longer: Together on the Journey of Hope* was published in 2003, the road to comprehensive immigration reform has been filled with potholes. With the effects of a major terrorist attack and a deep recession adversely impacting the political environment, progress has been slow. Despite the rough terrain, immigration reform continues to be part of our national discourse, and the elements of a "grand bargain" remain in place. With increased advocacy, soon our nation's elected officials will realize that they can no longer avoid the issue, and that the political cost of not addressing immigration reform exceeds the cost of moving forward.

While the skeptics and opponents of reform will continue to

work against it, supporters should not be deterred or lose heart. The indicators for success remain on the pro-reform side, provided ongoing advocacy efforts continue and increase. The economy will improve, security concerns will diminish, and public opinion in support of addressing immigration reform will return. In time, our elected leaders will do the right thing, both for our immigrant brothers and sisters and for the nation. The journey to immigration reform may be long, but it is filled with hope.

NOTES

1. Address by His Excellency Vicente Fox, President of the United Mexican States, U.S. House of Representatives (September 6, 2001), Congressional Record, H5411–H5412.

2. Comprehensive Immigration Reform has been used to describe changes in all parts of the federal immigration system, including the legal immigration system. For purposes of this article, the term "immigration reform" will be used. See Wikipedia, "Immigration Reform," at http://en.wikipedia.org/wiki/Immigration_reform.

3. Marc Rosenblum, "Immigration Policy since 9/11: Understanding the Stalemate over Comprehensive Immigration Reform" (Washington, DC: Migration Policy Institute, August 2011); http://www.migrationpolicy.org/pubs/RMSG-post-9-11policy.pdf (accessed September 6, 2012).

4. Ibid.

5. *Lou Dobbs Tonight*, "Catholic Church Pushes Amnesty" (April 2, 2007).

6. According to the U.S. Border Patrol, as many as six thousand migrants have died crossing the U.S.-Mexico border since 1994, the year the U.S. government initiated blockades of urban border areas. See Maria Jimenez, "Humanitarian Crisis: Migrant Deaths at the U.S.-Mexico Border," October 1, 2009, footnote 1, www.aclu.org.

7 In the past, these types of worker programs have been referred to as "guest-worker" programs.

8. Michael Chertoff, Secretary of the Department of Homeland Security, Testimony before the Senate Judiciary Committee (October 17, 2005).

9. Department of Homeland Security and Immigration and Naturalization Service, Annual Budget submissions, 2000–2010.

10. Pew Hispanic Center, U.S. Census Bureau, U.S. Census Reports, 2000, 2010.

11. Most Reverend John C. Wester, Bishop of Salt Lake City, "The Catholic Church and Immigration Reform," address at Stetson University (April 4, 2010).

12. Don Kerwin and Margaret D. Stock, "National Security and Immigration Policy: Reclaiming Terms, Measuring Success, and Setting Priorities" (November 9, 2011); http://www.aclu.org/files/fbimappingfoia/20111110/ACLURM002826.pdf (accessed September 6, 2012).

13. It should be noted that all 9/11 terrorists entered the country on temporary visas and not through the southern border.

14. Most Reverend Thomas G. Wenski, Bishop of Orlando (current Archbishop of Miami), "On Comprehensive Immigration Reform," Testimony before the House Subcommittee on Immigration, Citizenship, Refugees, and Border Security (May 22, 2007).

15. www.justiceforimmigrants.org.

16. Editorial, "The Gospel v. HR 4437," *New York Times* (March 3, 2006).

17. *PBS News Hour,* "Latino Communities Rally over Immigration Reform" (April 10, 2006).

18. Comprehensive Immigration Reform Act, S. 2611 (May 25, 2006).

19. S. 2611, www.thomas.gov, 110th Congress.

20. In Canada's immigration system, visas are awarded based on a point system. Immigrants with high-level skills, such as professionals with education, receive a higher number of points than unskilled workers. Family ties have little or no impact on visa issuance, which comes under a separate program. See "Canadian Immigration Points Calculator," www.workpermit.com.

21. Immigrants who had committed minor offenses or re-entered the country illegally were not eligible for the proposed program.

22. Robert Pear, "Broad Effort to Resurrect Immigration Bill," *New York Times* (June 16, 2007).

23. USCCB flyer to the U.S. Senate (June 13, 2007).

24. U.S. Senate Roll Call Votes, Second Session, 111th Congress (December 18, 2010).

25. "Senator Sessions: Immigration Calls Crashed Capitol Hill Phone System," June 28, 2007, www.democraticunderground.com.

26. See the websites of Federation of Americans for Immigration Reform, www.fairusa.org, and Numbers USA, www.numbersusa.org.

27. "Migrant Integration Policy Index" (Immigration Policy Center, Washington, DC, May 9, 2011); http://www.immigrationpol icy.org/just-facts/migrant-integration-policy-index-mipex-iii.

28. USCIS has distributed approximately $18.3 million in integration grants since 2009. See "USCIS Announces Citizenship and Integration Grant Opportunity," 3/20/2012, www.uscis.gov.

29. A poll conducted by the USCCB in 2008 found that 56 percent of Catholics supported a legalization program, provided the participants learned English.

30. "Coordinating Flags at Immigration Marches," *All Things Considered*, National Public Radio (April 11, 2006); http://www.npr. org/templates/story/story.php?storyId=5336799 (accessed September 6, 2012).

31. Samuel P. Huntington, *Who Are We? The Challenge to America's National Identity* (New York: Simon and Schuster, 2004). The controversial book makes the argument that immigrants—specifically Hispanics—are threatening American culture and identity.

32. According to the Social Security Administration, undocumented immigrants paid a net contribution of $12 billion into the Social Security Trust Fund in 2007 alone; see Edward Schumacher-Matos, "How Illegal Immigrants are Helping Social Security," *Washington Post* (September 3, 2010).

33. Focus groups organized by the U.S. Conference of Catholic Bishops in 2008 found that Catholics believed that undocumented immigrants received benefits unfairly. The groups strongly supported a path to citizenship which required immigrants to pay taxes, fines, and learn English.

34. The economic recession, an improved Mexican economy, lower birth rates in Mexico and Central America, and increased dangers from drug cartels and smugglers on the way to the United States are other factors contributing to lower rates of migration. Jeffrey Passell, D'Vera Cohn, and Ana Gonzalez-Barrera, "Net Migration from Mexico

Falls to Zero—and Perhaps Less" (Pew Hispanic Center, April 23, 2012); http://www.pewhispanic.org/2012/04/23/net-migration-from-mexico-falls-to-zero-and-perhaps-less/.

35. Robert Pear and Carl Hulse, "Immigrant Bill Fails to Survive Senate Vote," *New York Times* (June 28, 2007).

36. Ibid.

37. Since 2006, the number of Border Patrol agents has nearly doubled and close to seven hundred miles of fencing has been built along the southern border. "Border Patrol gets first new strategy in eight years," *USA Today*, May 18, 2012.

38. Jeffrey Passell, D'Vera Cohn, and Ana Gonzalez-Barrera, "Net Migration from Mexico Falls to Zero—and Perhaps Less" (Pew Hispanic Center, April 23, 2012); http://www.pewhispanic.org/2012/04/23/net-migration-from-mexico-falls-to-zero-and-perhaps-less/.

39. Ken Dilanian and Nicholas Riccardi "Border Security Trips up Immigration Debate," *Los Angeles Times* (June 15, 2010); http://articles.latimes.com/2010/jun/15/nation/la-na-border-security-20100615 (accessed September 6, 2012).

40. This statement does not include national security concerns, which, in some cases, would justify restrictions on immigration.

41. Bishop Thomas Wenski, "On Immigration Reform." See also "Border Impossible to Secure, Experts Say," *Fox News Latino* (December 6, 2011).

42. Polls have shown that immigration ranks behind jobs, the economy, and other related issues as a priority for Americans. Gallup Poll, March 3–6, 2011, "American's Worries about Economy, Budget Top Other Issues" (March 21, 2011); http://www.gallup.com/poll/146708/Americans-Worries-Economy-Budget-Top-Issues.aspx (accessed September 6, 2012).

43. Catherine Rampell, "The Job Market for Immigrants," *New York Times*, September 10, 2012; http://economix.blogs.nytimes.com/2010/08/14/the-job-market-for-immigrants/.

44. "Strength in Diversity: The Economic and Political Power of Immigrants, Latinos, and Asians in the U.S." (Immigrant Policy Center, June 2012).

45. For more information on E-verify, visit the National Immigration Law Center website at www.nilc.org and search E-verify for numerous articles.

46. Napp Nazworth, "Senator Marco Rubio Building Support for DREAM Act," *The Christian Post* (June 3, 2012); http://www.christianpost.com/news/sen-marco-rubio-introduces-dream-act-compromise-75972/.

47. His Eminence Theodore Cardinal McCarrick, Testimony before the U.S. Senate Subcommittee on Immigration (September 25, 2009), p. 6; www.usccb/mrspolicy.org.

48. Twenty-three thousand permanent visas are issued each year to married sons and daughters of U.S. citizens under the third preference; sixty-five thousand permanent visas are issued each year to adult brothers and sisters of U.S. citizens under the fourth preference.

49. USCCB has proposed adding category 2(b), immediate family members of U.S. permanent residents to category 2(a), immediate family members of U.S. citizens and giving those permanent visas to other categories. USCCB Components of Immigration Reform Fact Sheet, www.usccb/mrspolicy.org.

50. Stephen Dinan, "E-verify Bill Stirs Broader Immigration Debate," *Washington Times* (September 21, 2011).

51. Most Reverend José H. Gomez, Archbishop of Los Angeles, "The National Electronic Verification System," Testimony before the House Judiciary Subcommittee on Immigration Policy and Enforcement (February 10, 2011).

52. *Meet the Press*, NBC Network, "Meet the Candidates" Series (January 27, 2008).

53. Senator Jon Kyl and Senator John McCain, "Ten Point Plan for Enhanced Border Security"; http://www.kyl.senate.gov/legis_center/border.cfm#2 (accessed September 6, 2012).

54. Augustino Bono, "Study: Catholic Churches Key in integrating immigrants into U.S.," Catholic News Service, August 21, 2006; http://www.catholic.org/national/national_story.php?id=20973.

55. Robert Royal, "Catholics and Immigration," *The Catholic Thing*, May 2, 2010; http://www.thecatholicthing.org/columns/2010/catholics-and-immigration.html.

56. "Archbishop Discusses Catholic Church's position on immigration reform," *PBS News Hour* (August 15, 2006). Archbishop Chaput is currently Archbishop of Philadelphia.

57. "129th Knights of Columbus Convention—Archbishop José Gomez on Immigration Policy," *Salt and Light Blog* (August 3, 2011); http://saltandlighttv.org/blog/?s=gomez (accessed September 6, 2012).

58. Catholic dioceses and social service agencies serve the vulnerable based on "need, not creed." According to the late James Cardinal Hickey of Washington, DC, "We serve the least not because they are Catholic, but because we are Catholic." Kristen Hannum, "Why Social Justice? Because We're Catholic," *U.S. Catholic*, June 22, 2012.

Afterword

Archbishop Silvano Maria Tomasi

Archbishop Silvano M. Tomasi, CS, is an Apostolic Nuncio and Permanent Observer of the Holy See to the United Nations and Other International Organizations in Geneva.

On October 12, 1992, Pope John Paul II spoke to the Latin American bishops at the opening of their Fourth General Assembly in Santo Domingo, at which time he promoted the idea of convening a synodal meeting of the American bishops (EA 2–3). The positive response he received led him two years later to voice his intention to call together a series of continental synods, each of which would, respectively, focus on the Church in the Americas (1997), Asia (1998), and Oceania (1998) (TMA 38). An earlier continental Synod was held for Europe in 1991, followed by a second one in 1999, and another for Africa in 1994.

The Synod of Bishops, of which these continental Synods were an expression, was formally established in September 1965 in response to the desire of the Second Vatican Council Fathers to continue the sense of solidarity and collegial brotherhood that had emerged as a result of the conciliar experience.[1] As Pope Paul VI defined it nearly a decade later, the Synod "is an ecclesial institute, which we, questioning the signs of the times, and even more so in trying to interpret in depth Divine plans and the constitution of the Catholic Church, have established after Vatican Council II, to promote unity and collaboration between the Bishops of the whole world in this Apostolic See, through the common study of the conditions of the Church and in agreement on the questions pertaining to her mission."[2] From its establishment to the present, the bishops have on occasion met in such a forum to discuss pressing issues of importance in the life of the Church.

The most recent Special Assembly for the American Bishops was held in Vatican City from November 16 through December 12, 1997. Its primary purpose was aimed at the role of the new evangelization in

305

the Americas and on questions related to justice and economic relations in this part of the world (TMA 38). Throughout his opening homily to the assembly, Pope John Paul II repeatedly referred to the important role that the Church has played and should continue to play on the "American continent." While it was important to consider the unique contributions that the Southern, Central, and Northern parts of America had contributed to the life of the Church in the five hundred years since she began to evangelize in the New World, it was equally important to recognize this region as a single, organic reality.[3] In his Post-Synodal Apostolic Exhortation *Ecclesia in America*, which was the crowning point of the Synod, the pope referred to his decision to speak of "America" in the singular as "an attempt to express not only the unity which in some way already exists, but also to point to that closer bond which the peoples of the continent seek and which the Church wishes to foster as part of her own mission, as the she works to promote the communion of all in the Lord" (EA 5).

The publication of the joint pastoral letter *Strangers No Longer: Together on the Journey of Hope* (2003) by the American and Mexican bishops represented a further outgrowth of the spirit of communion promoted by Pope John Paul II in his convening of the American Synod in 1997. In its opening paragraphs the bishops highlighted this continuum and noted that "in the spirit of ecclesial solidarity begun in that synod and promoted in *Ecclesia in America*, and aware of the migration reality our two nations live, we the bishops of Mexico and the United States seek to awaken our peoples to the mysterious presence of the crucified and risen Lord in the person of the migrant and to renew in them the values of the Kingdom of God that he proclaimed" (SNL 3). While the Synod had addressed a wide range of issues pertinent to the American Church, the joint pastoral letter was narrower in its focus and picked up on the specific issue of migration.

Throughout *Strangers No Longer* the bishops appealed both to Scripture and to Catholic social teaching as a way to frame a Catholic response to the pastoral and policy implications of migration between the two countries. In the Old Testament God called on Abraham to leave the land of Ur to the promised land of Canaan (Gen 12:1–2), and commanded the Israelites to care for the alien who lives among them (Lev 19:33–34). In the New Testament the Holy Family is forced to flee into Egypt as refugees, while Jesus is often portrayed in his min-

istry as a migrant who has no place to lay his head. In his public teachings he established how we care for the stranger as a standard against
which we will be judged: "I was thirsty and you gave me something to
drink, I was a stranger and you welcomed me" (Matt 25:35). Taken
from a much broader perspective, our passage through life here on
earth can be understood as a long migration to the kingdom of heaven,
with Christ himself as an active participant in this process. Earlier in
this volume, Fr. Dan Groody highlighted the importance of this theme
to Christian thought when he noted "we come from God and are
called to return to God, and from beginning to end the Scriptures
reveal to us a God who migrates to his people, eliciting a response of
faith that does justice in its homeward journey."

Along with an appeal to Scripture, *Strangers* also provides a moral
framework that is rooted in Catholic teaching and which the bishops
believe should guide the formation of public policy.[4] Such a framework
includes a series of moral principles that are applicable to migration
and whose roots are evident in earlier papal teaching. While each of
these principles is intelligible on their own, each nuances the others
and provides a sense of balance to what might come off to some as
competing and contradictory claims. The first principle promoted by
the bishops in their letter is that "persons have a right to find opportunities in their homeland" (SNL 34). In his encyclical *Rerum Novarum*,
Leo XIII recognized the loyalty that one naturally has to her native
country so long as they are able to make a "decent and happy life" for
themselves (RN 47).[5] Being able to secure the goods necessary for existence in one's homeland is something that should to be respected and
pursued; individuals ought to have access to the basic necessities of life
that will help them to "live in dignity and achieve a full life through the
use of their God-given gifts" (SNL 34).

This claim is balanced by the recognition that not everyone is
able to secure such a livelihood in their homeland and thus, when such
situations arise, "Persons have the right to migrate to support themselves and their families" (SNL 35). In his noteworthy Apostolic
Constitution, *Exsul Familia*, Pope Pius XII specifically highlighted the
right of people to migrate when it is necessary to ensure their continued welfare. Here he quoted from a letter written to the American
bishops on Christmas Eve, 1948, in which he wrote that

the natural law itself, no less than devotion to humanity, urges that ways of migration be opened to these people. For the Creator of the universe made all good things primarily for the good of all. Since land everywhere offers the possibility of supporting a large number of people, the sovereignty of the State, although it must be respected, cannot be exaggerated to the point that access to this land is, for inadequate or unjustified reasons, denied to needy and decent people from other nations, provided of course, that the public welfare, considered very carefully, does not forbid this. (EF)

It is important to note that, while highlighting the obligation of the state to provide support to "needy and decent people from other nations," there are limitations on the obligations of states to respond to those who wish to migrate. Almost a dozen years later Pope John XXIII reaffirmed both points when noted that it is the "duty of State officials to accept such immigrants and—so far as the good of their own community, rightly understood, permits—to further the aims of those who may wish to become members of a new society" (PT 106). So long as the common good of the receiving nation is not being unduly harmed, there should be a predisposition to allow migrants to become contributing members of society. Nevertheless, and as is also evident from both quotes above, the right for individuals to migrate is not absolute. Recognizing this, the bishops of Mexico and the United States propose a third principle: "Sovereign nations have the right to control their own borders" (SNL 36).[6]

While the Church respects national sovereignty and the right of countries to maintain and control their borders, there has in recent years been the growing recognition that successfully dealing with issues such as mass migration cannot be achieved on the national level alone. Global problems require an international solution as individual states are not equipped to provide such solutions on their own. In dealing with the issue of mass migration, the question of scale is an important one to pursue. Consequently, it is not surprising that when suggesting solutions to unregulated and forced migration, the bishops recognize that the international community has an important role to play in this process.

Given the proximity of the United States and Mexico, the bishops of both countries called on their respective countries' leadership to "confront the reality of globalization and to work toward a globalization of solidarity" (SNL 57). Joint efforts to stimulate economic and political development in sending countries would contribute to the ideal condition in which migration is driven by choice and not by necessity. On a broader scale, the promotion of treaties and conventions that help to provide protections for migrant workers and their families could provide an important mechanism to help regulate migration patterns (SNL 77). Efforts to do so would likely require a degree of international cooperation that is at this time lacking but which is crucial if unregulated migration in particular is ever to be effectively managed.

Echoing this sentiment, Pope Benedict XVI noted in his encyclical *Caritas in Veritate* that the reality of mass migration confronts the world with a "social phenomenon of epoch-making proportions that requires bold, forward looking policies of international cooperation if it is to be handled effectively" (CV 62). While only 3 percent of the world's population is estimated to be migrants, in absolute numbers that equates to approximately two hundred fifteen million people, which would constitute the fifth largest country in the world.[7] Given the breadth of this problem the reform of international bodies like the United Nations and related economic institutions is crucial if the world community hopes to respond effectively to the problems that emerge as a result of forced and unauthorized migration in particular; there is, as the pope put it, "an urgent need of a true world political authority" that would be "universally recognized and…vested with the effective power to ensure security for all, regard for justice, and respect for rights" (CV 67).

It is proper for the U.S. and Mexican bishops to identify the issue of mass migration as an important topic that deserves attention in light of the moral teachings of the Church and to raise their voices in defense of those who are victim to the injustices that are often a consequence of the current system. The national, regional, and global characteristics that mass migration has taken on in the modern world points to the multifaceted and multi-leveled approach that is required if the international community hopes to manage migration flows. As is already evident from the comments above, the leadership of the Catholic Church is not naïve to this reality. Through its activities on behalf of migrants—evident in the recent efforts by both the Mexican and American bishops—the Church promotes a practical and yet morally grounded approach that responds to the pastoral and policy concerns of these communities. They also recognize that any attempt to deal with mass migration has to occur on the various national and international levels on which it occurs. In light of this, and as the bishops recognize in the conclusion of their pastoral letter, mass migration is a "sign of the times" that functions as a "call to transform national and international social, economic and political structures so that they may provide the conditions required for the development of all, without exclusion and discrimination against any person in any circumstance" (SNL 102).

NOTES

1. Holy See Press Office, "General Information on the Synod," March 9, 2012; http://www.vatican.va/news_services/press/documen tazione/documents/sinodo/sinodo_documentazione-generale_en.html (accessed September 25, 2012).

2. Ibid. For the entire text of Pope Paul VI's Angelus Domini from which this quote was extracted, and as it appears in the original Italian, see Santo Padre Paolo VI, "Angelus Domini," 22 settembre 1974; http://www.vatican.va/holy_father/paul_vi/angelus/1974/docu ments/hf_p-vi_ang_19740922_it.html (accessed September 25, 2012).

3. Pope John Paul II, "Homily: Opening Mass of the Synod for America," November 16, 1997, 2–3; http://www.vatican.va/holy_ father/john_paul_ii/homilies/1997/documents/hf_jp-ii_hom_ 19971116_en.html (accessed September 20, 2012).

4. Cfr. Silvano M. Tomasi, "Human Rights as a Framework for Advocacy on Behalf of the Displaced: The Approach of the Catholic Church" in David Hollenbach, ed., *Driven from Home: Protecting the Rights of Forced Migrants* (Washington, DC: Georgetown University Press, 2010), 55–69.

5. The full passage relevant to Leo XIII's claim in this regard reads: "no one would exchange his country for a foreign land if his own afforded him the means of living a decent and happy life."

6. A fourth and fifth principle, which we will not explore here, is also proposed by the bishops in the pastoral letter: "Refugees and

asylum seekers should be afforded protection"; and "The human dignity and human rights of undocumented migrants should be respected."

7. International Organization for Migration, "Facts and Figures"; http://www.iom.int/jahia/Jahia/about-migration/facts-and-figures/lang/en (accessed September 19, 2012).

Appendix

"Strangers No Longer: Together on the Journey of Hope"

A Pastoral Letter Concerning Migration from the Catholic Bishops of Mexico and the United States

INTRODUCTION

1. As we begin the third millennium, we give thanks to God the Father for the many blessings of creation, and to our Lord Jesus Christ for the gift of salvation. We raise our prayer to the Holy Spirit to strengthen and guide us in carrying out all that the Lord has commanded us. In discerning the signs of the times, we note the greatly increased migration among the peoples of the Americas, and we see in this but one manifestation of a worldwide phenomenon—often called globalization—which brings with it great promises along with multiple challenges.

2. We speak as two episcopal conferences but as one Church, united in the view that migration between our two nations is necessary and beneficial. At the same time, some aspects of the migrant experience are far from the vision of the Kingdom of God that Jesus proclaimed: many persons who seek to migrate are suffering, and, in some cases, tragically dying; human rights are abused; families are kept apart; and racist and xenophobic attitudes remain.

3. On January 23, 1999, at the Basilica of Our Lady of Guadalupe, Pope John Paul II presented his apostolic exhortation

313

Ecclesia in America, which resulted from the Synod of Bishops of America.[1] In the spirit of ecclesial solidarity begun in that synod and promoted in *Ecclesia in America*, and aware of the migration reality our two nations live, we the bishops of Mexico and the United States seek to awaken our peoples to the mysterious presence of the crucified and risen Lord in the person of the migrant and to renew in them the values of the Kingdom of God that he proclaimed.

4. As pastors to more than ninety million Mexican Catholics and sixty-five million U.S. Catholics, we witness the human consequences of migration in the life of society every day. We witness the vulnerability of our people involved in all sides of the migration phenomenon, including families devastated by the loss of loved ones who have undertaken the migration journey and children left alone when parents are removed from them. We observe the struggles of landowners and enforcement personnel who seek to preserve the common good without violating the dignity of the migrant. And we share in the concern of religious and social service providers who, without violating civil law, attempt to respond to the migrant knocking at the door.

5. Migrants and immigrants are in our parishes and in our communities. In both our countries, we see much injustice and violence against them and much suffering and despair among them because civil and church structures are still inadequate to accommodate their basic needs.

6. We judge ourselves as a community of faith by the way we treat the most vulnerable among us. The treatment of migrants challenges the consciences of elected officials, policymakers, enforcement officers, residents of border communities, and providers of legal aid and social services, many of whom share our Catholic faith.

7. In preparing this statement we have spoken with migrants, public officials, enforcement officers, social justice activists, pastors, parishioners, and community leaders in both the United States and Mexico as part of a process that lasted two years. Our dialogue has revealed a common desire for a more orderly system that accommodates the reality of migration and promotes just application of civil law. We seek to measure the interests of all parties in the migration phenomenon against the guidelines of Catholic social teaching and to offer a moral framework for embracing, not rejecting, the reality of migration between our two nations. We invite Catholics and persons of good will in both nations to

exercise their faith and to use their resources and gifts to truly welcome the stranger among us (cf. Mt 25:35).

8. In recent years, signs of hope have developed in the migration phenomenon in both Mexico and the United States: a growing consciousness of migrants as bearers of faith and culture; an outpouring of hospitality and social services, including migrant shelters; a growing network of advocates for migrants' and immigrants' rights; a more organized effort at welcome and intercultural communion; a greater development of a social conscience; and greater recognition by both governments of the importance of the issue of migration. Each of our episcopal conferences has spoken with great urgency to encourage these signs of hope.[2] We reiterate our appreciation for and our encouragement of manifestations of commitment to solidarity according to the vision inspired by *Ecclesia in America* (EA).

9. We speak to the migrants who are forced to leave their lands to provide for their families or to escape persecution. We stand in solidarity with you. We commit ourselves to your pastoral care and to work toward changes in church and societal structures that impede your exercising your dignity and living as children of God.

10. We speak to public officials in both nations, from those who hold the highest offices to those who encounter the migrant on a daily basis. We thank our nations' presidents for the dialogue they have begun in an effort to humanize the migration phenomenon.

11. We speak to government personnel of both countries who enforce, implement, and execute the immigration laws.

12. Finally, we speak to the peoples of the United States and Mexico. Our two nations are more interdependent than ever before in our history, sharing cultural and social values, common interests, and hopes for the future. Our nations have a singular opportunity to act as true neighbors and to work together to build a more just and generous immigration system.

CHAPTER I: AMERICA: A COMMON HISTORY OF MIGRATION AND A SHARED FAITH IN JESUS CHRIST

13. America is a continent born of immigrant peoples who came to inhabit these lands and who from north to south gave birth to new civilizations. Throughout history the continent has suffered through the expansion of other peoples who came to conquer and colonize these lands, displacing and eliminating entire peoples and even forcing unknown millions of persons and families from Africa to come as slaves.

14. It was precisely within the historical processes of forced and voluntary movements that faith in Christ entered into these lands and extended all over the continent. Faith in Christ has thus "shaped [our] religious profile, marked by moral values which, though they are not always consistently practiced and at times are cast into doubt, are in a sense the heritage of all Americans, even of those who do not explicitly recognize this fact" (EA, no. 14).

15. Our continent has consistently received immigrants, refugees, exiles, and the persecuted from other lands. Fleeing injustice and oppression and seeking liberty and the opportunity to achieve a full life, many have found work, homes, security, liberty, and growth for themselves and their families. Our countries share this immigrant experience, though with different expressions and to different degrees.

16. Since its origins, the Mexican nation has had a history marked by encounters between peoples who, coming from different lands, have transformed and enriched it. It was the encounter between Spaniards and indigenous people that gave rise to the Mexican nation in a birth that was full of the pain and joy that the struggle for life entails. Besides this, immigrants from all continents have participated in the birth of Mexico; they continue to do so now and will for years to come. Mexico is not only a country of emigrants, but also a country of *immigrants* who come to build their lives anew. It is important to remember the difficult experiences many of our brothers and sisters have of being strangers in a new land and to welcome those who come to be among us.

17. Since its founding, the United States has received immigrants from around the world who have found opportunity and safe haven in

a new land. The labor, values, and beliefs of immigrants from through-out the world have transformed the United States from a loose group of colonies into one of the leading democracies in the world today. From its founding to the present, the United States remains a nation of immigrants grounded in the firm belief that newcomers offer new energy, hope, and cultural diversity.

18. At the present time, the interdependence and integration of our two peoples is clear. According to U.S. government statistics, about 800,000 Mexicans enter the United States each day.[3] Cross-border U.S. and Mexican investment has reached unprecedented levels in recent years. Moreover, each year the United States admits between 150,000 to 200,000 Mexicans into the country as legal permanent res-idents, amounting to nearly 20 percent of the total number of legal permanent residents *admitted* each year.[4] A significant number of U.S. citizens live, work, and retire in Mexico. In addition to this present interdependence, Mexico and the United States have been bound his-torically by spiritual connections.

19. Our common faith in Jesus Christ moves us to search for ways that favor a spirit of solidarity. It is a faith that transcends borders and bids us to overcome all forms of discrimination and violence so that we may build relationships that are just and loving.

20. Under the light of the apparition of Our Lady of Guadalupe to the littlest of her children, who were as powerless as most migrants are today, our continent's past and present receive new meaning. It was St. Juan Diego whom our Mother asked to build a temple so in it she could show her love, compassion, aid, and defense to all her children, especially the least among them.[5] Since then, in her Basilica and beyond its walls, she has brought all the peoples of America to cele-brate at the table of the Lord, where all his children may partake of and enjoy the unity of the continent in the diversity of its peoples, lan-guages, and cultures (EA, no. 11).

21. As Pope John Paul II wrote in *Ecclesia in America*:

> In its history, America has experienced many immigrations, as waves of men and women came to its various regions in the hope of a better future. The phenomenon continues even today, especially with many people and families from Latin American countries who have moved to the northern

parts of the continent, to the point where in some cases they constitute a substantial part of the population. They often bring with them a cultural and religious heritage which is rich in Christian elements. The Church is well aware of the problems created by this situation and is committed to spare no effort in developing her own pastoral strategy among these immigrant people, in order to help them settle in their new land and to foster a welcoming attitude among the local population, in the belief that a mutual openness will bring enrichment to all. (EA, no. 65)

CHAPTER II: REFLECTIONS IN THE LIGHT OF THE WORD OF GOD AND CATHOLIC SOCIAL TEACHING

MIGRATION IN THE LIGHT OF THE WORD OF GOD

22. The word of God and the Catholic social teaching it inspires illuminate an understanding—one that is ultimately full of hope—that recognizes the lights and shadows that are a part of the ethical, social, political, economic, and cultural dimensions of migrations between our two countries. The word of God and Catholic social teaching also bring to light the causes that give rise to migrations, as well as the consequences that they have on the communities of origin and destination.

23. These lights and shadows are seen in faith as part of the dynamics of creation and grace on the one hand, and of sin and death on the other, that form the backdrop of all salvation history.

OLD TESTAMENT

24. Even in the harsh stories of migration, God is present, revealing himself. Abraham stepped out in faith to respond to God's call (Gn 12:1). He and Sarah extended bounteous hospitality to three strangers who were actually a manifestation of the Lord, and this became a paradigm for the response to strangers of Abraham's descendants. The grace of God even broke through situations of sin in the forced migration of the children of Jacob: Joseph, sold into slavery, eventually

became the savior of his family (Gn 37:45)—a type of Jesus, who, betrayed by a friend for thirty pieces of silver, saves the human family.

25. The key events in the history of the Chosen People of enslavement by the Egyptians and of liberation by God led to commandments regarding strangers (Ex 23:9; Lv 19:33). Israel's conduct with the stranger is both an imitation of God and the primary, specific Old Testament manifestation of the great commandment to love one's neighbor: "For the Lord, your God, is the...Lord of lords, the great God, mighty and awesome, who has no favorites, accepts no bribes, who executes justice for the orphan and widow, and befriends the alien, feeding and clothing him. So you, too, must befriend the alien, for you were once aliens yourselves in the land of Egypt" (Dt 10:17–19). For the Israelites, these injunctions were not only personal exhortations: the welcome and care of the alien were structured into their gleaning and tithing laws (Lv 19:9–10; Dt 14:28–29).

NEW TESTAMENT

26. Recalling the migration of the Chosen People from Egypt, Jesus, Mary, and Joseph themselves were refugees in Egypt: "Out of Egypt I called my son" (Mt 2:15). From this account the Holy Family has become a figure with whom Christian migrants and refugees throughout the ages can identify, giving them hope and courage in hard times.

St. Matthew also describes the mysterious presence of Jesus in the migrants who frequently lack food and drink and are detained in prison (Mt 25:35–36). The "Son of Man" who "comes in his glory" (Mt 25:31) will judge his followers by the way they respond to those in such need: "Amen, I say to you, whatever you did for one of these least brothers of mine, you did for me" (Mt 25:40).

27. The Risen Christ commanded his apostles to go to all nations to preach his message and to draw all people through faith and baptism into the life of God the Father, Son, and Holy Spirit (Mt 28:16–20). The Risen Christ sealed this command through the sending of the Holy Spirit (Acts 2:1–21). The triumph of grace in the Resurrection of Christ plants hope in the hearts of all believers, and the Spirit works in the Church to unite all peoples of all races and cultures into the one family of God (Eph 2:17–20).

The Holy Spirit has been present throughout the history of the Church to work against injustice, division, and oppression and to bring about respect for individual human rights, unity of races and cultures, and the incorporation of the marginalized into full life in the Church. In modern times, one of the ways this work of the Spirit has been manifested is through Catholic social teaching, in particular the teachings on human dignity and the principle of solidarity.

MIGRATION IN THE LIGHT OF CATHOLIC SOCIAL TEACHING

28. Catholic teaching has a long and rich tradition in defending the right to migrate. Based on the life and teachings of Jesus, the Church's teaching has provided the basis for the development of basic principles regarding the right to migrate for those attempting to exercise their God-given human rights. Catholic teaching also states that the root causes of migration—poverty, injustice, religious intolerance, armed conflicts—must be addressed so that migrants can remain in their homeland and support their families.

29. In modern times, this teaching has developed extensively in response to the worldwide phenomenon of migration. Pope Pius XII reaffirms the Church's commitment to caring for pilgrims, aliens, exiles, and migrants of every kind in his apostolic constitution *Exsul Familia*, affirming that all peoples have the right to conditions worthy of human life and, if these conditions are not present, the right to migrate. "Then—according to the teachings of [the encyclical *Rerum Novarum*—the right of the family to a [life worthy of human dignity] is recognized.[6] When this happens, migration attains its natural scope as experience often shows" (EF 50).

30. While recognizing the right of the sovereign state to control its borders, *Exsul Familia* also establishes that this right is not absolute, stating that the needs of immigrants must be measured against the needs of the receiving countries: "Since land everywhere offers the possibility of supporting a large number of people, the sovereignty of the State, although it must be respected, cannot be exaggerated to the point that access to this land is, for inadequate or unjustified reasons, denied to needy and decent people from other nations, provided of course, that the public wealth, considered very carefully, does not forbid this" (EF 50).

In his landmark encyclical *Pacem in Terris*, Blessed Pope John XXIII expands the right to migrate as well as the right to not have to migrate: "Every human being has the right to freedom of movement and of residence within the confines of his own country; and, when there are just reasons for it, the right to emigrate to other countries and take up residence there" (PT 25). Pope John XXIII placed limits on immigration, however, when there are "just reasons for it." Nevertheless, he stressed the obligation of sovereign states to promote the universal good where possible, including an obligation to accommodate migration flows. For more powerful nations, a stronger obligation exists.

31. The Church also has recognized the plight of refugees and asylum seekers who flee persecution. In his encyclical letter *Sollicitudo Rei Socialis*, Pope John Paul II refers to the world's refugee crisis as "the festering of a wound" (SRS 24). In his 1990 Lenten message, Pope John Paul II lists the rights of refugees, including the right to be reunited with their families and the right to a dignified occupation and just wage. The right to asylum must never be denied when people's lives are truly threatened in their homeland.[7]

32. Pope John Paul II also addresses the more controversial topic of undocumented migration and the undocumented migrant. In his 1995 message for World Migration Day, he notes that such migrants are used by developed nations as a source of labor. Ultimately, the pope says, elimination of global underdevelopment is the antidote to illegal immigration.[8] *Ecclesia in America*, which focuses on the Church in North and South America, reiterates the rights of migrants and their families and the respect for human dignity "even in cases of non-legal immigration" (EA 65).

33. Both of our episcopal conferences have echoed the rich tradition of church teachings with regard to migration.[9] Five principles emerge from such teachings, which guide the Church's view on migration issues.

I. Persons have the right to find opportunities in their homeland.

34. All persons have the right to find in their own countries the economic, political, and social opportunities to live in dignity and

achieve a full life through the use of their God-given gifts. In this context, work that provides a just, living wage is a basic human need.

II. Persons have the right to migrate to support themselves and their families.

35. The Church recognizes that all the goods of the earth belong to all people (PM 7). When persons cannot find employment in their country of origin to support themselves and their families, they have a right to find work elsewhere in order to survive. Sovereign nations should provide ways to accommodate this right.

III. Sovereign nations have the right to control their borders.

36. The Church recognizes the right of sovereign nations to control their territories but rejects such control when it is exerted merely for the purpose of acquiring additional wealth. More powerful economic nations, which have the ability to protect and feed their residents, have a stronger obligation to accommodate migration flows.

IV. Refugees and asylum seekers should be afforded protection.

37. Those who flee wars and persecution should be protected by the global community. This requires, at a minimum, that migrants have a right to claim refugee status without incarceration and to have their claims fully considered by a competent authority.

V. The human dignity and human rights of undocumented migrants should be respected.

38. Regardless of their legal status, migrants, like all persons, possess inherent human dignity that should be respected. Often they are subject to punitive laws and harsh treatment from enforcement officers from both receiving and transit countries. Government policies that respect the basic human rights of the undocumented are necessary.

39. The Church recognizes the right of a sovereign state to control its borders in furtherance of the common good. It also recognizes

the right of human persons to migrate so that they can realize their God-given rights. These teachings complement each other. While the sovereign state may impose reasonable limits on immigration, the common good is not served when the basic human rights of the individual are violated. In the current condition of the world, in which global poverty and persecution are rampant, the presumption is that persons must migrate in order to support and protect themselves and that nations who are able to receive them should do so whenever possible. It is through this lens that we assess the current migration reality between the United States and Mexico.

CHAPTER III: PASTORAL CHALLENGES AND RESPONSES

TOWARD CONVERSION

40. Our concern as pastors for the dignity and rights of migrants extends to pastoral responses as well as public policy issues. The Church in our two countries is constantly challenged to see the face of Christ, crucified and risen, in the stranger. The whole Church is challenged to live the experience of the disciples on the road to Emmaus (Lk 24:13–25), as they are converted to be witnesses of the Risen Lord after they welcome him as a stranger. Faith in the presence of Christ in the migrant leads to a conversion of mind and heart, which leads to a renewed spirit of communion and to the building of structures of solidarity to accompany the migrant. Part of the process of conversion of mind and heart deals with confronting attitudes of cultural superiority, indifference, and racism; accepting migrants not as foreboding aliens, terrorists, or economic threats, but rather as persons with dignity and rights, revealing the presence of Christ; and recognizing migrants as bearers of deep cultural values and rich faith traditions. Church leaders at every level are called on to communicate this teaching as well as to provide instruction on the phenomenon of migration, its causes, and its impact throughout the world. This instruction should be grounded in the Scriptures and social teaching.

TOWARD COMMUNION

41. Conversion of mind and heart leads to communion expressed through hospitality on the part of receiving communities and a sense of belonging and welcome on the part of those in the communities where migrants are arriving. The New Testament often counsels that hospitality is a virtue necessary for all followers of Jesus. Many migrants, sensing rejection or indifference from Catholic communities, have sought solace outside the Church. They experience the sad fate of Jesus, recorded in St. John's Gospel: "He came to what was his own, but his own people did not accept him" (Jn 1:11). The need to provide hospitality and create a sense of belonging pertains to the Church on every level, as Pope John Paul II said in his annual message on World Migration Day 1993: "The families of migrants...should be able to find a homeland everywhere in the Church."[10]

42. We bishops have the primary responsibility to build up the spirit of hospitality and communion extended to migrants who are passing through or to immigrants who are settling in the area.

- We call upon pastors and lay leaders to ensure support for migrant and immigrant families.
- We urge communities to offer migrant families hospitality, not hostility, along their journey.
- We commend church communities that have established migrant shelters that provide appropriate pastoral and social services to migrants.
- We encourage Catholics and all people of good will to work with the community to address the causes of undocumented migration and to protect the human rights of all migrants.
- We call on the local church to help newcomers integrate in ways that are respectful, that celebrate their cultures, and that are responsive to their social needs, leading to a mutual enrichment of the local church.
- We ask that special attention be given to migrant and immigrant children and youth as they straddle two cultures, especially to give them opportunities for leadership

and service in the community and to encourage vocations among them.

- The Church on both sides of the border must dedicate resources to provide pastoral care for migrants who are detained or incarcerated. The presence of the Church within detention facilities and jails is an essential way of addressing the human rights violations that migrants may face when they are apprehended.
- We encourage local dioceses to sponsor pertinent social services for migrants and immigrants, particularly affordable legal services.
- In many rural dioceses, the primary site of pastoral outreach for farm workers is the migrant camp, usually at a significant distance from the parish church. In this context we encourage local parishioners to be prepared as home missionaries and the migrants themselves to be prepared as catechists and outreach workers.

TOWARD SOLIDARITY

43. The building of community with migrants and new immigrants leads to a growing sense of solidarity. The bishop as pastor of the local church should lead the priests, deacons, religious, and faithful in promoting justice and in denouncing injustice towards migrants and immigrants, courageously defending their basic human rights. This should be true in both the sending and receiving churches. As leaven in the society, pastoral agents can be instruments for peace and justice to promote systemic change by making legislators and other government officials aware of what they see in the community. Working closely with other advocates for workers and with non-governmental organizations, the Church can be instrumental in developing initiatives for social change that benefit the most vulnerable members of the community.

44. The Church should encourage these broad-based efforts to provide both a comprehensive network of social services and advocacy for migrant families. Another important resource these communities can offer migrants, especially those seeking asylum or family reunification, is affordable or free legal assistance. A special call is issued to

lawyers in both our countries to assist individuals and families in navigating the arduous immigration process and to defend the human rights of migrants, especially those in detention. Parishes should work together to provide adequate services throughout the community, making every effort to invite parishioners with special expertise (lawyers, doctors, social workers) to assist generously wherever they can.

PASTORAL CARE AT ORIGIN, IN TRANSIT, AND AT DESTINATIONS

45. The reality of migration, especially when the journey entails clandestine border crossings, is often fraught with uncertainties and even dangers. As migrants leave their homes, pastoral counseling should be offered to help them to better understand these realities and to consider alternative options, including the exploration of available legal means of immigration.

Native Peoples Deserve Special Consideration

The one ancestral homeland of the Tohono O'odham nation that stretches across the United States and Mexico has no border. Neither does the homeland of the Yaqui nation. Tribal members' rights to travel freely throughout the land they have inhabited for one thousand years should be respected. They should be able to visit family members and participate in religious and cultural celebrations, observances, and other community events without harassment or multiple identity checks in both Mexico and the United States.

46. Prayer books and guides to social and religious services should be provided along the way and at the points of arrival. The migrants should be reminded of their role as evangelizers: that they have the capacity to evangelize others by the daily witness of their Christian lives. Special encouragement should be given to migrants to be faithful to their spouses and families and to thereby live out the sacrament of marriage. Support of the family that is left behind is also needed. Migration under certain conditions can have a devastating effect on families; at times, entire villages are depopulated of their young people.

47. Dioceses in Mexico and the United States need to work closely to provide a sacramental presence for migrants. Ideally, local

parishes should ensure that sacramental preparation is available to people on the move, making special provisions for them given their transitory lives of following work wherever it leads. Eucharistic celebrations or communion services and the Sacrament of Reconciliation should be available to migrants where they can easily attend, and at times that best suit working people with families.

COLLABORATIVE PASTORAL RESPONSES

48. *Ecclesia in America* recommends collaboration between episcopal conferences for more effective pastoral responses. Collaboration is most needed in the development of a more systematic approach to ministerial accompaniment of migrants. The numbers of migrants who leave Central and South America and Mexico and who enter the United States are so large that a more concerted effort is needed in the preparation of priests, religious, and lay leaders who accompany them.

49. In previous centuries, when immigrants from eastern and western Europe came to all parts of the American continent, the Church in some countries established national seminaries to prepare priests to serve in the lands where others in their country were settling, particularly in North and South America. In other countries, the Church developed religious communities of men and women to accompany emigrants on their way, to minister to them on arrival, and to help them integrate into their new homes from a position of strength, often by forming national or personal parishes. In still other countries, the Church has developed exchange or temporary programs in which commitments are made to supply priests for a period of three to five years. Up to the present there have been individual exchanges of priests between Central and South American, Mexican, and U.S. dioceses. The bishops from Central and South America and Mexico have visited the U.S. dioceses to which these priests and their people have immigrated, and U.S. bishops have visited dioceses in Central and South America and Mexico, reflecting the teaching of the Second Vatican Council that every local church is missionary, both as sending and receiving church. This exchange has built up the spirit of collaboration encouraged in *Ecclesia in America*. These efforts have been very positive, but the results have not been uniform.

50. Careful and generous cooperation between dioceses is impor-

tant to provide priests and religious who are suited for this important ministry. Guidelines for their training and reception by the host diocese must be developed jointly with the diocese that sends them. During their stay in the host diocese, international priests and religious deserve an extensive and careful orientation and gracious welcome. As immigrants themselves, they too experience the loss of a familiar and supportive environment and must have the support they need to adjust to the new environment and culture. Periodically, as resources allow, they should be encouraged to return to their home dioceses or motherhouses to rest and to reconnect with their communities.

51. A next step would be to study the possibility of a more comprehensive preparation and assignment of clergy, religious, and lay people who dedicate themselves to pastoral accompaniment of migrants. Such a study by representatives of both episcopal conferences should focus on the following:

- The needs of migrants on their journey and at the points of their arrival
- The dioceses most in need of priests, religious, and lay leaders
- The possibility of seminaries in Mexico to prepare priests for service in the United States
- The assignment of religious communities to accompany migrants

The study also should include recommendations on ways to build bridges of exchange between dioceses and on effective programs to orient ministers to the new culture they will enter. This formation should be an integral process of human development, educational enrichment, language acquisition, intercultural communication, and spiritual formation. In order to meet this critical need as soon as possible, cooperation with existing seminaries, schools of theology, and pastoral institutes is highly encouraged.

This study should also investigate ways to help the immigrants themselves to continue an active role as lay leaders in the new settings in which they find themselves and ways for the receiving church to animate and encourage them, especially those who served as catechists and community leaders in the country of origin. We recommend that a special academic subject on pastoral migration or human mobility be included as part of the regular curriculum in our seminaries, institutions, and houses of formation.

52. Another area of collaboration could be in the preparation of catechetical materials that would be culturally appropriate for migrant farm workers. Several examples already exist that reflect the collaboration of dioceses along both the United States-Mexico border and the Mexico-Guatemala border.

53. This cross-border collaboration has already reaped positive results, such as the development of legal services, social services, cooperation with houses of hospitality along the borders, and prayer books for the journey. Joint prayer services at the border, such as the *Posadas*, Good Friday vigils, and All Souls rites to cherish the memory of those who have died, also have been held.

54. To develop and continue the cooperation between the Church in the United States and Mexico, we bishops encourage ongoing dialogue between bishops and pastoral workers on the border, exchanges between dioceses, and continuing meetings between the USCCB's Committee on Migration and the CEM's Episcopal Commission for the Pastoral Care for People on the Move.

55. *Ecclesia in America* summed up these pastoral recommendations as follows:

> Migrants should be met with a hospitable and welcoming attitude which can encourage them to become part of the Church's life, always with due regard for their freedom and their specific cultural identity. Cooperation between the dioceses from which they come and those in which they settle, also through specific pastoral structures provided for in the legislation and praxis of the Church, has proved extremely beneficial to this end. In this way the most adequate and complete pastoral care possible can be ensured. The Church in America must be constantly concerned to provide for the effective evangelization of those recent arrivals who do not yet know Christ. (no. 65)

CHAPTER IV PUBLIC POLICY CHALLENGE AND RESPONSES

56. The United States and Mexico share a special relationship that requires focused attention upon joint concerns. The realities of migration between both nations require comprehensive policy responses implemented in unison by both countries. The current relationship is weakened by inconsistent and divergent policies that are not coordinated and, in many cases, address only the *symptoms* of the migration phenomenon and not its root causes.

57. Now is the time for both the United States and Mexico to confront the reality of globalization and to work toward a globalization of solidarity. We call upon both governments to cooperate and to jointly enact policies that will create a generous, legal flow of migrants between both nations. Both governments have recognized the integration of economic interests through the North American Free Trade Agreement (NAFTA). It is now time to harmonize policies on the movement of people, particularly in a way that respects the human dignity of the migrant and recognizes the social consequences of globalization.

58. With these goals in mind, we offer several policy recommendations for both nations to consider that address the root causes of migration, legal avenues for migration, and humane law enforcement. These recommendations focus upon both U.S. and Mexican government policies toward newcomers in their own nations, since both are receiving countries.

ADDRESSING THE ROOT CAUSES OF MIGRATION

59. As we have stated, persons should have the opportunity to remain in their homeland to support and to find full lives for themselves and their families. This is the ideal situation for which the world and both countries must strive: one in which migration flows are driven by choice, not necessity. Paramount to achieving this goal is the need to develop the economies of sending nations, including Mexico.

60. Only a long-term effort that adjusts economic inequalities between the United States and Mexico will provide Mexican workers with employment opportunities that will allow them to remain at

home and to support themselves and their families. The Church has consistently singled out economic inequality between nations as a global disorder that must be addressed. Within the United States-Mexico relationship, we have witnessed the application of economic policies that do not adequately take into account the welfare of individual proprietors who struggle to survive. For example, the North American Free Trade Agreement (NAFTA) has harmed small businesses in Mexico, especially in the rural sector. Both nations should reconsider the impact of economic and trade agreements on persons who work hard at making a living through individual enterprises.

61. The creation of employment opportunities in Mexico would help to reduce poverty and would mitigate the incentive for many migrants to look for employment in the United States. The implementation of economic policies in Mexico that create living-wage jobs is vital, especially for Mexican citizens without advanced skills. Targeted development projects in Mexican municipalities and rural areas that traditionally have had the highest rates of emigration are necessary. Projects and resources particularly should be targeted to the Mexican agricultural sector and small businesses.

62. As border regions are the focal point of the migration phenomenon, resources also should be directed toward communities on the United States-Mexico border. Such additional resources would augment existing efforts by border residents to aid migrants in meeting their most basic needs. We urge the initiation of joint border development projects that would help build up the economies of these areas so that border residents may continue to work and live cooperatively. Church leaders should work with both communities on the U.S. and Mexican border and both communities on the Mexican and Guatemalan border to help them to overcome fears and prejudices.

CREATING LEGAL AVENUES FOR MIGRATION

63. With both the United States and Mexico experiencing economic, social, and cultural integration on an unprecedented scale, it is important that both governments formally acknowledge this reality by enacting reforms in the immigration systems of both countries.

Family-Based Immigration

64. As pastors, we are troubled by how the current amalgamation of immigration laws, policies, and actions pursued by both governments often impedes family unity. While the majority of Mexican migrants enter the United States to find work, many cross the border to join family members.

65. The U.S. legal immigration system places per-country limits on visas for family members of U.S. legal permanent residents from Mexico. This cap, along with processing delays, has resulted in unacceptable waiting times for the legal reunification of a husband and wife, or of a parent and child. For example, the spouse or child of a Mexican-born legal permanent resident can wait approximately eight years to obtain a visa to join loved ones in the United States. Spouses and parents thus face a difficult decision: either honor their moral commitment to family and migrate to the United States without proper documentation, or wait in the system and face indefinite separation from loved ones.

66. This is an unacceptable choice, and a policy that *encourages* undocumented migration. In order to ensure that families remain together, reform of the U.S. family-based legal immigration categories vis-à-vis Mexico is necessary. A new framework must be established that will give Mexican families more opportunities to legally reunite with their loved ones in the United States.[11] This would help alleviate the long waiting times and, in time, would *reduce* undocumented migration between the United States and Mexico.

67. Family unity also is weakened when the children of immigrants are left unprotected. In the United States, birthright citizenship should be maintained as an important principle in U.S. immigration law. In Mexico, some children are being denied birth certificates and consequent Mexican nationality due to their parents' undocumented status. As the Mexican Constitution ensures and Article 68 of the National Law of Population codifies, such children have the right and protection to be documented at birth. Otherwise, their access to health, education, and other basic services may be denied later in life. Moreover, the right to an identity and nationality are enshrined in international covenants.

Legalization of the Undocumented

68. Approximately 10.5 million Mexican-born persons currently live in the United States, about 5.5 million of whom reside legally, and the remainder of whom have undocumented status. Each year, an estimated 150,000 Mexican migrants enter the United States without authorization, working in such industries as agriculture, service, entertainment, and construction.[12] Despite the rhetoric from anti-immigrant groups and some government officials, they labor with the quiet acquiescence of both government and industry.

69. A broad legalization program of the undocumented would benefit not only the migrants but also both nations. Making legal the large number of undocumented workers from many nations who are in the United States would help to stabilize the labor market in the United States, to preserve family unity, and to improve the standard of living in immigrant communities. Moreover, migrant workers, many of whom have established roots in their communities, will continue to contribute to the U.S. economy.

70. Legalization also would maintain the flow of remittances to Mexico and would give Mexicans safe and legal passage back to Mexico, if necessary. In addition, such legalization would promote national security by reducing fear in immigrant communities and by encouraging undocumented persons to become participating members of society. Legalization represents sound public policy and should be featured in any migration agreement between the United States and Mexico. In order to ensure fairness for all nationalities, the U.S. Congress should enact a legalization program for immigrants regardless of their country of origin.

71. In the case of Mexico, the legalization programs that the Mexican National Migration Institute have executed provide a good beginning. The benefits of legalization have been evident to the migrants themselves, since they may now work with the protection of their basic labor rights; and to the government, which can now gain a more realistic picture of the population present in the country. We hope that future programs will provide more publicity and information to the public, will increase the number of and better train those who administer them, and will decrease the cost to the applicant, which in the past has disadvantaged those with lesser means.[13]

Employment-Based Immigration

72. In the context of the United States-Mexico bilateral relationship, the United States needs Mexican laborers to maintain a healthy economy and should make a special effort to provide legal avenues for Mexican workers to obtain in the United States jobs that provide a living wage and appropriate benefits and labor protections. The U.S. employment-based immigration system should be reformed to feature both *permanent* and, with appropriate protections, *temporary* visa programs for laborers. A system that is transparent and that protects the rights of workers should be formulated. Visa costs of the program should remain affordable for all who wish to participate. Reform in worker programs must be coupled with a broad-based legalization program.

Remittances: The Lifeblood of Many Mexican Families

Mexican workers who labor in the United States send large portions of their wages, which they have earned by the sweat of their brows, back to their families in Mexico. Termed "remittances," these funds amount to as much as $8–10 billion a year, representing one of the largest sources of foreign currency in Mexico. These funds are an important source of support for many families in Mexico. Unfortunately, many Mexican workers in the United States must pay exorbitant fees (some as high as 20%) to send remittances to their families in Mexico. Perhaps a more efficient means can be devised for sending funds to Mexico that would result in more of the money reaching those in need. Furthermore, arrangements could be made with the organizations that process these remittances to channel some of their earnings from the fees to support community development efforts in Mexico, such as road construction, sewers, health clinics, and so on. Such an approach could be further expanded by making arrangements with the U.S. and Mexican governments to match developmental funds paid through fee revenues in order to augment the investment in sustainable community development programs.

73. A certain number of work visas should be created to allow laborers to enter the country as legal permanent residents. Family ties

and work history in the United States are two of the possible factors that should be considered in allocating such visas. A visa category featuring permanent residency would recognize the contributions of long-term laborers and would ensure that their labor rights are respected.

74. More problematic is the reform of U.S. temporary worker programs. The first U.S. agricultural temporary-worker program, known as the *Bracero* program, ended abruptly in 1964 because of widespread evidence of corruption and abuse of workers. The current program, which allows more than thirty thousand workers to enter the United States each year, is marked by a lack of enforcement of worker protections and by insufficient wages and benefits to support a family.

75. Nevertheless, we recognize that, as an alternative to undocumented migration, an efficient legal pathway must be established that protects the basic labor rights of foreign-born workers. In order to prevent future abuse of workers, any new temporary worker program must afford Mexican and other foreign workers wage levels and employment benefits that are sufficient to support a family in dignity; must include worker protections and job portability that U.S. workers have; must allow for family unity; must employ labor-market tests to ensure that U.S. workers are protected; and must grant workers the ability to move easily and securely between the United States and their homelands. It must employ strong enforcement mechanisms to protect workers' rights and give workers the option to become lawful permanent residents after a specific amount of time. In addition, the United States and Mexico should conclude a Social Security agreement that allows workers to accrue benefits for work performed during participation in the program.

76. A properly constructed worker program would reduce the number of undocumented persons migrating from Mexico to the United States, lessening the calls for border enforcement and the demand for the services of unscrupulous smugglers.

77. Moreover, in order to honor the labor rights of foreign-born workers, the United States should sign the International Convention on the Protection of the Rights of All Migrant Workers and Members of Their Families, which lays out principles for the protection of the labor and human rights of migrant workers.[14] Mexico, already a signatory, should implement its principles without current reservations.

HUMANE ENFORCEMENT POLICIES IN MEXICO AND THE UNITED STATES

Enforcement Tactics

78. As explained above, the Catholic Church recognizes the right and responsibility of sovereign nations to control their borders and to ensure the security interests of their citizens. Therefore, we accept the legitimate role of the U.S. and Mexican governments in intercepting undocumented migrants who attempt to travel through or cross into one of the two countries. We do not accept, however, some of the policies and tactics that our governments have employed to meet this shared responsibility.

79. The men and women of the law enforcement agencies charged with maintaining the United States-Mexico border have difficult jobs that require long hours in sometimes extreme conditions. Unfortunately, the enforcement policies that they implement have had the effect of undermining the human dignity of migrants and creating a confrontational and violent relationship between enforcement officers and migrants. Steps must be taken to create an environment in which force is used only in the most necessary circumstances, and only to the extent needed, to protect the physical well-being of both the enforcement officer and the migrant. This requires not only a review and reform of enforcement tactics, but also, more importantly, a reshaping of the enforcement policies of both nations.

U.S. Enforcement Strategy Fails to Deter Migrants

In 1994, the U.S. government adopted a new border enforcement strategy designed to deter migrants from entering the United States from Mexico. The Immigration and Naturalization Service (INS) has launched several blockade initiatives over the past several years, including "Operation Hold the Line," in El Paso, Texas, in 1993; "Operation Gatekeeper," in the San Diego, California, region in 1994; and "Operation Safeguard," in southern Arizona, in 1995. According to an August 2001 report by the U.S. General Accounting Office (GAO), the primary discernible effect of the enforcement strategy has been to divert migrants away from the largest concentration of enforcement resources, most typically to remote regions of the southwestern United

States. During the same period, the number of undocumented persons in the United States has more than doubled, from four million in 1994 to more than eight million in 2000.

80. Alarmingly, migrants often are treated as criminals by civil enforcement authorities. Misperceptions and xenophobic and racist attitudes in both the United States and Mexico contribute to an atmosphere in which undocumented persons are discriminated against and abused. Reports of physical abuse of migrants by U.S. Border Patrol agents, the Mexican authorities, and in some cases, U.S. and Mexican residents are all too frequent, including the use of excessive force and the shackling of migrants' hands and feet.

81. In the United States, documented abuses of migrants occur frequently. To be sure, the large majority of Border Patrol agents conduct themselves in a professional and respectful manner. But there exist those who perpetrate abuses and who are not held accountable by the U.S. government.[15]

82. In addition, the U.S. record of handling undocumented unaccompanied minors from Mexico and other countries is shameful. Mexican children intercepted along the U.S. border often are placed in dilapidated detention facilities for days at a time until they can be repatriated. Children from Mexico and other countries in Central America often are not given the option to contact an attorney, guardian, or relative, or to file for asylum. These practices must stop. Because of their heightened vulnerability, unaccompanied minors require special consideration and care.

83. Mexican enforcement of immigration laws, targeted specifically through racial profiling of migrants attempting to reach the United States, has been marked by corruption, police brutality, and systemic abuses of basic human rights. Migrants often are forced to bribe Mexican police to continue transit and, if unable to produce payments, are beaten and returned to the border. Because of the lack of rights and policies that drive undocumented migrants away from small urban areas, the migrants often are assaulted by bandits in the border area between Ciudad Hidalgo, Mexico, and Tecun Uman, Guatemala. We know of migrants from Central America who pay thousands of dollars to smugglers to shepherd them through Mexico but who, in some cases, are kidnapped. Their families never hear from them again.

84. Although we acknowledge that the government of Mexico has improved the administration of the migration system and is attempting to bring the rule of law to it, Mexican immigration policies remain unclear and inconsistent. Corruption continues to weaken the Mexican migration system and to hurt the common good. We urge the Mexican National Migration Institute to strengthen the participation of civil society organizations in its Delegation Councils as partners to bring healthy transparency to the country's migration system.[16]

85. In order to address these excesses, both governments must create training mechanisms that instruct enforcement agents in the use of appropriate tactics for enforcing immigration law. We urge the U.S. and Mexican governments to include human rights curricula in their training regimens so that immigration enforcement personnel are more sensitive to the handling of undocumented migrants.[17] Community organizations, including dioceses and parishes, can assist enforcement officials in this effort. In addition, the enforcement function in both nations should be left to federal authorities (the Immigration and Naturalization Service and Border Patrol in the United States, and the National Migration Institute and Federal Preventive Police in Mexico), not transferred to local police who necessarily have other priorities and who are untrained in the proper methods for enforcing immigration law. Military personnel from any branch or service should not be used to enforce migration laws along either country's land borders.

BORDER ENFORCEMENT POLICIES

86. Of particular concern are the border enforcement policies pursued by both governments that have contributed to the abuse and even deaths of migrants in both Mexico and the United States. Along the United States-Mexico border, the U.S. government has launched several border-blockade initiatives in the past decade designed to discourage undocumented migrants from entering the country. These initiatives have been characterized by a tripling of Border Patrol agents, especially at ports of entry, and the use of sophisticated technology such as ground sensors, surveillance cameras, heat-detecting scopes, and reinforced fencing.

87. Rather than significantly reducing illegal crossings, the initiatives have instead driven migrants into remote and dangerous areas of

the southwest region of the United States, leading to an alarming number of migrant deaths. Since the beginning of 1998, official statistics indicate that more than two thousand migrants have lost their lives trying to cross the United States-Mexico border, many from environmental causes such as heat stroke, dehydration, hypothermia, or drowning. The blockades also have contributed to an increase in migrant smuggling, in which desperate migrants pay high fees to smugglers to get them into the United States. In recent years, smuggling has become a more organized and profitable enterprise.[18]

"COME AND LOOK AT MY BROTHER IN HIS COFFIN"

José Luis Hernandez Aguirre tried desperately to find work in the maquiladora plants near Mexicali but was unable to do so. With a wife and two children, ages one and seven, José needed to find a job that would put food on the table. A smuggler told him of the high-paying jobs across the border and offered, for $1,000, to take him there. Joined by his brother Jaime and several others, the group headed for the United States with hope. After one day, brother Jaime called and reported to the family and José's sister, Sonia, that José was lost. Jaime could not make the trek in the desert, but José wanted to continue on the journey. He had to find a job for his family. Four days later, José's body was found in the desert. His sister Sonia borrowed a truck to retrieve José's remains. Upon her return, she encountered another group of migrants heading to the United States. "Why do you want to risk your lives like this?" she implored. "Come and look at my brother in his coffin."

88. In southern Mexico, similar policies have resulted in countless migrant deaths along the Suchiate River, most by drowning. Another cause for concern is the presence of Mexican checkpoints–far from most urban areas and difficult to monitor for human rights abuses–which are manned by military and federal, state, and local police agencies along the country's borders and interior. Because these checkpoints are used as "choke" points for arms, drugs, and migrant smuggling, there is an unfair tendency to associate migrants with criminal activity.

89. We urge both the U.S. and Mexican enforcement authorities to abandon the type of strategies that give rise to migrant smuggling operations and migrant deaths. Care should be taken not to push migrants to routes in which their lives may be in danger. The U.S. Border Patrol has

recently launched a border safety initiative to prevent migrant deaths. We ask the Border Patrol to redouble their efforts in this area and to work more closely with community groups to identify and rescue migrants in distress. We also urge more concerted efforts to root out smuggling enterprises at their source using a wide range of intelligence and investigative tactics. In other church documents, the U.S. bishops have also expressed concern about the increasing drug-trafficking industry.[19]

90. Similarly, we call upon both nations to undertake joint efforts to halt the scourge of trafficking in human persons, both within our hemisphere and internationally. Trafficking in persons–in which men, women, and children from all over the globe are transported to other countries for the purposes of forced prostitution or labor–inherently rejects the dignity of the human person and exploits conditions of global poverty.

91. Both governments must vigilantly seek to end trafficking in human persons. The U.S. government should vigorously enforce recent laws that target traffickers both at home and abroad. Mexican authorities must strengthen efforts to identify and to destroy trafficking operations within Mexico. Together, both governments should more effectively share information on trafficking operations and should engage in joint action to apprehend and prosecute traffickers.

Due Process Rights

92. In 1996, the U.S. Congress eviscerated due process rights for migrants with the passage of the Illegal Immigration Reform and Immigrant Responsibility Act (IIRIRA), which authorizes the detention and deportation of migrants for relatively minor offenses, even after they have served their sentences. IIRIRA has caused the unjust separation of untold numbers of immigrant families.[20] We urge the U.S. Congress to revisit this law and to make appropriate changes consistent with due process rights.

93. We also urge the Mexican government to honor the right to due process for all those who are in the country, specifically documented and undocumented migrants who do not now enjoy due process and who may be removed from the country for arbitrary reasons. Recognizing such a right only strengthens the rule of law in a country and further legitimates its institutions.[21]

94. Once apprehended, migrants often are held in unsanitary and crowded prisons, jails, and detention centers, in Mexico and the United States, sometimes alongside serious criminal offenders. Migrants without documentation should not be treated as criminals, should be detained for the least amount of time possible, and should have access to the necessary medical, legal, and spiritual services. Asylum seekers who pass an initial "credible fear" interview should be released.

PROTECTING HUMAN RIGHTS IN REGIONAL MIGRATION POLICIES

95. As defenders of those who flee persecution in foreign lands, we are increasingly troubled by the asylum policies employed by both the United States and Mexico. Most alarming is the prospect of creating a North American exterior boundary system in which asylum policies would be regionalized in such a way as to deny asylum seekers appropriate judicial remedies and protection.[22]

96. Increasingly, asylum seekers from across the globe are smuggled through Central America to Mexico and the United States. They come from as far away as China, India, Iran, and Iraq. In most cases, they have valid claims for protection, but many are swept up in anti-smuggling initiatives in Central America and Mexico and are sent back to their persecutors without proper screening.

97. The denial of asylum adjudication rights is an especially acute problem along the United States-Mexico border. Employing a U.S. policy known as *expedited removal*, U.S. immigration officers routinely detain and deport migrants without giving them a hearing before an immigration judge. In fact, expedited removal is most heavily used against Mexicans. Of the just over 180,000 total removals from the United States in FY 1999 and FY 2000, 81 percent of those deported were Mexican.[23] Moreover, Mexicans and others deported under expedited removal are subject to being barred from readmission to the United States for at least five years. Along the southern border of Mexico, migrants are returned on a regular basis to Central America without screening.

98. Denying access to asylum procedures, making them complicated, or not providing clear information about them in languages that

341

people can understand is a grave injustice and violates the spirit of international law and commitments made by both our countries.[24]

99. We restate our long-held position that asylum seekers and refugees should have access to qualified adjudicators who will objectively consider their pleas. We urge both countries to take a leadership role in the Regional Conference on Migration (*Puebla* Process) and to work with our Central American neighbors to ensure that asylum seekers and refugees throughout our hemisphere have access to appropriate due process protections consistent with international law.

CONSEQUENCES OF SEPTEMBER 11 TERRORIST ATTACKS FOR MIGRANTS

100. The terrorist attacks of September 11, 2001, which ended so tragically in New York, the Washington, DC, area, and Pennsylvania, have placed national security concerns at the forefront of the migration debate and have added another dimension to the migration relationship between the United States and Mexico. Certain security actions are a necessary response to credible terrorist threats, such as improved intelligence sharing and screening, enhanced visa and passport security, and thorough checks at the United States-Mexico border. Other actions, however, such as reducing legal immigration between the two nations, do not serve to make the United States or Mexico more secure. We urge both nations to cooperate in this area, but not to enact joint policies that undermine human rights, reduce legal immigration, or deny asylum seekers opportunities for protection.

CONCLUSION

101. As bishops we have decided, in the words of Pope John Paul II, to "put out into the deep"(NMI 1) in search of common initiatives that will promote solidarity between our countries, particularly among the Catholics of both countries. We are committed to the new evangelization of our continent and to the search for new ways of leading our peoples to encounter Christ, who is "the path to conversion, communion and solidarity" (EA, no. 7).[25]

102. We recognize the phenomenon of migration as an authentic

sign of the times. We see it in both our countries through the suffering of those who have been forced to become migrants for many reasons. To such a sign we must respond in common and creative ways so that we may strengthen the faith, hope, and charity of migrants and all the People of God. Such a sign is a call to transform national and international social, economic, and political structures so that they may provide the conditions required for the development for all, without exclusion and discrimination against any person in any circumstance.

103. In effect, the Church is increasingly called to be "sign and instrument both of a very closely knit union with God and of the unity of the whole human race" (*Lumen Gentium*, no. 1). The Catholic bishops of the United States and Mexico, in communion with the Holy Father in his 1995 World Migration Day message, affirm that

> In the Church no one is a stranger, and the Church is not foreign to anyone, anywhere. As a sacrament of unity and thus a sign and a binding force for the whole human race, the Church is the place where illegal immigrants are also recognized and accepted as brothers and sisters. It is the task of the various Dioceses actively to ensure that these people, who are obliged to live outside the safety net of civil society, may find a sense of brotherhood in the Christian community. Solidarity means taking responsibility for those in trouble.

The Church must, therefore, welcome all persons regardless of race, culture, language, and nation with joy, charity, and hope. It must do so with special care for those who find themselves—regardless of motive—in situations of poverty, marginalization, and exclusion.

104. We ask our presidents to continue negotiations on migration issues to achieve a system of migration between the two countries that is more generous, just, and humane. We call for legislatures of our two countries to effect a conscientious revision of the immigration laws and to establish a binational system that accepts migration flows, guaranteeing the dignity and human rights of the migrant. We ask public officials who are in charge of formulating, implementing, and executing immigration laws to reexamine national and local policies toward the migrant and to use their leadership positions to erase misconceptions about migration. We ask adjudicators who process immigrants' legal claims to

create a welcoming atmosphere that does not threaten their confidence or security. We encourage the media to support and promote a genuine attitude of welcoming toward migrants and immigrants.

105. We, the Catholic bishops of the United States and Mexico, pledge ourselves to defend the migrant. We also pledge to support the creation of the necessary conditions so that all may enjoy the fruit of their work and life in their homeland, if they so wish.

106. We stand in solidarity with you, our migrant brothers and sisters, and we will continue to advocate on your behalf for just and fair migration policies. We commit ourselves to animate communities of Christ's disciples on both sides of the border to accompany you on your journey so that yours will truly be a journey of hope, not of despair, and so that, at the point of arrival, you will experience that you are strangers no longer and instead members of God's household. We pray that, wherever you go, you will always be conscious of your dignity as human beings and of your call to bring the Good News of Jesus Christ, who came that we "might have life and have it more abundantly" (Jn 10:10). We invite you who are forced to emigrate to maintain contact with your homes and, especially, to maintain fidelity to your families so that you treasure your cultural values and the gift of faith and so that you bring these treasures to whatever place you go.

107. The appearance of Our Lady of Guadalupe to St. Juan Diego revealed the compassionate presence of God reaching out to Mary to be in solidarity with and to give hope to a suffering people. In the same spirit, we, the Catholic bishops of the United States of Mexico and the United States of America, have written this letter to give hope to suffering migrants. We pray that you will experience the same hope that inspired St. Paul in his Letter to the Romans:

> What will separate us from the love of Christ? Will anguish, or distress, or persecution, or famine, or nakedness, or peril, or the sword? As it is written: "For your sake we are being slain all the day; we are looked upon as sheep to be slaughtered." No, in all these things we conquer overwhelmingly through Him who loved us. For I am convinced that neither death, nor life, nor angels, nor principalities, nor present things, nor future things, nor powers, nor height, nor depth,

nor any other creature will be able to separate us from the love of God in Christ Jesus our Lord. (Rom 8:35–39)

108. And may the blessing of Almighty God come down upon you and be with you forever: the blessing of God the Father, who loves you with an everlasting love, the blessing of God the Son, who was called out of exile in Egypt to be our Savior, and the blessing of God the Holy Spirit, who guides you to extend Christ's reign wherever you go. And may Mary of Guadalupe, our mother, bring you safely home.

Delivered on the fourth anniversary of
Ecclesia in America, *January 22, 2003*
Washington, D.C., U.S.A., and Mexico City, Mexico

DEFINITIONS

Asylee: See Refugee, below. The definition conforms to that of a refugee except regarding the location of the person upon application for asylum: The asylee applies for protection in the country of asylum, whereas the refugee applies for status in either his or her home country (under certain circumstances) or in a country of temporary asylum.

Globalization: The process whereby the world's goods, communications, and peoples are more fully integrated, accessible, and interdependent.

Immigrant: A person who moves to another country to take up permanent residence.

Legal Immigrant: A person who has been admitted to reside and work on a permanent basis in the United States; admission is most commonly based on reunification with close family members or employment.

Migrant: A person on the move, either voluntarily or involuntarily, in the person's own country, internationally, or both. Unlike refugees, migrants are commonly considered free to return home whenever they wish because their lives are not in danger there.

Refugee: Any person, who, owing to a well-founded fear of being persecuted for reasons of race, religion, nationality, membership in a particular social group, or political opinion, is outside the country of his or her nationality and is unable or, owing to such fear, is unwilling, to avail himself or herself of the protection of that country; or who, not having a nationality and being outside the country of his or her habitual residence as a result of such events, is unable or, owing to such fear, is unwilling to return to it (source: United Nations International Law).

Undocumented immigrant: A person who is in a country without the permission of that country's government. Such persons are called "undocumented" because they lack the required paperwork.

NOTES

1. The synod was held in Vatican City from November 16 to December 12, 1997.

2. Cf. Conferencia del Episcopado Mexicano (CEM), *Del Encuentro con Jesucristo a la Solidaridad con Todos* (México, DF: CEM, 2000). United States Conference of Catholic Bishops (USCCB), *Welcoming the Stranger Among Us: Unity in Diversity* (Washington, DC: USCCB, 2000).

3. U.S. Department of Transportation, Bureau of Transportation Statistics, North American Trade and Travel Trends, BTS01–07 (Washington, DC, 2001), 19.

4. Immigration and Naturalization Service, press release, "INS Announces Legal Immigration Figures for FY 2001," Washington, DC, August 30, 2002.

5. V. Maccagnan, ed. Stefano de Fiores and Salvatore Meo, "Guadalupe," Nuevo Diccionario de Mariologia (Madrid: 1988).

6. "No one would exchange his country for a foreign land if his own afforded him the means of living a decent and happy life." From Pope Leo XIII's 1891 encyclical *Rerum Novarum* (On Capital and Labor), no. 47. Retrieved from Vatican website: www.vatican.va.

7. Pontifical Council Cor Unum and Pontifical Council for the Pastoral Care of Migrants and Itinerant People, *Refugees: A Challenge to Solidarity* (1992), nos. 13–14. Retrieved from Vatican website: www.vatican.va.

8. Pope John Paul II, Message for World Migration Day 1995–1996, *Undocumented Migrants* (July 25, 1995), no. 2. Retrieved from Vatican website: www.vatican.va.

9. "Immigrants from lands across the globe have helped build our great nation....Their presence has enriched our local communities, rural areas, and cities, and their faith in God has enlightened our increasingly secularized culture" (USCCB Resolution on Immigration Reform, November 16, 2000, no. 2).

10. Pope John Paul II, Message for World Migration Day 1993, Problems of the Migrant Family (August 6, 1993), no. 3, citing *Familiaris Consortio*, no. 77. Also see *Welcoming the Stranger Among Us: Unity in Diversity* for recommendations.

11. The bishops in the United States have consistently supported reform of the family reunification visa system. Numerical limits on visas have adversely impacted many nationalities, especially Filipinos. In the context of this statement, we focus on Mexican family reunification because of the proximity of Mexico to the United States and because of the unprecedented number of families separated between these two countries. The per-country limit for Mexico and other affected countries, such as the Philippines, should be increased without harming allotments for other nations.

12. U.S.-Mexico Migration Panel, Mexico-U.S. Migration: A Shared Responsibility (Washington, DC: Carnegie Endowment for International Peace, 2001). Jeffrey Passel, "New Estimates of the Undocumented Population in the United States" (Washington, DC: Migration Policy Institute/Migration Information Source, May 22, 2002).

13. Foro Migraciones, *Migración: México Entre Sus Dos Fronteras*, 2000–2001 (México: Foro Migraciones, 2002). The CEM's Human Mobility Commission is a member.

14. In the U.N. Convention, migrant workers are viewed as more than laborers or economic entities. They are social entities with families and, accordingly, have rights, including the right to family reunification. (See *International Convention on the Protection of the Rights of All Migrant Workers and Members of Their Families*, United Nations General Assembly, December 18, 1990. This document can be obtained from the U.N. Center for Human Rights, 8–14 Avenue de la Paix, 1211 Geneva 10, Switzerland.)

15. In 2000, the U.S. Office of Internal Audit (OIA) of the U.S. Immigration and Naturalization Service (INS) opened 4,527 cases of reported abuse by INS agents. Roughly 10 percent were referred to the

U.S. Department of Justice's Civil Rights Division, and less than 10 percent of those referred led to prosecutions. See Chaos on the U.S.-Mexico Border: A Report on Migration Crossing Deaths, Immigrant Families, and Subsistence-Level Laborers (Washington, DC: Catholic Legal Immigration Network, 2001).

16. The Mexican National Migration Institute has consulting councils for each of its thirty-two regional offices (one for each state and Mexico City) and national office. Such councils include representatives from broad sectors of Mexican society, including universities, shelters, and churches.

17. The U.S. Border Patrol does include some treatment of human rights protection in their training. More intensive instruction in the proper use of force and in appropriate engagement and retention techniques should be considered.

18. In Tecuman, Guatemala, along the Mexico-Guatemala border, smugglers have established offices to receive Central American migrants who wish to travel through Mexico to the United States. (Source: U.S. bishops' delegation to Central America, October 2000.)

19. See *New Slavery, New Freedom: A Pastoral Message on Substance Abuse* (Washington, DC: United States Conference of Catholic Bishops, 1990).

20. The law also applies retroactively for an offense committed years ago for which a person has already served his or her sentence.

21. "What article 33 of the Constitution does, is grant the faculty to the government of being able to arbitrarily expel a foreigner. It is arbitrary, firstly, because no due process is required, in other words, it is a faculty that may not be submitted to the scrutiny of constitutionality or legality, either ex ante or ex post. It is a direct elimination of the guarantees contained under articles 14 and 16 of the Constitution." (Foro Migraciones, *Migración: México Entre Sus Dos Fronteras, 2000–2001* [México: Foro Migraciones, 2002], 57).

22. The United States and Canada agreed to coordinate asylum policies on December 5, 2002.

23. U.S.-Mexico Migration Panel, Mexico-U.S. *Migration: A Shared Responsibility* (Washington, DC: Carnegie Endowment for International Peace, 2001), 28. Also see *Statistical Yearbook of the Immigration and Naturalization Service, Fiscal Year 2000* (online at www.ins.usdoj.gov).

24. The detention of asylum seekers without serious reasons is a violation of the letter and spirit of the "Conclusions on International Protection" of the UNHCR Executive Committee. Both Mexico and the United States are members of the UNHCR Executive Committee, and both have accepted the conclusions. References: No. 44 (XXXVII) 1986; No. 46 (XXVII) 1987; No. 50 (XXXIX) 1988; No. 55 (XL) 1989; No. 65 (XLII) 1991; No. 68 (XLIII) 1992; No. 71 (XLIV) 1993; No. 85 (XLIX) 1998; No. 89 (LI) 2000.

25. "Taking the Gospel as its starting-point, a culture of solidarity needs to be promoted, capable of inspiring timely initiatives in support of the poor and the outcast, especially refugees forced to leave their villages and lands in order to flee violence" (EA, no. 52).

About the Authors

J. Kevin Appleby is the director of Migration Policy and Public Affairs of the U.S. Conference of Catholic Bishops and has testified before Congress on immigration issues and represented the U.S. Catholic bishops on these issues at public events and with the media. Prior to joining the USCCB, Kevin worked as Deputy Director of the Maryland Catholic Conference in Annapolis, Maryland. He received his B.A. from the University of Notre Dame, an M.A. in International Affairs from The George Washington University, and a law degree from the University of Maryland.

Leticia Calderon Chelius is a professor and researcher at the Instituto Mora in Mexico City and a Doctor of Social Sciences FLACSO-Mexico. She is a member of the National Research System and at the Mexican Academy of Sciences, on the Board of the Civil Partnership, and a network coordinator of a group of experts who study the migration process (www.migrantologos.mx). Leticia is the author of three books on issues of migration and political rights and a score of articles and chapters on the international migration process.

Terry Coonan teaches at Florida State University's Law and Criminology Schools and is the founding Executive Director of the Center for the Advancement of Human Rights, an interdisciplinary center dedicated to human rights teaching and advocacy. As an attorney, Professor Coonan has served with the U.S. Justice Department, the U.S. State Department, and the UN Human Rights Commission. In addition, he served as the lead investigator in formulating the 2010 *Statewide Strategic Plan to Combat Human Trafficking* for the Florida Governor's Office.

Colleen Cross is a graduate student in theology at the University of Notre Dame. Her primary area of studies focuses on the intersection of migration, theology, and public policy. Her previous work experience at the United States Conference of Catholic Bishops has also provided her with the opportunity to work in the field of migration policy.

Jesuit Father **Allan Figueroa Deck** holds the Charles S. Casassa Chair of Catholic Social Values and is Professor of Theological Studies at Loyola Marymount University in Los Angeles. In 2007, he was named first executive director of the Secretariat of Cultural Diversity in the Church at the United States Conference of Catholic Bishops in Washington, DC, where he served until 2012.

Mark Ensalaco is an associate professor of political science and is the former director of the International Studies Program and, in 2007, became the director of the newly formed Human Rights Studies program at the University of Dayton. He has conducted human rights research in Latin America for more than two decades, is the cofounder of Abolition Ohio-The Rescue and Restore Coalition in the Miami Valley, a member of the Ohio Attorney General's Human trafficking Commission, and serves on the Association of Catholic Colleges and Universities' Peace and Justice Committee.

Fr. Daniel G. Groody is currently an Associate Professor of Theology and the Director of the Center for Latino Spirituality and Culture at the Institute for Latino Studies at the University of Notre Dame. Drawing on years of work in Latin America, particularly along the U.S.- Mexico border, he has authored various books and articles which have been translated into five languages, including *Border of Death, Valley of Life: An Immigrant Journey of Heart and Spirit* (2002), and *Globalization, Spirituality, and Justice: Navigating the Path to Peace* (2007).

Kristin E. Heyer holds the Bernard J. Hanley Chair in Religious Studies at Santa Clara University. Her books include *Kinship across Borders: A Christian Ethic of Immigration* (2012), *Prophetic and Public: the Social*

351

Witness of U.S. Catholicism (2006), and the edited volume *Catholics and Politics: Dynamic Tensions between Faith and Power* (2008).

Donald M. Kerwin, Jr., directs the Center for Migration Studies (CMS), a New York-based educational institute devoted to the study of migration. He is a non-resident senior fellow at MPI and an associate fellow at the Woodstock Theological Center, where he co-directs Woodstock's Theology of Migration Project. He is co-editor of *And You Welcomed Me: Migration and Catholic Social Teaching*.

Maryann Cusimano Love is Associate Professor of International Relations in the Politics Department of The Catholic University of America in Washington, DC. She is on the Core Group for the Department of State's working group on Religion and Foreign Policy, charged with making recommendations to the Secretary of State and the Federal Advisory Commission on how the U.S. government can better engage with civil society and religious actors in foreign policy. Dr. Love also serves on the U.S. Catholic Bishops' International Justice and Peace Committee where she advises the bishops on international affairs and U.S. foreign policy.

Todd Scribner has a Ph.D. in religious studies from The Catholic University of America with a particular focus on American Catholicism. He is the Education Outreach Coordinator in the Department of Migration and Refugee Services at the United States Conference of Catholic Bishops, where his work primarily examines the intersection between migration, Catholic social teaching, and the Church.

Patricia Zamudio has a Ph.D. in Sociology by Northwestern University and is professor at the Center for Research and Graduate Studies in Social Anthropology (CIESAS) in Xalapa, Veracruz, Mexico. Her main line of research is on the topic of international migration and its effects on citizenship and she is currently working on developing a non-exclusionary conception of citizenship that acknowledges the worth and equality of every person in the world. Her most recent book is *Rancheros in Chicago: Life and Consciousness in a Migrants' Story*.

Index